CIRCUS AND CARNIVAL
BALLYHOO

CIRCUS AND CARNIVAL
BALLYHOO

SIDESHOW FREAKS, JAGGERS AND BLADE BOX QUEENS

A.W. STENCELL

ECW Press

Published by ECW Press
2120 Queen Street East, Suite 200, Toronto, Ontario, Canada M4E 1E2
416-694-3348   info@ecwpress.com

LIBRARY AND ARCHIVES CANADA CATALOGUING IN PUBLICATION

Stencell, A. W
Circus and carnival ballyhoo : sideshow freaks, jabbers and blade box
queens / A.W. Stencell.

Includes bibliographical references.
ISBN 978-1-55022-880-9

1. Sideshows--United States--History. 2. Freak shows--United
States--History. 3. Carnivals--United States--History. 4. Circus--United
States--History. I. Title.

GV1835.S739 2009   791.3'50973   C2009-902534-5

Developing editor: Jack David
Cover and text design: Tania Craan
Typesetting: Gail Nina
Front cover photos from the author's personal collection:
(Left to right) Karl Cullison (talker and owner), Jim Cook (Sir James the Baron of the
Blades), David Wilson (the World's Smallest Guru), Vivian Elaine Wheeler,
(Malinda Maxey the Bearded Lady), lady hired for the day billed as Serpentina.

Printed by Shanghai Chenxi   1   2   3   4   5

Circus and Carnival Ballyhoo has been generously supported by the Government of Ontario through the Ontario Book Publishing Tax Credit, by the OMDC Book Fund, an initiative of the Ontario Media Development Corporation, and by the Government of Canada through the Book Publishing Industry Development Program (BPIDP).

PRINTED AND BOUND IN CHINA

ECW PRESS
ecwpress.com

Contents

Acknowledgements

Showman Dean Potter's astute comments on the operational side of the sideshow business from both a performer's and an owner's perspective were extremely helpful to me. Unfortunately Dean died before the book was published as did John Bradshaw. John started working on sideshows in 1970 and went on to owning sideshows into the early 1990s. His memories of those times gave me a good look into the last days of midway sideshows.

Sword swallower, illusion builder and sideshowman Red Trower provided me with valuable information in regards to his theories on sideshow operational techniques, blow-offs and pitches. Johnny Meah's insight on the use of "cat walks" was helpful. I spent a few days with Coney Island veteran Bobby Reynolds and have related several of his stories here. Phone converations with Jim Steinmetz and the late Walter Wanous revealed key information on pre– and post–World War II sideshow operations. I spoke with Charlie Roark numerous times and spent a day with him at his home. His tales of circus sideshows, the people on them and the grifters that hung around them were priceless. When he goes, another rare link to those that amused the masses from sideshow stages goes with him. Visits with the late Norm Johnstone gave me the information included here on sideshow mitt camps.

You can't write a book on sideshows on either circuses or carnivals without speaking with Ward Hall or Chris Christ. They have seen and done it all while still bringing the public the only big North American midway sideshow. Both have been generous in answering my questions and in letting me use photos from their archives. I'm very proud to call them friends. The same goes for showmen Dick Johnson and Floyd Bradbury.

In a similar vein, you cannot explore the world of weird entertainments, magic or the con without consulting performer/actor/historian Ricky Jay. My conversations with Ricky are always both entertaining and educational. Who else could tell you that Lentini The Three-Legged Man wore his socks high to cover up a mole on his lower leg that embarrassed him!

They are not mentioned in the text but Fakir Musofar and Doug Malloy, the fathers of the modern primitive movement, deserve credit for inspiring the new wave of pain enigmas. One of the first publications putting tattooists and sideshowmen together was Lyle Tuttle's tattoo fanzine in the early 1970s. Veteran sideshow performers Todd Robbins, Johnny Fox, Red Stuart, Harley Newman and the late Don Leslie keep the sideshow arts alive until the sideshow devotees weened on the coattails of the Jim Rose Circus Side Show came along. They continue to be sideshow heroes.

Joey Givens' contributions to my first book *Girl Show* were amazing. His candid and humorous stories of his time as a female sideshow performer, bearded lady and sword swallower are treasures that I'm proud to pass on. So are the sideshow stories told to me by the late Bill English, Bobby Fairchild, Henry Thompson and Harry Rawls. I also want to thank showmen Doc Swan, John Strong Jr. and Billy Martin who are still working in the business.

Carnival grind show information came from talks with show folks Malcolm Garey, Jack Sands and his late wife Ruth, Mickey Saiber, Jack Constantine, Jamie Allen, Lee and Pete Koloszy, Rick West, Jeff and Sue Murray, Lew Stemm, Barbara Pedrero, Dennis Gilli, Rick West and the late Frank Hansen of frozen-creature fame. Performance artist Matt "The Tube" Crawley's quest to find out what Hansen's frozen creature was really made of was a big help. My thanks goes out to Barth Littleton of the Littleton Funeral Home for his information on Eugene, and to Diane Phillips for all her help on grind shows.

I have been lucky to attend most of the sideshow gatherings put on by Frank Kossa and Marc Fairchild as part of their fall Ink'in in the Valley Tattoo Convention at Wilkes-Barre, Pa. I sincerely thank those I interviewed there over the years including Stepanie Monseu, Keith Nelson, George the Giant, the Lizardman, Sez Carny and Sideshow Bennie. Their stories have all helped in doing this book. Special thanks goes out to Jim Rose, Tim Cridland, Jan Gregor, Matt Boliver and his late wife Felicity Perez for all their stories about the triumphs and horrors of pushing today's sideshow troupes down the road. The saddest thing in doing this book was hearing of the early death of Felicity (Cha Cha) Perez.

I want to thank everyone mentioned in the photo credits and to those who sent me photos that did not make it into this book. Steve Gossard has been a friend and a help on all my books. I thank him and Maureen Brunsdale for all their help and for the use of images from the Illinois State University Special Collections, Milner Library. North American Carnival Museum and Archives founder Wayne Van de Graaff and archivist Jennifer Walker have been very generous in providing photos from the Conklin Archives. Erin Foley from the Circus World Museum library Baraboo, Wisc., and Terry Ariano from the Somers Historical Society, Somers, N.Y., have been a huge help. I have used several images from their respective collections.

Many images come from my collection. However the uniqueness of the book comes from photos and material supplied to me by private contributors.

Those include Bob Harris, Lee Koloszy, Bill Cooker, Richard Groggin, Diane Falk, Ken Harck, Charles L. Hansen, Karl Cullison,

Diane Phillips, the late Frank Hansen, Faye Renton, Mickey Saiber, Richard Syder, Rick West, Jeff and Sue Murray, and Jack Sands and his late wife Ruth. A special thank you to Laura Sedlmayr for use of photos from her Royal American Shows archives. The same to Barbara Childs Fahs for use of rare platform show photos from her C. W. Parker collection. Numerous sideshow images come from the late Bob Paul's collection.

Friend and sideshow specialist Bob Blackmar has provided numerous rare photos while generously sharing his vast knowledge on the subject. Years back, Chris Fellner started a sideshow fanzine. Bob continues its publication. I want to thank my friend Jan Gregor for his continuous help in keeping up with today's sideshow performers.

Information on early sideshows was greatly enhanced by reading the late circus historian Stuart Thayer's books, *The Annals of the American Circus*. Rare dime museum ads came from show historian John Polacsek. Circus historian/curator Fred Dahlinger not only provided information but read over the manuscript. I thank him for his many helpful suggestions. Historian Dick Flint's expertise on early circuses and sideshows was a great help. Many pages in the book have been enhanced by his photos of early circus sideshows along with his images of ads, broadsides and pitch cards.

My editor Stuart Ross is amazing. If I had a sideshow out today, I would feature him in the blow-off as the "Most Patient Man" — ALIVE. For your pleasure, he remains tremendously flexible in making sense of my stories of striptease gals, racecar-driving monkeys and men pretending to be women. Thanks to everyone at ECW PRESS including publisher Jack David, press agent Simon Ware, scanner Jen Knoch, researcher Steve Nesbitt, layout artist Gail Nina, and a very special thanks to Tania Craan and Rachel Ironstone whose creative skills have delivered this piece of eye candy.

Some of my long-standing friends I met when they worked on my circuses. Giovanni Iuliani was one of them. Giovanni continues to be a massive resource in the world of outdoor show business lore. He has generously let me relate here his touring presentation of the movie *L'Amour Chez les Montres* (*The Love of Freaks*). Gypsy Red arrived as concession help. John B. (Gypsy Red) Jackson passed away two years ago. He was a real show trouper in every sense of the word that went way beyond his love for the circus and carnival. Best of all he loved the con and hustling. I'm a better person for knowing him. I've dedicated this book to his memory.

Again, my heartfelt gratitude to my wife Shirley. Numerous times she has rescued me during my many brain cramps while operating a computer. She always comes up with positive encouragement and a welcome pat on the back at just the right times. She's simply the best.

Al Stencell

A 2005 advertising card for the Washington, D.C.–based theatrical sideshow troupe Cheeky Monkey. Among their artists were Harry Murphy, billed as the oldest living escape artist, and troupe founder Swami Yomahmi (Stephon Walker), who holds a B.A. in theater from Penn State University

Introduction

Uniformed ticket collectors in the 1940s have just opened the marquee gates to a jam-packed Ringling Bros. and Barnum & Bailey Circus crowd. People surged forward, ignoring the sideshow ticket sellers — they just wanted to get into the big top and get the best seat possible.

As the last years of the 20th century unfolded in North America, young guys and gals in clubs stood gawking at a man lifting weights with his penis. His act was the crowning glory of a night when the stage had been home to a troupe of light-bulb digesters, maggot glommers, sword swallowers and regurgitation specialists. Not the opera, but definitely guerrilla theater for a room full of tattooed and pierced folks who were barely legal drinking age. The Jim Rose Circus Sideshow was in perfect harmony with their audience's world of punk, techno, comic books, zines and nose rings, but most of the show's patrons didn't know that what they were witnessing had a long and colorful past. Midway 10-in-ones and circus sideshows had disappeared from America's show lots before these marks were even born.

Minus the freaks, Rose's spectacle relied heavily on the old working acts that were the guts of sideshows for close to two centuries. Rose's crew, in true sideshow tradition, didn't measure the success of their performance by the crowd's applause but by how many of them fainted, dropped to their knees, averted their eyes or threw up. The old-time sideshow had found a new home. And while Rose may have given the old showman's patter new twists and sprinkled it with profanity, his fixation on the after-show T-shirt sales indicated he hadn't drifted too far from the real heart of any sideshow operation: the inside money.

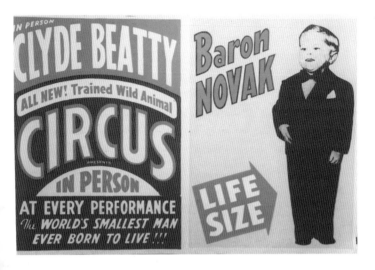

In the first years of touring menageries and circuses, freak attractions featured prominently in newspaper ads and on posters. That ended by the close of the 19th century. Few circus posters afterward featured freaks, though there were exceptions, such as Ringling in the 1930s, ballyhooing their "Giraffe Neck Women and Saucer Lip Ubangi" female tribe members, and, pictured here, midget Baron Novak adorning a 1947 Clyde Beatty truck circus poster.

The exhibition of freaks and curiosities in America has ridden a roller coaster of popular interest — positive and negative — since the sideshow's modest beginnings in wagons or small tents that followed early menageries and circuses. After the Civil War, the circus business grew quickly. The modern age of the big top began in the 1870s, when owner W. C. Coup devised a system for putting circuses on railroads. Not only did circuses expand into huge traveling enterprises but the sideshows that accompanied them were now recognized moneymakers that warranted their own prominent positions on the show grounds. They had their own bands and many employees — talkers, ticket sellers, doormen, freaks, working acts, dancing girls, concessionaires, tent workers and grifters.

The establishment and success of the organized traveling midway in the mid-

Ringling Bros. started replacing canvas sideshow banners with pictorial wood panels attached to a wagon in the 1920s. By the '30s, the long sideshow bannerline was made up of four wagons with foldout panels. The wooden wagons were replaced by steel ones in the mid-'40s. In 1953, illustrator, painter and show clown Bill Ballantine brightened up the midway by painting the sideshow bannerline, midway concessions and ticket wagons in the art deco theme shown here.

(Above) Midgets were always good eye candy for circus and carnival sideshows. Big carnivals often featured a revue show put on solely by midget dancers, singers, jugglers and strippers. Here, World of Mirth owner Frank Bergen poses with the show's midget performers in front of a display in the midget show tent that advertises Philco televisions.

1890s gave sideshowmen another stand-alone amusement enterprise to book with. By World War I, many of these ardent showmen were offering midway patrons 10 acts under a long skinny tent for one low admission price. The 10-in-one show became a carnival mainstay like the merry-go-round and cotton candy.

While there were no longer sideshows on circuses by the 1990s, several sideshow

operations with their long line of lurid banners still exist on carnival midways today. The largest, run by veterans Ward Hall and Chris Christ, features a dwarf waving torches on the bally stage much like in the old days, and talkers whose openings still stretch the truth of what you will see. Inside the contemporary sideshow, performers are packaged around illusions, freak animals and cased curios. At some fairs, a couple of dozen showmen still sell glances at tiny women,

(Above) The 1955 Ringling show shares its Philadelphia lot with a carnival. The circus sideshow tent is to the right of the ball diamond, and at the end of the sideshow bannerline are the show's five ticket wagons leading to the main entrance attached to the menagerie tent. The side-walled canvas alley known as the "Connection" leads patrons from the menagerie into the big top. The show's big cookhouse tent is behind the sideshow.

(Right) Royal American Shows stretches along the river of Memphis, Tenn., in the late 1940s. The show's front end (concessions) is out of the photo to the left, but the back end starts with the big motordrome, then the Lorow Brothers' large 10-in-one, then a funhouse setup adjacent to the main girl show featuring Sally Rand. Next to it is the show's midget revue plus a string of tented grind shows. Rides and the show's generator units topped with light towers are positioned in the rest of the street. The show's coaches and two stock cars are parked on rail sidings nearby.

headless ladies, midget horses and pickled babies inside small trailers or tents.

In the final years of my own tent circus in the 1980s I advertised: "See it now or miss it forever." The same pitch could now apply to sideshows a mere century after showmen first coined the word "ballyhoo" at the 1893 Chicago World's Fair, when they misused Arabic words to call their performers out front to give the audience a free peek at the entertainment offered inside. The word somehow stuck and never left the showman's lexicon. For future showmen, the platform in front of any show became known as the "bally stage" and the free show itself became simply the "bally," while the decorative

Bobby Breen starts a bally on Ward Hall and Chris Christ's sideshow in 2007. The show featured their new "Girl to Gorilla" illusion along with sideshow working acts and illusions. Seldom does the last big sideshow on carnival midways fail to make the Top 10 grossing attractions on a fair's midway.

During a carnival 10-in-one presentation some operators thought it was important to hold up a new crowd so they didn't come into the tent during the blade-box pitch or the blow-off spiel. Showmen called it "putting them in the pig pen." Here a tip wait to start their visit to Hall and Christ's World of Wonders at the Florida State Fair in 2005.

From the late 1880s until just prior to World War I, circuses were America's most popular amusement. But once every town had a movie theater the circus audiences waned. You wouldn't know it by this crowd of people in Las Cruces, N.M., waiting for the arrival of the 1936 Al G. Barnes circus train.

canvas hung around the stand to hide the support jacks became known as "bally cloth." Besides the showmen's spiels and bally acts, ballyhoo is also the gaudy and exaggerated artwork on sideshow banners and show fronts. It's the midget beating the bass drum or the mysterious hooded figure slumped in a chair on the bally stage. Midway and circus showmen appear to have a special ballyhoo gene inside them. Break down this DNA code and it reads: "Sell the sizzle — not the steak."

We are still a nation of gawkers. Although freakdom is rare on today's fairgrounds, there

is no shortage of it in our popular culture. A successful TV series titled *Carnivale* mixed the sideshow world and the paranormal, while several TV networks have aired sideshow documentaries. In the privacy of our own living rooms, we sit bug-eyed watching programs like *Jerry Springer*, slurping up stories of the damaged and sexually graphic lives of the 15-minutes-of-fame crowd who are skewered daily for our pleasure. At night we feast on reality shows to get our fill of worm eaters, underwater terrors and trailer-park inhabitants. For the so-called "normal folks," the midway never goes away.

In the politically correct '60s, your parents may have dragged you right past the sideshow bally and its lurid banners on the way to the fair's grandstand show to see the latest country-and-western star or the demolition derby. That's a pity. So it's time to show you what you missed. Here's your ticket — get behind the crowd lined up in the pig pen. As soon as the marks have left the blow, you will be let into the tent. Wonders await you. And you'll need cash!

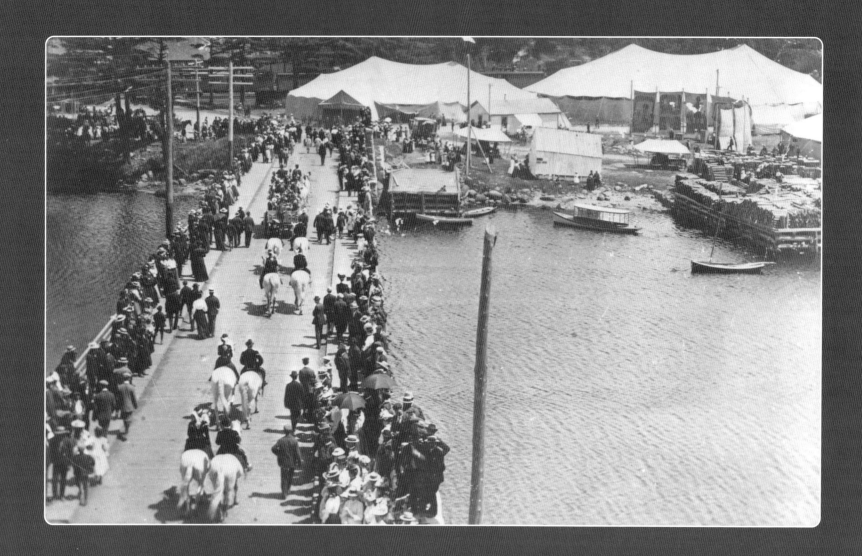

The Racket Begins

An 1880s circus near Bridgewater, N.S. The circus parade is returning to the lot, followed by the town's population. The menagerie and big top are both two-pole tents. The sideshow bannerline in the right corner of the photo has to be laid out in a curve to fit on the tight lot. Two tented concession stands and the ticket wagon are visible, and the circus's railroad stock cars can be seen behind the tents.

In the late 1700s, the spectacle called a circus made its debut in North America. In buildings crudely converted to accommodate spectator seating and the 42-foot ring established by Britain's Charles Hughes — a protégé of Philip Astley, the founder of English circuses — audiences were treated to displays of horsemanship, acrobatics, juggling and rope walking. Engagements were haphazard affairs until a group of outdoor showmen based around Somers, N.Y., launched the first traveling shows, which stayed in a community a day or two during a touring season defined by the warm-weather months. Until the canvas roof and side-walled pavillion arrived in the 1820s, their typical long stay exhibition spaces were built-up temporary amphitheaters with wooden walls and canvas tops.

Early pavillion showman Levi North ran his first circus in 1826, in a 50-foot round tent with little room for seats. An advertising agent traveled ahead of him on horseback with two saddlebags full of handbills. The show, featuring a half-dozen performers, with a brass drummer and a hand-cranked hurdy-gurdy providing the music, was pulled on the road by seven horses, and North's expenses were about $35 a day. He only put on afternoon shows, except in large centers. When the circus didn't perform at

night, the performers could mount an indoor exhibition and keep the money.

Menagerie showmen — whose shows featured exotic animals — were the elite among the roving fraternity of circus troupes, gypsies with performing bears, magicians, peep showmen and curiosity exhibitors. Circus historian Stuart Thayer records 41 menagerie companies on tour between 1813 and 1834. The 1813 company titled Museum of Living Animals consisted of merely a tiger, an ape and a marmoset. Two or three attendants and one wagon took it on the road. The word "museum," which referred to any collection, soon became loosely used in the titles of fairground shows, store shows (put on in rented vacant stores), hall exhibitions, circuses and menageries.

The Exhibition of Natural Curiosities, touring in 1821, listed among its animals a freak calf with six legs. Exhibits of wax figures, static cases of curios and freak animals, dead or alive, were part of early menageries and often deemed sensational enough to be placed in a separate enclosure — sometimes even off the lot in a rented hall — where visitors had to pay an additional price to see them. Patrons to the 1834 J. R. and William Howe Jr. and Co. Menagerie could view G. K. Nellis, "the Armless Man," in a separate tent for 12½ cents extra, while the 1835 Zoological Institute's Baltimore Menagerie carried a separate tent containing serpents and

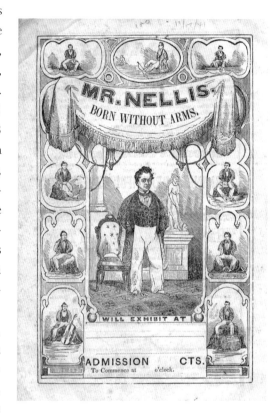

Handout advertising bill used by armless performer Mr. Nellis when showing in halls. Nellis was a prominent freak attraction with early menageries and circuses.

paintings. "Cosmoramas" were popular outside attractions, usually exhibited in a small tent containing a wagon with a proscenium, across which scenic paintings were moved past the audience by hidden end rollers.

An 1835 Dedham, Mass., newspaper noted that the museum carried with the June, Angevine, Titus and Co. Menagerie was a separate small affair consisting of two loads of wax figures, a live anaconda and a couple of chaps who sang nonsensical Negro songs. In contrast, the New York Zoological Institute's Mammoth Exhibition traveled in 1836 on three dozen wagons, nine of which carried an outside attraction titled the New York Museum and Exhibition of Fine Arts. This extra-cost show with its lofty title displayed wax figures, stuffed birds, serpents, and mineral and fossil specimens.

Many menageries were financed by investors until the 1837 stock panic. Then, some animal exhibitors struggled on while others threw their lot in with circus showmen. These two enterprises had already begun blending in the 1830s — menageries added ring acts to their static zoo displays while circuses exhibited cages of wild animals inside their performance tents. All of this took place under the watchful eyes of local clergy, who disdained circuses as a waste of time but viewed menageries as educational. The public, however, felt differently. Circus crowds grew bigger and bigger, necessitating larger tents, more seating and additional rings. To make room for extra seats, the wheeled animal cages were removed and placed inside their own tent.

This 33-page booklet relating the history of various species of wild animals along with poems and songs sold on the Oriental Circus and Egyptian Caravan operated by J. V. Cameron in 1874.

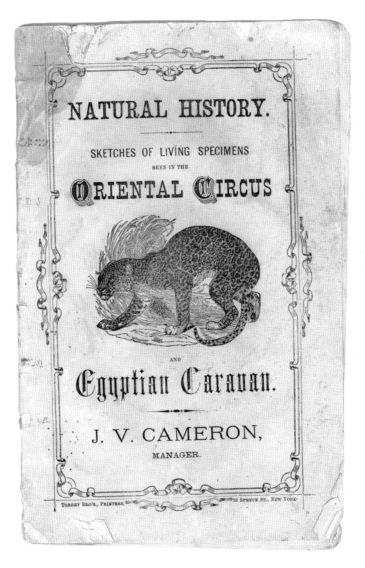

NATURAL HISTORY.

SKETCHES OF LIVING SPECIMENS

SEEN IN THE

ORIENTAL CIRCUS

AND

Egyptian Caravan.

J. V. CAMERON,

MANAGER.

TORREY BRO'S, PRINTERS, 13 SPRUCE ST., NEW YORK.

Newspaper ad for the Australian Children noting The Marvels of Nature — On Exhibition in a tent adjacent to Forepaugh's Menagerie and Circus Pavillion.

Gil Robinson in the John Robinson Circus ticket wagon at Brooklyn, N.Y., 1872. Note the mirror in the ticket-wagon window flap. Ticket sellers were masters at shortchanging patrons and those standing in line were fair game for pickpockets and other grifters.

Separate-charge attractions similar to those traveling with menageries were also found outside the main tent on early circuses and other tented attractions. Circus showmen referred to them as "outside shows." By the 1860s, exhibits and curios both living and dead featured in various outside shows became the sideshow or museum tent on the circus lot. Most sideshows were owned by independent showmen and many went back and forth between circuses and fairs and other public gatherings.

One local newspaper reported a score of sideshows traveling with the 1854 Franconi's Hippodrome. First on the lot was a wax show on two wagons that were joined together under a canvas roof. Next to arrive were Ethiopian singers, with a white man painted black and riding a mule to draw a crowd. By mid-morning, shows containing a "Living Skeleton," a "Wild Boy of the Woods" and a sea lion were open on the lot. Their admission prices ranged from a nickel to a quarter. All did good business until the Hippodrome opened, at which time they had to stop.

Fayette Lodawick Robinson — popularly known as Yankee Robinson — started his show-business career in 1845 at Danville, N.Y. By the early '50s he ran a two-wagon circus, and from 1859 to 1864 his show was a combination of circus acts and theater pieces. Robinson's answer to a jaded public who were tired of paying for outside instead of inside exhibitions was to offer his main show and three outside shows for one price. With this new strategy, his show drew well in every village.

In an 1890s issue of the *New York Clipper*, the show trade's weekly, Silas Robinson related his father's detailed description of outside shows. Yankee told his son, "In 1857 we started from Chicago with bills that read 'Yankee Robinson Quadruple Show.' Four separate shows in four separate tents for 40 cents. We had a 70-foot round tent with a 30-foot middle and in one end a stage nine feet by 15 feet. We had some scenery and the remains of Harry Waugh's 'Billy Faye the Shanghai Clown.' We put it and 'The Days of '76' on in the afternoon and 'Uncle Tom's Cabin' at night. We had posturing, tumbling, La Perche, ladders, rings, and trapeze before the drama. The only new features that year were the four shows and the overland calliope.

"We had three sideshow canvases large enough to hold one wagon and these completed the Quadruple. The menagerie had one cage with: a black bear, a wolf, a coon, two monkeys, a badger, white rabbits, guinea pigs and a parrot. The one-wagon museum with glass sides contained a large rib, some quartz specimens and petrifications. The minstrel organization was a wagon with the box off and planks on it for a stage. A middle man and two end men plus the orchestra on the ground were the show. When the crowds gave up their ticket at the main show they paid to see it all and wondered how they would see the rest without a ticket. When the big show was out, the side canvases of the

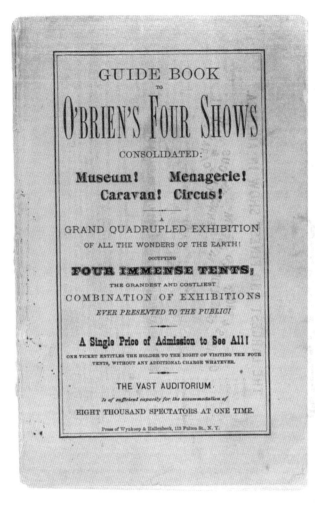

After the American Civil War, the circus business expanded rapidly and competition was fierce. Some operators combined all their tented features for one price. The flyer for O'Brien's Four Shows advertises one admission to all four tents, offering the museum, menagerie, caravan and circus.

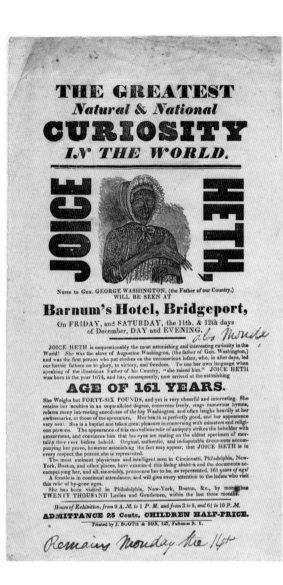

P. T. Barnum's first big hoax on the showgoing public was Joice Heth — billed as the 161-year-old former slave of Augustine Washington, the father of President George Washington. This bill is for her appearance at the Barnum Hotel in Bridgeport, Conn., where for two December days she was on exhibit from 9 a.m. until 1 p.m., 3 to 5 p.m., and 6:30 to 10 p.m.

— to set up on the circus lot. Some showmen tried to avoid paying these privilege fees by setting up on land adjacent to the lot or in the streets leading to the show. Circus owners viewed these "trailers" with more disdain than Civil War generals viewed the hookers following their troops. The milieu on and off the lot could include personal-hygiene product sellers, fortune tellers and hucksters of tinware, jewelry, figurines, religious tracts, cards with "God" written in 48 languages, bawdy parodies of popular songs, questionable poetry and lewd pictures. Caged rats shilled for the rat poisoners while jars of bed bugs attracted clients for the bug expeller. White cotton lambs on sticks were sold by hawkers like concessionaires sell balloons today.

The main tent's performance was just as eclectic. It was comprised of animals, freaks, talking clowns, equestrians and aerialists. The ring presentations of P. T. Barnum and Seth B. Howe's circus on their 1851 visit to Hartford, Conn., included the 28-inch-high Tom Thumb, Mr. Nellie "the Armless Wonder," a baby elephant, a Burmese bull and a cage of

six lions into which a performer entered for a short time. A display of wax U.S. presidents topped off the enterprise.

But there was a shadow over the colorful circus business: it was common for grifters, pickpockets and other hustlers to show up wherever crowds gathered. In an April 1873 *Clipper*, Barnum warned, "Although I will carry detectives with my show I advise everybody not to bring to the show jewelry or valuables and limit themselves to an amount of money not much more than sufficient for admission tickets and refreshments. Look out for all games."

An early look at show grift can be found in the journals of William Hunt. Hunt wasn't a self-aggrandizing promoter like Barnum but he was certainly America's most talented showman. Born in Lockport, N.Y., in 1838, Hunt, while still a child, moved with his parents to Port Hope, Ont., and on their farm he became a gifted acrobat and wire walker. Under the name Signor Guillermo Antonio Farini, in 1860 he duplicated the Great Blondin's feat of walking a rope across the

sideshows were dropped and all on the lot viewed the wonders."

Various concessionaires and small sideshow exhibitors paid a small fee — a privilege

Pitch booklet sold by Farini's Krao the Missing Link. Most showmen believed Krao came from the slums of Liverpool, U.K., and not a jungle as Farini proclaimed. Regardless, Krao was a major dime museum and circus sideshow draw.

The lot layout of this small early wagon circus shows the one-pole big top surrounded by a half-dozen smaller tents. Several are refreshment tents while at least two appear to be sideshows. Waterways were some of the best transportation corridors for early circuses. Wagons, animals and gear were loaded on and off steamboats, barges and small canal boats.

Niagara Falls, and while in Europe he invented the person-shot-from-a-cannon act.

Prior to walking across the Falls, Hunt was the bookkeeper on Dan Rice's Circus. There he witnessed a fakir — as showmen called con men and grifters — take a black patron's $10 bill but only give him change for a five. He told Rice, who replied, "That's all right, you'll get used to it. Keep yourself honest, that's all I ask of you. Every show has fakirs. I had one last year that came in with four thousand dollars. They may as well have it as them damn 'niggers' who don't know how to use it." Hunt soon noticed that all the ticket sellers, candy butchers and photo salesmen short-changed patrons, and pickpockets and grifters hung around the ticket wagon. Rice collected a weekly privilege fee from them and from the operators of the sideshow, lemonade and candy stands. When police caught a fakir robbing someone, the show owner would plead innocence, and the show's canvasmen would stage a fight, allowing the accused fakir to escape. He would return a few towns later.

Stereo view of Barnum's circus showing the sideshow bannerline with two connected tents behind it. A single ticket wagon for the main show sits near the canopy entrance to the big top.

Getting an early wagon circus over the road was often difficult. Workers and performers rode and slept on the tops of the wagons nightly, except when they reached steep hills or had to push the carriages through mud or streams. Most tied themselves to the wagon with their belts in case they tumbled off. Here, a cage wagon on the 1918 Mighty Haag Circus crosses a river via a wood ferry somewhere in the South.

There were, however, some honest (and perhaps less racist) owners. John J. Jennings's 1882 book *Theatrical and Circus Life: Or, Secrets of the Stage, Green-room and Sawdust Arena* quotes W. C. Coup: "I've been offered as high as a thousand dollars a week by camp-followers for the privilege of robbing my patrons. . . . The sideshows can be made to pay without robbery. Last season the sideshows that traveled with my show made

seventy-five thousand dollars, which was more than I made." Obviously many sideshows did well even without the grift.

Rarely did circuses and grifters run *Clipper* ads regarding their operations, such as the May 1874 ad stating, "Privilege of running a wheel of fortune in sideshow is wanted by J. J. Southworth." Usually such notices were cloaked in show lingo, like C. Whitaker's 1886 *Clipper* invite to grifters to join his

circus. It read: "Wanted — fakirs — good men only for tenting season. Show moves by rail and everything goes." Some circus owners merely condoned grift, knowing they would be blamed for it anyway. Others embraced it heartily as a way of leveling the playing field since farmers, local merchants and city officials habitually robbed them. Lawmen expected to be paid off, and town officials often demanded higher than pre-set

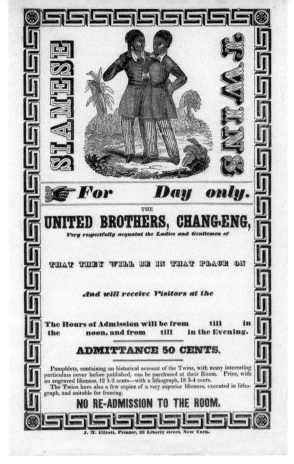

A blank handbill for a room showing of "Chang-Eng — the United Brothers," mid-19th-century American freak attraction. With admission a hefty 50 cents for everyone, they made a fortune. The ad informs patrons they will be able to purchase a published historical account of the brothers along with an engraved likeness for 12½ cents. The bio also came with a lithograph for 18¾ cents, and a limited number of superior lithographs suitable for framing were also for sale.

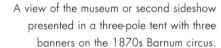

A view of the museum or second sideshow presented in a three-pole tent with three banners on the 1870s Barnum circus.

license fees once the show tents went up. Comp tickets were big items, maybe a quarter of the audience. Circus proprietors could only pay up, shut up, show and move on.

Still, the sideshow wasn't taken entirely seriously by many show owners. Tony Pastor, vaudeville's founding father, who as a child star played the tambourine in the 1847 Raymond & Waring Menagerie's minstrel

sideshow, recalled how the sideshow's night performance had to be put in a rented hall because the big-top tent crew would take down the sideshow tent before the main show started. Sideshows were still small affairs: the 1860 Cooke Circus Co. sideshow, for example, featured only fat lady Miss Hannah Barrister, weighing 500 pounds, as well as a living skeleton, a stone eater, a clog dancer, a comic jester and a female dancer. The next year, Professor Hyman's sideshow with Madigan's Great Show consisted of cages of animals, a Swiss stone eater, a sword swallower, a Gypsy queen and the Professor doing magic.

Circus performers were expected to double and triple — a company short of female performers made do with males in drag. An August 1873 *Clipper* relates how a circus playing out west advertised the only mermaid on exhibition, giving daily peformances of eating, drinking, sleeping and smoking — under water. When the mermaid was discovered to be a muscular canvasman in makeup and wig, all hell broke loose. Regardless, female impersonators — gay and straight — became a permanent part of circuses and sideshow operations. Some circus owners thought it was bad luck not to have at least one gay person on the show.

MIGHTY HAAG. 1918. SOMEWHERE IN THE SOUTH.

Elephants could pose difficulties for wagon showmen. Some elephants feared a bridge wouldn't hold their weight and refused to cross it. Here one of the Mighty Haag Circus bulls seems okay with floating across the river on a raft in 1918.

Many sideshow operators also ran the concert (or after-show) privilege and tried to hire "specialties" — musical, acrobatic and dance acts suitable for both shows. Magicians were ideal as they could do stage magic, Punch and Judy, and ventriloquism in the sideshow and acts of illusions or mentalism in the concert. Since magicians were good talkers, lecturers and pitchmen, many became early sideshow

After the 1870s many circuses became large railway operations, but there were still plenty of smaller shows, like the 1897 Campbell Bros. Circus. Note the one-pole sideshow tent with seven banners out front. The midway crowd is waiting for the "cloud swing" act that will appear between the two-pole setup before the entrance marquee and the menagerie tent. This is the showman's way of holding the tip so the sideshow can get a good crack at the crowd.

owners or managers. Coupled with a female companion presenting a large snake, assisting in an illusion, reading palms or appearing as the "Circassian Beauty," the magician could put on the whole show. The addition of a midget, a fat person or a giant upgraded the enterprise into a big-time display. Waxed, stuffed and mummified freaks extended the displays while providing additional subjects for outside banners. A wax two-headed baby required no lodging or salary and was easily packed away for transport. People were fascinated with snakes and they were easy to transport too. A small cage containing wolves, cats, dogs, birds and monkeys billed as the "Happy Family" could be seen on most early sideshows.

By the early 1870s, the physical layout of the modern tent circus was developing into its characteristic 20th-century look. The lining up of the sideshow, menagerie and big-top tents in a straight line replaced the multitude of scattered small tents. A photo from the period shows the 1872 P. T. Barnum's Circus sideshow housed in a small one-pole round tent fronted by a bannerline of eight banners of various sizes. Sideshowmen still preferred hiring acts with their own paintings, ensuring a mixture of styles and colors on sideshow bannerlines into the 1880s.

In spring 1873, the *Clipper* issued its first circus supplement, listing 22 touring shows. Most carried a sideshow, a museum or both. Joel E. Warner's circus trouped a free menagerie of 12 cages, plus an extra-charge museum tent that included more exotic beasts — three camels, one elephant and an English mastiff.

Early group photo taken inside the sideshow tent on a circus features a bearded lady and deformed midget, and almost as many women performers as men. The elaborate hanging purses on the two ladies suggest this is where they kept their pitch money when working.

Another stereo view of the five-banner sideshow on a circus with the show's concession tent and ticket wagon in the foreground.

The sideshow featured skeleton man John Battersby, fat lady Hannah Battersby, "Aztec Children," an "Egyptian Mummy," Punch and Judy and an "Educated Pig." Barnum's World's Fair boasted a regular performance tent plus a cookhouse and four sideshows, while the Great Eastern Menagerie's sideshow offered a Punch-and-Judy show, magician Professor Collier, two cages of animals, an "Albino Boy" and a "Four-Footed Four-Legged Child."

MARY JANE POWERS,

28 years old   Weighs 807 pounds.

200 pounds heavier than any Lady in America.

THE WORLD-RENOWNED
Kentucky Giantess.

JOHN H. POWERS,

Eighteen years old   Weighs 600 pounds.

The heaviest boy of his age in America.

The Wonderful Kentucky
GIANT BOY.

Front and back of the pitch booklet sold by John Powers and his sister Mary Jane while on tour in the early 1860s.

J. W. Orr was an ambitious outside showman. His attractions at the 1873 Van Amburgh & Co. Circus included a museum tent of inanimate objects, a tent sheltering the paleontological exhibit of life-sized animals long passed from earth and another holding a wax works and a gymnastic display, while views of European cities and principal American seaports were offered inside the cosmorama tent. Another pavillion held Capt. John Grimley's Australian Bird Show while Orr's Monstrosity Show featured the eight-foot-six giant Terrance Keough and his eight-foot-two sister Margaret. Other oddities included 673-pound fat lady

The first circus concert is credited to the 1836 Old Columbia Circus where a performance of magic feats and negro songs was put on after the main show in a separate tent. Show owners soon found the "after show" grossed more if put on in the main tent. The concert was announced several times during the show while vendors sold tickets in the seats. Western film stars like Tim McCoy became big circus concert draws in the 1930s. In 1949 Dailey Bros. Circus hired Doug Autry, seen here outside the big top. Lettering on the train and circus wagons screamed "AUTRY IN PERSON," with "Doug" in very small letters. Although Doug was a relative, Gene Autry soon had the show repaint the equipment with both names the same size.

Adelaide Hopwitt and Ella Bray, a child wonder who weighed 114 pounds at age 14 months. Dwarves included 19-year-old Willie Grant and 23-year-old Eva Henshaw, each just over two feet tall. Arthur Barnes, the "Living Skeleton," stood five-three but weighed only 34 pounds. Armless Lillie Deveneux, two "Circassian Beauties," Mungo Park ("the Spotted Boy"), bearded child Essay Blake, a "What Is It?" from Patagonia, a boy and girl aged 11 and 14 from Madagascar and an African "Earth Woman" rounded out the exhibit.

The Museum of Living Curiosities connected to L. B. Lent's Leviathan Universal Living Exposition, Metropolitan Museum, Mastodon Menagerie, Hemispheric Hippozoonomadon, Cosmographic Caravan, Equescurriculum and Great New York Circus featured a dwarf, a bearded lady, "Circassian Beauties," a "Living Skeleton," a "White Moor" and glassblowers. Lent's April 1873 Clipper ad trumpeted 60 carloads of curiosities and marvels, boasting, "All living wonders and attractions. No Wax works, no stuffed animals, no fictitious names, no ventriloquist frauds, no corpses, and NO HUMBUG!" The sideshows appearing with larger circuses began featuring more living human curiosities. The short, fat, tall, skinny and deformed became the Monstrosity Show's big draws.

Many freaks handled their own bookings and some had their own sideshows. Kentucky fat boy and teenager John H. Powers and his 807-pound-plus sister Mary Jane worked on circus sideshows until the fall of 1872. They then bought a tent and played fairs on their own. In 1874 their tent and animals burned, leaving them only a set of banners. Partnered with sideshowman John Fulton, who had a 25-by-35-foot tent, they paid a $2,500 privi-

Parading into town became the main advertising tool for wagon shows. Here is the second circus bandwagon used on a show in America carrying John Stowe's circus band in 1850. Stowe's Great Varieties featured the Hanlon trapeze act, Babcock Bros. acrobats and George Cutler, cannonball juggler.

lege fee to join the Melville, Maginley & Cook Circus, but business was so bad they couldn't afford fresh straw for their monkey cage. They left and paid $15 to set up at the Albany, N.Y., races where they took in only nine bucks.

In 1874, armless entertainer Prof. S. Greneley did better than the Powers siblings. His sideshow, which boasted new canvas and banners, featured himself drawing, writing and firing a gun with his toes, plus a child with two heads and a double-bodied pig, both preserved in alcohol. Small zoo animals and an educated hog topped off his hour-long presentation.

Up-front privilege money often got the show out in the spring, and many circus owners left the profits from the extras off the books. Owner Adam Forepaugh kept all

Photos of wagon circuses are rare. Here we see the Whitney Family Circus lined up in the 1880s. Note the lead wagon with a large tent pole hung low on its side and the canopy over the wagon driver to keep the rain off. Note also the limited turn radius of the front wheels!

Attractions in the 1888 Barnum & Bailey Circus sideshow included the armless Charles Tripp standing in front of the four Shield brothers (giants). Also seen here are a thin man, Rubber Skin Joe, the Bearded Lady — Anna Studard — and orator Bill Henshaw seated beside the Circassion snake lady.

the money from sideshows and banner sales for himself. He also kept the fees he collected from hustlers allowed to sell circus tickets for 10 cents more prior to the ticket-wagon opening and from a blind woman he let beg beside it. Many circus owners became fed up when privilege operators abandoned them to play fall fairs. Show owners began in earnest to run their own lucrative extras that included sideshows, pit shows, exhibition wagons, concerts, dollar stores, reserve seats, songster and program sales and prize candy pitches, along with souvenir, food and drink concessions. Circus owners hired managers to supervise these operations while performers and other workers received bonuses for helping out with the privileges, giving them more reasons for "being with it and for it." Behind the scenes, the legal adjuster — or "patch" — dispensed cash and tickets to city officials and police to ensure the grifters and sideshow hustlers were not interfered with.

Within several decades, the circus sideshow had gone from single exhibitions of small curiosities scattered around the outside of the main circus tent to its own large tented pavillion. The sideshow had become part of the circus, just like the menagerie and the "big show." More importantly, owners gave it a designated position on the show lot and considered the sideshow a serious money-generating portion of their circus enterprise. On stages inside the sideshow tent, lecturers' polished patter and descriptions became the speech templates for future freak and oddity showmen. The circus sideshow became the place to view human oddities of all kinds, new wonders of science and technology, outstanding variety acts, musicians of all sorts and nationalities and, for men, quick flashes of female nudity and an education in games of chance many would sooner have passed on.

Chapter 2

The Sideshow Matures

The cast and crew of the Buffalo Bill Wild West Show in front of the bannerline. Mr. and Mrs. Shields — giant and giantess — are in the group to the right of the bally while the male midget on the bally is Major Ray. The three-legged horse gets an extra-large banner as do the tall folks.

Many circus owners had started in the privilege end of the business as sideshowmen. For example, New York State resident Sig Sautelle, who'd been a teenage ventriloquist and Punch-and-Judy worker, had his own sideshow before trouping a full circus on canal boat, wagon, rails and finally trucks between 1870 and 1930. Sig said he built his whole show around Punch and Judy because the act was "clean and happy." He also watched expenses. One old-timer remembers him coming into the cook-house and yelling, "Give the boys all the eggs they want" — while holding up one finger.

By the 1900s, sideshows on large circuses were substantial operations whose revenues greatly helped to offset the show's operating costs. These circuses hired the best giants and midgets, along with the most unusual folks — those without limbs or with twisted spines, half-bodies or other physical blights. Showmen billed them as "Frog Boys," "Armless Wonders," "Half Humans," "Boneless Phenoms" and "Ossified Humanity." The talker's catchy phrases and rhymes describing the freaks were bettered only by the attractions' own billing: "Slats the Skeleton Dude," "Ho-Jo the Bear Boy" and "Flippo the Seal Boy." While the marks snickered, the freaks stared back, knowing they were earning a living and enjoying an independent life. However, the real entertainment meat in a sideshow sandwich was the bevy of oddball variety acts, cat and rooster orchestras, and illusions with lofty titles. These acts moved the show along and kept the audience upbeat all the way to the annex door.

The large double-deck bannerline of the Sig Sautelle Railroad Circus, with Sautelle's painted image over the doorway that advertises his "Parlor of Fun, Dog Circus, and Museum. 3 Monsters Shows" for one price. The ticket boxes are storage boxes with a canvas-covered front frame to hide the ticket seller's feet.

Fat folks, midgets and dwarves — or "runts," as sideshowmen called them — along with giants were circus sideshow mainstays covering the "freak" lineup. Siamese twins were a rarity and by the 20th century, circus sideshow goers preferred dancing girls, minstrel bands and novelty acts.

Sex was a powerful draw, and from the start women played a prominent role in sideshow exhibitions. Although good-looking dames on the bally were extremely effective in selling the show, circus ladies proved to be more than passive hangers-on. Inside they were snake handlers, weight lifters, club swingers, bell ringers and illusion helpers. A male knife thrower and a shapely female target put sex into the performance, and an older woman made the perfect mind reader — her wrinkles merely reflected years of experience that convinced marks she could sort out the lines on their outstretched palms.

1895 *Clipper* ad for one of the great freaks of all time — Jo-Jo the Dog Faced Boy. Note that he has a new painting by Tucker Bros., one of the leading banner firms of the time. For years, circuses and dime museums required acts to have their own banner or had ones painted for them and charged them for it.

GREAT OPPORTUNITY
For Summer Resorts and Side Shows,
JO-JO,
THE DOG FACED BOY,
AT LIBERTY for July, August or September. Address
NICH. FORSTER, Manager, No. 1,190 Third Ave., N. Y.
P. S.—New painting by Tucker Bros.

Even small shows like Lincoln Bros. Circus had substantial sideshows. Depicted on the banners are an escape artist, mind reader, snake handler, Duke the Fighting Lion and more. Note the sideshow band out front.

Snakes were a mainstay on any sideshow and ladies were the preferred presenters. Note the elaborate backdrop, stage cloth valence and stage railing.

Circassians, from the mountainous regions of the Black Sea, were believed to be the purest form of the white race. For a time, "Circassian women" were hot attractions. Some were legitimate imports, while more were sideshow workers' wives or girlfriends outfitted with a glorious mop of frizzy hair. Others followed the instructions in *Shaw's Book of Acts* for making Circassian hair: "Soak the ladies' hair in one quart of stale beer. Do up the ends in the ordinary way. Leave the hair up for three days, soaking it twice a day. After three days, carefully remove the leads and comb the hair upwards. The hair will remain standing, and will be long and wavy like that of Circassians." Some weren't ladies at all; an 1887 *Clipper* ad stated: "Champion amateur female impersonator wants engagement as Almolette the Circassian."

The Barnum & Bailey Circus, the "Greatest Show on Earth," was the leading circus of late-19th-century America. Their 1891 sideshow, run by W. D. Hagar and William Henshaw, featured a 10-piece band and Lew Graham as the talker. Working acts included marionettes, magicians, performing birds, a snake charmer and an expansionist who, by stretching his limbs and neck, could make himself appear taller. Legitimate freaks were C. H. Vreck "the Hungarian Giant," Charles B. Tripp "the Armless Phenomenon" and Asbury Ben "the Spotted Boy." A tattooed couple, along with "Zip" or "What Is It?" and Waino and Plutaeno, the "Wild Men of Borneo," rounded out the cast. Gone were the curios and small cages of animals.

The sideshow bannerline was the first and most colorful thing patrons saw coming onto the grounds. It faced toward town, or in the direction that people came onto the lot. A colorful circus midway put visitors in a carefree mood and opened their wallets. As the 20th century approached, efforts were expanded to color-coordinate valences, trims and bally

"HOME, SWEET HOME."

Freak attractions got people inside the sideshow, but working acts such as cat orchestras were needed to provide the entertainment content.

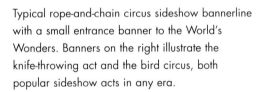

Typical rope-and-chain circus sideshow bannerline with a small entrance banner to the World's Wonders. Banners on the right illustrate the knife-throwing act and the bird circus, both popular sideshow acts in any era.

Poster for the Barnum, Bailey & Hutchinson Circus. James L. Hutchinson was hired by P. T. Barnum in 1872 as a press agent. He went on to be an extremely good sideshow operator and teamed up with James A. Bailey to create the Greatest Show on Earth. Freaks and other sideshow performers were featured on early circus advertising but less so as the wild animals and spectacular pageants became the circus drawing cards.

been creating banners since 1848. Both were highly rated by showmen.

Ringling Bros.' 1892 route book claimed their sideshow was the only one with scenery and other stage apparatus necessary for a first-class theatrical exhibit. The writer suggests if the compilers of *Webster's Dictionary* visited, they would surely be impressed enough to put the word "sideshow" into the dictionary. A series of 1890 route books for the Hunting's Circus compiled by sideshowman Charles Griffin not only gives us a look into the "Wizard's Den," as Griffin called his sideshow there, but also into who supplied the sideshow trade with costumes, magic supplies, animals, snakes, illusions, pitch books and photos. Griffin, a magician, ventriloquist and Punch-and-Judy man, advertised lessons in these arts at his N.Y.C. Conjuring College. Among the other advertisers was the New York canvas-making firm of M. R. Kunkely that held the patent to "lap lacing," an innovation that let showmen piece together large tents from small, manageable canvas sections, an important invention for the expansion of the circus.

cloths on food stands and sideshow platforms. One banner painter or scenic firm would do the bannerline, ensuring all banners had the same borders, highlights, shading, lettering, color combinations and pictorial styles. From 1894, E. J. Hayden and Co. led the way in circus and carnival scenics. Their star artist was 25-year veteran Charles Wolfe, whose sideshow fronts Hayden hailed as "a traveling art gallery." His rival was J. Bruce, who had

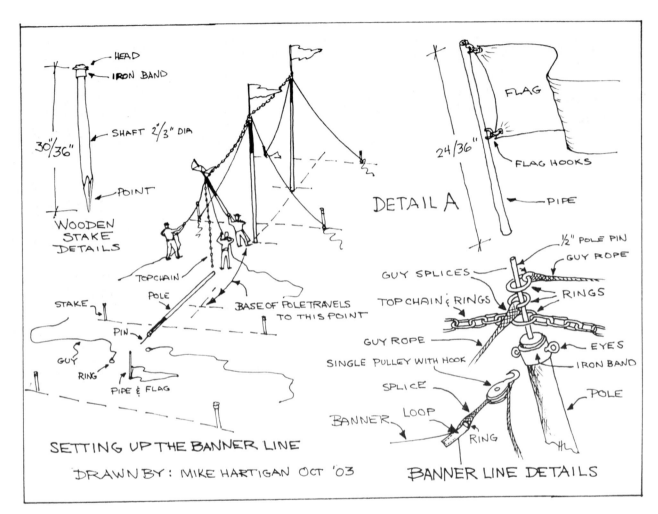

HEAD
IRON BAND
SHAFT 2"/3" DIA
30"/36"
POINT
WOODEN STAKE DETAILS

TOPCHAIN
POLE
STAKE
PIN
BASE OF POLE TRAVELS TO THIS POINT
GUY
RING
PIPE & FLAG

SETTING UP THE BANNER LINE
DRAWN BY: MIKE HARTIGAN OCT '03

FLAG
DETAIL A
24/36"
FLAG HOOKS
PIPE

1/2" POLE PIN
GUY ROPE
GUY SPLICES
RINGS
TOP CHAIN & RINGS
GUY ROPE
EYES
SINGLE PULLEY WITH HOOK
IRON BAND
SPLICE
POLE
BANNER   LOOP
RING

BANNER LINE DETAILS

Mike Hartigan's sketches showing how a rope-and-chain bannerline is put together. Once you get the first pole up, the hard part is done. These appeared first in a copy of the magazine *Little Circus Wagon*, published by the Circus Model Builders Association.

Despite the color and action it added to the circus lot, the sideshow was rarely mentioned in publicity. Crippled, deformed and diseased folks were odd to look at but didn't make for positive advertising material. But regardless of what was in the sideshow, someone or something had to draw the crowd to the bally stage so the talker could convince them to pay money and go inside. Snare drums, bugles and hand organs were the main noisemakers outside early circus sideshows, and banjo players came along after the Civil War. In the early 1900s, shaker chimes and Una-Fons were popular, and the metal triangular gong rang on the bally into the 1950s.

In the late 1870s, some circuses carried both a main circus band and a brass or high-

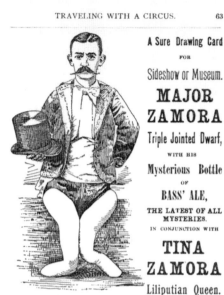

A Sure Drawing Card

FOR

Sideshow or Museum.

MAJOR ZAMORA

Triple Jointed Dwarf,

WITH HIS

Mysterious Bottle

OF

BASS' ALE,

THE LATEST OF ALL MYSTERIES.

IN CONJUNCTION WITH

TINA ZAMORA

Liliputian Queen.

TO WHOM IT MAY CONCERN.

The little Major has done the lecturing in our Annex past two seasons to universal satisfaction, and with his Mysterious BOTTLE TRICK has proven to be a great drawing card. He is a little gentleman at all stages, and I can heartily recommend him as pleasing to all classes. We always have an opening for him.

CHAS. E. GRIFFIN, Manager Annex, Hunting's Circus.

Per. address, MAJOR ZAMORA, 123 W. Madison St., Chicago, Ill.

Chas Griffin put out several Hunting's Circus route books. Here is an ad, on the back of the 1893 route book, for Major Zamora, the triple-jointed dwarf. Another, placed by N.Y.C. animal dealer W. A. Conklin, stated: "African Snakes Always on Hand."

Shaw's Book of Acts included ventriloquist dialogue and instructions for several sideshow acts including sword swallowing. W. H. J. Shaw was a Canadian magician who moved to Victoria, Mo., in the late 1800s where he became a prominent supplier of sideshow materials, including deformed wax babies, vent figures and mechanical wax figures.

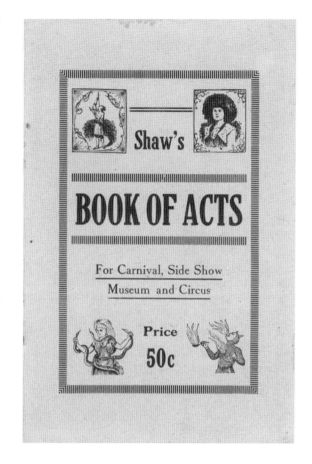

Shaw's

BOOK OF ACTS

For Carnival, Side Show
Museum and Circus

Price
50c

land band just for the sideshow. The morning circus parade on the town's main street was a big part of selling the public on the show, and parading several musical groups enhanced the show's status. The proliferation of black minstrel troupes, which became the band most associated with circus sideshows and the nation's main conductor of popular songs and dances, didn't start until after the Civil War

years. The Georgia Minstrels, the cream of these black shows, was formed in 1865. The 1880 Sells Brothers Circus had one of the earliest trouping black sideshow bands, while the 1894 Walter L. Main Circus sideshow had an eight-piece North American Indian brass band. The next season they featured Joe McNutt's 12-piece Colored Minstrels and Jubilee Singers. Hunting's Circus sideshow in 1893 presented

Griffin's Famous Congo Band, composed of two white and two black musicians — a fife player and percussionists. The next season Charles Griffin carried Professor W. H. Jacobs's seven-piece Colored Band.

The sideshows on both the Barnum & Bailey's and the Ringling Bros.' circuses used Italian bands until 1907. The next year, Ringling installed Rob Roy Pope as its first

THE MORNING OPENING.

Sketch from 1893 Hunting's Circus route book depicts sideshow manager and performer Chas E. Griffin making an opening with his Punch and Judy figures.

black sideshow band leader. From then until the 1940s, Ringling featured a large black minstrel organization that, for novelty, noise, comedy and dancing, couldn't be beat, until the last few years of the Ringling sideshow when they were replaced by Hawaiian and Latin American musicians and dancers.

Inside the front flap of the 1893 Ringling Bros. World's Greatest Shows' route book was a quote from Shakespeare: "Men's eyes were made to look and let them gaze." And they sure did. Almost every sideshow featured oriental or dancing cuties. "Peggy from Paris" had been exciting saloon and theatrical patrons since the 1850s. The 1893 Chicago

(Left) The 1909 Norris and Rowe Circus sideshow band heads out in the circus parade the show is staging in Los Angeles, Calif., March 19. Ornately carved wagons gilded with gold leaf and drawn by a four-to-eight-horse hitch were the big flash in the parade, which usually ended with a long procession of elephants and the steam calliope.

Minstrel entertainers had been a part of circus and circus sideshow performances from the beginning. Once "black" music took off in the later part of the 19th century, the black minstrel band with its comedians and girl dancers was a must on every circus sideshow.

By the beginning of the 20th century, vaudeville theaters were big, and sideshows made sure they covered anything popular. Here the sideshow entrance banner promises "Museum Wonders, Vaudeville and Minstrel Shows." No mention of dancing girls, but they were in there.

World's Fair icon Little Egypt ensured hoochie-coochie dancers a place in sideshow annexes. The same fair also ignited interest in exotic races as attractions. The Reverend J. Coleman Adams of Brooklyn's All Souls Church said a tour of the Chicago World's Fair midway "was equal to a voyage around the world." He preached, "'The Midway Plaisance' is an object lesson in the method of evolution. The savage is just a man child and a child of man. He is a case of arrested development." Showmen soon made sure rubes everywhere, even those Americans that hadn't traveled further than the ends of their local streetcar lines could mentally escape to distant islands or African bushlands to view Fiji Cannibals, South Sea Islanders, Zulu Tribesmen and Congo Headhunters.

Ethnological attractions — big-lipped "Ubangis," "Giraffe-Necked Women," "Wild Zulus," "Dahomey Warriors" and a slew of American black performers in various tribal mufti — became circus sideshow fixtures. Showmen ballyhooed them as educational exhibits, fully aware that the semi-nude female tribe members on display were merely peep shows. Fortunately for showmen, the same folks who picketed local vaudeville houses to protest tight leotards on female performers saw nothing wrong with gaping at bare-breasted African villagers to advance their education.

Both Charles Darwin's 1859 publication *On the Origins of Species* and the 1926 Scopes Monkey Trial ensured showmen a captive audience for any dark-skinned humans with lots of body hair and odd-shaped craniums.

Many early sideshows featured talking animals. Educated pigs told time, added up sums and answered your questions. In this "Pick-out act," the animal gets his cues from the trainer in very subtle ways. Here is the 1893 Great Adam Forepaugh Sideshow's *N.Y. Clipper* ad promoting Mazeppa the Talking Horse.

The 1903 and 1904 Barnum & Bailey Circus sideshow featured Signor Guillermo Antonio Farini's protégé, "Krao the Missing Link." Krao's bio claimed Carl Bock had found him in the jungles of Laos, but rumors hinted that Farini had found him in a Liverpool, England, slum. Farini's lecture related Krao's closeness to the primate world by showing

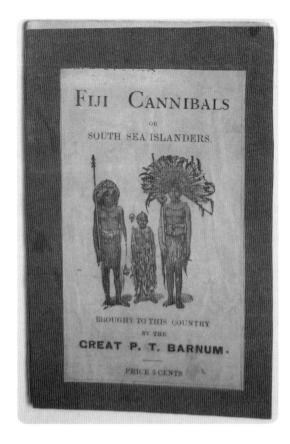

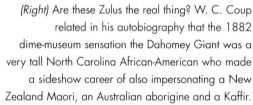

(Left) Pitch booklet for Fiji Cannibals exhibited at Barnum's Museum. By the start of the 20th century large rail circuses were ballyhooing their "Ethnological Department" and advertising in *Billboard* for Zulus, Ubangis, Dahomeys and other dark-skinned races wishing to work in their sideshows.

(Right) Are these Zulus the real thing? W. C. Coup related in his autobiography that the 1882 dime-museum sensation the Dahomey Giant was a very tall North Carolina African-American who made a sideshow career of also impersonating a New Zealand Maori, an Australian aborigine and a Kaffir.

that his feet were prehensile like the tail of a monkey, while the hair covering Krao's body highlighted his simian features. The lecture convinced many that Krao was a superior ape. In reality, he was a good-hearted, well-educated person, and, for over three decades, a formidable sideshow act. In 1926, he died of influenza at age 49.

Well-off freak exhibitors scouted the world or hired overseas agents to find the unusual, but ordinary showmen didn't have the time or money for such extravagance. Makeup, wardrobe and a bit of coaching quickly transformed a black circus or fairground workman into "the Fiji Cannibal" or a "What Is It?" Overnight, a black can-

vasman on the Sells Brothers Circus became "South Sea Island Joe," while Calvin Bird, a black farmer from Georgia, had two silver plates surgically placed under his scalp into which he inserted goat horns. He earned thousands of dollars as a sideshow curiosity.

The height of act–manager co-operation was Barnum's "Zip," who never spoke in

Old Zip—Barnum's what is it?

ZIP — What Is It? William Henry Johnson was born around 1840 in Bound Brook, N.J. His sideshow career lasted from 1859 to 1926. He was often referred to as Barnum's "What Is It?" However, an 1864 *N.Y. Clipper* relates how sideshowman A. M. Ballard opened a few seasons back a basement exhibition space known as "What Is It" and was the first to show the Wild African Boy there two years before Zip worked at Barnum's. In later years, Zip was managed by his friend O. K. White, whose sister was Violetta, the Armless Girl.

public. William Henry Johnson's career as a fictional link beween ape and man lasted from 1859 to 1926, when he was a premier attraction at circus sideshows and in dime museums. Zip was only four-foot-five. Zip's mental faculties may have been questionable, but he certainly grasped the idea that not speaking advanced his career considerably. For Zip, silence became golden, and offstage he conversed with only a couple of close friends. In May 1926, W. W. Dunkle recalled for the show-biz weekly *Billboard* a backstage visit to Ringling's Madison Square Garden date: "Here we stood as Zip, museum attraction grizzled and gray, feeble of step and plainly exhausted, came off from his last appearance in public. . . . Fred Warrell (Ringling executive) said, 'What's the matter, John?' 'Very sick man,' replied Zip. A few minutes later he was stripped of his fuzzy, brick-red garment and hurried off to Bellevue Hospital. Doctors said he had pneumonia and was in critical condition. . . . Weeks earlier he was laid up in Bellevue for a rest. The first night Ringling opened, he was on his stage in the basement being greeted by old friends. Many asked questions, but his only reply was a grin. Zip died before the month was out."

The main reason for drawing customers into the sideshow, besides the initial ticket-box revenue, was to get additional money out of them. The show's percentage from a sideshow act's souvenir sales was piddling compared to the cooch-annex revenues that were enhanced by the grifters' take.

The cooch annex always made money since the grift worked on percentage and the dancers were often wives of sideshow employees or big-top showgirls. Canadian-bound shows usually loaded up with grift to offset high provincial licenses. When Ernest Haag's Mighty Haag Circus opened at Welland, Ont., on June 8, 1910, Inspector William Mains was on the grounds. The next day he wrote to Ontario Provincial Police Superintendent Joseph Rogers: "In the sideshow, I found that after each performance the men were invited to pay ten cents and go behind a curtain where they would see some performance that would be interesting to look at — a number of the men present as well as myself were admitted to the apartment — where we found a female dressed in female attire on a platform who went through what

The Mighty Haag Circus on the lot around 1912. This was a tight medium-sized rail circus designed to make money — and it did. The midway has the sideshow on the left, where the opening is just getting underway. On the right, the ticket wagon is between the pit show and the marquee that leads to the menagerie tent, and the big top is in the background.

These two sideshow midgets are barely as tall as the bandsman's horn.

is known as the hoochie kouchie [sic] performance. Part of the performance struck me as being out of place." Mains instructed Haag to cut the cooch, and Haag complied.

Each time Haag remitted his license money to Rogers, he begged for a reduction, claiming lost revenues without the cooch. His June 15 letter stated, "The female impersonator that did the dance at Welland hasn't done

Nude dancers and grifters with games of chance occupied many 20th-century circus sideshow blow-offs. You seldom found one without the other.

Receipts at Oakland, Neb. June 9, 1915

Big Show	757 25
Side Show	66 55
Concert – afternoon	27 90
Reserve Seats – afternoon	134 50
Reserve Seats – Night	84 00
Pit Show	12 15
Dance	26 75
Concert – Hartington	12 40
Cushions	1 80
Candy Stand	59 25
Patsy Zingaro Privledge	20 00
Side Show Privledge	2 30
Banners	10 00
Cash Brought forward	373 928
	495413

A copy of the Gollmore Bros. Circus daily wagon sheet for Oakland, Nebraska, June 9, 1915. Out of the show's take of $1,214.85, a third of the money came from the extras including $26.75 from the cooch annex.

anything since, only sit on his stage with his make-up on like a woman. These people sell their pictures such as the snake charmer, tattoo lady and the female impersonator. This last one sold some pictures which were not too nice but still not nude as they had tights on. . . . On the picture between the limbs is a shadow. One of your men, Mr. Connors, thinking they were nude arrested the hoochy-coochy

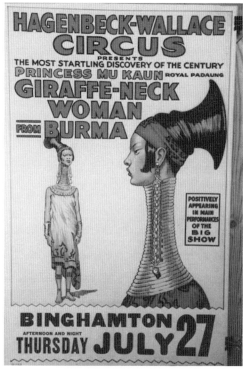

The "free act" on the Downie and Wheeler Circus gathers people on the midway before the sideshow opening. The bicycle rider is about to race down the wooden incline, jump over an elephant and several camels and continue safely down the ramp onto the ground. While people in the crowd tilt their heads upward, the heads of the animals are cast downward, eating the field grasses.

A one-sheet upright poster for Princess Mu Kaun, Giraffe-Neck Woman, on the Ringling-owned Hagenbeck-Wallace Circus in the early 1930s. The Ringling sideshow featured three or four of these ladies. One was sent over to the Ringling-owned Hagenbeck-Wallace show.

dancer." Pleading, Haag wrote, "Not one dance since Welland, nor did I allow these pictures sold. This was done when I wasn't looking. They are not bad. Plenty of art pictures hanging around on walls in public places and art galleries with women with little on them. I shall see that no pictures are sold except nice ones." In a few days Haag wrote again: "Mr. Rogers — let me put the dance on with that man, not woman, to help out. . . . I won't be able to get back to the States unless business gets better."

Big sideshows were excellent entertainment value for your money, despite the grifters' games, the sales pitches for souvenirs and the men being dinged to pay extra to enter the cooch annex to see partially nude women. During your 30 minutes inside, the freaks

Ringling office wagon ledger. After the ticket windows closed, front-door collectors took whatever cash (noted here as "door cash") they could get from latecomers. The concerts, sideshow, candy stands, lunch car and sales of balloons and giant rings make up a quarter of the day's gross.

The 1900 Campbell Bros. Circus sideshow featured Lulu the Tattooed Venus. Notice the lettering on the banner next to hers, beginning with: "A Card to the Public." Sign painter J. Bruce often stated in his banner-painting ads that he wanted to hire "cards" for dime museums. This was another name for sideshow acts and maybe why Coney Island sideshowmen called their banners "Valentines." Notice the simple ticket box similar to those used by the reserved seat sellers inside the big top. Sideshowmen called them "field boxes" because on the big days they put one or two of them out by the end of the bannerline and literally "in the field."

were discreetly lectured on and non-talking acts like the sword swallower or fire-eater were accompanied by tunes from the minstrel band. The children loved the midgets and Punch and Judy, and their parents the antics of the black comedians and the wiggling of the Hawaiian dancers. While most patrons came to the showgrounds to see the circus, those who visited the sideshow were satisfied with how they spent their money.

AL. G. BARNES CIRCUS - SIDE SHOW - SEASON 1930

Chapter 3

Make Way for the Mud Showmen!

The 1930 Al G. Barnes Circus sideshow cast poses before the annex curtain. A giant and two dwarves are the only freaks. Being Ringling-owned, the show had no dancing girls in the blow-off. Manager Art Windecker's "Mr. 'X' — Crime Doesn't Pay Exposé" featured an ex-convict's short lecture and an electric-chair demonstration. Later, when Mel Smith managed it, he installed a large stage divided into three sections where Fay — The Man of Mystery — presented three large illusions. Art Hubbell's wife was one of the box jumpers.

Sideshow manager and big-top announcer Lew Graham was a circus legend. His November 1921 *Billboard* ad seeking a marionette act and "non-repulsive human oddities" reflected the Sunday School image of Big Bertha, as Ringling was known. The rustling of the hula dancer's skirt was the only exotic thing a dad's eyes would see at a Ringling show. There was no extra-charge show, no blade box and no glassblowing joint. The only concession was a small drink stand with its bowl of orange flukum beside the sideshow band's platform.

In the '30s, Charlie Roark worked on Ringling doing vent, Punch and Judy, and lecturing. "I broke into the sideshow business when the sideshow managers were gentlemen," he recalled. "They wore a coat, vest,

tie and carried a cane. You behaved yourself on Ringling. No grift. Any stealing that went on around there was from the show or each other. It wasn't from the public. They had a notice in the sleeping cars: 'No loud noise after 11 o'clock. No pets. No alcohol.' Ringling didn't pay the best, but still wanted the very best to maintain the majestic splendor of this organization.

"They had women-only cars with lady porters worse than a convent," continued Charlie. "You couldn't fraternize. There was one guy who worked as a butcher [concessionaire who sold items in the circus seats] and was in love with one of the ballet girls. He told me if the show was going to have the next Sunday off and they wanted to get together he had to send her a telegram: 'Meet

Clyde Ingalls replaced Lew Graham as Ringling's sideshow manager in 1926 after Lew developed TB. Clyde is seen here on the bally June 18, 1938, in Watertown, N.Y., in his last years in the business.

Assistant sideshow manager John (Doc) Oyler on Ringling in 1938. He had been sideshow manager on Miller Bros. and the 101 Ranch before joining Ringling in 1937. His contemporaries were sideshow legends A. L. Salvail, W. F. Palmer, Cal Towers, J. E. Ogden, Henry Emgard, George Oram and the great Sterling S. (Duke) Drukenbrod.

Charlie Roark on the Ringling sideshow bally with his dummy Jerry McGuire. Charlie also did an adult-only nightclub act with a dummyhe called Mr. McNasty.

me next Sunday at such-and-such drugstore.' He'd better not be seen in the backyard talking to her. Backyard people, especially performers in wardrobe, were never allowed up on the front end."

Five ticket boxes fronted the Ringling sideshow. "The first guy would make an opening and then the next guy, right along," recalled Charlie. "Even the manager stood in the ticket box to make his opening. You couldn't take your coat off no matter how hot it was, until the manager took his off. You'd better not chew gum or smoke. If you

wanted to smoke, you hollered to the manager, and when he okayed it, you got down and sat behind the box and smoked. I was lecturing one time in Chicago — it was 110 degrees inside the sideshow tent on the Soldier Field parking lot — and I got up there without a coat on. I got called out front by Fred Smythe, who said, 'You look like half a shirt. Go back and put on your coat and tie and don't take it off.'"

But Charlie liked rail circuses. "On a big circus like Cole Brothers, when the big show started you kept working right through," he recalled. "The cookhouse fed the night meal around three to three-thirty in the afternoon. They would let half the acts go. We ate in rotation. If you came into the sideshow at mealtime, you would see some vacant platforms, but by the time the lecture brought you around to them, there were acts on them. You came back from supper, washed up and put your best wardrobe on for the night show. In the round end where the

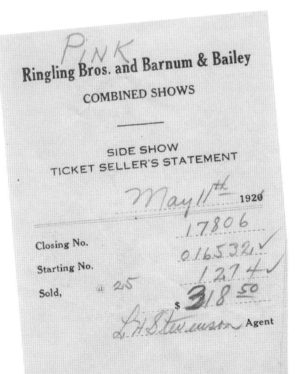

cooch was presented you also had a small curtained dressing room area. All your trunks and water buckets were in there when you came to work in the morning. You had one or two buckets of water to clean up with.

"You gave a working guy 50 cents a week to load and unload your trunk each day. The whole system worked on tips. You tipped the waterman, the mailman, the cookhouse waiter and the car porter. You gave the porter 50 cents weekly, and a dollar if you wanted your shoes shined each night while you

Inside the 1942 Cole Bros. Circus sideshow, the sword swallower has just finished. Showgirl, dancer and sometime cooch artist Leona Teodorio shimmies and shakes before the seated Hawaiian performers that include Marion, Duke Kamakua and Frances Vandercook. Note the sparse light chandelier hanging from the tent's center pole and the striped material hanging from the sidewall as decoration for the back of the stages.

slept. He would take your laundry out, and it would be on your bunk that night. You didn't have time to do it yourself and most times you never saw the downtown. The marks would ask, 'Where are you going from here?' I'd tell 'em, 'Hell, I don't even know what town I'm in *today!*'"

The most excitement on Ringling's sideshow was often caused by "Eko and Iko." "Sometimes the cookhouse would be a way down the road," Charlie said. "They couldn't turn those sideshow people loose to walk down there. The gilly bus took them, waited and brought them back. Returning as the bus neared the sideshow, Eko and Iko

Arthur Windecker, another fine all-round sideshowman, takes up his position in a Ringling sideshow ticket box in 1941. It was not unusual for the Ringling sideshow to staff their ticket boxes with former sideshow managers because they knew the daily volume of traffic through the Ringling sideshow would generate extra money in walk-aways (folks who left their change on the ticket counter), etc., for them.

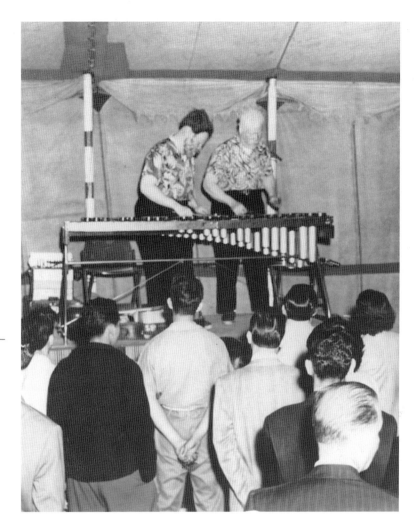

From the '30s into the mid-'50s Willie Muse and his brother George were on every major circus and carnival sideshow, billed as "Eko and Iko, the Ambassadors from Mars." Here they are working for Charlie Cox on a Pete Kortes sideshow at the Coney Island park in Havana, Cuba, 1952.

would holler, 'Monkey house, city hall, all off.' They were southern albino black people, only they had pinkish-blue eyes and hair as yellow as gold that stood out like an afro. They could play any musical instrument you gave them. They couldn't write their own names or read music but they could play it."

Coo-Coo "the Bird Girl" was on Ringling when Charlie was there. "Her real name was Betty Green," he recalled. "She had skinny legs — shaped like a bird's legs — and a nose that looked like a beak. They tied her hair up high on her head and made a set of shoes for her that were like clown shoes but bird feet. The

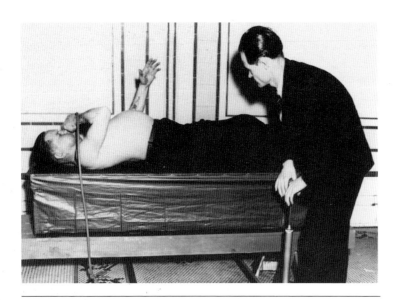

Art Hubbel was sometimes billed as the Human Bellows. His contract called for him to not perform until an hour after his meals. Charlie Roark said when he worked with him on Ringling, the sideshow manager sent Art to eat as soon as the cookhouse opened for supper.

A Ringling sideshow ticket seller makes an opening with Harry Doll perched on the ticket counter. Most sideshows made their openings from a bally stage, but Ringling's midway was a long one and they got better results from having all five ticket sellers make one opening after another.

Early bally noisemakers included snare drummers, banjo players and the talker banging on a metal gong, or, in dire circumstances, beating his wooden cane on the side of the ticket box. Carny showmen preferred a bass drum. The New Deagan Una-Fon that arrived on the market in 1918 provided something unique that could be played right on the bally.

lecturer told people she was the bird girl and she would do a "chicken dance" — that's all she did. When she went to the cookhouse, she left her bird shoes on the stage. One day while she was eating, Archie Hubbell 'the Human Bellows' nailed her shoes to the platform. She came back just as the lecturer was coming to her stage. She hurried up there and put her feet back in her shoes. The lecturer started in his spiel and the band played her music but she couldn't budge. She knew right away what had happened and started cursing Archie."

"Hubbell's wife worked with him dressed in a nurse's outfit," Charlie continued. "Archie put the end of the rubber tubing from a tire pump in his mouth while the lecturer asked an audience member to come up on the platform and pump his stomach up. When it looked like Hubbell's stomach might burst, the volunteer was told to stop. Hubbell would stand up and push his sides in. This big 'woosh' of air would rush out like gas escaping. You heard it all over the tent."

Franz Taaibosch, aka Clicko the Dancing Bushman, of Dutch-African blood, born in Cape Colony. Irishman Capt. Paddy Hepston brought him to England to perform in music halls around 1908. In Cuba, a friend of Frank Cook, Ringling's legal adjuster, alerted him to the clog-dancing sensation Taaibosch, and he was hired for the 1917 Ringling sideshow. Cook legally adopted Taaibosch and he remained one of the family until he died at Cook's daughter's Hudson, N.Y., home in 1940. Clicko was known for smoking big black cigars, drinking beer and loving the girls.

Dwarves and giants were often used in the show's spectacles or parades around the track inside the big top. Johann Petursson and a dwarf get ready in the backyard on Ringling.

There are few good interior photographs of sideshows. Because acts sold their photos, they didn't allow marks to snap pictures of them. This shot depicts the canvas-decorated stages of the 1937 Ringling sideshow. On the right is the Hawaiian troupe on a large stage, then a smaller stage for the lady sword swallower, then a mentalist act using a blackboard. Note the dropped sidewall meant to cool the place and the colored pennants hanging from the tent's quarter poles as added decoration.

Charlie Roark first mistook Clicko for Southern black despite his billing as an Australian or African bushman. "He jabbered away in a strange tongue and needed a guardian," recalled Charlie. "One day on Ringling, Martin Johnson, an African authority and filmmaker, came in the sideshow and went right up to Clicko. They started talking in this strange language Clicko used. He turned out to be a genuine bushman. Ringling sideshow manager Fred Smythe described Clicko as "an inebriate and a wolf, everything a sideshow performer shouldn't be. I was never able to tell when he was drunk until, in flawless English,

The sideshow manager on the 1917 Al G. Barnes Circus has dragged the bally platform across the midway to stop the crowd coming from the big top. The all-girl bally indicates he is selling the oriental display to a mostly male tip. The sideshow marquee and bannerline have been taken down on this matinee-only date.

When Ringling folded mid-season in 1938, they sent equipment and Gargantua (gorilla) over to beef up their Al G. Barnes–Sells–Floto Circus. The wagon on the right is Gargantua's cage.

Arthur (Abe) Wright playing on the 1937 Ringling sideshow. He was their sideshow band leader for two decades. Nothing could beat the minstrel musicians, comics and dancing girls for sideshow entertainment.

Clicko started to make indecent proposals to ladies in the tip. Austin King was lecturing on him one day when he just fell backwards off the platform, drunk." Clicko was believed to have been over 100 years old when he died — perhaps pickled.

On big shows, the sideshow would remain open the whole day. On smaller shows, it would close before the main event, as some of the people had other jobs to do. During the circus performance, the announcer would promote the sideshow: "On your way home today, if you haven't already visited our vast sideshow, don't fail to do so after this performance." While this announcement was being made at the 1903 Barnum & Bailey Circus, its 30-some-strong sideshow troupe walked around the big top in the show's second number, billed as "The Queerest Parade on Earth." At the 1927 Ringling sideshow, managed by Clyde Ingalls, the two dozen attractions paraded around the hippodrome track and filled the rings. The giant came through the back door carrying the midget, and the skeleton dude marked time alongside the fat lady.

For the "come out," many old-time sideshow managers tried to stop and corral the crowd by dragging the bally stand and ticket boxes across the midway and placing them perpendicular to the bannerline. Both Charlie Roark and sideshow manager and performer Henry Thompson told me they often tried to build a human wall using lot lice — the name show folks gave to locals who hung around the circus lot. Henry would get up on the bally with the fire-eater, with their backs to the marquee. The fire-eater would be waving his lighted torches while Henry invited the lot lice down in front for a "free" show. He timed this to coincide with the elephants going into the big top to conclude the performance. When the first patrons exited the marquee, they would turn around and face the new arrivals. The new tip, as the crowd was called, was held in front of Henry by the wall of lot lice behind the bally stand, and the "sucker netting" on the sides of the midway. There was nowhere for them to exit the midway until Henry turned some of them into the sideshow and the lot lice watching the free show dissipated. The rest of the trapped crowd could now squeeze past the ticket boxes to go on home. These strong-arm tactics helped sell a few more sideshow tickets.

Circus advance agents sent back synopsis sheets for each town that included where the show train unloaded, a diagram of the lot and the shortest way to it, the location of the water supply, a list of town officials and goods suppliers, and specific instructions, such as: "Keep the end of the sideshow bannerline close to the street or front of the lot, leaving no space for trailers." Trailers were

SIDE SHOW		
1		70-ft. round top with 3 30 ft. middle pieces
4		pipe center poles- 30 ft.
16		quarter poles- 14' 6"
50		side poles- 12'
92		wooden stakes
64		iron stakes
12		sledge hammers
4		bale rings
4		sets rigging for center poles
17		banner poles 22'
15		sets rigging for banner poles
1		12 X 12 stage
1		8 X 12 stage
1		8 X 10 stage
3		8 X 8 stages
3		6 X 6 stage
3		4 X 6 stage with curtains
7		back grounds for stages
1		dressing room curtain
1		proscenium curtain- 70 ft. wide
4		pieces 12 pole wall- 12' high
3		grub hoes
4		shovels
1		rake
28		chairs
30		chair covers
13		stage ladders
2		10' side wall ladders
1		12 X 12 barber shop
2		8 X 8 toilet tents
1		front door posts 4'
6		nickle plated posts 5'
4		flag staffs
12		banners 12 X 20
1		20 X 20 door piece
3		ticket boxes

The inventory for the 1920 Sells-Floto Circus sideshow. Somehow, all this equipment fit into one show wagon.

not welcome. At one time, Red White's parents, Doc and Zelda, trailed Ringling with a complete sideshow, and a July 1933 *Billboard* reported a mermaid show set up near the Ringling lot in Fitchburg, Mass. Concessionaires and hustlers working around large cities were particularly bothersome and cut into souvenir, food and drink sales by selling to people heading for the show lot.

Fletcher Smith's December 1927 *Billboard* article, "Evolution of the Mud Show," stated there were 11 rail shows and 24 truck circuses out. Increased railcar charges plus unionized strikes by train and coal workers had enticed showmen to convert to trucks. By the 1930s, improved roads and stronger trucks made moving the truck circuses' heavy loads of wet canvas and elephants much easier.

Ray Rogers's 1928 Barnett Brothers Circus, originally framed in New Glasgow, Nova Scotia, became a successful American truck circus. One of Rogers's canvasmen was still living in New Glasgow when I showed

By the 1920s, circus and carnival owners were experimenting with moving their shows by truck. Once trucks were strong enough to move elephants and heavy wet canvas from town to town, the growth in truck circuses increased while those traveling by rail declined.

The 1930s Seal Bros. Circus was a small mud show on a dozen or so trucks. Note that all the sideshow banners are for animal attractions inside. Looks like everyone in the tip had put on clean white shirts and blouses to attend the show. Old-time boss canvasman Shorty Lynn, who'd been with the circus, gave me this photo.

there in the '70s. The big problem with early truck shows, he explained, was the lack of places for the crew to sleep. The canvasman related Rogers's solution. After tear-down, during the cold spring and fall days, the crew all piled into the back of a show truck and were transported to the town's rail station. They slept in the warm waiting room overnight. In good weather they slept in the truck cabs or underneath them. Most staff and performers hoteled it. A few had homemade boxes on truck bodies to live in, or dragged small single-axle trailers behind their cars.

Early truck circuses carried all the trappings of the big railroad shows, including cooch dancers in the sideshow. Long-time female impersonator and cooch dancer Billy Dick (William F. Treem Jr.) explained why the owners of the Seils-Sterling truck circus, who ran a relatively clean operation, put cooch in their sideshow. On their first visit to Louisiana in the '30s, the state made them pay an occupation tax and buy license plates for all their trucks. The owners were not happy about this and quickly hired two visiting carny cooch dancers to work in the King Baile–managed sideshow. The extra blow-off money paid for the tax, license plates and more.

While rail circuses continued to decline, mud showmen — the dismissive name given to truck showmen — found fresh towns and prospered. Not all places had rail service and

The front end of the large Hagenbeck-Wallace Circus in the fairgrounds at Manchester, Iowa, July 5, 1922. The sideshow is on the left and the pit show on the right. It's a windy day (note the flags) as the pit-show banners have been left down and the sideshow double-decked banners have been lowered right to the ground with only the top half showing.

many small centers hadn't seen a circus since the wagon-show days of the last century. Motorized shows played a "high grass route," meaning they avoided the cities and stuck to smaller towns. These circuses relied on local kids to help in the morning in exchange for show passes. At night, men and young boys were recruited from the audience to stay and help tear-down for cash. A show veteran called a "punk pusher" directed the extra help.

Many large truck circuses were run by former rail circusmen and mirrored their previous big operations in every way. They carried big tops, a menagerie tent, pit shows and big sideshows. They paraded too, but parading soon became a problem for all shows, as downtown lots became harder to find. Once

The form used by the sideshow manager of the large Hagenbeck-Wallace Circus to report the day's income to the office manager. The lower price ticket was for kids. Note the space for income from the cooch annex and sword box.

Kids help carry seat planks into the big top of the 1940 Hunt Bros. Circus. You can see the unplanked seat stringer to your left. One board is placed on the top riser and one on the bottom to level it — then you board up. These midsize truck shows were designed to get up and down with circus staff who directed kid power.

1984.4.8.75

Hagenbeck-Wallace Circus

Form SSS 500 7-15-32

Number Tickets Sold	TOWN			Totals
	DATE			
	Tickets at 25c			
	Tickets at 15c			
CASH REGISTER				
FRONT DOOR TOTAL				
	ORIENTAL DEPARTMENT			
	Tickets at 25c			
	Tickets at 15c			
	ORIENTAL TOTAL			
	SWORD BOX			
	GRAND TOTAL			

Charlie Roark was married to Betty Broadbent, seen here in the Ringling sideshow. Their first winter together they visited her adoptive parents in Florida. One day, when Charlie was out back of their house repainting his Punch and Judy figures, the mother said to Betty, "What kind of man did you marry? He's out there playing with dolls!"

Ringling Bros. 1919 season contract for O. K. White to present Zip in the sideshow. They split the $40, ate in the cookhouse and slept on the train. Ringling charged White $21 for painting Zip's banner, and White split the money from the sale of Zip's photo cards 50/50 while the show paid for the printing of the cards.

truck showmen stopped parading, they dropped the menagerie tent since they no longer needed to carry cages of exotic animals as parade flash. Many shows, however, retained a couple of cages of such animals for the morning lot lice to gaze at and to justify the line in the circus herald that stated, "Come and see the animals fed circus morning." The cages were put in the sideshow along with the lead stock (camels, llamas, ponies, donkeys and bulls); this increased the sideshow's appeal and solved the owner's problem of having to provide shelter for them.

The 1935 Seal Brothers Circus was a good example of a high-grass circus. The double-bannered sideshow was managed by Earl Sinnott, and inside lecturer Ralph Noble was later a renowned big-top boss and superintendent on the Dailey Brothers Circus. Working acts included sword swallower Bertillion, the bird circus of Evelyn Drey, snake handler Lucille King, magician Abadella, and Jolly Kitty squeezed into the sword box. Professor Louis Harlem's "Night

These Ringling sideshow panel wagons are from one of the seasons that Charlie Roark was on the show. Two wagons were placed end to end on either side of the sideshow entrance to make a front over 100 feet long.

James M. Cole from Penn Yenn, N.Y., was a circus owner for over half a century. Numerous generations of N.Y. state school kids attended his wintertime school circuses. Here is Jim's tented circus on a tight lot in 1956. The midway is jammed and the sideshow is sporting new banners painted by Snap Wyatt.

Club Revue" provided the minstrel show, and two dancers worked the annex.

Charlie Roark recalls, "On those smaller truck shows, when I had the elephants in the sideshow, I'd feature feeding a peanut to them. I'd tell the tip in my opening, 'Do you remember the first circus you saw? I'll bet you can't remember the names of any of the performers, but if you fed a peanut to a big old elephant, you remembered that. How about the kid you got by the hand there? Don't you want him or her to have those same memories?' Candy butcher 'Old Iowa' with his big tray of peanuts would be standing in the doorway. When I made the turn he would lead them right in there. He'd stand by the elephants handing out those peanuts. It was the strongest thing you had in there."

The sideshows on the big rail shows remained huge, such as that on the 1937 Ringling Bros. and Barnum & Bailey, managed by Clyde Ingalls. The midget troupe numbered eight performers — four members of the Doll Family, plus Baron Paucci and three others. The "South Sea Islanders" Hawaiian troupe featured six dancers and three musicians, while Arthur A. Wright's minstrel band had 19 performers. Among the attractions were Mossad Habib the "Egyptian Fakir," Sam Pappalardo as "Popeye the Sailor Man," giant Jack Earle, Eko and Iko "the Ministers from Dahomey," Miss Jean in the "Iron Tongue Act," Egan Twist "the Man with the Rubber Arms," plus Madame Rhonda, a crystal gazer and sand diviner.

Also on the bill were giant Al Tomaini and Jeannie his half-lady wife, billed as the "World's Strangest Married Couple." (The Tomainis were also the earliest residents of Gibsonton, Fla., and founders of Giant's Camp, a fishing camp and restaurant.) Miss Susanne did Punch and Judy, Paul Williams was billed as "the Man with the Largest Mouth," and Chang was the "Jungle Demon Ape." Betty Broadbent "the Tattooed Lady" and fat girl Baby Lee rounded out the cast. The big show's employees numbered 76, more than some truck circuses had in their whole roster.

The Depression years saw most people struggling to feed their families. Even the inexpensive entertainment provided by touring circuses was beyond most people's finances. Nineteen thirty-eight was an especially bad year for shows. Shortly after Ringling left their indoor venues in New York City and Boston, the tent tour became a bust. In June, when the show proposed a 25 percent wage cut, the Actors Federation of America backed a performers' strike. At Scranton, Pa., the night show was canceled and management sent the show home. Some weeks later, the show's big top, extra seats, menagerie tent and "Gargantua the Gorilla" joined the Ringling-owned Al G. Barnes–Sells–Floto Circus in Redfield, S.D. Ringling's main competition, the Zack Terrell–owned Cole Brothers Circus stumbled along for 16 weeks before closing early. Business on their stands had been down 30 to 50 percent. The all-new 1938 Tim McCoy Wild West Show closed in just a few days.

Charlie Roark, like many performers and workers on shows that closed early, had to scramble for whatever jobs were open. "I went over from Ringling to Duke Jeanette's 10-in-one on the Cetlin and Wilson Show," he said. "It was a gilly [boxcar] show and a come-down for me. No warm bunk on the show train. We slept on cots in the blow-off. When it came time to make the jump, all the stuff was gillied down to the rail yards and loaded in box cars. It was against the railroad rules to ride in the box cars but we had to. We also couldn't open the door for air in case the railroad bulls found us. On one of the jumps when they were switching us around, the jar containing the two-headed baby in formaldehyde broke. What a smell! We couldn't open the door until we got to the next town."

Ringling got back on track in 1939 and remained the "big one" until it closed under canvas in 1956. The show continued to be moved on three trains, with the sideshow equipment on the second section and the personnel on the third. "Most mornings when we got up to the cookhouse on the lot, the sideshow was pretty well set up," Charlie Roark said. "We ate breakfast, and by 10:30 the sideshow was open and ran continuously until the spec [spectacle] started on the track for the 8 p.m. show. We had plenty of acts, so you could send two or three at a time for lunch or supper. As soon as you heard the night spec music, you started tearing down. Ringling had one guy whose only job was to take a horse and plough and go around the tents making a ditch so that in heavy rains the water wouldn't run into the tent's interior. But when it rained, all the tents leaked. The only dry place on the sideshow was inside the small marquee. I used to tell them on the midway, 'It's high and dry on the inside,' but it never was."

Meanwhile, motorized circuses lumbered on, using a new promotion called "the Merchant's Guest Ticket." While the advance billing crew was placing piles of these ducats on store counters, the advance press agent was at the newspaper office laying out ad space the local business community helped pay for. Circus ads instructed the public to patronize the merchants and pick up complimentary circus tickets at their stores. Fine print on each ticket revealed that a 10-cent service charge was payable on the show grounds. But the "free" tickets put bums in the seats, which was the main object of the circus game. The sideshow, pit shows, candy pitch and concessions all did well. Good crowds turned out daily — some shows had to do three or four performances to handle the crowds. Performers complained about doing the additional shows without being paid extra, but management reminded them of the three meals served daily in the cookhouse, and the fact that they were lucky to be working.

Chapter 4

Post-War Boom and Bust

For showmen, World War II had meant shortages of tires, sugar, labor and fire-proofing chemicals. Show trains gave way to troop trains. Late arrivals meant even Hoppie the Frog Boy was up in the sideshow wagon hauling lumber. But the post-war baby boom was a salvation for both circuses and carnivals. Carnivals now carried large "kiddielands" and rail circuses enjoyed an upswing, with the Austin Brothers, Arthur Brothers, Dailey Brothers, Sparks, Russell Brothers–Pan Pacific and Clyde Beatty among the new railers, though only the Dailey Brothers and Clyde Beatty lasted beyond their initial tour.

In 1949, the Mills Brothers Circus lay claim to the smallest sideshow on tour. It contained only the Great Hugo swallowing live mice and fish, and Buffalo Ben, a 91-year-old ventriloquist. The Clyde Beatty Circus sideshow was larger. Owner Marvin Smith lectured and did an anatomical act, and his wife swallowed swords. Other acts included mentalist Madame Rose, snake girl Rose Lee, armless Francis O'Connor, half-boy Wesley Upperman, indestructable Verna Stewart, Bozo "the Monkey Man," the frog family of Hazel and Jacqueline Morris, and Oscar C. Jones' seven-piece minstrel band.

Over on King Brothers Circus, other than the sideshow annex dancers, the big act inside was Captain Dwight Nifong battling a lion. The fighting lion act, a staple of early English menageries and later circuses, was presented inside a cage wagon with doors on both ends. The trainer would try to get in one door while the snarling lion barred his way. The

Frances Vandercook entertains the marks inside the 1942 Cole Bros. Circus sideshow. Leona Teodorio on the end and Duke Kamakua and another musician provide the music.

(Left) A tip gathers in front of the 1951 Al G. Kelly–Miller Bros. Circus sideshow somewhere in rural America. Like most truck circuses of the late 1940s and 1950s, the biggest attractions were the show's exotic animals.

(Above) Jon Friday did a low-wire act before becoming a big show announcer and sideshow manager. Here he is on the bally of the Wilson Story–managed Sells & Gray Circus in 1967 at Jacksonville, Ill., the home of the Eli Bridge Ferris wheel company.

(Left) Despite banners advertising Dixie Minstrels, fire eaters and Femme de Paree dancing girls, on the 1951 Al G. Kelly–Miller Bros. Circus, the main part of the show was the display of wild animals inside, including a hippopotamus and a rhino.

In 1950 Ringling sideshow manager W. R. McKitrick arranged a deal with NBC for Howdy Doody. The show paid a small flat fee on the indoor dates and a percentage of the sideshow gross under canvas. Howdy was a big flop and was soon dropped. Not everyone had a television set back then and the small figure was hard for children to see in a crowded sideshow tent.

The Fighting Lion Act worked by Éloïse Berchtold in the 1952 King Bros.–Cristiani Circus sideshow. Note the small entrance cage for the performer to get in before entering the lion's den proper.

trainer would then run to the other door and the lion would bounce to that one. Finally the trainer got in, and a mock battle ensued. When it was all over, the lion licked the trainer's face through the cage bars. Frank C. Bostock introduced the act to American audiences in the 1890s, with Wallace his fighting lion heading his midway wild animal shows. The act's noise and fierce action made it a natural sideshow presentation. To circus showmen, the fighting lion act became known as the "Wallace act."

Sideshow acts didn't care which circus they were on but followed sideshow managers

Frank Bostock's 1894 *Clipper* ad offering Wallace the Untamable Lion act for theaters during the winter.

they trusted from show to show. Sword swallower Capt. Don Leslie, who was on the 1955 King Brothers Circus, recalls manager Tommy Hart, who went back and forth between circuses and carnival sideshows: "Tommy was a powerful talker. He didn't rely on the bullshit to get them inside. He didn't lie to them. I would see him outside his house trailer scribbling openings and introductions, and working with a thesaurus to find interesting words. The sideshow had the fighting lion act — Carlos Leal went in the cage with a chair he used to poke Leo to get a reaction from him rather than for protection. Leo was old and just wanted to sleep. All the cages on the show had padlocks, but the door on the sideshow lion truck just had a pin through a hasp. They weren't worried about Leo getting out!"

Sideshowman Norman Carroll expressed in a 1947 *Billboard* that he didn't think freaks were a necessary part of the modern sideshow. He felt lecturers singing the sympathy angle in presenting malformed people undermined the happy, carefree circus image. Still, many large circuses, including Ringling, had lots of freaks in their sideshows. Red White's 1949 Ringling sideshow featured freaks that included Rose Westlake "the Sheep-Headed Girl," "Sealo the Seal Boy," Johann Petursson "the Viking Giant," armless and legless Frieda Pushnik, the Doll family midgets, fat lady Baby Jane and Sam Alexander, "the Man with Two Faces."

Red also ran the 1952 Clyde Beatty sideshow, with Charles Cox as the talker. Red's roster had Sam Alexander in the blow with Freddie "Manipo" Harris as lecturer. The freak lineup was as strong as you were going to get on any sideshow — circus or carnival: Zola Williams "the Bearded Lady," "Laurello the Man with the Revolving Head," Danny Danesi

"the Penguin Boy," Julius Grauhart "the Aztec Pin-Head" and "Sealo the Seal Man." Working acts were "Chief Jerome Red Cloud" with tribal dances and shrunken heads, Shackles Horrell's escape act, Freddie Harris's puppet theater and illusions and David and Alola Naeole's "Hawaiian Revue."

In contrast, Bobby Hasson, the sideshow manager on Cole Bros. in 1949, had lots of working acts but only one freak — Joe Nawrath, billed as "the Musical Midget." Bobby's big act was Joe Carvalho and Duke Kamakua's Hawaiian troupe with four dancers, including veteran Leona Teodorio. Duke had made it big in the 1930s on the RKO circuit. His "Paradise Radio Hawaiians" were heard on more than 100 radio stations. Show girl, stripper, chorus dancer and cooch artist Leona worked in Duke's troupe when she

A young Bobby Hasson sells tickets on the 1937 Ringling sideshow with Baron Paucci standing on the ticket counter. Bobby later went on to own his own carnival sideshow and managed the Cole Bros. sideshow as well as the 1955–56 Ringling sideshows.

RINGLING BROS AND BARNUM & BAILEY
SIDE SHOW
WANTS FOR ITS GIGANTIC SIDE SHOW AND ANNEX
Freaks, Oddities and Novelty Acts of the Highest Caliber. Attractive Hawaiian Troupe, Colored Musicians and Minstrel Men. Ticket Sellers capable of making openings from boxes. Write, giving full particulars. Send photos, will return same.
All Replies to:
BOB HASSON, RINGLING BROS AND BARNUM & BAILEY CIRCUS
SARASOTA, FLORIDA

1955 *Billboard* ad placed by Bobby Hasson for acts on the Ringling sideshow.

wasn't in the cooch annex at Cole Brothers. She also rode horses or elephants in 'Spec' and did web and ladder acts. During the off-season, Leona worked Chicago club and burlesque dates.

Sideshows had to carry at least a drummer or flutist for the cooch dancers, but the main musical entertainment since the jazz era were black bands playing the hottest tunes. "On Ringling, when you made the first sideshow opening, you brought out the band," said Charlie Roark. "The public would come down to where the band was. After they went back inside when an outside talker finished his spiel, he would push a button and ring the bandstand's bell inside. They'd begin playing. 'There they go, they're starting now,' cried the talker. 'The band's playing. See the first part and all of it.' It worked like a magnet. If you were walking down the midway and heard the band playing inside the sideshow you at least knew something was going on in there.

"Inside, the band wouldn't play for the talking acts like the magician and Punch and Judy. Punch with the pitch took eight to 10 minutes. Sometimes the sword swallower didn't talk during his or her act and the band would play. They played for the fat lady because she did a little shimmy dance. The minstrel band's own act lasted 10 minutes.

"Most big rail circuses also had a Hawaiian troupe. Ringling had 'em too. They were

One of the foremost black sideshow band leaders was P. G. Lowery, standing second to the left in the front row of minstrel troupe on Cole Bros. Circus. He was on Cole 1935–1942 and 1944–1948.

Hawaiians, or looked Hawaiian, and made a lot of flash on the bally with their grass skirts and ukeleles. The girls in the troupe, between shows, would make leis from color paper. They sold them for 50 cents."

How long was a sideshow performance on the big rail circuses? "About a half hour to see it all," Charlie said. "That's before the big

show starts. If there were enough lot lice, you stayed open, but you slowed it down as there was no hurry for them to get into the big top. Fifteen minutes before the big show started, the inside man had to get up and say, 'The circus in the main tent will start in 15 minutes. If you are going, I advise you to leave now. Be there when the first horse kicks his

PERFORMANCE AGREEMENT

THIS AGREEMENT made at Sarasota, Florida, this......6th......day of.......January,.................19..48..,
by and between RINGLING BROS.-BARNUM & BAILEY COMBINED SHOWS, INC., a Delaware Corporation, having its principal
office at Sarasota, Florida, (hereinafter called "The SHOW," and ......The Doll Family..................
.... (hereinafter called "The CONTRACTOR").

WITNESSETH:

In consideration of the mutual covenants and agreements and warranties hereinafter contained the parties hereto agree
as follows:

1. The CONTRACTOR agrees to appear and to produce its act or acts (as hereinafter described) on all performances
of the circus operated by the SHOW during the season of 19...48... in accordance with and subject to all the terms and conditions hereinafter contained. The term "season," as used herein, shall mean the normal operating season of the SHOW's circus
extending from approximately the beginning of April through approximately the beginning of November, such approximate limits
being subject to exact determination by the SHOW.

2. The SHOW and the CONTRACTOR agree that payment by the SHOW to the CONTRACTOR for producing its act
or acts, as aforesaid, shall be based on the actual number of the public performances of its act or acts and, for their mutual convenience, shall be made by the SHOW weekly in the amount of ......One Hundred and Forty Dollars(Joint)......
....($140.00......) Dollars for the aggregate number of performances given in the preceding
calendar week less, with respect to any such week in which a full number of performances is not scheduled, one-twelfth (1/12)
of such amount for each unscheduled secular day performance; provided, however, that the SHOW shall hold back the sum of
....($..................) Dollars
as security for the strict performance of this agreement by the CONTRACTOR. By a "full number of performances" is meant
twelve (12) secular day and two (2) Sunday performances.

3. The SHOW agrees that it will offer, and that the personnel and employees of the CONTRACTOR may at its option
accept, but only during that part of the season in which the circus operated by the SHOW plays under canvas, meals, carloading
and transportation common and customary in the circus business; provided, however, that animals or pets not used in performances shall not be carried except by special permission of the SHOW and on terms of Ten ($10.00) Dollars a week for each
animal or pet so carried.

4. The CONTRACTOR warrants that its act or acts so to be produced by it as aforesaid will be as follows and will
constitute first-class and excellent performances:

"The Doll Family" consisting of Elly, Hilda, Frieda and Kurt
Schneider, to appear in the Side Show at all times during the operation of same, presenting their full and complete Act.

Wardrobe to be first class and in perfect condition at all
times.

5. The CONTRACTOR represents and warrants that it constitutes a permanent amusement organization; that the act
or acts produced by it are special, unique and extraordinary; and that such act or acts, by reason of the CONTRACTOR's skill in
production and presentation, constitute a "feature" performance. And the CONTRACTOR further represents and warrants that it
has full rights to the production and presentation of such act or acts and agrees to indemnify and hold the SHOW harmless
against any and all claims and demands of third persons with respect thereto.

6. The CONTRACTOR represents and warrants that it is fully familiar with the conditions obtaining in the circus business, that it recognizes the necessity for safety of premises and equipment (including apparatus, paraphernalia, costumes, animals, etc.), and that its employees and personnel are fully conversant with and suitably skilled for its act or acts. And the CON-
TRACTOR agrees that it will keep all premises used by it, including the premises for performance of its act or acts, in a first-
class and safe condition; and assumes exclusive supervision and control with respect thereto.

7. The CONTRACTOR agrees to furnish and maintain in first-class and safe condition and at its own expense any and
all equipment (including apparatus, paraphernalia, costumes, animals, etc.) used in the production and presentation of its act or
acts. The SHOW agrees that during the season, and for convenience only, it will pack and transport and deliver such equipment
to the CONTRACTOR and that it will erect any apparatus in a preliminary fashion, all as is common and customary in the circus
business and all in accordance with the directions of the CONTRACTOR. But the CONTRACTOR agrees that it will assume final
supervision and control with respect to such erection and that it will construct and present its act or acts under its own exclusive
supervision and control in all particulars with respect to personnel, employees, property men, assistants and in every other respect whatsoever.

8. The SHOW and the CONTRACTOR agree that the CONTRACTOR's undertaking hereunder is only with respect to ex-
cellency of the results produced by its act or acts and that the means and methods by which such results are accomplished shall
be at all times within the exclusive supervision and control of the CONTRACTOR. And the SHOW and the CONTRACTOR agree
that the relationship between them is that of Independent Contractor and that under no circumstances shall the CONTRACTOR,
or any of its employees or personnel, be or be deemed to be an employee of the SHOW. The SHOW and the CONTRACTOR
further agree that this agreement embodies and constitutes the entire agreement between them and that the same shall be gov-
erned and construed in accordance with the laws of the State of Florida.

9. The CONTRACTOR agrees on behalf of itself and its personnel that in the presentation of its act or acts and in its
other association with the SHOW, it will maintain the ordinary standards of morality and decency and that it will not permit
inebriety on the part of any of its employees or personnel.

The 1948 Ringling sideshow contract for the Doll Family, a Ringling sideshow fixture from the 1930s. Note the $140 salary for all of them — you see why their photo-card pitch was so important.

heels up on the hippodrome track.' The main show was the main thing, but the sideshow stayed open.

"One time on Cole I had a big tip in the sideshow. It came up to 15 minutes before the main show but I didn't tell them. I hurried them down to my Punch act, did the act and made the pitch. During the pitch I saw owner Zack Terrell standing in the corner hitting his cane on the ground. He walked over and said, 'Charlie, have you got all the money you're going to get out of this bunch?' I replied, 'Yes, sir, Mr. Terrell.' He took his hat off and bellowed, 'Ladies and gentlemen, the circus in the big tent will start in 15 minutes.' At that

Arthur Hoffman, sideshow manager, and the Joe Carvalho Hawaiian troupe making an opening on the 1940s Cole Bros. bally stage. Hoffman had once owned a rail circus, toured whale-car shows and, in Charlie Roark's words, was "one of the best showmen around."

time two big-top acts had already worked. He liked to see people making money."

One of the many eight-by-ten framed photos on Charlie's circus-room wall in Malvern, Ark., shows him in a tuxedo with midget Daisy Doll. Charlie saw me looking at it and said, "On Ringling I'd make the Doll family's pitch. Being tall, I looked good up there next to them. 'Now, folks, here are Mr. Harry Doll, Miss Tiny Doll, Miss Graisy Doll and Miss Daisy Doll. No doubt you have seen these little people many, many times on the silver screen. Harry co-starred with the late Lon Chaney in *The Unholy Three* — he was the unholiest one of them.' Harry would give me a dirty look. I'd go down the line and get to Daisy on the end. I'd say, 'She's known in Hollywood as the vest-pocket version of Mae West.' She'd say, 'Come up and see me sometime.' I'd reply, 'I do, but you're never at home. Now they are going to do a little dance choreographed by Miss Graisy Doll.' They'd do their little dance, and the band would play 'We Are Dresden China Dolls.' 'If you'd like to have

a souvenir photo of the entire family, it's auto-graphed and 25 cents.' All of them grabbing money like hell. They sold a lot of pitch cards with four of them selling.

"Ringling had two lecturers," Charlie continued. "The job kept you busy going up and down those stage ladders. It was tiring. On a big day you would start one lecture at one end and the other at the other end. Two bunches of people going around at the same time. You met and crossed over. When you got them all the way around you raised the wall up in the back and let them out. You couldn't get out the front for the people coming in." On Cole Brothers, Charlie's workload was lightened when management hung big speakers above the bandstand so he could stand there doing the lectures and pitches on the microphone.

"On Ringling you opened at 11 in the morning and you didn't close until the circus started that night," recalled Charlie. "At 8 p.m. you did one fast show that took about 10 minutes. By the time you got that done they

A rare inside view of the 1940s Cole Bros. sideshow. The drink stand is in the foreground; to the left is the minstrel band and across the back of the tent is the decorated proscenium curtain behind which the cooch dancers work. The rest of the show stages are not pictured.

had jerked half the sideshow platforms out of the tent and folded down the front wagons because the sideshow went on the second train section. On the Cole show you didn't close until after the night blow-off because the Cole show had the grifters. You kept open for them."

The 1940s Cole Brothers sideshow had one of the better grift operations. Charlie admired fixer "Big" Joe Haworth. "He could go downtown in the morning and square it so he could pick people's pockets on the court house steps at noon hour," claimed Charlie. "He personally knew every police chief in the country. He was a big loudmouth Irishman — one of those guys you couldn't help liking. Most days, Haworth sat in the sideshow marquee watching out for police. Somebody would come up and ask him if he was the manager and he would say, 'Yes, sir. My name's Mr. Cole. What's the trouble?' The mark would tell him that some fella beat him out of $50,

and Joe would say, 'Oh, there were two of you. You were gambling?' The mark usually said he wasn't gambling. Joe would counter with, 'Did he just take it from you? You know it takes two to gamble. I better take you both down to the police station.' That was usually the end of it.

"You had a guy with a skillo at one center pole and other grifters carrying bute boards and tripes working the crowd. The show got a good percentage. Old-time candy butcher

Gus (Nosey) Schwab noted the big scores so Terrell could compare the grift's nightly turn-in. Mickey O'Brien was the head grifter, along with broad tosser 'Little Reno' Marchette, Peek'em John and Whiskey Bob. The grift had their own codes. The outside man and the dealer were hollering and fair-banking the mark. A stick would catch a glimpse of a policeman coming in under the sidewall and he would say loudly, 'Well, I was downtown this morning at the restaurant

Leona Teodorio was a veteran showgirl around the Cole Bros. Circus. She rode elephants and worked in production numbers and the Hawaiian troupe. She was also a great cooch dancer when needed. In the winter she danced in Chicago clubs and burlesque theaters.

The sideshow cooch dancers were the lures used to get men into the men-only blow-off where the grifters could work the strongest. One sideshow manager was quoted as saying, "Any gal can learn the art of annex dancing if she can master the movements necessary to get into the third berth on a show train." Cole Brothers was noted for its cooch annex. "They had a big hand-painted proscenium across the back of the tent with scenes from the *Arabian Nights*," recalled Charlie. "The painted minaret towers had mess windows. Behind each window was a platform with steps up to it. At one point the guy making the cooch pitch from the ticket box would point and say, 'Look!' The girls would all be up on those platforms waving, bumping and grinding. When you saw that, you knew you weren't going to go back there and see just one little ol' cooch girl. They had five or six plus the flageolet player and a guy beating a drum.

"When I was there and they'd make the cooch pitch, an old guy with no teeth would

The cooch dance in the sideshow blow-offs was usually short and sweet. Male patrons sometimes saw total nudity but often just quick flashes of bare female flesh before the lecturer or the lone musician hollered, "It's all out and over, gentlemen!"

and all they had was BEEF, DUCK and LAMB.' They'd all run. O'Brien kept a clown suit hung over by the big top. Dodging a bad beef, he would put the clown suit on and sit by the back door. He wintered in Fort Lauderdale and later had a dry cleaning business there. His business interests never veered far from cleaning suckers."

holler out, 'I ain't going. I ain't going. I was in there yesterday night and seen the gull darn thing. Those women were in there just as

The cooch dancers with a lady accordian player bally on the 1949 Dailey Bros. Circus sideshow during its Canadian tour.

naked as the palm of your hand! None of you guys are going, are you?' He and the grifters led the rush to the ticket box." Inside, the grift operated a skillo, three-card monte (tossing the broads) and the pea game. The pea was called "the nuts," "blocks," "greasy pig" and sometimes in the South "the dinx." Skillo was a wheel game that the operator could control by pushing his stomach or finger against a hidden button that activated a brake in the wheel's base.

John B. "Gypsy Red" Jackson turned up to work concessions on my 1980s indoor circus. When Jackson was a teenager he ran away from a Southern orphanage and joined

John B. (Gypsy Red) Jackson with trombone to the left in the Clyde Beatty–Cole Bros. sideshow band. An orphan, Gypsy Red ran away in his teens from a Southern orphanage and grew up on shows. He recently passed away in his 90s at a hospice in Stuart, Fla.

BEATTY-COLE Side Show Band has, from left, Red Jackson, trombone; Rabbi Dixon, trumpet; R. L. Watts, trombone; Buck Able, drums; Willie Rogers, tuba, and Buddy Conway, leader and tenor sax. Not pictured is Al Grauls, trumpet.

Milt Robbins managed the sideshow on the Dailey Bros. Rail Circuses in the late 1940s. His father, Frank A. Robbins, had toured his own circus from 1880 through 1917. Milt's stepbrother was the Toronto-based Frank A. Robbins Jr., who had carnival sideshows in Canada and lived with half-and-half Albert-Albertine. Milt last worked for Ward Hall and Chris Christ. He was 84 when he died in St. Petersburg, Fla., in 1981.

Jimmy Eskew's Wild West Show as a pony punk on the famed Rubin & Cherry Shows. Except for occasional prison stretches, he spent 60-some years working as a trombone player and concession help. He spent a season on the Dailey Brothers Circus, playing in the sideshow band for bandleader Johnny Williams, who placed him at the back of the bandstand inside the tent. Peering over the sidewall onto the midway he watched for police. Any sign of them and he'd yell to

Williams who directed the band into "Deep in the Heart of Texas," while "Gold Tooth" McCarty, "Deep Sea" Red (when he was drunk, show folks called him "Shallow Water Pinky"), "Slim" Farley and the rest of the gang scattered.

In retirement in Indiantown, Fla., Red recalled, "Once the night performance started, the sideshow crew took down the marquee and bannerline. The sideshow bally stage and ticket boxes were dragged across

the midway. Inside, they only left up a stage for the band, another for the snake girl and one for the cooch. After manager Milt Robbins had gotten what he could inside from the come-out crowd, the band played a chorus for the two tap dancers and a chorus for the girl dancers. The comic told three jokes and sang a comic song. The band then played for the snake girl, and when she finished, the lecturer made the cooch pitch. It cost a dollar to step behind the proscenium.

The snake girl holds up a good-sized Burmese python to stop the blow-off crowd as they exit from the matinee performance of Dailey Bros. Circus in Marysville, Kans., in 1947. It's a windy day — the big double-decked bannerline has been lowered. Two of Johnny B. Williams's minstrel band musicans are seen behind the bally platform.

One of Johnny B. Williams's dancers on Dailey Bros. Circus sideshow, 1948. Before showtime these gals cleaned the show coaches or helped out in the cookhouse. You didn't have just one job on a circus.

"They held the cooch off until the grift got some scores. By the time the dancers came on, the sideshow crew had all of the tent sections down and rolled except the round end over the cooch area. The girls took off their bras then flashed their pubic hair, as a worker unplugged the lone light hanging from the centre pole. The crew dropped the tent on the marks' heads. The marks scrambled out from under the canvas as the gilly van hauling the girls and the grifters drove off toward the show train."

Recalling the 1950 Biller Brothers Circus, Ward Hall said, "It had a big sideshow. Marvin Smith 'the Anatomical Wonder' out of San Antonio, Texas, was manager. Reno Marchette and Rebel had the joints. Joe Haworth was the fixer. He later became head of the phone

1940s Cole Bros. cooch dancer in the blow-off.

The David Naeole Jr. Hawaiian troupe works the bally on the Bobby Hasson–managed Ringling sideshow in 1955. Bobby had given up his 10-in-one on Royal American Shows and thought he had it made until the show closed for good early the next season.

Ad seeking grifter. Dales Bros. Circus was the first circus my parents took me to. It was owned by one of the best "broad tossers" in the business, Mickey Dales, whose real name was Michael Joseph Dalesio. His wife, Lucy, handled the snakes in the sideshow. Later Mickey was a legal adjuster with joints on various carnivals. He died in 1971.

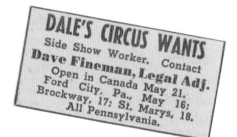

DALE'S CIRCUS WANTS
Side Show Worker. Contact
Dave Fineman, Legal Adj.
Open in Canada May 21.
Ford City, Pa., May 16;
Brockway, 17; St. Marys, 18.
All Pennsylvania.

promoters on the Beatty show — many grifters ended up working phones."

Magician and organist Floyd Bradbury broke in on the 1953 Wallace & Clark Circus sideshow, managed by Lee Aldrich. Owner Norm Anderson took the show into Canada and was rumored to have come home with a hundred grand. Bradbury, who did magic and vent, recalls, "The show had two blow-offs. The first had dancer Pearl Philips. Lee's cooch opening went, 'Now, the next part of the show takes place behind this curtain and for men only. Not that we have anything against ladies but it would not be fair to charge you for something you can look at in the mirror and see for nothing at home. Behind this curtain you will meet lovely Miss Pearl, who'll do the 'Dance of the Seven Veils,' except she has forgotten them today. This is an extra added attraction for all the men in the audience who are not narrow-minded and who feel there is nothing wrong with seeing a pretty girl in the raw. The cost is 50 cents and it starts in three minutes.'

"Dee would beat a bass drum for Pearl's few minutes of dancing in bra and panties, then announce, 'The rest of the performance is for those over 18, because in this part of the show Miss Pearl dances completely nude. That's right, gentlemen — hide, hair and pussy! If you care to stay, it's 50 cents more and starts right away.' Nearly every guy stayed. The second blow-off featured 'Amok the Living Monster from India.' Aldrich touted, 'Five hundred teeth but kills with its tail.' Amok was a fifteen-foot python. Grifters Mickey O'Brien and Eddie Moore were in the sideshow and Reno in the entranceway to the big top. Mickey worked three-card monte and the other two the blocks [the shell game]. Frank Ellis had a pit show on the midway and was the patch. The grift worked every day."

In 1953, artist/clown Bill Ballantine gave the Ringling midway a much-needed makeover. Ticket wagons, concession stands and the sideshow bannerline sported art deco colors and designs. Four different cut-out metal frames adorned each bannerline wagon and held bulb lighting behind them. Ballantine called it a "shadow box effect." It paid off. In Philadelphia, Penn., on May 29, 1954, a one-day all-time sideshow attendance record was set, with 21,976 people paying to see it. Most truck circuses at the time were lucky to see that many patrons over a few weeks.

Most circus owners put up with unionized bill posters, musicians and performers but resisted any attempts to unionize staff, concessionaires and workers. In the '50s, the teamsters vigorously pushed to organize circus labor. Union pickets greeted the Ringling trains and the public coming onto the showgrounds. During the 1956 tour, the show's trains often ran late due to equipment sabotage and other union tricks. Sick of too many canceled matinees, John Ringling North closed the show on July 16, 1956, in Pittsburgh, saying, "The tented circus as it exists today is, in my opinion a thing of the past."

Billboard outdoor editor Tom Parkinson asked in a November 1956 article, "Did the circus sideshow slip away while the public attention was diverted by the passing of the

Teamsters picket the Ringling circus lot beside the Cow Palace during the show's September 1955 visit to San Francisco. Sabotage of circus equipment and other distasteful tactics by the union caused the show to miss matinees. The show finally closed the next season at Pittsburgh, Pa., on July 16.

The 1954 Ringling sideshow managed by Richard Slayton. Back row has Stanley "Sealo" Berent, Harold Smith on musical glasses, whip cracker Johnny Kirk, Mom Pushnick with armless-legless Frieda in front of her and tattooed Lyda Akado next to her. Next to Frieda is the Doll Family. At the right end of the back row is knife-thrower Fred Bancroft with his sword-swallowing wife, Elizabeth. In front are magician and Punch-and-Judy worker Fred L. Harris, snake lady Josephine Rosal and fat lady Thelma B. Amand. MacFadden's Highlanders pipe player James A. Roche and drummer James McCarthy are on the right.

big tops?" Parkinson wrote, "Three circuses opened in the spring of 1956 with traditional sideshows, and all three — Ringling Brothers Barnum & Bailey, Clyde Beatty and King Brothers — closed early. Despite people moaning about the loss of the big-top circus, there were plenty of other tent circuses enjoying a good season. What disappeared was the old-time sideshow. The 20-odd tent circuses out still had midway pit shows and sideshows with bannerlines, but the sideshow features were animals."

Most Ringling sideshow acts found work on carnival 10-in-ones, while a few went to circuses. Don Leslie recalled, "On Cristiani we had a clean sideshow. They didn't want any frightening freaks. Betty Broadbent 'the Tattooed Lady' and the Doll family came over from Ringling. I did fire and sword and we had an armless guy. The one odd act was Charlie Hunter. He had been around Jerry Lipko's sideshow, billed as 'the Gorilla Girl.' Charlie had a lot of facial hair and dressed in drag with lots of lipstick and rouge. A dental plate made with fangs stuck out and down over his lower lip and he wore a wig. You could see the hair on his legs balled up under the nylons. He sat draped in a cape until it was his turn to work. Then he stood up, took off the cape and told the audience that when his mother was carrying him in the womb she'd been scared by a big monkey. We giggled away behind the sidewall listening to his spiel. Charlie was always telling us to shut up during his act, but it was hard to keep a straight face and hear what he was telling the marks."

Chapter 5

Roller-Skating Penguins

The Clyde Beatty–Cole Bros. sideshow in the late '60s, when Stu Miller managed it. On the bally to the left of Stu are Percilla and Emmett Bejano, the world's strangest married couple. The net sideshow sign replaced a huge steel monster that the sideshow crew were not fond of putting up each day.

By the 1960s, acts in circus sideshows had shrunk dramatically. "I was sideshow manager on Cole and Walters around 1961," said Charlie Roark. "We had grifters Fred Brad and two other guys, but they didn't work every day — some of those towns were too small to patch. Some carny came along with his wife who did cooch and I put them to work, but it didn't go over. I did Punch and Judy and the sword box and had a tramp clown come over from the main show and juggle. That was it besides the three elephants, llama, camel and a cage of bears and monkeys. We left the sidewall down until showtime. People who had been out to watch the setup and had seen all the animals still paid to see them when they came to the show later."

Local officials were still coming around with their hands out. Bill English recalled, "Even on Sells and Gray in the 1960s, I was propositioned in the deep South by sheriffs: 'Don't you have any games, any girl shows?' When I told them no, they weren't pleased, but we gave them a bunch of passes and they went away." During the King Brothers Circus's few weeks in Ontario in 1968, manager Jimmy Cole put a couple of carny flat joints on the midway, and in the 1980s John "Gopher" Davenport carried flat joints with his various circuses. And that was the grifters' last stand.

The reputation of the Kelly–Miller Brothers Circus, founded in the late 1930s by Obert Miller, rested on their huge menagerie and large elephant herd, but in the '50s, they went along with that decade's trend of putting the animals in the sideshow. Then in

The King Bros. Circus, piloted and partially owned by Floyd King in the 1950s, was a huge truck show. Here Charlie Roark makes the opening with some of the Doll Family, who had come over from Ringling when that outfit folded in 1956. The Dolls made a couple of seasons but, tired of driving their car and pulling a house trailer, they left the business.

1959, Obert's son Dores, who liked people to see the animals — even for free — put them back into a separate tent, leaving only acts in the sideshow. He told a *Billboard* reporter he was getting more satisfied customers than ever before, but the sideshow gross had dropped by two-thirds.

You couldn't have found a circus that was more deserving of the title High Grass Show than the 1973–76 Royal Bros. Circus that I operated with Johnny Frazier. Here Harry Rawls makes the sideshow opening in Western Canada. Next to him on the bally is his daughter, clown Bonnie Bonta, "Burf" the fire-eater and bagpipe player Dave Knodderer. Check out the Academy Award–nominated National Film Board of Canada documentary *High Grass Circus* to see this crew in action.

On most 1960s truck circuses, canvas bannerlines were eliminated in favor of labor-saving folding metal panels mounted on the sides of a show semi that was used as employee sleepers or show animal transporters. A semi like the one here on the 1970s King Bros. Circus was placed on each side of the sideshow bally platform to make up a long bannerline. They also never needed to be lowered in high winds.

The Carson & Barnes Circus, jointly owned by Jack and Ann Moore and Dores Miller, had grown from a wrestling-bear/tented-film show to a midsize operation. It was a typical Hugo show that opened with a lion act and had the elephants working three or four times during the performance. Aging Western star Tim McCoy did the concert, and the midway had two pit-shows and a sideshow that featured two semis of caged animals and ex-Ringling bull elephant Joske as the world's largest elephant.

In 1967, Carson & Barnes offered a splendid sideshow managed by Chuck Fuller. On the bally, the first person to name the

The 1961 Al G. Kelly–Miller Bros. Circus sideshow was mainly comprised of animals plus Diamond Jim DeLock and his wife Martha. He did magic, Punch and Judy, and a pick out pony act. Martha was the target in their knife-throwing act.

tune the bagpiper was playing ("Man on the Flying Trapeze") got in free. Inside, Cliff King served as lecturer and fire-eater while his wife, Mamie, did the electric chair act as "Celeste the Lady from Mars." Pietro Canestrelli and his wife, Joyce, did their knife-throwing act and she also worked in the blade box — they were one of the last good working acts around circus sideshows. Jack Smith played the bagpipes inside and Vernon Goin appeared as "the Tattooed Man." Besides the show's five elephants, there were four lions, a coatimundi, a tiger, a jaguar, a hyena, six bears, a camel, two llamas and a guanaco. A lot to see for 50 cents.

When Jack Moore died of cancer late in 1968, Dores Miller took over. He brought over more bulls, a couple of cat acts and added a separate menagerie tent, but with help shortages, it was not always up. The sideshow had a petting zoo and a hippo on display plus eight or so working acts and the

King Charles Weatherby and his sideshow band were one of the last minstrel outfits playing tented circuses. He was on the late-1950s Jack Moore's Carson & Barnes Circus and on the '60s Von Bros. Circus, where his band also played for the big-top performance. King Charles stayed on the road until 2007, when he was in his late 70s. In his latter years he was the 24-hour-man on a number of Bob Childress–owned circuses.

Jim Steinmetz was an old-time 10-in-one operator. Near his last days as a sideshowman, he had his show over on the Carson & Barnes Circus for a season in the early '70s.

The last sideshow on Dores Miller's Carson & Barnes Circus in the late 1970s was one owned by Harry Nelson and his wife. The long metal front folded out from one semi-trailer, while the back of the trailer opened up as a stage. Here Harry's wife lets a young sideshow goer feel the snake. Individual stages held the blade box, sword ladder and nail board.

blade box. The annex attraction was a midget calf, and the midway had a turtle show, Ken Gottschalk's snake show and Vernon Goin's "What Is It?"

Over the next decade, the show grew into a large five-ring wild animal show with over 20 elephants. The animals were exhibited open-air style after the public gave up their

The Beatty–Cole spring date in Philadelphia, Pa., at Front and Erie Streets was a big sideshow date for the circus. In May 1962 a packed midway listens as Ward Hall makes a matinee opening. On stage, *left to right*: sword swallower Ricky Ricardo, magician Fred "Mannipo" Harris and Ward; behind Ward is tattooed lady Betty Broadbent, on the bally steps is manager Tommy Hart, and behind him Dingo, the show's fire-eater.

FAT GIRL W. 632¼

ALIVE

Clyde BEATTY-COLE B
combined
SIDE SHOWS ANIMAL
WILD
CONTINUOU ENTERTAINMENT

Showman Bill English makes the sideshow opening in the late 1950s on the Beatty–Cole sideshow. An unidentified hula dancer stands next to fire-eater Carlos Leal.

WANTED
SIDE SHOW ACTS
Inside Lecturer
Fire Eater
Sword Swallower
Mid-December Closing.
Wire: ROGER BOYD, JR., Side
Show Mgr., Per Route
CLYDE BEATTY/COLE BRS. CIRCUS

tickets at the marquee. The last two good sideshow operators there were Jim Steinmetz and Harry Nelson. Harry's show was in a square-end top behind a beautifully painted metal front. Charlie Stevens's big-top band came out and played until a crowd formed for Harry's opening. He barely made the turn when management sprung open the front doors to the main show. That ended the sideshow operation there.

In the spring of 1957, the Clyde Beatty Rail Circus had emerged from its DeLand, Fla., base as a large truck circus. The Clyde Beatty–Cole Brothers Circus soon became the top tent circus in America and the last one to carry a large sideshow. Over the next two decades, the cream of the sideshow crop — Roger Boyd, George White, Stuart Miller, Charles ("Chuck") Fuller and Ward Hall — served as managers. Bill English put in four

seasons. His 1960 lineup included tattoo queen Betty Broadbent, sword swallower and inside lecturer Alex Linton, Benny Bernard doing magic and Punch and Judy, "Wild" Bill Cody's impalement act, "Whitley the Man with the Miracle Mind," Hawaiian dancer Lurline and Adrienne Ash as the blade-box lady. Jelly Roll Roger's seven-piece Dixieland band, dressed in red-and-white-striped coats, provided the music. The show's giraffe, six

The last place to see a big minstrel sideshow band was on the Clyde Beatty–Cole Bros. Circus. They played for the bally on the come-in, and inside they played for some of the sideshow acts as well as doing their own presentation. Seated in the back row on the right in 1962 is leader and sax player Buddy Collins.

bulls, two camels, two guanacos and two horses were the animal content.

The only freak that year was Buck Nolan, billed as "the Seven-Foot-Five-Inch Boy." Born Charles Logan Buxton, he was a seasoned kleptomaniac — if it wasn't made of concrete, Buck made off with it. Addicted to flea markets and various substances, he could be a handful. He had a habit of standing in the sideshow marquee while English made the openings. Infuriated, English would yell at him, "Buck, for Christ's sake, you're the feature giant I'm describing — get the hell back inside!" Buck would calmly reply, "Bill, they don't know I'm the boy giant!"

Ticket selling was one of the more lucrative jobs on the lot. In the winter of 1958, Jon Friday wrote Bill English asking for a ticket-selling post on the Clyde Beatty sideshow. Bill replied, "We use two ticket sellers, both of whom are to make second openings. A job of this sort can lead in the managerial direction more easily than an actor's job because it is on the business end of the show.

"Many veteran ticket sellers have never advanced or wanted to advance beyond that

The colorful 1960s Sells and Gray Circus sideshow front with its prominent red, orange, yellow and blue painted banners. In the middle of the midway is the show's cotton-candy stand, and at the top of the midway is the souvenir stand (garbage joint). Opposite, out of the photo, are the show's pony ride, Spidora pit show, ticket wagon and main concession tent.

level. While it is a white-collar job where your appearance on the box must be tops (we provide uniform), there is a limited amount of Chinese labour with it. Ticket sellers set up and tear down the front, including their ticket boxes and the bally stages. They do not touch any canvas or any part of the show except the front. We have a veteran sideshow boss canvasman and a crew of six men. You would be expected to drive a truck.

"The show moves at night and the cookhouse is in the air before dawn, serving a sit-down breakfast at 7:30 a.m. Service is by table waiter and ticket sellers and butchers each pay their waiter a two-dollar-a-week tip. You occupy a regular sleeper berth similar to berth facilities of a rail show. Salary is small — just enough to cover your personal nut: $25 a week. Here lies the big difficulty. For a skilled and experienced ticket seller, with the volume we handle, this box is worth an additional $50 to $200 a week. To an amateur it might be worth next to nothing. We will be using a 50-cent ticket this coming season. If I were to put you on a box, I would be putting you on in place of some old-timer who could make a good living on it. I would like to have you. On the other hand, it would be no favor to you and no advantage to me to have you in a capacity where you could not make a living for yourself. The answer lies in your own attitudes, aptitudes and abilities."

In June 1964, I joined my first circus — Gene Cody and Kipling Brothers, owned by Bill and Dick Garden. It didn't have a sideshow. Instead, a gruff old veteran named Freddy Jones had two trailer-pit shows on the midway. "Flexible" Freddy had been around — first as a contortionist in vaudeville and Hubert's Museum, and then on circuses as a legal adjuster. One season he managed the Beatty-Cole sideshow. On this show he came into the ring halfway through the circus performance and proceeded to dislocate his shoulder. With one arm dangling awkwardly by his side, he delivered a Swiss warbler pitch.

"Flexible" Freddy Jones in the doorway of his snake-pit show on the 1963 Dick and Bill Garden–owned Gene Cody and Kipling Bros. Circus in Canada.

I don't know his real name, but around circus and carnival sideshows in the '60s and '70s he was known as Hi-Ti the fire-eater.

The next season, the show had a small trailer of caged animals onto which was loaded the sideshow tent, with its six small banners that made up the front. Inside, Carlos Leal did fire-eating while his boyfriend walked barefoot on broken glass. The show's lone elephant was staked out in one corner. That was it. Business was lousy.

At 18, I jumped ship when the concession manager offered me the outside cola and hot dogs on Sells and Gray's Canadian tour. Bill English was manager and one-third owner. The first morning there, I was busy chopping lake ice when a short guy with a beer belly appeared. "Hey, kid, fill this up with ice," he demanded, shoving a silver milkshake container toward me. Alex Linton tipped me weekly for keeping his ice glass full. A borderline alcoholic, he went through lots of ice. Each morning when I asked him how he was, he always replied, "Never felt better and had less." He also said, "Once you can swallow a sword you can swallow anything." I laughed off his pickup lines.

Half-loaded on the bally, Alex would effortlessly drop a sword down his throat when Stuart Miller turned to him and said, "Down the hatch without a scratch." English called Alex a great "rain or shine" trouper. Over the years he had been on every major carnival and circus sideshow. In 1975, Alex was found dead in his Sarasota cottage. He had lots of money and property but no will. No one came forth to claim his body. As president of the Showfolks of Sarasota Club, Bill English stepped in and rounded up enough cash from the club's bingo fund to inter Alex.

I doubt any 20th-century sideshow trouper had been around longer than Alex Linton. Here he waits beside the "rubber skin girl" for his turn to perform on the 1960s Sells & Gray Circus. He preferred circuses to carnivals, but he had worked in dime museums, amusement parks, 10-in-ones and everything in between, besides doing a stint in the army.

The Beatty-Cole sideshow remained the only big one. In 1973, Tommy Hart managed it with Ward Hall as the talker. Inside, Ward was the target for his partner Harry Leonard's knife-throwing act. Midget clown Pete Terhurne worked the bally and inside did his sword-ladder walk, and a seven-piece minstrel band provided the music. Other acts were noted freaks Emmett Bejano "the Alligator-Skinned Man" and his wife, Percilla, giant Ed Carmel, as well as a ventriloquist, tattooed lady, sword swallower, magician, fire-eater, clay modeler and the omnipresent Punch and Judy, electric girl and blade box.

As the '70s ended, Frank McCloskey, the driving force behind the Beatty show, died, and partner Jerry Collins, not wanting to run it alone, donated it to the University of Florida. Within months, manager John Pugh rounded up enough cash to get the circus back from the university, put it on the road again, and by 1981, John boasted they were carrying the only real sideshow left. It lasted 25 minutes and admission was $1. When I last talked to sideshowman John Bradshaw he told me he looked after the sideshow animals that year: "I didn't make the whole season as I got bit by the baboon. They had the menagerie cage truck plus the bulls in there. I sold peanuts to feed to the elephants. We opened in DeLand, Florida. No money, and no seconds in the cookhouse! Freddie Logan and the bull crew were in the sideshow top when I was feeding monkey chow to the baboon and monkeys. The bull hands asked if it was good to eat. I told them it was a complete diet for primates. They ate five pounds of it!" The sideshow was dropped two seasons later.

The last circus sideshows were managed by husband-and-wife teams who received

Knife-throwing act on a truck-circus sideshow in the '60s, when such working acts were rare. Most sideshows by then were managed by a couple — the husband did the openings and a little magic inside, while the wife handled a snake and went inside the blade box. Additional acts, if any, were usually a fire-eater or sword swallower.

25 percent of the ticket sales and whatever inside money they could get. Henry and Sandra Thompson were among the best. Henry was a short, debonair Errol Flynn lookalike, a Southern gentleman from Vicksburg, Miss., while Sandra was a tall, shapely blonde. Both were good talkers, and Sandra was once the target in their impalement act. When Henry finished his openings, he would duck inside and start the show by swallowing one sword, then do his Punch-and-Judy routine. Sandra would grind and make the second openings. Henry usually added a fire-eater and a lady big-top performer to do the electric girl act and work in the blade box. He was a first-class show painter and often did all the painting, including the bannerline.

Old-timers knew you could make a lot of money around little circuses because they often played more fresh towns. Ted LaVelda was a sideshow vet who, in 1966, was on Clark and Walter Circus. His sideshow bally partner was veteran Sonny Burdett, billed as "Professor Conroy" with his vent dummy. A quarter got you inside, where Ted and his wife, Frieda, worked a small knife-box illusion on her head, followed by Sonny's short vent act. Before doing his mechanical-man routine, Ted explained that time did not permit him to don makeup and a tuxedo to enhance it. The 10-cent blow-off pitched by Ted was a "Tate" figure (a shrunken body

For a few months, Hall and Christ put their sideshow over on Jim Roller's Roller Bros. Circus in 1984. Here Ward makes an opening. Previously they had a sideshow on Circus Vargas but the show found it hard to find room for them on the shopping-center lots they usually played.

made by Homer Tate) billed as "the Little Man From Mars." The show also had three bulls and a llama plus a cage truck and trailer that held various animals and doubled as the show's bannerline.

Kentucky showman Hoxie Tucker was another traditionalist. He opened his Hoxie Brothers Circus in the '60s and carried an adequate sideshow for many seasons. His 1973

sideshow, managed by Stuart Miller, included Stu's second wife, Sara Diaz, handling snakes and her sisters Leticia and Andrea doing the blade box and electric girl routines. Stu did "Punch" and a short magic routine ending in his sale of a magic package for a quarter. Eleven elephants and an assortment of other exotic beasts justified the 50-cent admission. Three years later, the ticket price jumped to a

Mud shows couldn't exist without performers like Dot and Sonny Burdett. Into her late 60s, Dot did three or four acts in the big top, and Sonny could be found with a big cigar selling sideshow tickets and then doing vent inside. Here they pose by their truck and trailer on the Famous Cole Circus in 1961 at Washington, Kans.

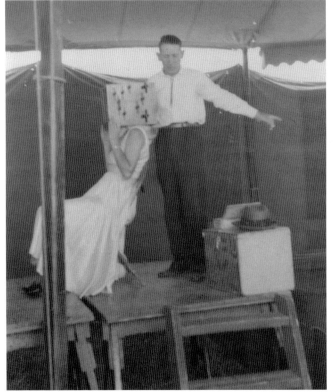

Ted LaVelda and his wife doing an illusion act on a small circus sideshow. Ted was one of those showmen who could do just about everything around a circus.

buck, when they obtained "Mongo the Gorilla," from Bob and Mae Noel's primate zoo in Tarpon Springs, Fla. Gorillas were extremely rare on touring shows. Mongo's 24-foot semi-trailer home was equipped to keep the air-conditioning running at all times.

Ward Hall, Chris Christ, Stuart Miller, Jim Windland and Bobby Hasson were a few of the sideshow managers who easily moved back and forth between a circus sideshow and a carnival 10-in-one. "Some of us were cross-trained," said Chris. "You couldn't make a carnival-style opening on a circus nor could you make a circus opening on a

The late Bobby Fairchild makes an opening on the Circus U.S.A. sideshow in the late 1970s. Bobby was a talker, knife thrower, magician and circus performer. With him are clown Jackie LeClare, tattooed Lorette Fulkerson and dwarf Pete Terhurne. Late 1970s.

carnival. The opening on the circus was longer."

Carl Conley, Mel and Jim Silverlake, Mike Martin, Bobby Fairchild and Billy Martin were the last generation of tent-circus sideshow managers and talkers to come along in the '70s. For the 11 seasons I owned a tent circus, there was a sideshow of some sort. Animals were its main attractions. You paid one of the clowns $10 extra weekly to come out and make bally. The two ticket sellers were backyard people getting five percent of their sales. One year we had fire-eater and magician Brian LaPalme.

We also had the show's camel, llama and mule, the liberty act horses and a half-dozen small wood cages set on jacks inside. The latter

Doc Swan does the electric lady act with Kathy Wilson on the 1980 Martin and Downs Circus. Kathy joined out in 1975 when we played her hometown of Nipawin, Sask. She became an all-round showgirl and stayed with us until the tent show closed in 1983. She also did aerial work, presented animal acts, helped in the cookhouse and sold sideshow tickets. That year Doc did fire-eating in the sideshow and played drums in the show band. He's still performing across America.

Bill Martin is on the microphone and I'm in the ticket box catching the latecomers on the Martin and Downs Circus sideshow in the late 1970s. Bill went on to take over the James M. Cole Indoor Circus, which Cole had run during the winters in schools in New York State for half a century. Bill and his wife, Angela, have continued the tradition with their Billy Martin All-Star Circus.

Carl Conley and one of his "big birds" make the 1977 sideshow opening on my Martin and Downs Circus. In the background are Wayne and Stretch, two long-time working guys. The banners were painted by Bobby Rawls.

contained a pair of coatimundis, a South African porcupine, a family of monkeys, some pheasants, two crows and a turkey. Baby sheep and goats made up the petting zoo part of it. Windland's openings always included mention of the nonexistent "roller-skating penguins." When we played my home town, I asked him to ixnay the penguins.

The folksy, low-key talkers, like Carl Conley, got the best grosses. Once a big-time riding act, Carl and his father managed sideshows and provided a few exhibition animals from their wintertime business of showing animals in schools. Carl also did rolla-bolla, juggled and presented a four-horse liberty act. On the bally, Carl looked like a big goofy kid. His wardrobe appeared slept-in and rarely was his tie without food stains. When he stepped on the bally to make his opening, he carried a big macaw in one hand

and the microphone in the other. Folks broke from the lines and came right over to him. A few minutes of his folksy spiel and all you saw were their behinds crowding the ticket boxes.

In the early '50s, many circuses had changed from lot and license contracts to sponsored dates. Service clubs received a percentage of the ticket sales in return for providing all licenses, a lot and their goodwill, plus allowing the circus phone crew to use their names to sell advance children's tickets. The

Sandy Windland handling a snake in the sideshow of the new Al G. Kelly–Miller Circus, operated by David Rawls in the 1980s. Her husband, Jimmy, managed the sideshow.

In the 1990s Dick Garden put out a large, new tent circus he called Toby Tyler, which featured Hall and Christ's sideshow one season. Here, Chris Christ makes the opening in Joliet, Ill., with dwarf Pete Terhurne, tattooed lady Lorette Fulkerson and clown Walter Stiemax. This was the last big canvas bannerline you would see on a tent circus.

callers told merchants if they didn't want the tickets delivered to them, they would be donated on their behalf to the area's "under-privileged children." "That ruined the sideshow business," complained Roark. "People already had their UPC tickets and knew what time the show started. They didn't come an hour before, but arrived just at showtime."

I didn't use phones, but still had to cope with people forming lines on the midway. You wanted people to arrive early and walk around spending money on the concessions, pony rides or the snake show. Closer to show time, people formed two lines in front of the marquee gates. The hardest thing for the sideshow manager to do was to get the public to come over in front of the sideshow bally.

Years ago, some circuses would use a high act setup beside the marquee. To see it properly, the gate huggers had to back up as far as the sideshow ticket boxes.

Patrons worried about not getting a seat in the big top. The side show manager's spiel started with, "If you have come out to the show grounds to see the circus and have your circus tickets, it starts over here.

The corporation that owned the Beatty-Cole Circus also owned the King Bros. Circus and the Sells & Gray Circus. These medium-sized circuses moved on a dozen trucks and had two elephants. Both had sideshows. Here, Harry Rawls makes the opening on the King Bros. Circus sideshow in the mid-1960s; he soon graduated to concession manager and then show manager.

Nothing happens over there until this show is all out and over. The same man who owns the big show also owns this show and he isn't going to run competition with himself. Don't worry, when it's time to go in the big show we have enough seats in there so each of you can lie down if you want to. You won't miss any part of the big show by going in here. For goodness sakes — if you have brought the children out to see the entire circus, then your visit starts right here at this tent."

The spiel closed with, "This is the only place on the circus grounds where you can safely feed one of those big old elephants a peanut. If you have brought your children out to see the animals, this is where you want to go first." The talker then used the jam — "Ticket sellers, put away those adult tickets. For the next five minutes and five minutes only, everyone out here today goes in on a child's ticket. Come along, it's circus day and it starts right here."

The public started arriving later and later, with most showing up just before the advertised showtimes instead of the preferred hour which gave circuses time to sell them concessions and draw them into the sideshow. I tried intermissions, but they didn't increase the sideshow gross by much. A few operators

Brian LaPalme, a sideshow manager and performer on both carnival and circus sideshows over the years, still does his excellent fire act and announces on circuses today.

One of the last tent circuses with a sideshow was the David Rawls–run Al G. Kelly–Miller Bros. However, the political correctness of the time had forced him to rename it the Children's Theatre. The old showman's term "kid show" for the sideshow had finally hit home.

brought a sideshow act into the ring, pitched it like a concert and sold tickets in the seats, but that didn't work either. The sideshow was dead, and without it, circus midway revenues fell off, but eventually recovered thanks to people willing to pay more for a ride on ponies, camels and elephants. Some circuses put moonwalks, petting enclosures and face-painting stands on the midway. New dings were tried in the main tent. Some owners invited patrons to step into the circus ring at intermission and pay to have their photo taken with a python or baby chimp. Some put the blade box on at intermission.

I visited Bill English as he was dying of lung cancer. Lying in bed, trying to get his breath, his old gravelly voice still remained his most identifying feature. As we talked about shows he recalled, "I fondly remember standing on the bally before a packed midway when I had the sideshow on Beatty and having all those suckers hanging on your every word. It gave you a sense of power, and when you turned the tip and they surged on the ticket sellers, it was sure thrilling."

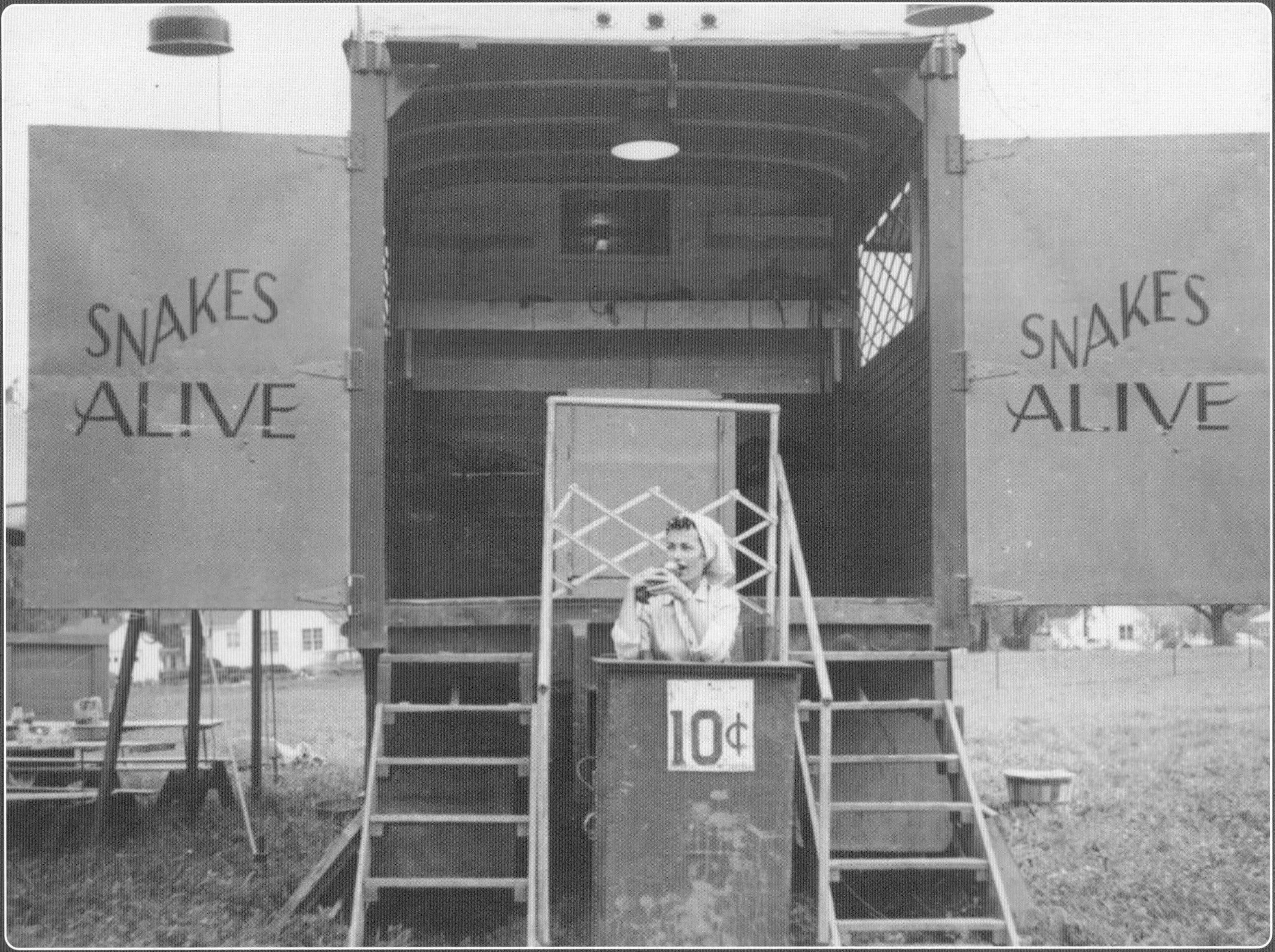
SNAKES ALIVE
SNAKES ALIVE
10¢

Chapter 6

Shows on Wheels

Franconi's European Museum in a small tent and wagon set-up in a town square. This is an unusually long wagon for the time. Note the wood brace between the front of the wagon and the back wheels to support the wagon in the middle.

Your basic circus-style pit show built into a truck, trailer or semi-trailer in the 1960s. The back doors serve as the panels advertising the snakes. Just behind the lady in the ticket box on the truck floor is the walk-around pit that houses the snakes — one set of steps in and one set out.

Peep shows — carried on the back, trundled along cart-style — or pushed like wheelbarrows were perhaps the first mobile exhibitions. Exhibiting in their own horse-drawn wagon was a big step up for showmen who previously had to rent a room over a store or tavern and hire a talker to draw folks in to their attraction. The wagon solved all their problems of transportation, lodging and a secure exhibition space. After the Civil War, many American showmen popped up in town squares, public markets, vacant lots, street fairs and on or near circus lots with exhibition wagons.

An April 1875 *Clipper* offered for sale two elegant museum wagons holding a large collection of first-class wax figures and views, while another in a March 1892 issue described a curiosity-exhibition wagon as "the most convenient ever built." The wagon-bed dimensions were 7-by-14 feet and 6.5 feet high, complete with steps and banner poles, and the wagon could be used open-platform style or in a tight space with the drop sides closed up, still allowing passage around the inside pit.

A "combination wagon" for sale in the January 31, 1903, *Billboard* had a sliding adjustable top easily raised high for exhibition, or lowered to pass through tunnels and under bridges when loaded on a show train. And in 1916, W. H. Hann of Arapahoe, Neb., advertised for a 50-foot tent in exchange for his street wagon containing an octopus, a porcupine, a raccoon and other small animals,

Two wagons that made up Col. F. M. Smith's Stupendous Aggregation of Wild West and Medieval curios. I suspect the latter consisted of instruments of torture. Note the front porch suggesting Mr. and Mrs. Smith and their dog also lived in the wagon on tour.

The Haviland family out of Mt. Auburn, Iowa, toured various exhibition wagons from the late 1800s before switching to a tented movie show operation. Here, their museum wagon contained a replica of Jesse James's body with built-in breathing mechanism. The high wheels, typical of overland show wagons, allowed them to cross small creeks and shallow rivers.

as well as an Indian woman and child mummies.

The two-wagon Haviland's Museum toured out of Mt. Auburn, Iowa, from the late 1800s into the early 1900s. One wagon bore lettering across the bottom that read, "Jesse James' Last Breath and Other Curios and Monstrosities." A December 1917 *Billboard* ad offering Haviland's show for sale, including Jesse James, states that the figure was in good order, but the breathing machinery needed repairs. Someone may have indeed witnessed Jesse James's last breath in Haviland's wagon.

The mid-morning circus parade was the best show-day advertising event, and many shows carried an uptown exhibition wagon. The wagon was unloaded from the show train early and set up along the parade route. Afterward, it was hauled to the lot and opened up. Midgets were good uptown wagon attractions, as they were easily concealed behind low pit walls. Giants were out, except for fake replicas laid out flat. Chimps or baboons billed as "gorillas" always did well, while live or taxidermed freak animals were a good bet too. Hoochie coochie dancers, despite being

limited to an all-male clientele, never failed to do well, as did "wild men" and women with big snakes. In the 1920s, the Kansas City, Mo., Horne's Zoological Company advertised sloths — ballyhooed as the Upside-Down Family" — as the best pit attraction on earth.

In the 1870s it was common for a circus to have both a sideshow and a "museum tent." The 1873 G. G. Grady's Circus sideshow featured a Circassian girl, an albino, an armless woman and a decapitation act called "Life in Death," while the museum tent offered patrons five cages of curiosities, including a

The Gollmar Bros. Circus's uptown wagon set up to catch the parade crowd in the early 1900s. The attraction inside appears to be a wild boar.

Miller Bros. 101 Ranch Wild West Show wagon. A chimpanzee stands on top of his cage as the workers assemble the canvas roof over the wagon.

living six-legged bull, a stuffed double-headed calf and the original "Cardiff Giant." On the 20th-century circus lot, the uptown wagon or a small pit show replaced the museum tent. It was usually set up opposite the main sideshow on the circus midway, and breakfast was hardly over before the pit-show operator was taking money from the lot lice watching the tents go up and the animals being watered and fed.

Ideal pit-show attractions were those that were cheap to buy and non-breathers, although 1880s animal dealer H. R. Overton's offer of a pair of monkeys for 10 bucks was hard to resist. Wax anatomy specimens in glass cases made excellent pit-show exhibits.

Thomas C. Rogers operated his wax "Museums of Anatomy" pit shows on circuses from 1869 until he died in 1904, the last of the anatomy

Besides trained monkeys and dogs, Buck's Animal School offered platform showmen a 15-foot alligator and the smallest bull alive.

Rare photo of the 1922 pit show carried on the Ringling Bros. Circus midway. The banners indicate it featured a wild baboon or big mandrill. Note the show even had its own bally platform.

museum operators with circuses. A February 1874 *Clipper* ad offered, on short notice, double-bodied girls, doubled-headed babies and other curiosities, while a January 1889 ad pitched showmen the "original 'Cleveland Child,'" known as the "Devil Child." The pit show came with a 30-by-50-foot tent, an 8-by-10-foot Tucker Brothers banner, plus pictures of the child's condition from his day of birth to the present. The child was made of either papier-mâché or wax.

Even the smallest 20th-century circus had some kind of a pit show. On larger circuses some held single attractions while others were mini-sideshows. The 1927 Christy

Often the small-time showmen are not only the most successful but also the most interesting. Clayton Hawkes took out small shows while he ran a movie theater near Binghampton, N.Y. Here he has Queenie the three-legged hen at the 1941 Owego, N.Y., fair.

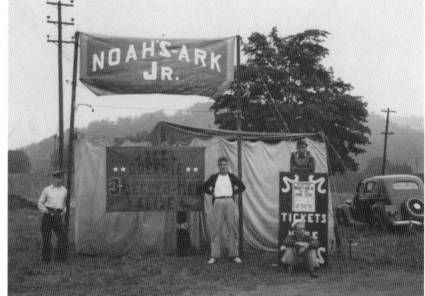

Some showmen liked to put their exhibits in buses they could also live in. Here is a snake pit show mounted in a bus on the 1955 King Bros. Circus when it played Brantford, Ont. It's parked on the midway beside the circus ticket wagon.

Brothers Circus had a pit show that featured fat girl Jolly Eva, a 16-legged horse and a cage of monkeys. The spiel for Duke Drukenbrod's "Petrified Man" pit show on the 1920s Hagenbeck-Wallace Circus midway described how the subject had turned to stone and was later found in the Ohio River in 1905. Some clever showman had it carved with well-detailed toenails, rope marks and a hole like a dagger wound. It was then plunked into the river and later discovered by fishermen. Newspapers across the country ran with the story. Years later, it was exposed as a hoax, but the figure and copies of the original newspaper articles were passed on from one showman to another for decades.

The April 1921 *Billboard* classifieds ran one of the earliest sales ads offering a motorized pit show — an uptown wagon built on a two-ton Mack truck with platform sides that opened to make a 14-by-20-foot deck. The owner had it on World's Fair Shows exhibiting "One Fisher Mummy." In the spring of 1935, some lucky showman spent $500 and picked up Bill Bahnsen's four-wheeled trailer show. He pulled it behind his car and inside was a mechanical figure that breathed and rolled her eyes, billed as Jane Wayers, "the Ossified Woman."

Anything to do with sex sold best, making the half-and-half a solid winner. Frank Fuller, who claimed to have originated the act, was born in Grand Rapids, Michigan, in the 1870s and known as "Lala Coolah." *Billboard* noted that the act "made carnival and circus pit shows famous." He was on the Barnum &

Bailey Circus for five seasons and many other prominent circuses and carnivals.

Truck and trailer exhibitions shows were quick to set up. There were no stakes to drive, and banners were replaced with solid wood or metal panels on hinges that in transit could be folded against the ends or sides of the unit. Sky panels folded down onto the roof and raised to give the front added height. All panels were back-braced with rods attached to the trailer or truck.

Some exhibits still had to go in a tent. Big-game adventurer Tony Diano was asked by the 1950 King Brothers Circus to put a giraffe pit show on their midway. Both it and his "Lost Canyon Dwarf Cattle" were exhibited in tented enclosures. The giraffe did well, except when the show played near cities with zoos.

Joe Lewis went from exhibiting a chimp billed as a "Killer Gorilla" to the big papier-mâché whale seen here on Howard Suez's 1960 Hagen Bros. Circus midway.

The next season, the Kelly-Miller Circus giraffes were in a pit-show tent. Semi-trailer pit shows became the normal setup. In the '60s, the Clyde Beatty–Cole Brothers Circus had two fine semi-trailer pit shows, one of which displayed a hippo, but not many shows toured a hippo. I'd had my own run-in with one. In 1975, my partner Johnny Frazier and I were into our third season operating Royal Brothers Circus in Canada. We headed west that year with a blood-sweating hippopotamus leased from Fisher Brothers Circus. For $100 a week we got a huge beast, a semi-trailer with a built-in pool tank, a not-so-late-model tractor to pull it, plus Harold the driver and hippo attendant. It was a toss-up some days which smelled worse, Harold or the hippo.

The hippo started out inside the sideshow, but we soon realized that with four live acts, a couple of elephants plus a semi full of caged wild animals, we had enough in there, so we

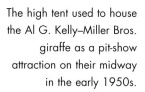

The high tent used to house the Al G. Kelly–Miller Bros. giraffe as a pit-show attraction on their midway in the early 1950s.

put the hippo on the midway as a pit show, where it turned in respectable daily grosses. Around matinee time, on a hot July day, the hippo died in Rosthern, Sask. He was standing up in his pool with just his eyes and the top of his head visible, and an absence of air bubbles in the water indicated things weren't right. We exhibited him dead on the matinee and again at night. After the night show started, I drove out to the local vet, hoping he had a dead-stock area. When I told him I had a dead hippo, he got very excited. "Can I keep the head?" he asked. "Sure thing!" I replied. Once the lot cleared after the night show, Harold went in the murky pool in his underwear and got a chain around the hippo. We built a sloping ramp of seat boards from the raised truck doors to the ground. A large back-

From the early 1960s until the late 1980s the Clyde Beatty–Cole Bros. Circus carried two midway pit shows, both of them successful. One housed a hippo and this one exhibited large snakes.

The rhinoceros pit show featured on the 1958 Famous Cole Circus midway. The exotic beast on a small tent circus was expected to do well, but for some reason it wasn't a big winner cash-wise.

hoe with a bucket on the front dragged the body out and it was then scooped up by the bucket and deposited onto a flatbed truck. Turned out the hippo had died of natural causes, which squared us with its owner. Several years later, when I was back through Rosthern, I stopped at the vet's office. The hippo head adorned the waiting room. It had cost him $500 in dry ice to keep the head until the taxidermist mounted it — it was a lot cheaper than going to Africa.

Floyd King's truck circuses usually had his wildlife show at the front of the midway. It could be a straight pay attraction, but he usually operated ding-style. The big King Bros. show was the second circus I saw as a child. I remember going into the wildlife show with my mother — the signs outside the tent read "Free Entrance." We went down past two lines of small cages and turned the corner to view a few more cages before exiting out the front. When we got to the exit area, a mob was

shouting at a circus employee who wanted a donation. Finally, someone threw some change in the employee's box and the first guy in line knocked the collector back into the sidewall. We all stampeded by before the guy regained his balance. The idea of charging folks to leave a free show made my mother furious. She refused to buy me a program, ignored the reserve-seat squeeze and when the sucker netting was dropped around the reserved seats she led the charge from the end blues into the better seats.

The most consistent pit-show money-maker has always been the big snake. On my Martin and Downs Circus from 1977 to 1983, the snake show occupied two-thirds of an 18-foot Wells Cargo trailer. When not on exhibition, the snakes were kept in a wicker basket that sat beside the furnace in our house trailer. Once the snake show entertained more than 3,600 people in a Newfoundland outport at 50 cents a head.

Captain Scott, manager of the pit show on the 1927 Sparks Circus, handles a new arrival.

The show world has a long history of large chimps being passed off as gorillas. John Francis's 1950s "Gorilla" pit show featured two large chimps. In an ad selling them, Francis stated, "One black face that passes for a gorilla." Jack Turner had his own ape show over on Carson & Barnes in 1959, while the 1959 Kelly-Miller midway had Shorty Shearer's "Canyon Horse" show, E. L. Robb's "Gorilla" and R. Moses's snake show. Shearer and his wife operated pit shows for several decades — their "Gorilla" show was a fixture on the Carson & Barnes midway for over a decade.

Manuel King, son of Snake King, the famed Texas snake-farm dealer, was one of America's youngest wild animal act presenters. Later on he had several pit shows on circus midways. Here is his "Giant Mummy" exhibit on the 1981 Carson and Barnes Circus midway.

A rare penguin pit show on the 1960s Cetlin & Wilson Shows midway. The signs say: "See Willie The Penguin and His Family." When the show was for sale, an ad said it came with four penguins, a freezer for fish, a light plant (generator) and the know-how to keep the penguins alive. The owner said it did big money as a street exhibition.

The new Sells & Gray Circus was launched in the winter of 1962 by Bill English and the owners of the Beatty-Cole Circus. For a couple of seasons the show carried a "Spidora" pit show — a giant spider with a woman's head — in a 20-by-30-foot top fronted with three Snap Wyatt banners. Bill's daughter Kathy was "Spidora." One winter in Sarasota, Fla., I asked Bill about pit shows he'd worked around. "I was a good friend of Dick McLaughlin," he related. "I remember his penguin show. It drew okay, but the problem was the short lifespan of the penguins. They did not take well to travel and Dick had to keep sending for new birds. The same

A May 1953 ad placed by veteran back-end showman Tom Hughes offering his penguin show for sale. Besides Willie the Penguin, it came with Oscar the giant South American tame condor with a wingspan of nine feet. Also inside the trailer on exhibit were a Jap Atomic Mummy and Wax Communist Warrior Figure.

The "Big Otto" hippopotamus pit show was a strong draw on the Clyde Beatty–Cole Bros. Circus midway. For years, the hippo was featured on one of their window cards.

problem was encountered on the Beatty show when they briefly tried an alligator pit show — the varmints kept dying.

"But the best animal pit shows were the big snake and the hippo show. The hippo worked well on the circus where the tank could be flushed daily, but it drew a blank on a carnival midway where it could not move and quickly developed a smell that kept everyone away in droves. Of all the animal pit shows, though, probably the greatest money-getter was Joe Lewis's 'Gorilla' show, on Kelly-Miller Circus in 1954. Others have copied the operation but Joe Lewis was the master.

"Kelly-Miller heavily advertised the feeding of the wild animals and drew a lot of lot lice each morning. His grind spiel told

In the '70s, the Himalayan Monster was a pit show on the Hoxie Bros. Circus, billed as "Neither man or beast — Homopongodies." Regardless of what the thing was, the creator has sculpted it with a very large and erect penis.

Joe Lewis's famous "Killer Gorilla" pit show in the 1950s on the Al G. Kelly–Miller Bros. Circus midway, where it opened early and closed late. Joe and his wife slept up front.

the marks the "Killer Gorilla" had been raised from a baby by a wealthy lady, but the gorilla killed her and had been sentenced by the courts to imprisonment in Joe's semi-trailer. He had impressive blow-ups of the fake newspaper story. When it was time to turn the tip, a slight tap on the ape's cage was enough to send the animal, which was actually a large, vicious chimp, into an impressive fit of screaming and pounding on the walls. At 15 cents, it had turned as many as 2,000 suckers a day. Joe liked to refer to rural audiences as the "bib-overall aristocracy." As they mounted the pit-show steps, he would say to them, "Take off your hats — you're entering the presence of an intellect greater than your own."

THAT WONDERFUL LITTLE GIRL
PEGGY
THE STRANGEST GIRL ON EARTH ALIVE
THAT STRANGE GIRL
PEGGY
THAT STRANGE GIRL
PEGGY
AN OPTICAL ILLUSION
PEOPLE
C. W.
World's Largest
Amusement Devices.
KANSAS.
10841

Chapter 7

"It's Never Out – It's Never Over"

Basic platform-style exhibition show set up in the yards of the C. W. Parker factory in Leavenworth, Kans., in the teens. The only hint of what makes "That Strange Girl PEGGY" different are the words "An optical Illusion," lettered on the back roof canvas valance.

Mid-19th-century showmen with small fairground sideshows had been around as long as sideshows on circuses. An August 1860 *Clipper* reported: "We are glad to hear that the proprietors of the smaller or curiosity shows expect to reap a good harvest in the fall, on the occasion of their visiting the agricultural fairs." The *Clipper* noted several shows at the Indianapolis, Ind., fair: "Some with more monstrosities than people could ever imagine exist. Men without arms or legs who could play the flute. Three bearded children, a skeleton man, hogs with nine legs and a calf with six!" During the winter, the Macon, Georgia, December Cotton Plantation Fair was the big date, featuring Chinese jugglers, L. Hubbell "the American Samson," Jane Campbell "the Connecticut Fat Girl" and Colonel Vedder and

Major Burnell's Museum of Living Wonders. The latter featured "Vantile Mack," an infant giant, as well as a dwarf family, a massive anaconda, Japanese mice and wax "figgers."

Fairground and circus sideshows of this era were similar in both appearance and content. Noted in a spring 1879 *Clipper* was Ben Potter's New and Greatest Show, a Richmond, Va.–based sideshow using two tents and moving via rail baggage car service. One tent held eight monkeys, 12 birds, three snakes, Tom Thumb "the Educated Pig," a Punch-and-Judy show and an illusion in which a woman was cut in half. A wire-walker and an 11-member minstrel troupe worked in the other tent. The other staple attraction for fairground showmen was freak animals from the nation's farms. Six-legged cows, double-

GREAT ATTRACTION!
AND
GRAND RECEPTION LEVEES
OF THE
WORLD-RENOWNED
FRENCH
GIANT
In this City, for a short time only.
TO BE EXHIBITED IN HIS
PAVILION!
At Martin-street Gate Eentrance, near the Fair Ground,
during the Agricultural Exhibition.
AT THE SIGN OF THE GIANT!
THE FIRST VISIT TO THE "CITY OF ELMS,"
OF
MONSIEUR BIHIN
Having earnestly desired to visit this city before returning to Europe, he will be happy to receive
visitors, and make their acquaintance at the above-named Pavilion.
THE
FRENCH GIANT!
FROM LYONS,
Is said to be the TALLEST and BEST PROPORTIONED
man in the world, being nearly eight feet in height,
and weighing 350 pounds!
Fail not to visit him. Monsieur BIHIN has had the honor of appearing in the principal cities, and
before the nobility of Europe, also in New York, Boston, Philadelphia and Baltimore, in which places he
was daily visited by Thousands of astonished admirers, who, one and all, awarded to him the well-deserved
title of THE CHAMPION GIANT OF THE WORLD. For extraordinary altitude, beauty of form,
muscular development, and symmetrical proportions, it is impossible to conceive a more perfect represen-
tative of the Giants in olden times.
☞ The Ladies and Children are particularly invited to visit this extraordinary specimen of our race.
In every city on the Continent of Europe, and where he has been exhibited in America, the Press has
spoke loudly in his praise, as far exceeding in proportions any and every giant they have seen.
Admission, - - - 12 1-2 Cents.
NO HALF PRICE.
N.B. This Giant appears in Roman Toga Costume of the Second Century.
BENHAM, STEAM PRINTER, 55 ORANGE ST., NEW HAVEN.

This single-banner pit show exhibiting Handsome Johnny Webb on the 1914 Parker and Kennedy Shows midway was typical of how freaks and curiosities were shown on early midways. Johnny Webb was just a very fat young kid. His manager, A. V. Maus, had him on carnivals in the summer and on the movie and vaud theater circuits in the wintertime.

This mid-19th-century broadside for the "French Giant" (Monsieur Bihin) informs the public that he is being exhibited in a tent outside the fairground's gates in this New England town — the rent inside the fairgrounds may have been too high. The advertisement says, "At the sign of the giant," which refers to the painting or banner. Admission for all was 12½ cents, the going rate for such attractions at the time.

An early 20th-century pit show using a concession-style tent features a midget lady — Princess Carita. The front is made up of painted wood panels for banners.

Freak attractions were found around early beaches and other locations for fun parks. This broadside for fat lady Big Hannah notifies the public of her appearance at Bullock's Point next to the "Flying Horses," an early merry-go-round where the horses hung from the top of the frame and swing out when the ride is in motion. Besides gawking at Hannah, the viewers were entertained with plantation melodies by the Jubilee Singers.

headed calves and more were cheap and good draws.

The *Clipper* seemed oblivious to the approaching 1893 Chicago's World's Columbian Exposition. Except for acts and shows claiming to be "World Fair Class," there was little hoopla. The Panopticum Co. of Hamburg, Germany, sought an operator for its

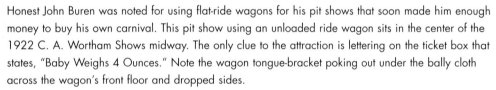

Lala Coolah
THE FREAK
THAT MADE
THE "PITSHOW"
FAMOUS.
Half Man — Half Woman
SELLS-FLOTO CIRCUS
1916

Honest John Buren was noted for using flat-ride wagons for his pit shows that soon made him enough money to buy his own carnival. This pit show using an unloaded ride wagon sits in the center of the 1922 C. A. Wortham Shows midway. The only clue to the attraction is lettering on the ticket box that states, "Baby Weighs 4 Ounces." Note the wagon tongue-bracket poking out under the bally cloth across the wagon's front floor and dropped sides.

Lala Coolah (Frank Fuller) claimed he first presented the half-man, half-woman act in America, but that is false. However, he certainly was the best pit-show attraction going for years and spent five seasons with the Barnum & Bailey Circus. He was born in Grand Rapids, Mich., in the 1870s and when he died in 1931, he had a mummy and python show at Savin Rock Park in New Haven, Conn., and left his wife a large Texas estate.

"Mirror Labyrinth," saying only, "Good for the Chicago Exposition," and Neal Van Doomum wanted investors to get his 50,000-pound "California Big Tree" section from New York City to Chicago, saying that all the extra log wood could be turned into sale novelties.

The 1892 season was business as usual for fairground showmen. Professor Lowande started his 12th year by exhibiting his "World of Wonders" at the Detroit fair, before continuing west. During the winter he sold used show equipment — from spirit cabinets to stuffed freaks and more. In late July, Doc Gibb's Olympic Museum opened in Middleton, Md., housed in two 30-by-60-foot tents, with an 18-picture bannerline.

Doc's wife presented dogs and birds, while another woman showed snakes and iguanas, and manager S. A. Kennedy did magic. Three more performers and four canvasmen rounded out the crew.

During the same era, Pete Conklin and his son left the Barnum & Bailey Circus sideshow to go onto the fairgrounds. Their show

The early 20th-century midway business got a positive boost when Elks and other community-minded organizations started putting on street fairs. A midway company was contracted for and set up on the town's main streets, like this one. On the left is a big carved show front, then the loading steps for the camel rides and further along a Ferris wheel. A row of concessions is across the street.

The attractions on one of the first big carnival companies — the Gaskill-Mundy Shows — are listed here in a 1902 Elks Jubilee Carnival ad. The only freak attractions are the Burmese Midgets and Wild Rose, the ½ Monkey Girl. The mainstays of the midway are the big wild animal show, the circus acts, the stadium show featuring thrill acts and a number of shows based on illusions, plus the "dancing girls." You got in the gate for a dime.

consisted of a knife-throwing act, a magician, a den of snakes, two clowns, a six-piece band and weightlifter Professor Leonard on the bally. Conklin continued to pull against a team of horses as the feature act.

A carnival manager advertises for attractions for the Lockport, Ill., 1906 Firemen's Street Carnival. Note in brackets: "Wide Open Town." Hustlers with no equipment and just a pad of contracts jumped into the "street fair" business and soon the Elks were condemning the carnival racket. Things didn't improve much until the next decade, when big carnivals with their own rides and shows started to dominate the business.

George Hall Jr. had two sideshow units out in 1894, playing Michigan and Wisconsin, including the Wisconsin State Fair. He and his wife, traveling on the first unit, presented magic and Punch and Judy, along with a lecturer, a female hypnotist, a musical albino lady, a sword swallower and a mindreader. The other unit, managed by Theo Grouper "the Fire King," carried a tattooed man, magician Mons Lorena, Bohemian glassblowers, a mindreader and a lecturer, plus an eight-piece band.

Inspired by the Chicago World's Fair's "Midway Plaisance," scenic artist Otto Schmidt launched the first touring carnival company in 1894. Within a couple of seasons there were a half-dozen carnival companies on the road, and within the decade these enterprises became stand-alone outfits like the circus. The new midway companies consisted of a cluster of independently owned rides and shows organized by a showman or promoter. Their main attractions were wild animal shows, oriental theaters, open-air water arenas and tented coliseums offering high divers and loop-the-loop bike riders. Freaks and other sideshow attractions appeared as single attractions in small pit or platform shows.

The popularity of midway companies developed hand-in-hand with the street-fair business. Street fairs were sponsored by downtown merchants or fraternal clubs who signed a contract with a carnival promoter for show attractions. The sponsors received a small percentage of the gross, and in return, they provided street locations, print advertising, electricity and most everything else, including building materials.

One of the most practical show setups for curiosity exhibitors playing street fairs were platform shows. The platform show's base was a square or rectangular wooden floor raised a few feet off the ground and surrounded on three sides with canvas walls, with a roof. A single banner ran above the front. The open front provided a view of the walled pit and the people looking into it. It was an ideal show for city streets because it didn't need any stakes or guy lines and could be butted up against sidewalks or buildings. Many platform showmen traveled by train with their gear in the baggage car. Just a few crates were needed to hold their gear, and one crate could be converted into the show's ticket box. On the train, human attractions rode with the showmen in passenger service.

Some exhibitors preferred the single-banner pit show, with their attraction in a small 20-foot-square tent. The front was open, revealing a waist-high, four-sided canvas wall or pit in the center, keeping midway walkers from getting a free glimpse at the oddity. The show could be enlarged with additional banners and a bigger tent. A November 1913 *Billboard* article, "The Evolution of the Pit Show by One Who Knows," stated, "Profit is what counts in show-business and in that regard, pit shows have more than held their ground. Credit is given to Walter E. Sibley as the originator of the multiple pit show attractions idea exhibiting two-in-one, four-in-one, five-in-one and seven-in-one shows."

In his teens, Boston-born Sibley worked at B. F. Keith's Vaudeville Theater, followed by

A showman could easily transport this platform show in a few crates via a railroad baggage car. Note the frame ticket box with canvas covering and small box with rope handles as a platform for the talker. The midget lady Ina, the showman and any other help rode in coach.

stints as a professional bike racer and fireworks promoter. In 1893, he partnered with Bill Hicks to exhibit a two-headed baby billed as "Taka-Tama" at Coney Island. Next, Sibley promoted fat men Jack and Jill Karns and exhibited them as "Cliff and Eddie, the Fat Twins." Next, he was showing the Karns twins, Hugo the big snake, and "Zeno the Man-Ape" platform-style.

Sibley played all the major fairs, but wasn't accepted at Toronto's Canadian National Exhibition (CNE), which had had problems with previous American curiosity showmen. Anxious to perform at North America's largest fair, with its annual attendance of over a half-million, Sibley's wife kept sending in applications. Finally CNE manager Dr. J. O. Orr booked Sibley's shows for the 1906 fair, so long as he could inspect each one before letting them open. Orr passed two shows, but objected to Corela "the Two-Headed Baby," until Sibley agreed to tone down the outside spiel. Orr had been to Africa and also knew "Zeno the Man-Ape"

This is a lot scene of the T. A. Wolf Superior Shows, a noted rail carnival of the era. The big WHIP ride in the foreground has just come out from the Mangel's amusement ride manufacturer company of Coney Island, N.Y. The 10-in-one show in the background is typical of ones in this era when a lot of operators used painted wooden panels rather than banners.

was merely a baboon presented as a gorilla. To get the Zeno show open, Sibley had to drop all use of the word "gorilla" — he still did well.

Next season Sibley arrived at the North Vernon, Ind., fair and found the cost of renting space extremely high. Regardless, Sibley ponied up, buoyed by the recollection that Snakey Thorton used a bannerless, open-front tent, housing four pit attractions at Kankakee, Ill., in 1901, and by another showman's suggestion that a large platform show with many pits viewed for one admission might do well. Sibley put his four attractions under a long canvas enclosure, and at 10 cents' admission, he outgrossed everything on the fairgrounds. He operated the same way at another date to make sure it wasn't just a lucky occurrence, and again did bang-up business.

That winter, Boston's Hoyt Company made Sibley a red-and-white-striped tent, 40 feet wide with two 30-foot middles, and Charles Wolfe painted a new set of banners. Eight German flaming arc lamps were ordered, four for the inside and four for the outside. Special burgees, or triangle flags, adorned each banner

Walter Sibley's early platform shows featured the Karns Twins. Some members of the Karns Fat Folks who may or may not have been blood relatives are shown inside their exhibition tent. Into the late 1940s, Cliff Karns was the main force in putting together and booking their fat show.

pole. The Wappler Electric Company in New York City made Sibley an electric chair, which he claimed was the first exhibited in a sideshow. His 1907 show used four talkers, a seven-piece kiltie band and a large band-organ, and he augmented the acts with 30 cages of small animals. Sibley built a 16-section scenery front, each with a five-foot-square opening three feet above the ground filled in with a banner. Sibley believed this provided the open-front look of the old-time bannerline but gave the front more class.

Sibley played Toronto again, now in competition with Billy William's famous "Mamie" show, Charlie Abrams' "African Mummy" and Col. Francis Ferari's "Animal Arena." Located across from Ferari's outfit, Sibley did 10 times more business than the big show. At the Louisville, Ky., fair, Col. Percy Mundy's wild animal show and Doc Turner's geek show were among his competitors. Both protested Sibley's low entrance fee of 10 cents, but then quickly adopted his style of operation for their own shows.

In 1909, Sibley added more pits and a $1,000 band organ. Soon, every midway company wanted to book a five-, seven- or 10-in-one show. Many carnivals built their own and hired an operator with the acts. Said Sibley of his show's popularity, "A show has evolved that is so diversified and yet so cheap to see, that almost anyone can be pleased and satisfied."

At the 1909 Minneapolis Fair, Sibley met Harry Metz, another 10-in-one pioneer whose show was set up on the Great Parker Shows' midway. Metz's "Annex" featured "Radion the Armless and Legless Wonder," "Serpentina the Boneless Girl," plus an educated baboon. In 1911 when Coney Island's Dreamland Park burned down, Harry wired future Coney Island sideshow king Sam Gumpertz and was soon operating amid Dreamland's ashes. His "Freakatorium" became an annual fixture, grossing $60,000 a season. Metz put his profits into movie and vaudeville houses in New

Jersey, while his brother Ted remained on the road until the 1940s, operating 10-in-ones, circus sideshows and winter museum shows. When Metz's main Coney Island competitor, King Karlo, expanded his show into a 20-in-one, Gumpertz adopted Karlo's setup, putting out his own 20-in-one on the Ferari Shows.

10-in-ones and circus sideshows both had bally stages and bannerlines advertising virtually the same acts. However, they were like night and day in operation style. Circus sideshows were housed in large, closed-up,

(Above) This five-banner sideshow on the 1920s Abner Kline Shows is typical of the early midway four-in-one and five-in-one shows. A sideshowman would take one outstanding attraction like Donny the half-boy on the bally and put a couple more acts with him. Those extra acts here appear to be a two-person jazz orchestra and a magician who also presents the electric-chair act.

(Below) A 1929 ad placed by showman Neil (Whitey) Austin, one of the pioneers along with Slim Kelly of the big 10-in-one carnival sideshows that featured all the dings, traps and blow-offs needed to get the mark's money. Neil doesn't need acts — he wants people who will pay him to work, like glassblowers, a tattooist and someone with a lung-testing machine.

Early carnival sideshow features banners depicting the "Human Fish" and the "Cigarette Fiend."

A string pit show on the C. A. Wortham midway in the early 1920s. The high pit curtain on the front side hides the acts from midway walkers. The idea was to keep folks lined up along the front curtain as lures for more customers, but on big days you had to let them into the tent. There appear to be risers to stand on along the back wall of the tent so those folks can see over the people lined up along the back pit curtain.

round-ended tents, entered through a small marquee behind the bally stand. The acts inside occupied individual stages. In contrast, the carnival 10-in-one tent was long and narrow with an open front. Patrons stood along the opening looking over a waist-high curtain where the acts worked in pits before them.

The circus sideshow's main business time was limited to an hour before the big show, while the 10-in-one opened mid-afternoon on still dates and mid-morning at fairs, continuing until closing late at night. These longer hours were a boon to pitches and dings. Sibley remarked, "Circus men were speculating as to whether the pit show as a circus sideshow would get as much money as the old-style closed-in sideshow. I booked my pit show on the 1911 California Frank's Wild West Show. Circuses were doing perhaps 10 percent of the business of the main ticket gross with the old-style sideshow. I did around 25 percent of the gross over there." Despite Sibley's success, few circus sideshows converted.

"The first sideshow I ever saw was on Lewis Brothers Circus, in 1938 or 1939," Ward Hall recalled. "It was pit-style — all just one big pit divided down the center poles — and I remember not seeing much except the tattooed man. You could only see what was right in front of you unless you were right up on the rail or were really tall. The people were three or four deep." The pit-style sideshow wasn't suited for big circuses where a good sideshow manager could turn 300 or 400 people at one time. You needed a big tent to hold them.

Ben F. Karr held the "X" — the exclusive — for pit shows on the Tom Allen Shows. His May 1915 ad said they were worth $7,000, but he was offering them for half-price. The 10-in-one equipment listed included a 22-by-140-foot khaki tent plus a new glass-front tank on a 7-by-14-foot wagon for the famous "Divona" human fish act; a pump for pumping water and his own patented heating device; four laughing mirrors, an electric chair and three mummies.

The old "embryo and stiff" showmen who dominated the late-19th-century fairgrounds believed there was no need to pay good money for a living curiosity when a dummy in a pit would do. That all changed with operators like Sibley, Metz and Max M. Klaus. Klaus exhibited his sideshows with plenty of quality acts. His 1915 pit-style sideshow on the Sells-Floto Circus in a 26-by-120-foot tent featured the Aztec-Indian midgets, Emo "the Turtle Boy," Lala Coola the half-and-half, armless wonder Barney Nelson, glassblower Geo Schmidt, mental marvel Princess Maxine, magician Ali Budah and a monkey family.

For many years, the sideshows and girl revues booked into the CNE by Patty Conklin came out of Coney Island, other East Coast

A 1920s string show on the Conklin & Garrett Shows midway. The acts work on the wooden floor in the center. The wooden frame along the back of the tent supports lighted signs covering the spaces in front where each act works. Note the mitt camp in the middle with stairs leading up to it and the possible blow-off area behind the striped side wall at the far end.

operators to put out a sideshow unit to catch the last of the fall fairs. From 1913 to 1919, the main park sideshowman was C. H. Armstrong, who often had as many as 35 acts signed up for Chicago's Riverview Park and another road unit. The fair unit closed in November and acts were then given work in his dime museums in Philadelphia and Washington.

Manpower shortages during the World War I years resulted in most 10-in-one operators using illusions and other time-fillers. Fred Mintzer tried to overcome the labor shortage when he invested $15,000 to frame a large carnival-style pit show on motor trucks in 1919. Mintzer used three trucks and one trailer, all with telescoping pits. Placed end-to-end, they created a 125-foot exhibition space complete with pits, bally, steps and walk-around platform. Rather than on banners, all the paintings were on steel panels, and there was no tent to set up, so the whole show could be erected in an hour. A *Billboard* writer described Mintzer's business as good, though no other 10-in-one operators followed Mintzer's idea.

parks, parks in Chicago and in the 1950s from Montreal's Belmont Park. After Toronto, they played the London, Ont., fair before going on to the southern U.S. fairs. Lou Dufour, Pete Kortes and Sam Alexander kept up this tradition into the 1970s. It became a normal routine for park sideshow

In 1919, the Iowa-based Tangley Company offered pit sideshow operators a new novelty. Tangley turned out excellent air calliopes used on circuses and sideshows and offered showmen an act that would allow the performer to "melt, weld iron from electricity

A talker makes an opening on a 10-in-one while the bally girl tied to the cross freezes the tip in front. Jim Steinmetz said, "We used bally girls in as skimpy a costume as we could get away with. This helped the sale of the blade box inside. We tied the girl to the cross with rope that was in two sections and had snap releases."

FREAKS --- CURIOSITIES

WANTED—For my Riverview Park Circus Side Shows, high-class Freaks and Sensational Acts that can work in Pits. State all, including salary wanted. 18 weeks at Riverview Park and long road season after park closes. Will buy or place on percentage a large Mechanical Show or Funny House. Also want a strong Ballyhoo for my Road Pit Show with the World at Home Co.

C. H. ARMSTRONG,
4846 NORTH CLAREMONT AVE., - CHICAGO, ILL.

Pioneer 10-in-one showmen C. H. Armstrong, Harry Metz and the Detroit-based Claude Hamilton were Walter Sibley's main competition at fairs during early years of his operations. Amstrong worked out of Chicago and had a summer sideshow at Riverview Park and a road sideshow booked on the World of Home Shows during the 1916 season. Wintertime he had museums in Market St. in Philadelphia and on 9th Street in Washington, D.C.

Ted Metz's 10-in-one sideshow, booked onto the 1930s Tom Mix Circus. Notice the high pit wall inside the tent. The drawback with a carny-style sideshow for big circuses was that the circus sideshowman only got a couple of shots at the public at each showtime. You had to jam half the "circus midway" crowd into the tent on the first opening to make any money, and these long, skinny 10-in-one sideshows just didn't have the room inside. It was better than nothing and required no investment on Mix's part.

During the 1920s, many big 10-in-one sideshow operators favored these highly carved and decorative sectional bannerlines where the center bracing for the banner uprights went right through the middle of the tall banners. This is a show photo of all employees, so not everyone is from the sideshow, but you can pick out midgets, a fat lady and a giant.

The 1927 Johnny J. Jones Shows' 10-in-one sideshow at Youngstown, Ohio, featured Sesrad the Psychic Scientist standing on the left of the bally next to the sword swallower and behind Eagan Twist, the contortionist. The second man from right standing on the bally with cigar in hand is Laurello the Man with the Revolving Head. The entrance banner says: "You never wait. Show positively going on all the time."

Robert Ripley's freak and sideshow act cartoons added both national publicity and needed respectability to sideshows. Many operators, including Alfred Renton, used the Ripley's Believe It or Not title on his sideshow, seen here in 1938 on the Mighty Sheesley Shows midway. Note the four ticket boxes and three bally stands. Because of the long skinny tent, showmen called such operations "string shows."

through the body." Every operator wanted one. Sideshows desperately needed new gimmicks and acts that a bally girl could work, since the boom in 5- and 10-cent vaudeville theatres which gobbled up so many variety acts was blamed for the number of poor 10-in-ones of this era.

The biggest problem was that same illusions appeared over and over. In a 1928 *Billboard* article titled "Fair Midways and Sideshows," Joe Tracy related, "If you saw 10 sideshows on midways this summer you no doubt saw at least ten fire-eaters, 10 blade boxes, 10 Buddha camps, and 10 or twelve dilapidated, rusty-looking illusions." Many of these had already been exposed for a nickel in the blow-off or right on the bally platform.

Midway patrons saw the same banners on different shows — each proclaiming to be "The Only One" or "The Original." Shows with dead banners — banners for which there were no acts — didn't help win the confidence of midway patrons. There were other negatives too. On one rag-bag 10-in-one, the glassblower remarked, "The joint looks so big from the outside that they think

Alfred Mark Renton was a big-time sideshow operator from the 1930s into the 1950s. Al, nicknamed "Around the World Renton" for his love of shortwave radio, stands in the center at the microphone. A young Sealo the Seal Boy, dressed in all-white, stands next to him. The tall chap with the boater hat and dark suit is the show's mechanical or wax man.

there is something going on in here and come in on purpose." One mark said, "No wonder that fella could dance on broken glass. If he ever washed his feet he would have to break in a new act." Another noted, "A little elbow grease and 25 cents of varnish could save the lecturer a lot of squaring on the mummified attractions!"

Regardless of the negativity, the 10-in-one arrived on midways at the right time, just as the business was trying to soften the nudity and rigged games. The big carnivals needed more independent showmen with quality shows, and they were willing to make deals to keep good sideshowmen. The public began shying away from the bigger walk-over bally shows — they didn't like waiting in hot tents while the talker made three ballies to fill the venue before starting the show or being confronted with the candy pitch in every sit-down show. When *Billboard* reps visited the Wortham Shows at the 1921 Canadian National Exhibition, they noticed the

majority of shows were either open-front pit shows or walk-through shows. Wortham maintained, "If they want to sit down, let them ride the rides." The climate was ideal for the walk-in–walk-out sideshow.

Large string-illusion shows and 10-in-ones had similar acts, illusions, blow-offs and dings. Faye Renton Frisbee recalls how Slim Kelly had encouraged her dad, Alfred Mark Frisbee, a.k.a. Al Renton, to take an illusion show out: "My mom, Jean McMillen, was a showgirl. My dad was stage manager on the New York Hippodrome when they met. My dad worked as a magician for Slim Kelly in Coney Island. He framed an illusion show — a half-lady and a four-arm girl, and that's what he had when he built the sideshow. He kept both, and Alfred Lee, my oldest brother, ran the illusion show. We were on World of Mirth four seasons in the '30s and then 14 years with Captain Shesley's Greater Shows."

Faye says her dad was a good talker who used various bally stunts. "When we ballied

we did the chain escape — the girl tied to the cross and the gully can," she recalled. "The gully can — you keep pouring water out of it. You can pick water out of the air with the can, then dump it into a bucket. During the war years, my dad had a big wooden 'V' on the back of the bally light up with red, white and blue neon tubes for victory. He'd chain or tie one of the bally girls to it while he made his opening. Sometimes he used the chair, broom or sword suspension. It was called 'the brace,' because the bally girl wore a brace that attached to the ratchet end of the suspension devices.

"A guy out there with a hood over his head was billed as 'the Mystery Man.' He worked the electric chair inside. And my father often had bird men. One guy was six-foot-six, and Dad shaved his head and glued a feather on top and had him yell, 'Koo-koo . . . koo-koo' on the bally. It was hard to keep a straight face sometimes."

Chapter 8

A Strange Business for Hustlers

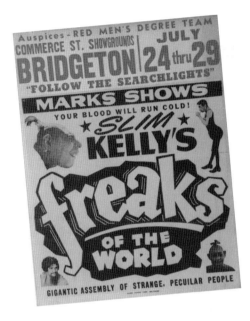

Window card for Slim Kelly's sideshow on the John L. Marks truck carnival. Slim started in the sideshow business in 1912 on the C. A. Wortham Shows. In 1918 he and Neil (Whitey) Austin invented the "jam," a circus and pit sideshow operational tactic still used today. In 1935 he tried out a 183-foot bannerline using 22-foot-high banners painted in black and white. This "comic book" bannerline was one of the few innovations of his that didn't work out.

Midget wedding on Thomas W. (Slim) Kelly's 10-in-one on the Rubin and Cherry Shows at Louisville, Ky., May 3, 1930. Slim stands next to the right-hand ticket seller. Notice how part of the ticket counter folds over to protect tickets and money when not in use and that the far ticket seller has tickets ready to sell as soon as the tip is turned. The carnival band in the background and customers stand on the catwalk, looking over the pit curtain.

In 1916 a Chicago firm offered showmen a nifty bally stunt. The new "Parrot Bally" featured a live caged parrot that talked to potential 10-in-one customers. But the key to any midway show's success was a human talker with a pleasing personality and clean appearance. Good ones projected intelligence and geniality, and were masters at finding the right words to paint vivid mental pictures. The talker's biggest challenge was knowing when the tip had heard enough and it was time to turn them. Enthusiasm helped, but the clincher was sincerity: the hayseed talker often did better in putting over the show than the well-dressed Slick Willie. Press agent and show humorist Star DeBelle's idea of a perfect opener was an old man who got up on the bally and said, "This is a family show. You won't see it advertised on telegraph poles, barns, fences and outdoor privies. Our show is right in yonder on that stage. It's me and my wife, her folks, our youngest boy and his wife and her folks and a hired comedian. If you don't have the money, don't worry about it. We take butter, milk, alfalfa hay and canned goods!"

The wax or mechanical man works on the bally of Slim Kelly's 10-in-one in the 1930s. Slim's behind him, waiting to make the opening.

Billboard ad offered $20 weekly for a talker who'd be responsible for setting up the front of the show, making the openings, grinding, setup and tear-down, seeing the show off and on the lot, paying for his/her own hotel and for the ride on the show train on the long jumps. One talker recalled his expenses, saying it cost him $3 a week for a hotel, $4.50 to eat, a dollar for his laundry, 30 cents for the barber and a couple more dollars for incidentals. If he could save half of his pay, he was in pretty good shape. The real bonus was in the "walk-aways"— folks who left some of their change on the ticket-box counter. Only pros got away with deliberately short-changing — any slowdown or beefs at the ticket box made the operators angry.

The July 1905 Billboard carried 37 ads for talkers. Only one asked for references.

To attract a tip, early talkers resorted to foghorns and other noisemakers. In 1917 the Deagan Company of Chicago's Una-Fon was said to be the fastest-selling instrument for sideshow ballies. Light and easy to pack, it sounded like a big band, and any amateur pianist could play it. Joseph E. Ori was an early maker of pneumatic calliopes, used by many sideshow operators. Many bally showmen also stayed healthy by banging on a gong or bass drum to draw a tip.

Talkers could earn an average wage on salary and did extremely well if paid on percentage of tickets sold. A July 1905

The bally begins on Slim Kelly's sideshow with a dwarf in makeup: the famed magician and sideshow performer Bluey Bluey, one of the best at a magic trick known as the Thumb Tie. The feature was Mary Whitaker, Double-Headed Girl — no doubt pickled. Note people standing on the cat walk.

Lou Dufour related in an October 1976, *Amusement Business* column, "When old-time talker Johnnie Bejano had trouble turning a tip, he would resort to this: 'Folks, we also have on the inside a laughing hyena. He eats only once a month. He moves his bowels only once in six months. He mates only once a year. They call him the laughing hyena. Now, ladies and gentlemen, I have a proposition for you. There's a free seat inside for any man or woman who can tell me what the hell he's got to laugh about!'"

Al Moody's huge, three-banner-high freak animal show in the 1970s included a live double-bodied cow, a two-headed cow, an eight-legged cow and 40 other freak animals. Al was self-conscious about how he sounded as a talker. Recalled Chris Christ, "I've seen the

The talker has told the tip that when he and his assistant pull the ropes around this young man's neck, they could possibly strangle him. Not politically correct today, but it was a good bally trick in the '50s.

Al Renton behind the suspended lady on the bally of his 1936 World's Fair Freaks. There's lots here to capture the tip's imagination and curiosity, including the hooded man, the lady tied to the cross and the painted-faced dwarf. Note the canopy over the bally protecting the show's staff from rain or sun.

most articulate guys that couldn't turn three people and I've seen the 'them, dese and dose guys' that could turn everybody. Moody's own tape was right out of central casting: 'See what the H-Bomb done did to the animal kingom: the two-legged cow, the eight-legged cow. Smell the aroma, you know they are ALIVE, living and breathing.' He sounded like an old farmer from Tennessee and it sold like gold."

On 10-in-ones, the talker's job was to keep the front hot. Bally followed bally. Talker Charlie Roark related his own carnival experiences: "I went over for a few weeks one time on 'Bad Eye' W. T. Collins' carnival sideshow. They'd open in the morning at those fairs when the first FFA [Future Farmers of America] boy brought feed out for his hogs and they stayed open until the grandstand emptied late that night. You would get hoarse working on the front. Dust blowing in your face all day while making a bally every 20 minutes. Bill Chaulkas had the 10-in-one and his talker Blackie Haskens had been with him all his life. He was good on still dates: right there and sober. The first fair, he was lying face-down drunk under the bally. I was second talker, so had to do it all — sun drenching down on you all day."

Charlie related how talkers and lecturers were both still "leather lunging" it on Ringling in 1938: "Some of those old-time talkers could be heard five miles around when

Banners visible in image: NATURE'S MISTAKES ALL ALIVE, FREAK ANIMALS, FREAK ANIMALS ALIVE, HALF RHINOCEROS & HALF ZEBRA, SCAVENGER OF THE BATTLEFIELD, HALF TURKEY-HALF CHICKEN, COW WITH NO EYES NO HORNS NO TAIL WHAT IS IT?, SMALLEST MONKEY, DUCKS WITH 4 WINGS, HALF MONKEY & HALF SQUIRREL, HALF RAT & HALF RABBIT, 5 LEGGED COW, MIDGET BULL, 5 LEGGED SHEEP, HALF TURKEY-HALF CHICKEN, ALIVE

they spoke in a normal voice." It was tough work. Long days of loud talking hurt the vocal cords. The Horne Chemical Co. of Chicago in

Al Moody was the train master on the large World of Mirth Shows, which folded in 1962. Afterward, Al and his wife toured one of the largest and finest freak animal sideshows going at the time. Four sets of three-high banners on each side of the doorway made it an impressive sight on any midway.

The inside of a 1950s Pete Kortes or Lou Dufour 10-in-one at the Toronto CNE. Inside the large rectangular tent, there is a solid stage across the left end and another along the back wall. The blow-off would be to the right, out of the photo. The tip is watching a young lady getting into the blade box, while the fat lady looks on from stage left and, in the right-hand corner, Percilla the Monkey Girl waits to work.

1903 offered "Voice Tone," while another outfit advertised "Voxin" as voice aids. Some talkers claimed whiskey worked best.

One of the first mechanical aids for talkers was the cone-shaped megaphone. When amplified sound replaced it in the 1930s, talkers could talk at a normal level. In 1931, some circuses began using canned music. The same

season, manager Duke Drukenbrod of the Hagenbeck-Wallace Circus sideshow, which had its biggest week ever while playing in New York City, told Billboard, "The loudspeaker system used on the sideshow front is an important part in the good business this department is having this year." Pen pitchman Harry F. Gilliam had been one of the first American showmen to use sound amplification. In 1923, he employed a "dynamo diaphragm" speaker, a mounted phonograph turntable for musical records and a large, single-button carbon telephone-shaped microphone.

Gilliam sold a set to Carl Sedlmayr, who used it on the Hilton Sisters pit show. Gilliam told Billboard, "I showed him how to play records to fool the folks into thinking they were hearing the Hilton Sisters live." Later, Sedlmayr's press agent transcribed girl-show operator Raynell Golden's regular openings with a machine carried in the press wagon. "When crowds were small, Raynell would use the record, holding the mike close to her face and barely moving her lips, saving her voice for big crowds," said Sedlmayr. Raynell was the first to use a Hammond organ to cut an outdoor show. She also had RCA in New York City make her a large electrical transcription-disc called a Victrola Record. With its inherently low surface noise, this large, 33⅓-speed disc had the complete inside narration for her "Expose" posing show.

"I believe our 10-in-one was the first to use loud speaker equipment," Sedlmayr told *Billboard* in November 1937. "When it was installed, one talker after another would try it out and at first didn't like it, but soon it became the standard. We put single microphones on our revue stages and could use a far higher type of vocal performer. We then put three or four microphones around the stage and made them so the sound completely filled the large tent theaters." Although recordings couldn't beat a good talker, finding good talkers became hard during the war years. A

One of Carl Sedlmayr's first adventures into the carnival business was this pit sideshow. He's the last man on the left side of the bally. Carl made sure both his son and first grandson — Carl II and Carl III — all served their apprenticeship as sideshow talkers. Up until the end, the sideshow layout stakes on Royal American Shows always said, "Pit Show."

1945 *Billboard* article by Ernest Sylvester lamented, "There are few Duke Drukenbrods on the fronts at present, so I am using recordings made by professional announcers from radio stations."

On the left is Paul (Mush) Wunder, one of the greatest sideshow talkers ever, and another good talker, Bill Thompson, holding up Zandu the Quarter Boy in 1960 on Dick Best's sideshow on Royal American Shows (RAS). Mush also broke in his nephew Bill Stewart as another good talker. Mush died at age 48 in 1968, and both Thompson and Stewart were around long enough to be put out of work when the central ticket box system arrived on midways in the 1970s.

Mickey Mansion's sideshow on James E. Strates Shows in 1952 featured Emmett Bejano the Alligator Skin Man and his wife Percilla the Monkey Girl. Mansion was the tattooed man in the 1926 Miller Bros. 101 Ranch Wild West sideshow. He died in 1958 and his show, with a 160-foot bannerline and 30-by-140-foot tent transported in a 28-foot Fruehauf semi, was sold off.

The show world's dirty laundry was aired out in *Billboard*'s letter columns, but most show folks paid more attention to humorous pokes

at the business in press agent Star DeBelle's 1940s columns "One Horse and Up" and "Ballyhoo Bros. Exposition." One time he suggested that rail shows put glass roofs on the coaches to kill the bed bugs. His description of "Judd Emptypit's" operation in a January 1943 *Billboard* was a great send-up of the sideshow business. Judd believed that if an act didn't have a sideline to pay itself off and give him a cut, he should can it. His magician did one mechanical trick followed by a long pitch that always grossed well.

Tall cardboard window or pole card used by World of Mirth Shows in the 1950s for the Viking Giant.

However, his glassblower never had a fire going and it seemed he'd only hired three shelves of glass knick-knacks. The glassblower's demonstration consisted of a six-word lecture: "Glass is made out of sand," followed by his pitch.

Judd's whittler had shelves laden with wooden chains, carved mermaid bookends

Pete Kortes and his brother George Courtis from Nafplion, Greece, were major sideshow operators and managers of many freak attractions, including Schlitzie. These photos of Pete and his triple-deck-banner 10-in-one are from the 1936 Beckmann & Gerety Shows pictorial magazine. Pete started as a fire-eater in the World War I years.

Veteran sideshow folks Art Converse and his wife, Mickey, gather a tip on the bally platform of the 1956 James E. Strates Shows sideshow. Note the big bass drum behind Mrs. Converse. "Grab a snake and get out there on the bally" was a constant cry by old sideshowmen to their help.

and ships in bottles, but no wood shavings lay in the pit. One of his men, needing to borrow a knife to splice a rope, asked the whittler, who then confessed to not owning one. Judd exploded: "This is it. I have stood still for magicians who couldn't do magic, glass-blowers without fires, experts on handwriting analysis who couldn't read or write, strong men who pitched health books but were always too weak to help put the tent up, but when I get a whittler who doesn't own a knife — I'm ready to fold."

The most remarkable aspect of outdoor show business was its ability to heal itself and keep rebounding time after time. After a few seasons' rest, a burnt town was fresh again. Gallons of paint, new fronts and tents took the curse off worn-out midway attractions. Competition kept everyone on their toes. By the 1930s, there were over 300 midways, and competition for the best fairs was ferocious.

Show agents battled it out at fair conventions for the plum dates. They tossed cash, cars, booze and hookers at fair-board members. The most potent contract closer was often the midway's reputation for carrying a solid lineup of first-class back-end shows. A ride was still just a pile of iron — fair managers were most impressed with shows that offered top-notch burlesque dancers and extraordinary freaks whose names were bathed constantly in media ink.

A May 1928 Billboard write-up called Dick Best's 10-in-one pit show on Royal American Shows' midway "formidable." It was long and narrow, with a flashy striped-awning front. Big balls, crescents and stars studded with lights hung inside the tent. The shows' banners were illuminated by floodlights at night. It appeared to be a miniature affair, but framed to do as much business as a bigger outfit. The pits were close to the front so when there was a small bunch of people it would appear filled, and when patrons came in big numbers, there would be plenty of room for them on the other side of the pits.

The years between the world wars saw some of the finer 10-in-one innovations. The "jam" was introduced by Thomas (Slim) W. Kelly, who announced to the tip that the advertised show price would be cut in half for a limited time. In a 1930s Billboard story, Slim

This dwarf, or "runt" as Slim Kelly called them, is doing an opening and describing the giant to the tip. He emphasizes the giant's size by holding up one of his shoes.

explained, "We found it very effective in keeping an open-front pit show full. We used it only when the crowd thinned out. It was a great asset to the pit show. Now, every show

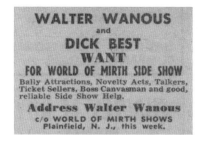

Two of the premier sideshow operators from the mid-1930s were Walter Wanous and his brother-in-law Dick Best. Sometimes they were partners, as listed in this Billboard ad seeking help for their World of Mirth Shows sideshow. Mostly they had separate 10-in-ones on big railroad carnivals.

that ballies, uses it in their closing, and many patrons won't go into a show on the grind at regular price. They wait for the talker to make an opening, knowing he will reduce the price at the end."

Greenfield, Ind.–born Ralph H. (Dick) Best was 96 when he died in Sarasota, Fla., on April 24, 1994. He had entered showbiz as a candy butcher in a Detroit theater in 1889. During World War I he was badly injured in an army truck crash. He discharged himself from the army hospital and went back to butchering at a circus. Several years later he owned a fun house and then a pit show. In 1939, with help from ride inventor Elmer Velare, Dick changed his 10-in-one on Royal American. They built two 32-foot light towers with six revolving

1947 Hennies Bros. Shows ad. For two decades starting in the mid-1930s, the show was one of the premier rail carnivals. When it sold in the late 1950s, the title changed to Olson Shows. The show took a big gamble on paying stripper Sally Rand a weekly fortune, but it paid off with huge increases in midway revenue at their fairs. Girl shows and 10-in-ones remained the top-grossing attractions on midways for years.

1950s Billboard ad placed by Dick Best seeking help on Royal American Shows. The midway's big spring date was a Shriner-sponsored event held beside the Mississippi River in Davenport, Iowa.

banners that flanked the bally. Between the towers hung a large neon "Freak" sign. The front was 150 feet long and 22 feet high, the panels separated by heavy wood frames decorated in chrome metal and neon-lit. Inside, all acts worked on a center stage that was raised three feet. A railing kept the crowd back. The 60-foot round top with a 30-foot middle had 16-foot walls to accommodate 20 sections of three-tier-high seats. Best dropped all inside dings and raised the outside ticket price to 50 cents. The season was a bust. He learned quickly that you needed the cheap ticket and the dings inside to survive. However, he may

Pete Kortes's 1951 lineup at the Toronto CNE. First row, from right: Grace McDaniels's son, then famed sword swallower Mimi Garneau. The next girl is holding up the neon-light swords Mimi swallowed in her act. Musical act Sally Vagge holds the accordian. Next to the black vent act is Grace McDaniels, the World's Ugliest Woman, and next to her is Hezekiah Trimble, the Congo Jungle Creep. Behind Mimi is bag-puncher Milo Vagge and on the far end Pete Kortes and lecturer Woody Dutton. In the center is fat man Jack Connors, and next to the clown is Shorty Hinkle.

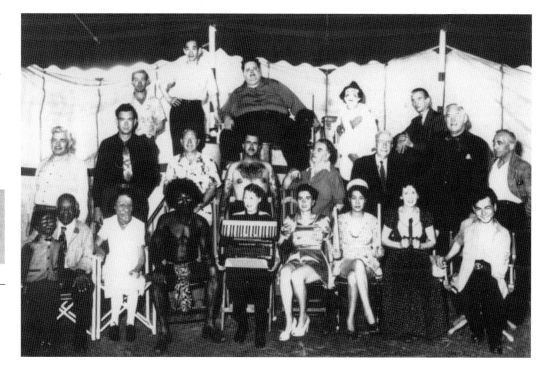

Ad seeking acts placed by Ward Hall and his first partner, Harry Leonard, for their sideshow. Ward became the target in Harry's knife-throwing routine after the 1946 Dailey Bros. Circus closed, and Harry took Ward with him onto the Ray Marsh Brydon winter store shows. Ward is still going today with the last big sideshow, operated by him and partner Chris Christ.

During the season, the weekly *Billboard* would have ads from sideshow owners seeking help. Up into the '60s most carnivals had some sort of a sideshow.

Dick Best's All-Girl 10-in-one on RAS in the 1960s. Note the girl tied to the cross as the talker makes his opening. Lettered on the teaser curtain hanging down from the front side of the tent are the words "Continuous Performance." The Monkey Girl was Percilla, the sword swallower Sandra and the spotted girl Sadie-Victoria.

have been the first 10-in-one to go from pits to a single stage.

Walter Wanous was Dick Best's brother-in-law. As the last big sideshows faded from the midways, the Wanous family was still out there with a big 10-in-one. Walter, in retirement in Montgomery, Ala., related, "We had a 150-foot bannerline, a bally stand and two ticket boxes. The right-hand box usually did the best business, as people tend to walk to their right like traffic on the highway. We used the cross, tying a girl's arms and feet to it with break away ropes. It worked good on the bally for us. We also had an old Navy bell we rang to draw attention to starting a bally. When the talker turned the tip he said,

'Watch the girl on the cross. . . . One . . . two . . . three — there she goes. . . . Follow her inside, folks!' You had to know when to turn the tip and you could see when they were bored or antsy. You knew when to make an opening short and sweet or to draw it out. . . . If you had them in your grip and saw them fidget, turn them! If you needed more people in the tent you jammed . . . cut your price in half, from a dollar to 50 cents or from 50 cents to a quarter — whatever you had to do to keep a crowd in there as bait for the next crowd."

Every operator stresses that you had to keep people in the sideshow to make money. Walter Wanous recalled, "On the first show, most all the people went to the blow-off and then left the show. That was a hazard, as you now had to put more people in there right away to keep the tip building and to keep selling tickets all day. As you did continuous shows, more stayed in after the blow to see the rest of the show. The more people visible in there, the more people bought tickets outside and came in."

In the late 1940s, when many 10-in-one showmen adopted the long back-wall stage in their shows, they faced new problems. If the front of the tent was left open so midway walkers could see customers inside, the acts onstage were visible. Showmen fixed the situation by installing two items: the "teaser curtain" and the "catwalk." The teaser curtain was

We don't know whose sideshow this is, but the bally is full of interesting characters plus two dressed-up dogs. You rarely see carnival sideshows advertising Oriental dancers. I'm sure the show inside was highly entertaining without any freaks other than the Ossified Girl.

With this coupon and 25 cents you could get in to see Percilla the Monkey Girl. Someone would be hired to give these out on the midway.

This is Jimmy Chevanne's 10-in-one on Royal Crown Shows at the 1953 Winter Haven, Fla., fair. Standing on the ground at the right is Jimmy himself, and the lady on the left side of the bally is Jimmy's wife, Louise. The gentleman on the far right is Jack Frost. Seated are pinheads Sniki, Chief and Gothu.

a separate piece of canvas that hung from the outside tent valance all the way across the front. It blocked the midway crowd's free view while still allowing the backsides and legs of folks lined up on the show's catwalk to be visible.

Catwalks were long, narrow walkways with a railing about chest-high that the customers could lean their elbows on. "When you only had a few people, you left them up on the catwalk," Red Trower commented. "They could see the stage, and people on the midway could see their legs and asses and it looked like your tent was full."

Ward Hall stated, "The first sideshow I ran was an office-owned pit show and the first one I owned in 1951 was pit-style. Before going on Cavalcade of Amusements in 1953, we had pits with a bally cloth across the front and a 20-by-80-foot top with an open front. You didn't have any teaser — you didn't need to. You put the tent as close to the bannerline as possible. Real pit shows had a walk-around pit with little individual stages barely raised off the ground inside the pit. On Cavalcade, we put panels between the bannerline uprights and built individual stages — doing away with the pit. We had four or five stages in there plus the blade box and the blow-off.

"Sometime around June I built one big stage, because it was easier to handle. Individual stages look bad if you don't have someone sitting on one. On the circus that is okay because the acts work the come-in and then have a break until the circus blow-off. On carnivals, you are working all day. With one long stage against the back wall of the tent you could bring up just one act at a time. Acts didn't have to be on the stage all the time. The first one I saw framed that way was Lorow Brothers in 1950 on Royal American. The show ran an hour. Most of the acts didn't last longer than five minutes. Then the act had 50 minutes to rest, relax and be away from the public."

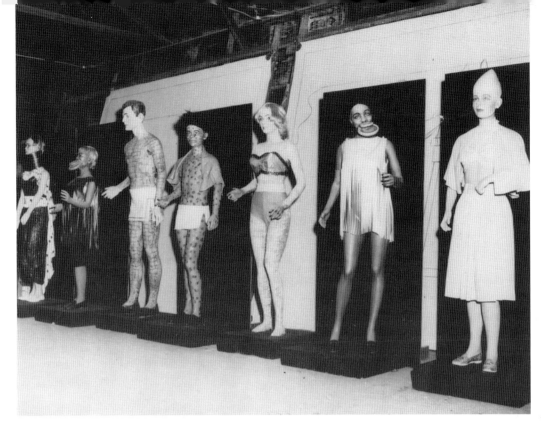

Snapp Wyatt, besides being one of the best banner painters, also specialized in making anything from papier-mâché, including these sideshow figures. Often billed as Barnum's Greatest Freaks, the show was okay for those willing to take the constant heat from disgruntled marks who assumed the freaks were alive. This set was made in 1975 for showman Harvey L. Boswell.

This huge 10-in-one is probably on the James E. Strates Shows at Ithaca, N.Y., in the 1940s. The two big banners on each end of the bannerline advertise the main attraction, the Viking Giant. Note the neon letters making up the FREAKS sign in the center, and the "Unbelievable But True" lettering under each banner.

Harry Doll handing over to the director of Happiness House in Sarasota a check from the Greater Tampa Showmen's Association. Onlookers are, from left, Dick Best, Daisy Doll, Bob Hasson, Grace Doll and Texas Jim Mitchell.

In 1961 Ward Hall ballyed and worked his ass off on his sidehow, but met with only limited success. At the Orlando fair that winter, he noticed Slim Kelly never ballyed, but used a grind tape. Slim told him how to make money without a bally: "You must have a catwalk. Put the catwalk so that immediately when they step inside the tent they have to step up onto it. When you are not doing any business you block the catwalk at either end so the people have to stay on the catwalk. Once you start doing big business you open the ends of the catwalk so the people can either stay there or come clear up to the stage because you have all that space in there.'"

I ventured into sensitive territory, asking Ward how he handled pitches with the catwalk. He quickly shot back, "I never missed a pitch! In later years Chris and I had a 30-foot top and we always used the catwalk. You had 15 feet between the front of the catwalk and the front of the stage. When you ma[d]e a pitch you would have someone pass out the item and collect the money. A couple of the girls would work the catwalk and I would work anyone in front of the stage. You had to be able to service all the people."

Chapter 9

The Inside Money

Chris Christ lecturing on fat man Bruce Snowdon on the Hall-Christ 10-in-one. Note the decorative diamonds on the valence along the side of the tent.

Toronto Star columnist Roy MacGregor found the timeless sleaze of sideshows an irresistible Canadian National Exhibition attraction. "The true beauty of the sideshow is deceit itself," he wrote in 1983. "The paid freaks stare out at the freaks for a day, usually ordinary people who have come here with the full knowledge and agreement that they are here to be taken." MacGregor had hit the nail on the head: sideshows were all about making money. The 10-in-one, like the carnival itself, was a business based on who got to count the money first. In a world where hustlers garnered the most respect, any showman who gathered a group of marks inside his exhibit and didn't try to sell them something was just a notch above mark status

himself. As MacGregor observed, even the marks would have been disappointed if it had been any other way.

Much like the five-and-ten-cent store, sideshows were designed to nickel and dime you to death. Woolworth's lunch counter's 59-cent mac-and-cheese special ballooned to over a dollar if you had the pie and coffee, while the 10-in-one's dime admission spiraled upward after the marks bought postcards, miniature Bibles, horoscopes and Buddha papers, had their fortune told or saw the blade box or the blow-off. For years, the inside scratch was the only money the sideshow operator didn't cut up with the show or fair board. When you gave up as much as 50 percent of your out-front ticket-

Early bio booklet sold by dwarf Colonel Chaffin.

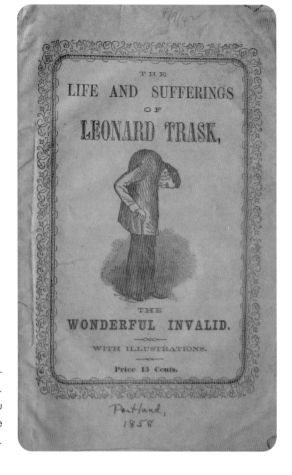

This clever 1858 pamphlet is not a freak pitch item. Leonard Trask was a handicapped person. If you helped him out with a small monetary gift he gave you this little history of his sufferings.

box money, keeping all the inside money was a big deal.

While getting people inside the sideshow was the talker's job, maximizing the inside gross depended on the lecturer. He was more than an announcer moving the tip from one act to another. Besides handling most of the pitches and doing the blade box and blow-off openings, a good lecturer made sure every act was presented in the best way possible. That meant everything he did or said focused on promoting the sales of the act's pitch item. Charlie Hodges' 1949 *Billboard* ad for a sideshow lecturer summed it up best: "Must be able to sell freaks unable to lecture on themselves, along with other duties." The lecturer knew when to inject humour into the show to alleviate any guilty feelings the tip held while viewing the handicapped or the deformed. Referring to a fat guy, some lecturers would use this line: "Now, Big Jim here has never seen his . . ." He'd look down and pause a few seconds before saying, "Feet!" It always got a laugh.

Squaring beefs and deflecting negative remarks was also part of the lecturer's lot. Mentalist Norm Johnstone said, "It was his job to please the customers after the outside talker promised them far more for a quarter than they got." The job could be stressful. A tip that had followed the lecturer from one act to another for a half-hour, enduring endless pitches, often saw the blade box or the blow-off spiel as the final slap in the face. Marks' tempers flared and some became verbally abusive, and lecturers had to quickly judge how best to handle such outbursts. Many had polished lines to quell hecklers and complainers.

Good lecturers knew how to get the money without creating too much heat — they put the extras dings over in a way that made people feel it was a pleasure to help out the cause. Recalling Don McGiver's lecture on the two-headed-baby blow-off, Norm said, "Inside the blow, Don would stand with his hat on beside a box covered with a black cloth. 'You want to know, is it alive? There can only be one answer — no! No two-headed baby ever lived more than 17 hours. This one lived only 15 hours. Now, let us remove our hats in the presence of the departed.' There wasn't a dry eye in the place as he took the

The 1937 Ringling sideshow contract for giant Al Tomaini and his half-lady wife, Jeannie, lets them sell their booklet describing married life for a dime and keep all profits. However, the lecturer made the pitch for them, for which they would have had to tip him weekly. If the show was so busy that he had to hurry through the acts, the Tomainis had to sell the booklets without his help.

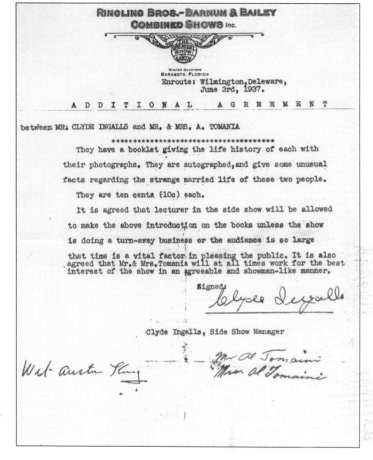

baby out of the box while saying, 'It's a blessing the good Lord called her home.'"

Sideshow salaries were never big. Operators negotiated an act's salary down to the lowest amount, in exchange for letting them pitch something. Almost everyone in the show depended on the inside dings and pitches, or merchandise sales for their winter bank rolls. In 1958, while working on a 10-in-one, Woody Dutton, the husband of famed sword swallower Mimi Garneau, received $75 a week for doing magic and lecturing. His five percent of the blade box and two percent of the blow-off monies went a long way toward boosting the meager wage.

Before photo cards were of decent quality and could be bought in large quantities at reasonable prices, these small printed bios, such as the one for the Albinos' 1861 exhibition at P. T. Barnum's Museum, N.Y.C., were what most freaks used for a pitch item.

Ward Hall loved to work his magic and vent routines so he could pitch something. Here he performs in his Hall-Christ sideshow on the Gooding Million Dollar Midway playing the Atlanta, Ga., Southern Fair in 1969.

Old-timers claimed sideshow manager and master talker Duke Drukenbrod, with Val Vino as the inside lecturer on the 1930s Hagenbeck-Wallace and Forepaugh-Sells, were the best combination for securing big sideshow grosses. Vino, a Coney Island veteran, had a reputation as the best freak lecturer around. He'd spent 1911 to 1920 on the Ringling sideshow, and in 1939 was still going strong, impressing the crowds in his 75th year. Doc Foster, P. J. Stauton and Homer Sibley, who managed Hubert's Museum in Times Square, were also larger-than-life characters remembered for their extraordinary handling of inside crowds.

Talented lecturers could work on any kind of show, and did. In a May 1874 *Clipper* ad seeking work, Professor Hutchins "the Lightning Calculator" stated, "Open for circuses, museums. Can lecture on any living curiosity or mechanical novelties, impromptu!" When the Ford Brothers, slayers of Jesse James, appeared at G. B. Bunnell's Museum in New York City in fall 1882, the *Clipper* noted the lecture delivered by Hutchins was such "to command for them sympathy." Set pieces of dialogue often remained unchanged for decades and were used by everyone. A line used to introduce the fat lady — "It takes a whole crowd to hug her and a box car to lug her" — went back to the rail circus days.

New spiels, pitches and novel catch-phrases, when they did come along, quickly spread among sideshow workers. To keep up with them, a lecturer or talker had only to look in the *Billboard* classifieds for ads selling new patter. The El Paso, Texas–based Progressive Door-Talkers Association's January 1911 ad offered for a buck a book featuring hundreds of up-to-date openings and talks by the nation's best lecturers. The same year, William Duke of Michigan publicized his standard book, *Learn to Be a Spieler*. In 1933, he advertised "Spielers, talkers, announcers — the Chicago Fair will need hundreds, while in the 1960s, beginners relied on Don Boles's *The Complete Pitchman*.

A good lecturer's strength lay in his ability to make a "blind opening," a spiel that would fit almost any attraction, with only slight adjustments. Even if the act had just joined the show, the lecturer could step right in and deliver the goods. Anything dead,

stuffed or mummified in the blow-off could be made to live and breathe with the right opening. The lecturer's blow-off spiel touting the most unusual sexual attraction you would ever see could easily turn out to be just the tattooed lady.

In 1902, Frank Coyle accepted a job lecturing, at the Chutes Amusement Park in San Francisco, on the infant incubators. Management didn't want to carry a large number of

anemic prematures, so the demonstrations were often done with robust babies. During Frank's lecture on a baby with a particularly healthy growth of hair, a woman spoke out, wanting to know why a newborn would have so much hair. Frank retorted that it was normal for a baby to start growing an abundance of hair after a brief stay in the incubator. The lady suggested Frank stick his own head, which was like a light reflector, into

Sideshow manager and magician King Baile sold this stock double-printed page of magic-trick instructions on various sideshows he was with, including the 1930s Seils-Sterling Circus. He refolded it to look like an eight-page booklet and stamped his name and address on it in case folks needed more.

the incubator. If it grew hair, she'd bring her bald husband back!

Barry Gray's 1932 *Billboard* article recalled his first time lecturing while performing in Pennell's London Ghost Show at Kohl and Middleton's West Side Museum in Chicago in 1886. "Between shows," Gray wrote, "I visited the Curio Hall to chat with the lecturer Smith Warner. One evening he asked me to relieve him for a half hour. I mounted the platform of the next-to-be-announced attraction, which was Oscar and Charlie 'The Zulu Warriors.' They stood at attention with deadly-looking 'assagais' in hand. They gave me a savage look and muttered words, I suppose in Zulu, which sounded like, 'Killum quicko, eatum alivo.' After my brief introduction, they sang a weird Zulu ballad, danced a war dance and then demonstrated their dexterity in throwing the sharp-pointed spears at a wooden target, while at the same time hurling their gibberish talk at me. Later I ascertained that the cause of their flare-up with me was my failure to announce their photos for sale, an error I have never since repeated."

One sideshow magician stated, "Patter packs easier than props." Magicians made good lecturers. If neeeded, their routines could be lengthened to stall or stretch a show. Most sideshow magicans used simple sleight-of-hand tricks with cards and coins. A standard trick involved swallowing razor blades or needles one by one, then pulling them out of the mouth a few minutes later, spaced out on a piece of string. Doing a dozen or more shows a day in a sideshow was the best way for budding magicians to practice their craft and patter. Early in his career, Houdini worked in the sideshow on the Welch Brothers Circus. A stone-swallower taught him how to swallow keys and bring them back up. Irene Lorraine, widow of the late magician Syd Lorraine, said, "The upper crust of magicians would put down sideshow magicians, but when you asked them where they saw their first magicians they would reply, 'In the sideshow!'"

One popular pitch item was the "traveling mouse," which went back to the turn of the 20th century. Street hustlers sold them for two cents, including instructions. One end of a short length of fine thread was attached to a wax mouse, the other fastened to the operator's shirt or coat. When you placed the mouse on the back of your hand and moved your hand away from your body, the mouse would run freely. Magician Eddie Dennis said the mouse ran better if you attached one end of the thread to your belt or fly. He made the string less visible by using black thread striped with black felt marker. M. Faught, of New York City, claimed he was the original manufacturer of traveling mice. His 1921 *Billboard* ad offered them to showmen at $3.50 a gross. Chris Christ used Arch McCaskill's molds, which made six mice at once. John Bradshaw, an excellent mouse pitchman, also made them. His biggest client in the 1990s was Tim Deremer, who sold a few thousand mice each season on his 10-in-one illusion show.

An older traveling-mouse box and a newer version made and packaged in the 1990s by showman John Bradshaw.

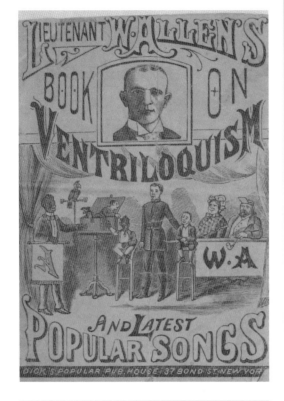

Vent performer Lieutenant W. Allen's instruction pitch book for learning ventriloquism, made even more saleable by the addition of the words to popular songs. Popular song booklets sold well anywhere a musical act worked, such as in a sideshow or concert.

A lecturer stands under the arm of Johann K. Petursson the Viking Giant while he tells the audience briefly about the giant's history. Their main focus will soon be the selling of giant rings on the display behind the lecturer or photo postcards on the table marked "CARDS" to left of Johann.

At the edge of all the hoopla during the first-ever sideshow convention held in August 2002 in Wilkes-Barre, Penn., stood Red Trower. "Little Red's" quiet demeanor didn't offer a clue that since the late 1940s he had done about everything there was to do around circus and carnival sideshows. He was a first-class knife-thrower, sword swallower, lecturer and builder of props and illusions. "How many pitches and dings could you could hit patrons with?" I asked him. "Probably no real limit," Red replied. "Even some sword-swallowers pitched miniature plastic swords, like the ones used as martini olive skewers. Easy pitches were around

149

freaks you could make people feel sorry for. That's how you make a freak pitch work so they could sell their pictures, rings, pennies, miniature Bibles, whatever.

"When you made the pitch for them you had to explain, this was how the freak survived in the wintertime. This was the only way they could remain completely independent when this show closes. That was the story you told. Some handled their own picture sales. If they didn't get too big a salary, you let them keep it. When the freak was on a big salary, you kept most of the pitch and gave him a little of it. It was up to the guy who made the pitch and collected the money to keep track of it so both the show and the attraction got their respective shares.

"If there were five pitches in the show and you got two of them, you could donate your two acts. That's basically what you were doing — donating your acts, because the salary wasn't much. You made it on the pitches. You got 15 percent as lecturer and pitchman. The blade box was always good money — a big weekend on the blade box was good for $300 to $500 a day. That was your nut and then some, as you stayed on the showgrounds in them days. The annex (blow-off) would double the blade box. If you got in on the annex money, you did all right.

"Overall, the inside should equal or do a little better than the front door. You look at

PERCILLA

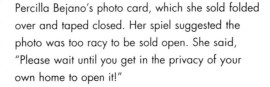

Percilla Bejano's photo card, which she sold folded over and taped closed. Her spiel suggested the photo was too racy to be sold open. She said, "Please wait until you get in the privacy of your own home to open it!"

the tickets sold to the show and you immediately knew what the shit brought in. Sometimes within a few dollars. Some people went for everything and some just one thing.

Percilla the Monkey Girl onstage in Whitey Sutton's 10-in-one. The sign behind her reads: "NO PICTURES TAKEN PLEASE." She wanted to sell you her photo — period.

If you had a $1,000 day on the front you should have the same on the inside. Best part of that thousand dollars was that it all went into the operator's pocket." I suggested that

CHIEF AMOK
Genuine Bontoc Headhunter

Now appearing in the World's Largest Museum or the World's Biggest Circus Sideshow.

P.S.—If you want another ring in the future write to permanent address: Care Billboard Publishing Company, 25-27 Opera Place, Cincinnati, Ohio.

Chief Amok's pitch card called him a "Genuine Bontoc Headhunter" but his main occupation besides demonstrating how fast he could climb a fake palm tree, was carving wooden Igorot rings. Note the address on the card in case you need more rings.

many carnival owners didn't realize the power of the inside money. Red responded, "Nobody let them."

Leonard Farley sold tickets for Hall & Christ sideshows. An avid letter writer, he wrote to a show enthusiast in January 1985: "The last year I worked with Percilla Bejano 'The Monkey Girl' (1978), the gray in her hair was starting to show, but such marks of age didn't embarrass her one whit. . . . She was also brutally frank in her presentation. . . . Her every word was devoted to 'selling her pictures,' including threatening her audience to eternal damnation in the event they failed to purchase her picture! She was highly successful in selling her photos and never split any of the money with Ward."

All the giants Charlie Roark worked with sold rings, including Jack Earle on Ringling. Charlie was six feet tall, but he stood under Earle's outstretched arm while making the ring pitch, and Earle would take off his ring so Charlie could pass a 50-cent coin through it. Charlie ended the pitch by saying, "He will gladly sell you one of his rings for 25 cents. There is enough good metal in that ring that even the meanest junkman will give you a quarter for it." "Earle made a ton of money," says Charlie.

Veteran lecturer Homer Sibley usually worked New York City museums in the

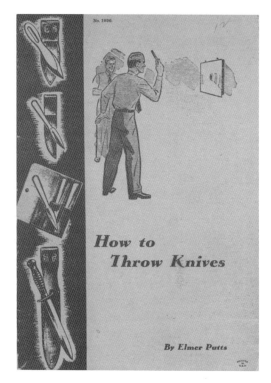

How to Throw Knives by Elmer Putts was one of the pitch booklets sold to sideshow workers by the Detroit-based Johnson Smith Co. Despite the author's name, the booklet offers a good introduction to knife-throwing.

winter and Coney Island in the summers. In 1917, while working on Sam Gumpertz's Dreamland sideshow, he noted Amok, billed as "a Bontoe Head-Hunter from the Phillipines," stopped the show every time with

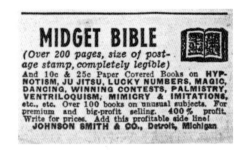

Billboard ad for Miniature Bibles manufactured by Johnson Smith Co. in Detroit, Mich. They also sold pitch books on various sideshow topics.

his tree-climbing act. However, Amok's main endeavor took place between shows, when he carved wooden figures and made Igorot lucky rings to sell.

Religous patrons were good marks. Acts would take shoe eyelets, fill the center with wax and stick a straight, flat-headed pin in them. The head of the straight pin would have been filed to roughen it up. It was pitched as "the Lord's Last Supper on a Pinhead." The lecturer told the tip to take them home and put them under a magnifying glass. Chris Christ recalled that "Emmett Blackwell 'the Armless and Legless Man' pitched 'the Lord's Prayer on a Pinhead.' He paid $60 a pound for them — over 2,600 in a pound. They were the size of a match head and he put them in little white envelopes."

Various acts have sold how-to booklets. Larry Benner played a saw, and after his act at Hubert's Museum, sold a booklet on saw playing. Manuals for learning magic, mind-reading, ventriloquism, weight lifting, club swinging, bag punching and knife throwing all sold well. A 1920s illustrated guide written by George "Steamboat" Steward, titled *Anybody Can Whistle and Imitate*, sold for 25 cents and taught the reader how to imitate birds, fowls, animals and steamboat or locomotive whistles — no instruments necessary. On the 1931 Conklin & Garrett Shows' sideshow, featured "Sex Enigma" half-and-half Madlyn-Arthur sold her fully illustrated booklet to adults only for a buck, while most other pitch books sold for just a nickel or a dime.

One year, Pete Kortes's 10-in-one with the Beckmann & Gerety Shows featured columnist Barney Oldsfield, who'd appeared in *Ripley's Believe It or Not* comic as the man

Nat Eagle was a "midget showman." In 1952 he managed the Ringling sideshow where his troupe provided half the acts. When his midget show closed after a summer season on carnivals he would take the troupe into schools — the show was free as long as the principal put it on just before lunch. Nat claimed he got most of the kids' lunch money with his Miniature Bible pitch.

who had seen more motion pictures than anyone alive. He made four daily appearances between "Athelia the Monkey Girl" and Doris and Thelma Patent "the Albino Twins." Like the others, he came up with a pitch item — copies of the cartoon Robert Ripley had drawn of him. Faye Renton recalled another unusual pitch: "On my dad's sideshow we had a guy who lifted things with hooks attached to his eyelids. We called him 'Stinky Beans.' He pitched beans from India, saying they were holy beans. For a dime he handed you a bean and a small story card to go with it."

"Look-Backs" made a good pitch item for sideshow contortionists. These cardboard cube viewers had two holes on one side and another on an adjacent side. Inside, a small piece of glass ran diagonally in front of the two holes. To see an image behind you, you held the Look-Back up and looked in the small hole. The pitchman suggested, "Standing on a windy street corner when the girls go by, what you are doing is nobody's business! You could spy on things you shouldn't be seeing!"

Miniature Bibles are long gone. For years, marks recognized the little Bible's uniqueness and gladly paid a quarter for one. Midgets and dwarves did well with them; the armless and legless even better. The Johnson Smith Co.'s 1949 *Billboard* ads claimed their stamp-size

Here Dolly Reagan, billed as half-woman/half-baby, does the lecture and pitch for handicapped Dick Brisben while the bally girl sells Dick's photo card. Leonard Farley recalled that when, during the 1983 Texas State Fair, Dolly had to go into the hospital, she was miserable because she was missing her postcard sales.

illustrated bibles had over 200 pages. A gross sold for $6.70. On the Cole Bros. sideshow in the early 1940s, Charlie Roark bought Johnson Smith Bibles: "When pitching mini-Bibles for an attraction I'd say, 'If you have a loved one that is going overseas, this minia-ture Bible makes an ideal gift,'" he explained. "'Pray to God nothing happens to them, but if something should, it is nice to know they had this in their pocket when their time came.'"

Chris Christ recalled, "Percilla pitched her photo as if she was photographed nude. She

Miniature Bibles and Giant Johann Petursson's pitch ring.

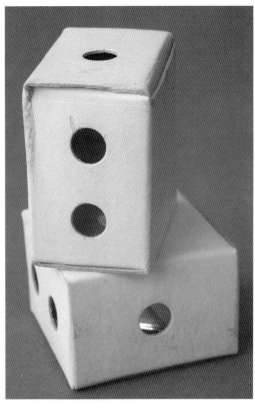

Look Backs pitched by contortionists and other sideshow performers.

Swiss warblers: instructions for use were to soak them in water before using.

either had the photo already in an envelope or had it folded over with a seal on it. She told the tip, 'Please don't open this until you get home.' She used a 1950s photo of her in a bikini posed under a tree." Chris points out the better an act went over, the more pitch money it made: "One year Bill Cole "the Half

Man" came to us after working the CNE for Sam Alexander. He asked us if we wanted him to do what he did on Sam's show. Before we could reply, he pulled out a harmonica and began playing it, rather badly.

"I suggested he should try something else. The girls made him professional wardrobe. I

built him a little chrome chin-up bar and stand, then worked out his routine. Within days, he was doing chin-ups, one-armed push-ups and a handstand. Now he was a rare freak — one that was not only physically unusual to look at, but more important, entertaining to watch. His new routine sold four times the number of pitch cards."

Punch-and-Judy workers always pitched the device that helped them make the puppet's shrill voices, called a "swazzle." Charlie Roark used to made his own swazzles by putting a piece of tape between two small pieces of metal and wrapping an elastic band around it. On Ringling, he had the whole Doll midget family making them. Beginners were advised to fasten one end of a string to the swazzle and tie the other onto a safety pin, then pin it to their shirt front. Prior to World War II, Charlie got a dime for them.

Later on, a quarter. "One year, Chas Bisbee wanted me to do vent, Punch and Judy, and be the leading man on 'Bisbee's Comedians,'" said Charlie. "It was a fine, outdoor, repertory canvas theater troupe, but I couldn't pitch anything. I turned him down. What he was paying a week I made in a day pitching on the circus."

The "Swiss warbler," a little reed device used to imitate animal and bird noises, was first sold with instructions under the name Ventrillo. First made in Germany and Switzerland, later in Japan, they had to be pre-

soaked to work properly. Dennis Michaels, on the 1975 Royal Brothers Circus sideshow, was the last person I saw pitching them. Dennis used a rubber chicken like a vent doll, while making a lot of zany animal noises. Taking the warbler out of his mouth and holding it up, he explained, "Boys and girls, all you need to make the animal sounds is this secret device. I'll gladly sell you one. Just pass up your quarters to defer the cost of shipping them from the Orient."

Chapter 10

Buddha Workers, Jaggers and Blade Box Queens

Rice writers, tattooists, fortune tellers, glass-blowers and other hustlers paid sideshow operators a percentage or flat fee to work inside. Most were as entertaining as the acts. E. L. Blystone, born in 1882 in Pennsylvania, won an automobile in the 1930s when he was selected as the "most unusual act" in Robert L. Ripley's *Believe It or Not* column. When working in sideshows, "Blyth" would show the tip the Lord's Prayer he had written on a grain of rice in 2,871 letters. For a small sum, he would write your name on one and give it to you along with a certificate of authenticity. When he grew bored with rice, he switched to writing on mustard seeds.

A mentalist's outside banner read, "The Lady with a Hundred Eyes." Inside, Madame X did a quick mentalist routine, ending in her offer to read palms. But many people were skeptical about fortune tellers. A report in a June 1877 *Clipper* about the lady billed as a "Phrenologist" on the Wonder World Show sideshow gave them good reason. The phrenologist enticed gentlemen into a closed-off section of the tent, with the promise of providing a free consultation of their character by studying their craniums. Behind curtains, she threatened to scream if he didn't come up with some cash. Sometimes she pulled a revolver on them. Show folks called her the "Screamer" and reported she made between $50 and $200 a day.

New York City resident S. Bower claimed to be the originator of "invisible fortune paper." His 1909 ads boasted a $10 investment could earn up to $125 a day. Supplying showmen

Mack's portable tattoo stand with his "flash" along the back is an ideal setup for this 1920–30s 10-in-one sideshow.

Bly the rice writer at work in 1939. He worked for many sideshowmen, including Lou Dufour, and was featured on many Ripley World Fair productions.

Rice writer Professor Wells and his attractive workstand. You could set this joint down anywhere — hotel lobby, conventions, trade shows, amusement park, circus or carnival sideshow.

with "Buddha papers" at $3 per 1,000, he warned, "Anyone else who has tried making them has ended up hurting their customers. All our stuff sells for a dime or more and only costs less than one cent." Bower's 16 kinds of Buddha papers offered 300 different readings.

From the 1920s to the '70s, the Nelson Enterprise Co. of Ohio, was the major supplier of fortune-telling supplies. In 1939, Nelson advertised new one-pound bottles of "Buddha Flukem" with restricted fumes, lessening the amonia smell in the developing fluid. Another Nelson invention was the "Phantom Tube Buddha Outfit," which could be worked indoors. For $1.50, Nelson sold big bottles of transparent Buddha ink to those making their own papers with customized fortunes that bore the worker's own signature.

"They smelled like rotten eggs," recalls Charlie Roark. "At first, they were small black pieces of paper. When you sold them you had the buyers sign it and you put them into a jar, usually a fish bowl. The chemical in there made a fortune appear on each paper. They came in books of 10, and you had a second book of them with different fortunes so you could rehash the crowd."

Another racket was "future photos," which dated back to early photography. Horace Petrie sold them in New York City in 1885 — he claimed his genuine future-husband-and-wife photographs could be pro-

duced on blank paper in a second. You took the plain card home and dipped it in water. A photograph of your future husband or wife appeared along with your lucky number and the date of your upcoming wedding.

Gypsy camps were popular store shows in the 1880s. The mitt camps' — or fortune-telling booths'— real home became the show lots. Some called it the oldest joint, predating the pea hidden under one of three thimbles. At best it wass a low-key racket, despite today's boom in psychic fairs held in hotel ballrooms, which legitimized fortune telling as harmless fun. Early carnival mitt camps were run by gypsies whose 10-foot-square booths had a curtain dividing the space in half, length-wise. Another curtain divided the rear half of the joint into two small reading rooms. There was a chair for the reader only — the customer stood. A reader leading a male customer back to the closed-off area (women were given readings out front) would tell her accomplice, "This man wants his fortune told." The other reader would reply, "He wants you, not his fortune." While the reader fooled around with the guy, the other reader went into the other room, reached through the curtain and lifted his wallet, taking out the money and returning the wallet undetected. The reader with him would give him a quick "free" reading and send him away rejoicing in his good fortune. Other scams had the reader

Your basic gypsy-style carnival mitt camp. Some gypsies used light wooden frames covered with thin canvas so the whole works could be quickly bundled up and thrown on top of a vehicle's roof for a fast getaway. By the time the mark came back with the police or fair officials, the gypsies were gone.

Norm Johnstone and his father standing beside Norm's banner on a sideshow on the Canadian prairies.

asking the mark if he wanted to see her "pussy" for $2. Once he'd paid, she'd pull a cat ornament from inside her blouse or show him a cat tattoo on her leg.

Harry Houdini's early 1920s cross-country seminars exposing mind-readers heaped new suspicions on the trade. The 1927 *Billboard* ad placed by C. R. Leggette Shows for pit-show attractions stated, "No mitt camp inside. Mind-reader okay, but no fortune telling." Many midways advertised, "No gypsies." Show owners advertised for "American-style readers only," and wanted their "Temples of Knowledge," which had wooden floors with rich carpets and drapes plus chairs for customers and waiting patrons. A lady outside sold tickets for 25 cents, entitling each customer to a brief reading. For $2 to $5 you got a better reading, while $25 got you the deluxe treatment.

Norm Johnstone grew up on the Canadian prairies learning magic and practicing fortune-telling. He began working sideshows in the 1930s and for years had mitt camps on them. A fixture on CNE 10-in-ones for 25 years, he often worked with an elderly gypsy woman named Vanita, who spoke many languages and had worked at World's Fairs. Norm described her as "a very tough little lady whose feet didn't reach the ground when she sat in her chair. She was raised by gypsies but gave her own version of American-style reading. A gentleman would pay his quarter to see her. She'd begin with, 'I'll tell you your mother's name, your father's name, your own name for $2.' No mention was made of the quarter entry fee. If he handed her a five and asked for change, she'd holler, 'Bad luck to ask for change!' She'd then say, 'You will never be rich, you will never be poor. . . . One long journey . . . one short journey, 8-6-4 are your lucky numbers. . . . Saturday is your lucky day. That's all.' When the mark asked, 'What about my name?' She'd reply, 'You crazy man. You don't even know your own name? Get out!'"

In his 70s, Norm was still reading in a Toronto tea room to a loyal following, including a former prime minister. He lived in a small apartment with his carny mitt camp folded up under his bed. "Sideshow mentalists," he told me, "usually wore turbans and Eastern-style wardrobe and were viewed more as magicians rather than people capable of foretelling the future. In a sideshow, I often used the crystal ball to get them in, then turned to palmistry. I sold $1 tickets, on the understanding I would call them by name or refund their dollar. When the customer came in the joint I called him by his given name and gave him a short reading. Then I tried to sell him a better reading."

The Great Lorenzo and his work area in a corner of a 10-in-one sideshow.

Norm described a typical mental act: "The lecturer or medium's assistant took various items from the audience and asked the blindfolded mentalist what they were. He holds up a coin and the mentalist tells him it's a coin and the date. The mentalist can tell the assistant the name and number on a driver's license he's holding. A simple code between them is the gimmick. The words *tell*, *give*, *let*, *now*, *go*, etc., mean certain things. *Tell* means *watch*, so if the assistant says, 'Tell me what this is,' she answers, 'Watch.'

"They finish the act quickly, then sell tickets to readings. Inside the booth, some mentalists gave the customer a pen and a slip of paper along with an astrology magazine to put under the paper for a hard surface to write on. The mark writes his question and is told to put the slip of paper in his pocket. The reader takes back the magazine. Holding it below table-level, he opens a few pages in to where a piece of carbon paper and blank paper have been inserted. He reads the question off."

With mitt camps, Red Trower said, "the sideshow operator doesn't get any money because he doesn't know how many come back after for extra consultations for serious money. You only find out when the police arrive that she's tapped some guy out for $300 or $400." Mitt camps became hard to book onto a sideshow because they didn't give the operators enough money to offset the beefs.

The simplest means by which a person could become a sideshow act was getting his or her body heavily tattooed. Many did so upon seeing or hearing about Captain George Costentenus's success on the 1870s P. T.

Barnum–titled circuses. The heavily tattooed Greek claimed the 888 designs put on with thousands of skin punctures was a punishment inflicted on him in China. The invention of the electric tattoo machine made things easier. Prof. "Tat" Mitchell on the 1917 Colonel Francis Ferari Shows advertised, "Only tattoed Indian in America and also electric tattoo artist." During this era, N.Y.C. tattooist Prof. Charles Walker tattooed a lot of sideshow subjects and sold tattoo supplies too.

On circuses it was a hit-and-miss proposition, as the show was only there one day. Carnivals usually stayed one week and word of the tattooist's arrival soon spread. I asked

Tattooing banner on the 10-in-one with the 1942 Penn Premiere Shows.

Back-end showman Jack Sands went by the name of Trader Jack when he did tattooing on midways.

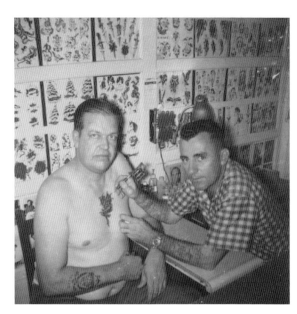

"Tattooing" in big letters right across this sideshow's bally curtain lets the marks know they can get tattooed inside. Often tattooing had to be disguised as an "act," so the banner would simply depict a heavily tattooed figure, but no mention of tattooing, which was illegal in some areas.

Unknown tattooist working in the Sutton 10-in-one on the James E. Strates Shows in 1983.

Walter Wanous if he had a "jagger," or tattooist, in his shows. He replied, "Numerous ones. They all paid me a good percentage to work there. I would put the tattooist's booth down in one end of the tent, away from the platform acts so the noise of the tattoo machine wouldn't distract the show. They were always busy no matter what the rest of the show was doing."

"They'd do minors," complained Red Trower. "They sold themselves as being able to remove tattoos by going over the tattoo with a machine to make it scab up. Ten or 12 days your tattoo was supposed to be gone, but it wasn't. All they did was place milk over the top of it. They would be gone by the time the scab came off." On the positive side, Red admits, "You saw a little bit of money because

he had to give you something. Every bit helps and a tattoo banner gives you another banner on the front."

In the early '90s, I visited tattooist and banner painter Jack Cripe before he died. The day I visited him, he had been back in his trailer a few weeks after open heart surgery, lying on the sofa in his underwear, a long red scar vertically bisecting him. Nearby was a

A jam-packed Lorow Brothers 10-in-one on Royal American Shows in the 1940s. Anatomical Wonder Analto Hayes entertains onstage. The Lorows' glassblowing stand occupies the whole end of the tent, and Cortez Lorow in a white shirt stands by the first center pole.

1916 *Billboard* ad for something new — an electric tattoo machine. It ran on four dry cells and was sold for $1.10 by Prof. J. F. Barber of Detroit.

case of beer and a fifth of booze. We had a great visit with lots of laughs, but Jack knew things weren't good, health-wise. He hoped to make it to the Florida Keys to spend his last days with "a mean dog and a bad woman." He'd been a showman, a tattooist and a banner painter. He had most enjoyed painting tattoo banners: "Look on any of those Sigler or Wyatt banners of tattooed women — if there's a heart on one of their tits and it says, 'I love Jack,' it's mine."

Humour helped workers through the long 10-in-one workday. Denny Gilli recalled tattoo artist "High-Stepping Jack" Wilson: "He and Sailor Bill were tattooing one night, and a guy came in and asked him, 'Would you tattoo a fly on the end of my dick?' Jack said, 'Yeah, I'll tattoo it but you'll have to hold it.' Then he looked at Sailor Bill and added, 'And you'll have to hold him!'"

Since the mid-1800s, one of the strongest joints on a sideshow was the glassblowing stand. Glassblowers sold more glass than they could make themselves, so a number of regional U.S. glass firms supplied them with ships, pipes, baby bottles, buds, fruit, animals and more. In the 1880s, H. O. John's Moundsville Bohemian Glass Novelty Co., in Moundsville, W. Va., specialized in glass supplies for those glassblowers working the pick-out box racket. The company's glass ornaments sold by the gross included three- and two-mast ships, crosses, shaded baskets, animals of all kinds, wineglasses, pipes and cigars. The company's six workers guaranteed fast delivery of any size order.

In the 1920s, Sam Gumpertz wrote *Billboard*, admonishing showmen who were complaining one of the worst rackets around

sideshows was the glass-stand pick-out box. In truth, Gumpertz's was the worst of them. The blower's short demonstration turned out a small glass pipe, dog or deer, and he told the tip that the dozens of pieces made daily had to be disposed of. Displayed behind him on velvet-draped shelves were dozens of big and small, plain and intricate glass pieces,

Cortez Lorow holds up some of the intricate glass pieces blown on his glass stand in the 1952 sideshow on Royal American. Early glass blowers also sold artificial eyes for humans or eyes for taxidermists.

Armless girl Joan Beach blowing glass, with Cortez Lorow on her right and Nate Skeeter Lorow on her left. The Lorows also operated a big glassblowing tourist shop in Miami.

Direct sales items have always done well in sideshows — the quirkier, the better. Wax flowers were a big sideshow sales item in the late 19th century while Chinese horn nuts sold well in the first half of the 20th century. The Dayton, Ohio–based Canton Chinese Horn Nut Co.'s 1922 *Billboard* ad claimed, "Non-growers, but can furnish growing sample for demonstration. Fifteen cents for sample." In the 1920s, wax-figure maker W. H. J. Shaw supplied operators with "Lord's Prayer on a Pinhead" engraving outfits. Until jewelry concessions with prize-every-time wheels and "free engraving" came along, you could often find jewelry joints in sideshows. The wire worker would take a coil of gilt wire, and with a small pair of round-nose pliers make you a bracelet, brooch or necklace.

But the best of all sideshow dings was the blade box. Ricky Jay told me its precursor was the "Hindu Basket Trick," in which a girl was placed inside a wicker basket while the magician repeatedly thrust a sword through it. The girl then stepped out of the basket unscathed.

each with a numbered card on it. Patrons paid a quarter to reach into a box full of folded-over paper pieces, which, when opened, bore a number corresponding to the stand numbers. If you didn't get what you wanted on the first try, you were urged to pay and pick again. The numbers for the big pieces were usually not in the box.

Circus sideshow lecturer putting in the blade-box swords. The success of the operation is in the patter.

Known as a "squat box," this blade box was similar in size to the Hindu Sword Cabinet offered for sale in 1921 by Western Show Properties. Again, circus sideshowmen liked the squat box for its speed as the customers just paid and walked behind it.

American audiences first saw it in 1834 — for years it was a regular sideshow act.

The "Hindu Sword Cabinet" listed for sale by Western Show Properties in a March 1921 *Billboard* ad measured three-and-a-half feet high and two feet square. Twelve cavalry swords were run through the box at various angles, making it appear impossible for anyone inside it to survive. The vaud section of a November 1924 *Billboard* pictured magician La Villette's new "Sawing the Woman in Half Mystery." In construction, the box used for this act was similar to the blade box, only it stood vertically on a square-wheeled base. La Villette put his lady assistant into the cab-inet and inserted 17 swords along with 16 flat pieces of wood through it. At the illusion's first appearance, a *Billboard* scribe noted many New York City magicians taking notes.

William Turtle's May 1925 letter to the *Billboard* magic column claimed "Leah, Maid of the Mist," where a girl is placed lengthwise in a box and knives and swords are stuck through the box without injuring her, was an illusion just like "Sawing a Lady in Half." But the illusion part didn't last long. Jack F. Murray wrote in an August 1925 *Billboard*, "We notice quite a few exposures of the sword box at beaches and parks these days." Coney Island sideshow magician De Lenz's *Billboard* response letter explained that he and a couple dozen others started exposing it inside various shows. The talker on the bally put the girl in the box before the tip's eyes, and while shoving the swords in he gave his spiel about the wonders inside. The swords were removed

In the early 1970s this South American showman reintroduced North American midways to the Girl to Gorilla illusion show, only the transformation was Girl to Skeleton. He also had a family-run sideshow. Instead of metal blades in his blade box he used wood saws.

For the Hall-Christ sideshow's 2009 season, Dick Johnson designed this upright blade box. It cut down the time needed to present it. The tip paid and walked behind it to see Natelli Zarelli imprisoned inside.

and the girl stepped out. The talker finished by telling the tip they would see how the trick was done inside for a dime.

The exposed blade box routine quickly spread through show business. In April 1939, *Billboard* reported that carnival owner Johnny J. Jones never permitted a blow-off on his midway. When sideshows there started exposing the sword box for a small fee, he stopped it immediately. He finally gave in and let it work as long as the operator gave each blade-box patron a small gift.

The Sedlmayrs were also against blow-offs. In the 1960s, sideshow operator Dick Best on Royal American Shows got around them by using what he called "a blow-off in a box." He put "Mona the Alligator-Skinned Girl" in the blade box and charged a quarter to see her. Said Ward Hall, "The Ohio State Fair was one of the better blade-box spots,

MYSTIQUE

Billy Martin working the blade box on Hoxie Bros. Circus sideshow in the 1970s. 10-in-ones placed the box on a stage and let the marks come up a set of steps, peer in and descend another set of steps. To save time, on some circus sideshows, they simply dropped the back of the blade box and let the marks pay and walk around the back of the platform.

The card given out inside the Hall-Christ 10-in-one at the Ohio State Fair so they could get around an Ohio law that would have stopped them from using the blade-box ding.

but a state law made using the blade box in the conventional way illegal. Ducking the law was as simple as giving each blade-box viewer a free photo pitch card showing the girl inside in three different poses. The girl in the photo wore a half mask so if she blew they could use any girl. Most people coming down off the platform threw the photo on the ground. The sideshow crew

169

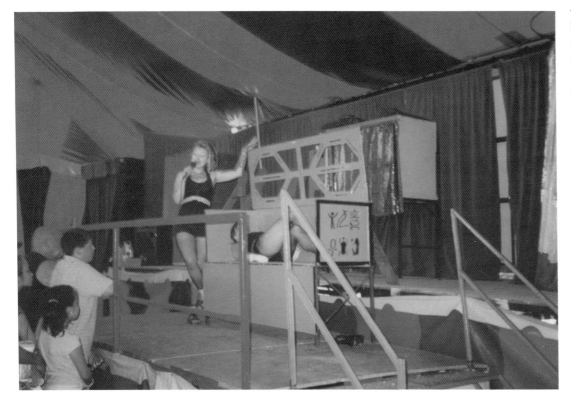

Blade boxes disappeared for a time in the late 1980–90s, except for showman Jimmy Dixon, who continued to work one inside a center joint on a midway. Hall-Christ put it back in their sideshow at one end of the tent in 2005. In 2006 they put it right in front of the main stage so they didn't have to move people over to it. The talented Chelsea Grammer is presenting it here.

was kept busy scooping them up before the next pitch."

There were different ways of working the blade box, as Red Trower explained: "You sell a story, not the blade box. Without the proper story, you get nothin'! Some sell the sex angle. I never did because you lose your family trade. If you do it right, you get the mother, the children, and they even give you a quarter for the little baby. Back 25, 35 years ago, you didn't have the family trade you have today. Still,

using the sex angle, the wife didn't want the husband to go and the girlfriend wouldn't let her boyfriend go up. All you get is the unattached rangs [rowdies]."

Sword swallower Andre "Pancho" Raymond spent 27 years working in sideshows at Montreal's Belmont Park for Pete Kortes and later Sam Alexander. He revealed how Kortes employed full-time shills, or "sticks": "Everywhere there was money there was a stick. The blade box was not always an easy

sell. The stick mingled with the tip and would be the first up the blade-box steps with his money out." Charlie Roark recalled presenting a blade box and noticing there wasn't a shill in the tip. In the middle of his spiel he inserted, "Give me a stick over here, quick!" A show roughy standing nearby took off and came back with a big piece of wood.

Dean Potter related, "We used to do it with the panties and bra. The girl would come onstage with a sheet around her. She got in the box and the lecturer took out the sheet. While putting in the swords, he would say, 'Oops, I have to make room for this sword,' and pull out her bra. We also had the pole that went all the way through the box from the ends. The girl would put the panties on the end of the pole as it was coming through. When it came out the end, the panties would be hanging from it. We asked for a silver donation to come up. She wasn't nude. The panties and the bra had been loaded in the box.

"One time we had a girl doing it that wasn't pretty. She wore big thick glasses. We couldn't make her look pretty so we used the sympathy angle, telling them she was blind. We made more money with her than with a pretty girl!"

Only in the last year or so have the new-wave sideshow troupes begun incorporating the blade box into their acts. Captain Don never abandoned it. "That's your hamburger money," he told me. "In night clubs I had the girl in a two-piece sequined outfit. I kept an identical outfit inside the box. When putting in the swords, I pretended one won't go in. The girl throws out her top and I shove the sword in. A few more swords and another sword sticks. She throws out her bottom. I tell the audience that the little lady in the box has decided to expose the trick. Give me a dollar, come up and look inside. You have to gather the money first, as the first mark up usually beefs when he sees she has clothes on! Then you look shocked and tell him, 'This is a family club!'"

Could a blade box act as a shrine? A few seasons back I visited Bobby Reynolds at the Hamburg, N.Y., fair, where his sideshow/museum was on the James E. Strates midway. Bobby's show, with a huge banner-line, was next to the giant wheel. At night, shadows from its long spokes swished across Bobby's tent roof. Inside, on an elevated stage, Bobby had displayed several illusions, including a blade box. "It's too bad you're not using it," I remarked. Bobby smiled, then he explained how it was a shrine to his late partner Jack Waller, who was a real gash hound. One of Jack's last wishes was that some of his ashes be placed in the blade box about where the girl's buttocks would lie. Bobby had mixed some of Jack's ashes with paint and coated that portion of the box with it. I bowed and left.

Chapter 11

Nothing but a Crack of Fat

Contemporary half-and-half banner painted by Glen C. Davies.

A small sideshow on Model Shows of Canada operated by Frank A. Robbins Jr. seen here in the ticket box. He lived with half-and-half Albert-Albertine seen here on the right end of the bally. Photo was taken in Halifax, N.S.

Sideshowman Artie Steinhart's 1920s outdoor education came from his father and uncle, both of whom were long-time Coney Island sideshowmen. In 1939 Artie told *Billboard*: "The blow-off was not an original feature in early sideshows. Business was so good you didn't need one." The Depression made operators put in blow-offs as additional money-makers, but it was not a smooth addition. New York City license commissioner Paul Moss constantly harassed the city's burlesque theaters and Coney Island showmen, and in 1934, he banned sideshow blow-offs. The Code of Ordinances regarding blow-offs stated that a holder of a freak-show license had to display a sign in a prominent location on the front, stating in large and contrasting-colored letters, "ADMISSION FEE: _____ CENTS. THIS FEE IS THE TOTAL FEE CHARGED, COLLECTED DIRECTLY OR INDIRECTLY, AND ENTITLES THE PATRON TO VIEW ANY AND ALL EXHIBITS ON THE PREMISES." You had to look around, but the sign was usually there, somewhere. Regardless, operators continued to sneak in blow-offs when they felt it was safe.

When business tanked, the circus owner would fire a couple of acts and hire more bill-posters. 10-in-one operators turned to the "jam," with additional stabs at the marks' wallets using the blade box and blow-off dings. Slim Kelly double-whammied them by using two blow-offs — his mid-'30s sideshow featured half-and-half Ramona Raye ("Bert Roberts") in one blow and the film *Mystery of Birth* in the other. Other showmen followed his lead.

173

Drag and bearded lady Laverne Martin worked on sideshows in the summer and in Phoenix City, Ala., in the winter. It was a wide-open town with a large army base. In the movie *Phoenix City Story* about the vice and corruption there, he introduced himself as Kitty and said he was the "French expert in town!"

Laverne Martin waiting in the sideshow blow-off. The drawings on the back scenery suggest a barbershop setting. He later lived in Gibsonton, Fla., where he had a small zoo on his property. He also had a fat girl show on tour.

Listings of show rosters in *Billboard* rarely mentioned the blow-off acts, and if so, discreetly called them "annex attractions." Sometimes the bullet of a 10-in-one banner might have the caption "Extra Added Attraction" in small letters. Some date the idea of blow-offs to B. F. Keith's Bijou Theater in Boston in 1891, where the former road showman originated the idea of the "annex" — a small theater on the ground floor. The annex entertainment of curiosities and small stage performances was designed to appease people waiting for seats in the main upstairs theater. Some writers suggest the sideshow "blow" was designed like Barnum's museum sign "To the Egress" — a way to free up a crowded exhibition space. However, 10-in-ones worked best when crowded. Putting the blow-off in its own small enclosed space in one end of the tent made it seem special and helped sell what was just another ding in a long line of swipes at the mark's pocket. Operators placed it last on the bill before the whole show repeated itself, because blow-offs were rarely as strong as the lecturer made them out to be.

"You always had people complaining about the extra charge, but if the act was good you got very few beefs," Walter Wanous recalled. "When we presented it, we told them it was an extra-special show not advertised on the outside. If people beefed, we gave them their money back. It slowed your ticket sellers down to have to deal with a beef around the ticket box — it didn't look good."

In the late 1960s when the law clamped down on 10-in-one sex blow-offs, some operators tried using a tattooed lady while many others switched to pin cushions. Sideshow Bennie is one of the best new sideshow acts out there who has been working on the Hall-Christ sideshow. Besides doing a number of acts on the main stage he also does pins in the blow-off.

Red Trower is more blunt: "When it came to the annex, you had to entertain them first, then you could rob 'em. They had to get happy before they got to the blow-off. Down there, you had to give them a blind opening so they really didn't know what they were going to see. You can't tell them what's back there, because if you do, nine out of 10 are not going to go. In the last years you had a tattooed lady, blockhead or pin cushion behind the curtain. Most people are not going to pay an extra buck to see that. So you have to camouflage it with a smooth, colorful story. I used to never crack the price until the end, and then as time went on, I got better results by telling them in the beginning."

Red reeled off his stock blow-off spiel: "The next attraction is behind this curtain. We are *all* going to go back there in the next few minutes. I'm going to tell you now in advance — in order to go see this next attraction there will be an additional charge of a dollar. However, if you listen for a few moments you can make up your mind whether you care or dare to go back there." Red explained, "You have already implanted the price in their mind. If they stay listening, you stand a chance of doing something. The other way, if you crack the buck at the last minute, a lot of them walk. The minute you ask them for money in the annex they don't come back into the tent, even though you tell them they can. They've had it."

Those not going into the blow were directed to the other end of the tent for the next act. Operators didn't want disgruntled blow-off customers on their way out chilling incoming customers. Some dumped the blow-off crowd out the back or side of the tent. Many operators held up a new crowd outside a couple of acts before the blow-off and the blade box, until it was over. This was called "putting them in the pig pen."

Two show guys who had one time made a living in drag. On the left is sideshow owner and half-and-half Dean Potter. Beside him is Jimmy Estep who ended his performing career running a sausage joint. He was the cook and clown on my Royal Bros. Circus in 1975.

Dean Potter recalled, "Slim Kelly never held up people coming into the show and I let people in the tent at all times, because holding them up caused just as many beefs as if they came into the show and were hit with an extra charge their first few seconds." Dean had been one of the best half-and-half acts in the business — very classy. During the winter Dean stripped at a Scranton, Penn., coal miners' bar called Slams, billed as "Chris-Dean, Queen of Them All." Dean recalled the years he worked the blow for Slim Kelly and Whitey Sutton: "In the 1970s they operated a very powerful 10-in-one — almost every act a feature freak. The show opened with Melvin Burkhart, followed by four feature freaks, then the first blow-off. Those who didn't go inside the blow were entertained by the electric-chair act. The blow-off crowd would be dumped out before the finish of the electric chair act so they saw some of it. Then four more freak attractions and the last blow-off.

"Slim decided to do away with ballies and work the show with just a grind tape and four ticket sellers. He no longer needed a bally girl. The bally girl usually doubled in the blade box but rather than hire a girl just for it, he decided that two blow-offs at opposite ends of the tent would produce far more revenue. As further belt-tightening was needed to keep going, he eliminated the girl from the electric chair act by using a volunteer from the audience."

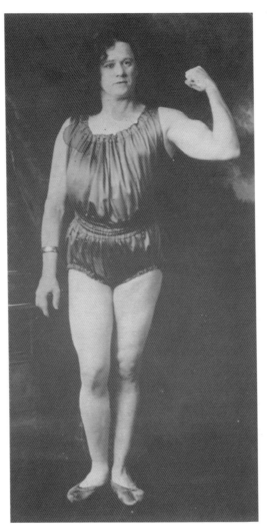

A late-1920s Hubert's Museum blow-off favorite was "Joseph-Josephine," managed by George Dexter Jr. Billed as "Sister and Brother in One Body," the act was presented, in Dexter's words, "[in] the manner that cannot

Elsie Stirk, a woman who claimed to have a daughter was a famous half-man half-woman pit show attraction in the 1920s. She had physically over-developed her muscles in her left arm to appear like a man's. She was born in France.

offend the susceptibilities of the most fastidious. Not a female impersonator. No display of costume lingerie or feathers or wigs to misdirect attention. No padded body cover. Nature's work only — every point demonstrated in the flesh." On the Columbia Burlesque Circuit, Dexter claimed the act took in $2,500 weekly.

In 1928, Anna-John Budd was advertised as the "Original, Uncomparable Half-Man Half-Woman," the only gaff-free attraction of its kind. Eugene Sutton (working as "Claude-Claudette") advertised himself as a "Strong worker — no gaff." James Keating (a.k.a. "Jean-Jeanette"), formerly a circus clown and wire-walker, worked half-and-half for Ray Marsh Brydon for 15 seasons, until he was killed by a streetcar while working at Riverview Park in Chicago in 1948. Harry Caro ("Albert-Alberta") was a famed half-and-half fixture at Coney Island sideshows and Hubert's Museum who also ran a Manhattan antique shop. Bobby Kork's last name came from how he used the gimmick — he wound a length of elastic with a cork at one end around his penis, then pulled it back and inserted the cork in his rectum to keep everything in place.

Jerry Lipko's sideshow on the East Coast in the 1960s with two banners featuring Charlie Hunter as Charlotte the Gorilla Girl.

When Charlie Hunter was out of work , his "At Liberty" ads read: "'Charlotte' sideshow annex. A-1 flash, blow-ups, intelli-gent, lecturer." Bobby Reynolds was a kid when Charlie worked on his dad's sideshow. "Charlie came on the lot dressed like a detec-tive," recalled Bobby. "He would take me around to junk stores. He'd say, 'Bobby, look at these shoes — they're wonderful.' He'd bring them back, swish alcohol around in them to kill any germs and let them dry in the sun. He'd tell me, 'You get very dirty out here on carnivals. Make sure you wash your dingus.' My step-parents warned Charlie in carny, 'Ixnay with the umpfray — no copping the ointjay!'"

Hunter also worked the blow for Jim Steinmetz in the early 1960s. "Charlie was a big, heavy-set guy with a very hairy body,"

Half-and-half Bobby Kork in his work clothes. In his era, (1940s–50s) he was one of the best along with Lola (Leola) Conklin. Another famous one was Bernie Rogers (Titsi Mitzi). Bernie went to Vienna where a doctor injected water into his breasts to create tits the size of tea cups. Claude Bentley, who had his own sideshows, worked half-and-half as Claudie-Claudelle. In the blow he had a small table beside him and the first thing he did was to grab his testicles and smash them down on the table.

the blow-off, which we split 50-50 with the person doing the act."

"They were the best moneymakers, depending on the individual," Ward Hall said about sex enigmas. "The best one I had was 'Diane' (George Searles), a very heavy-set guy who dressed in female wardrobe, but didn't overdo it, preferring expensive clothes from good women's shops. His father was a gangster and his mother a mitt camp worker. He was with us from 1948 through 1960." Ward explained how "Diane" was presented: "We had two banners on the front reading, 'Diane Is Here.' We put up tack cards around the grounds with the same message. I built a special six-foot runway off the bally stage into the tip. The bally production number had girls in ruffled Cuban outfits shaking maracas while I juggled torches to draw a tip. At the end of my spiel I introduced Diane by telling the tip, 'Walter Winchell says she is the strangest

Bobby Kork in street clothes. Joey Givens on being asked about gays as midway performers, said: "It was artistic temperament, natural for any of the drags that were any good. The only one I knew that worked joints worked in drag, then had the sex change operation. Her first name was Julie but everybody called her Sawed-Off."

person on earth.' Diane came up the back steps fluttering a six-foot fan. As she crossed

Jim recalled. "He covered his face in fake hair that he put on with spirit gum. Full-bearded, he dressed in a long gown with a cape. He added fake fingernails that looked like claws. He worked some years as a half-and-half, talking in a high-pitched voice. Half-and-halfs were good money, as we could get a dollar for

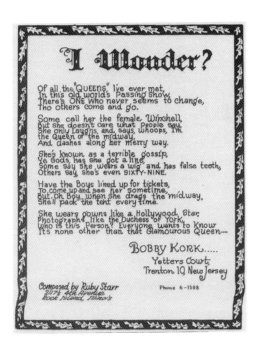

Poem on the back of Bobby Kork's souvenir photo card.

the bally, all the lights on the front bannerline were turned off.

"I proceeded to describe her as 'the world's only true hermaphrodite — all woman and all man. Diane can either marry a man or a woman. In fact, Diane is married. Tonight inside this tent in a separate theater, away from the eyes of children, she will be shown undraped and unashamed.' I handed the microphone to Diane, who said, 'Like this gentleman just told you, I am a true hermaphrodite. If I am not what I say I am, we will not only apologize for taking up your time but refund your ticket and give each and every one of you $100. We will give doctors $10,000 if they can prove I am not real.' Diane gave the microphone back to me, sat on the top of the ticket box waving her fan and held up two fingers in the 'V' salute as we sold tickets.

"Diane wore a bra with birdseed in one cup. She would show the crowd her big feet and joke, 'If they get any bigger I will have to wear the boxes they came in.' Then she told them, 'At this time I am prepared to show you both sexes, and without apology I must ask you for 50 cents if you want to stay. This silver-haired gentleman will collect the money.' Once a doctor from Johns Hopkins in Baltimore passed up his card, wanting to examine her. She told him he could, but she would have to guide his hand. Meantime, she reached back and unsnapped the gimmick. She placed his hand on her dick and balls, then shoved his finger up her ass. He came away convinced she had both sexes."

Guy in drag working as the Lion Faced Girl. The piece that you attached to your face to add hair was called "The Mush." Lionel, who had a late 19th-century sideshow act, had hair completely covering his face. He inspired numerous imitators over the years.

In the '60s, fair officials and police began clamping down on girl shows and sex blow-offs. Dean Potter remembers being busted the same day the law closed down the girl show. Nature has blessed us with few real bearded ladies, but midway politics turned many half-and-halfs into bearded females overnight. "Lola Conklin grew a beard so she could work to kids," Dean relates. "She was losing too

Lola (Leola) Conklin (Leiu Laverne Conklin) died at age 75 in drag on her stage in Karl Cullison's sideshow at the Shelby, N.C., fair September 28, 1975. Johnny Meah convinced the coroner to let them bury her as a woman in a local cemetery near the fairgrounds.

Lola Conklin's funeral was held in the sideshow tent. She wore a dress and turban, and she held a single rose and a white Bible in her hands. Her open coffin stood beside a tattoo display. Pallbearers included Dean Potter, Joey Givens, and another sideshow worker named Kim.

much money on kids' days. Charlie Hunter changed to 'the Gorilla Girl — one-third gorilla, one-third man, one-third woman.' If there were a lot of kids in the audience, he would just work simply as 'the Gorilla Girl.' I never grew a beard, but my bosses would have me put on that phony baby-growing-out-of-the-stomach gaff. I never felt comfortable doing it and never sold it good because I felt so damn self-consious. That was so we could work to kids. All economics. Money, money . . . money!

"When I was with Earl Meyers we couldn't work the sex angle in Gaithersburg, Maryland. I worked the baby-growing-out-of-my-stomach for him. You wore a cut-off T-shirt, and the whole thing went on like a corset. The end of the stomach and the baby were all one piece with lace at the back. The baby had a diaper on it."

Dean Potter believed Selma Woods "the Pony Girl" was the best blow-off of his time. "Her body was marked like a palomino pony — white with dark spots, out of which hair grew," he says. "She didn't like half-and-halfs and would fight for the blow-off because when she worked center stage she had to wear a little costume. In the blow she worked in a G-string and pasties, like a stripper. She liked that. She had a half-dozen kids and married a merry-go-round foreman. I saw her husband

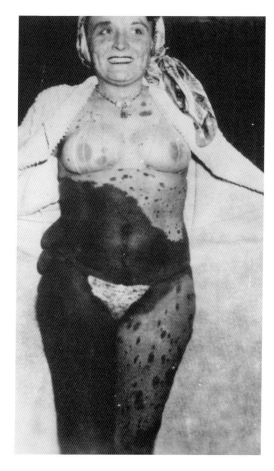

Thelma Ward the spotted Pony Girl was from Johnson City, Tenn., She was a highly rated sideshow attraction. Dressed like this, she'd get no beefs in the blow-off.

Dean also recalled one that few people mention: "Dick Best had a woman named 'Bit Tee the Human Tree.' Her hands and feet had tree-like branches growing from the ends of her toes and fingers. She was found with her son, begging on the streets in India, and brought over here. I was told her son had to saw the branches off her toes and fingers so they wouldn't get too cumbersome. She had an overabundance of calcium in her body which produced the growths. She was a sensation here, but was only out a couple seasons before she died."

A drag queen/stripper/half-and-half/ bearded lady career seemed a logical route for Joey Givens. "You're stuck in the middle of nowhere," he says. "The carnival comes to town and here is this cute guy that looks like a girl. Soon as you walk through the back end, 14 people are going, 'Hmmm — my, he'd look good in a dress!' Most of us were very versatile . . . . We worked as strippers, half- and-halfs and bearded ladies — anything involving girls."

In the late '50s, Joey's first employer was Leola Conklin, who had the sideshow with the John Marks Shows. "I was 17," Joey said. "I stood on the bally with a snake. Leola liked a boy up there rather than a girl. The pay was $3 a day and a pack of cigarettes. I didn't smoke, but sold the cigarettes for a nickel each. I always came off the road with a little money."

The versatile Joey Givens worked drag in Chicago nightclubs for years as well as being a carnival girl-show dancer. He also appeared as a half-and-half, bearded lady and lady sword swallower with various sideshows. He had his own single-o show out appearing as Josephine Tate the Monkey Girl or Dog Faced Girl. Here in 2006 he stands outside a candy wagon he operates.

and asked what happened to Selma. He said all those spots turned cancerous and killed her."

In his early 20s Joey was shown the half- and-half act by Paul LePage ("Paul-Paulette"), but watching Leola helped refine it. "She was an old-fashioned worker — no gimmicks," he explained. "She exposed the male organs, then turned around and bent over to show them the female organs behind the testicles. This was simply done with what was known as the 'finger gaff.' You take your finger and slide it between your balls and push in hard. All that extra skin folds right over. Most testicles have hair on them and it looks very real. When Leola worked, she dressed in a bra and panel like a stripper. The panel hid any skin imperfections. She was a quick, clean and clinical worker.

"We brought everybody we could possibly bring into the blow-off for a quarter — men, women and children. I then worked 'Bearded Lady' or 'Dog-Faced Girl' or 'Monkey-Faced Girl'— whatever you happened to be using at the time. Then you would ask the children to leave and the adults to stay. You worked to the adults for 50 cents. We had a curtain right down the middle of the blow, and we separated the men from the women. You worked to the women first — it was always very quick. 'There's a little penis up inside, not too big, nothing to get excited about — is it, ladies? Thank you. If you will now step outside, I'll flash for the gentlemen.' We'd pull the curtain back so the guys could get closer to the stage. You hit them for a buck to see the 'hole' thing, as we use to say. Again it was very quick and right out."

Fair boards and local law enforcement made it harder to work sex blows. Joey explained, "On Peter Hennen's Helles Belles show we played this spot with Specs Groscurth's Blue Grass Shows. I was working as a bearded lady. Specs came down before we even opened and said, 'The sheriff doesn't want any flashing here.' I said, 'I'll never make any money — that's what they are coming in there to see.' I didn't flash the first day — didn't make any money. Second day I gave out little peeks. Soon the word got around and I started making real money. Here comes Specs: 'Got a complaint you were flashing. You do it again, you got to leave.' I flashed, and he came down again: 'You got to go.' 'I can't. I don't have any money to leave with!' Next day the same thing. He says, 'Okay — work straight and Saturday you can flash.'

"Saturday I flashed all day. Specs came along: 'People are complaining at the office but it's 10:30 p.m. — I'm not going to worry about it!' You can tell the crowd all about it but that's no good. You have to flash. When I worked the bearded lady, I used to sit in a chair. My skirt was split all the way up the front. I'd say, 'Notice the hair on the legs.' Of course they didn't notice the hair on my legs, they were looking somewhere else."

Sign painter Denny Gilli recalled '60s performer Lester Swift, a.k.a. Ester-Lester:

Many fairground shows besides sideshows ran blow-offs. The blow-off on Ike Rose's midget show allowed patrons to look at a midget's bedroom and the bathroom.

"When 'Ester-Lester' worked, they divided the blow in half — women on one side and men on the other. The lecturer told them, 'So as not to embarrass the fastidious among you.' She presented it more like a medical exhibit, wearing a little apron-type thing around her waist with a question mark on it to signify she was unknown to what she really was. She had a very nice spiel about the doctor examining her when she was a child

1971 *Amusement Business* ad for the sale of Doc Hankins's *Madame X* (Child Birth Film) blow-off act while he was still on the Sutton Sideshow with James E. Strates Shows.

and pronouncing her 'the most perfect union of male and female he had ever had the privilege to examine!'

"Ester worked with the tie-back. It sounded painful to me. It was a string tied around the head of his penis. At the end of the string was a hook. He worked in a one-piece lady's outfit and used birdseed in the little bags for the breast, commenting that of all the things he had tried, the seeds gave him a full, natural look. A cape that came down over his shoulders right above the bra line hid a harness around his shoulders that crossed over his back. He would wait until just before he went onstage to pull the penis tight between the testicles, giving an appearance of a vagina. The hook on the tie-back slipped over the harness. When it came time to show both sexes he could reach way back and show a little bit of the penis head. Joking with his audience, Ester would say, 'My mother wanted a little girl, my father wanted a little boy. Both were satisfied.'"

For sideshow owners, the best blow-offs were the cheapest. Faye Renton said her dad often used the "Crucifixion Fish." There was nothing to it: viewers peered into a catfish skull's mouth to see two bones crossed in a "T," while the lecturer gave a spiel about the crucifixion. Phony mummies, fake bodies and *Birth of a Baby* films required no salaries. "I was working for Peter Hennen as a half-and-half," recalled Dean. "One day I got mad and left. I ran into Peter later. He told me, 'When you quit me I was really upset. Then I recalled Doc Hankin's birth-film blow-off. I put the film in there and I didn't have to split the blow money with anybody. You did me the biggest favor.'"

Denny Gilli added, "I picked Doc Hankin up once and he had his whole blow-off in a trunk — his lab coat, back drapes, screen and 8mm movie projector. His spiel informed the tip that he was a Washington, D.C., doctor who, at fair time each year, left his staff at such-and-such Washington clinic to come out to this dirty, filthy fairground in order to show *Madame X: The Mystery of Life* as an educational

There have been only a few legitimate four-legged girls. However that didn't stop showmen from presenting such an attraction. Here Doc Tripp and his wife present the four-Legged Girl blow-off on the 1936 Lewis Bros. Circus.

Man as bearded lady working for Lou Dufour at his John Hix Strange As It Is N.Y. World's Fair sideshow. I don't know how he explained the chest hair.

This is possibly a photo card of Leola Conklin working as Leo-Leola. Many show folks just called her Lola but her sideshow billing was usually Leola. In the '50s she had her own sideshows on various carnivals. Besides being one of the best half-and-half acts she also used torches from her fire-eating act to create smoke paintings on porcelain.

Leo   Leola

exhibit. Doc hinted that what they were going to see was extremely sexy. On his stage, the back curtain would open to reveal his movie screen. Before starting, he pointed out a couple of guys dressed in white lab coats who carried smelling salts. Doc informed the tip, 'During this performance, should any of you become light-headed or dizzy, just kneel on one knee and one of my orderlies will come around to assist you.' I never failed to be in there when at least two or three men dropped down. Doc carried two films about five min-

utes long, one black and white and the other in color. He'd brag, 'They were dropping like flies in there last night. I think I'll show them the color version tonight and really knock them down.'"

There were many sex angles and enough workers with raucous panache to carry them off under a 25-watt blue bulb. "On occasion, I worked the chastity belt in the blow for Peter

Hennen," admitted Joey Givens. "'Burn's Torture Show' used a chasity-belt blow with a real topless girl. If a drag worked it, they used foam rubber from old car seats for tits. Where the seat curves in rolls, you just take that section and glue a nipple from a baby's bottle on it, smear makeup all over it. You wore black chiffon over it like the black mesh bras that strippers wore — looks just like nipples and tits. You wore that and the chasity belt. You throw your shoulders back — it was a quick flash, that's all. Under the chastity belt was a G-string with hair sewn onto it. If the police said anything about the nudity, 'Hey — here it is. What am I showing?'"

Some operators stayed away from sex, preferring to use a featured freak in the blow. "I used Bob Melvin 'The Two-Faced Man' from Lancaster, Missouri," Walter Wanous said from his home in Montgomery, Ala. "He drew a lot of people. Alligator-skinned people were good blow-off attractions." But Dean Potter snickers about alligator people: "Years ago we used to paint a gazoonie [workingman] with glue. If Emmett 'the Alligator Man' was standing next to the guy, you couldn't tell the difference. It was a wood glue and hard to get. Earl Meyers would mix it up and paint the guy from the waist up, an hour before showtime. When it dried, he took the guy's skin in his hands and cracked it into little squares. You washed it off at night, but some of these guys wouldn't even bother. Earl hired this guy and painted him up, cracked him, and the guy took an epileptic seizure. I never seen Earl so scared. He didn't want to call the law or an ambulance in case they asked him what he was doing painting this guy with glue. Lucky for Earl, the guy came through it. When he did it again, he asked the new guy, 'Are you subject to seizures?'"

Line-up of acts on the 1952 Clyde Beatty Circus side show taken at Los Angeles, CA. On the bally are Sealo, Zola Williams, Augustus the pinhead, Danny the Penguin Boy, Shackles the escape artist and Chief Jerome Red Cloud. In front with his dog and cat are Martin Larrello, Freddy Smith holding the "Crocodile with Punch" in his mouth, and manager Red White and his wife, then a Hawaiian troupe next to Sam Alexander wearing a white plastic mask.

There were other approaches, too, when sex was taboo. Ward Hall used Antoria Gibbons "the Tattooed Lady," in the 1980s. "Red Gibbons, her husband, was a tattooist and he had done the work on her," related Ward. "She was billed as 'Artora.' The blow pitch was, 'Ladies and gentlemen, behind this curtain we have the strangest one of them all. She is not a freak, not born a freak, but a man-made freak. Her husband has marked and disfigured her body so none will lust over her.' Once the people were in the blow, it was the regular tattoo pitch. She heard me making the blow and was upset with me. She

185

said, 'I am not a monster, I go out to eat, get laid.' She was 86, deaf and going senile. When I told her I wasn't taking the show out next year, she was very upset."

In 1981, Sam Alexander's sideshow was on Bill Lynch Shows, playing the Bridgewater Fair. My circus was within an hour's drive of them and one day I went over. The young sword swallower made the blade box and blow spiels. One end of the tent was curtained off for the blow with a section of 10-foot sidewall. Inside was a rough guillotine illusion and this horrible-looking papier-mâché "Cardiff Giant" propped up at a 45-degree angle against the center pole. It looked awful. Was Sam losing it?

Sam's "Cardiff Giant" bothered me the whole drive back, until I concluded that he didn't care how it looked. He wasn't paying the giant a dime. Sam just wanted to keep all the blow-off scratch. He'd been one of the best all-time blow-off features himself: in the '30s, a propane water heater exploded in a garage and blew off the lower half of Sam's face, literally propelling him into the freak world. Don Leslie, who worked with Sam, told me, "When Sam's face healed, a derma-

tologist who was an amateur sculptor made him a mask to wear in public. Out, he would just drink liquids by pushing the straw up under his mask. As he aged, the mask didn't quite fit right."

I'd first met Sam at the CNE in the 1970s. Hearing I had a circus with a sideshow, Sam's manager took me back to his trailer, warning me that Sam's appearance could be shocking. Sam's nasal voice came toward me across the table in garbled bits through the flutterings of a white-cloth surgical mask. It was like carrying on a conversation with a hand puppet. He wanted to unload 3,000 miniature bibles he didn't want to take back into the U.S.

A friend had seen Sam's act at the CNE. When everyone was inside the blow, Sam turned his back on the tip, whipped off his mask and turned back around quickly. Several people fainted. What amazed my friend came afterwards. Sam opened up his coat and, standing there shirtless, he pointed to what looked like a big, fleshy hot-dog hanging off his left side. Sam pinched and poked it, explaining that it was growing flesh for a skin graft to fix his face. Sam assured the tip that their 25-cent admission to see him was being used to cover his plastic surgery costs.

Without a featured freak or sex in the blow-off, showmen had to revert to a non-human curiosity. "My best blow-off act was at Coney Island with a doubled-body pig in formaldehyde," John Bradshaw told me. "The blow would fit 40 people at the most. On a Sunday we started at 50 cents, then up to 75, and then a dollar. I told them it was an inhuman oddity still on public exhibition 25 years after its demise. They never caught that. When I went in to square it I told them, 'Ladies and gentlemen, I said it was a non-human oddity. You have all guessed by now that it is a freak animal. I said it died 25 years ago. Please understand that this poor creature suffered and she is not suffering now.' I asked, 'Are there any questions?' One lady in the tip said, 'Yes sir! Can we have our dollar back?' 'No! Any other questions?'"

Chapter 12

"Here I Am – There I Go"

FEATURE FREAK—FEATURE FREAK
WANTED
On account of sickness, would like to hear at once from Freak that can be featured and talked on, or a Sensational Act. Salary is no object if you have what I want. Write or wire at once. **JOHNNIE BEJANO, care Morris & Castle Show.** Show opens at Fort Smith, Ark., April 12; Tulsa, Okla., April 21.

April 12, 1924, *Billboard* ad placed by legendary 10-in-one operator Johnnie Bejano. Sideshowmen will tell you that you sell the show with the freaks but it's up to the working acts inside to square it.

Shown here on the lot of the Mighty Sheelsey shows midway is Robert Huddleson the Pony Boy featured in Al Renton's sideshow for several seasons in the 1940s. He was physically handicapped with back-bending knees, but managed to get around on all fours by using wooden blocks in both hands to avoid scraping his hands and fingers.

A tabloid cover featuring a freak photo still sells as many copies as one sporting Hollywood cleavage. Fred Dahlinger, curator of circus history with the John and Mable Ringling Museum of Art, suggests the public's viewing of deformed folks made them feel good about their own kids. He said, "Ask any new birth mother and the first thing they do is count their baby's fingers and toes, make certain that they are 100 percent normal, whatever that might be."

Today, except for a few small people, there are no freaks on the showgrounds. By the '60s, the last of them were either dead, too old to work or in their own single-O shows. Giants, Siamese twins and people who were three-legged, double-bodied or lobster-clawed once comprised the freak aristocracy of showdom. Next came midgets, dwarfs and fat people, with the armless, legless and all the "minuses" trailing.

Most 20th-century circus and carnival sideshows needed only a couple of freaks. Operators preferred those who didn't demand a big salary and who were easy to get along with. Dwarfs and midgets were the most common. In 1912, Ike and Mike "the Look-a-Like Midgets" became naturalized American citizens. Born in Hungary, they were promoted here first by showman Ike Rose. In the spring of 1925, when Ike and Mike were 24, they worked at Ringling's Madison Square Garden date, the Sells-Floto Circus sideshow during its Chicago Coliseum stand and then under canvas on the Hagenbeck-Wallace Circus sideshow. They never stopped working.

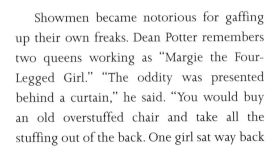

Mike and Ike were first managed and put on midways by midget promoter Ike Rose. Later, these two became the mainstays in the many sideshows and winter-store shows that Ray Marsh Brydon assembled. It was not unusual for a freak attraction to stay with the same promoter for years.

Diagram from Mahatma for working the three-legged-girl act.

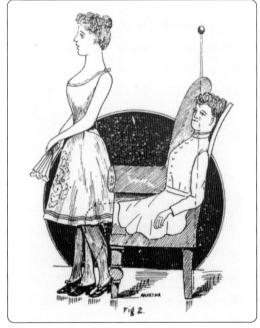

Showmen became notorious for gaffing up their own freaks. Dean Potter remembers two queens working as "Margie the Four-Legged Girl." "The oddity was presented behind a curtain," he said. "You would buy an old overstuffed chair and take all the stuffing out of the back. One girl sat way back and extended her legs and the other girl just sat on top of her. When they got in place, you opened the curtain. These two began arguing one day and kept it up, until during one of the night shows the one on top walked off in the middle of the presentation, leaving the other two legs just sitting there!"

Touring shows often took performers into hospital children's wards where they gave impromptu shows to cheer the kids up. Royal American Shows was the only show with a traveling Shrine Unit. In some towns, they'd take the whole sideshow and the girls from the girl shows out to a children's hospital where they would put on a special show on the grounds. Here Little Col. Casper and giant Johann K. Petursson are seen working a street corner in Tampa, Fla., in 1955 during the Polio Fund drive.

Chris Christ represents the last era of sideshowmen. A native of Buffalo, N.Y., he joined up in the 1970s when the few freaks left in the business were mostly midgets, giants, fat people and ballyhoo-able folks, missing legs or arms or both. "I never had a lot of freaks," Christ explained. "The best combo of stuff I had was a giant girl, a midget woman and a fat man. They gave me the strongest quotes for the bally because you're going from tall to small to big. Slim Kelly, Walter Wanous and others had a lot of acts that I called 'Here I Am, There I Go' acts. They were all the same: 'I was born of normal parents in so-and-so, Alabama, and I am so-and-so old and I have four normal children and I am happily married. Thank you! Here's my souvenir postcard for a quarter.' They'd have a whole show of that! Most of the attractions that I had would do something entertaining, no matter how frugal it might be."

Asked about freaks, Charlie Roark replied tersely, "Their deformity was all the act they had. Some fat ladies did the shimmy." But he

Zandu the Quarter Boy, is seen here balancing on one hand out back of the Dick Best 10-in-one tent. Note the extra padding on the bottom of his jacket.

Armless and legless performer Frieda Pushnik on her stage in the 1955 R.B.B. and B. Circus sideshow managed by Bobby Hasson. On the ground are her mom Erma and her sister Eileen. One or both often traveled with Frieda.

Ossified men showed unbelievable courage in touring. This photo should be posted in every club and theatre dressing room. Any entertainer that says he or she can't go on stage for any reason should be made to look at this guy before canceling the gig.

liked Frances O'Connor "the Armless and Legless Girl," the only freak on the 1944 Cole sideshow: "She was the perfect lady and did do something. Typed with her feet. Showed you how she fed herself by holding a bowl in one little stub hand and an eating utensil in the other."

Recalling half-lady Frieda Pushnik, Charlie said, "She was a good person. Both her mother and sister traveled with her. They were real nice, high-class, educated and well-bred people. On Ringling, Frieda worked a typewriter with a pencil in her mouth. While she typed away, we sold photos of her for a dime. They made a good living as she was probably the highest-priced act in there."

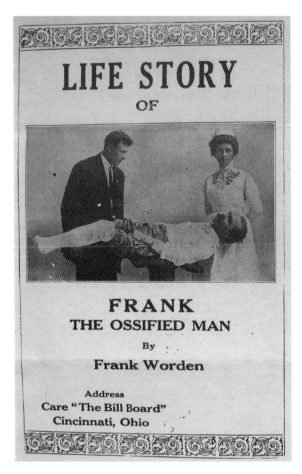

LIFE STORY

OF

A 1937 R.B.B. and B. Circus backyard scene with giant Al Tomaini and his half-lady wife Jeanie surrounded (from the left) by Major Mite, Daisy Doll, Tiny and Harry Doll and sideshow manager Clyde Ingall's son John.

FRANK
THE OSSIFIED MAN

By

Frank Worden

Address
Care "The Bill Board"
Cincinnati, Ohio

Pitch bio sold by Frank The Ossified Man.

Frieda was born in 1923 in Conemaugh, Penn., and her arms and legs had been severed in a botched appendectomy on her pregnant mother. She was first exhibited at age nine at Ripley's sideshow at the 1933 Chicago Century of Progress fair and from 1943 through 1955 she appeared mostly in circus sideshows. She died at 77.

Ossified humans were featured in many sideshows. Billboard obits in 1903 included one for Jonathan R. Bass, who lived to 62, having worked the week before his death at Hubert's Palace Theater in N.Y.C. Billboard related, "At age 16, while rafting logs on the Erie Canal, he was seized with ossific rheumatism but the doctor treated him for inflammatory rheumatism. He spent the next nine years in bed, as his body started turning to bone. He was in acute agony for a year as the ossification set in. He went blind. Showman Fred Lattia was his manager and first exhibited him at the Globe Museum in New York City. Fred read the papers to him every day. He was carried in the same bed all over the country for forty-six years."

A July 1921 Billboard noted the appearance of Frank Woods "The Ossified Man" at Columbus Park, N.J.: "With the exception of his forearms and hands he is rigid from the tips of his toes up to his neck — even his jaw is locked shut. He is fed only liquids and soft food. Manager Dan Nagle, several times a day, takes him out of the pit and carries him down to the ocean and places him in the water. He floats well and with a paddle glides along the surface. Nagle returns him to the pit followed by a big crowd who buy tickets and go in."

As late as the '60s, Joe Kara toured Capt. Bob Tait, "the Man Slowly Turning to Stone,"

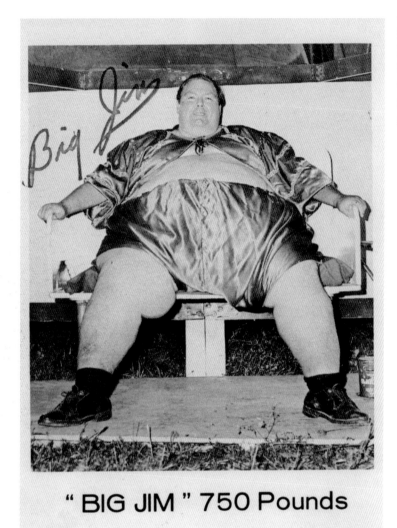

"BIG JIM" 750 Pounds

Floridian Big Jim a.k.a. Harold Spohn trouped for many seasons with Ward Hall and Chris Christ–produced sideshows.

Here's Big Jim's daily meal plan. When asked about certain sideshow acts, showman Jim Steinmetz said fat folks were easy to find. They appreciated being where someone else picked up the weekly grocery tab.

BIG JIM'S DIET !

BREAKFAST
- 1 Quart Orange Juice
- 1 Pound Bacon
- 1 Dozen Eggs
- 1 Loaf of Bread, Toasted
- 1/4 Pound Butter
- 1 Dozen Sweet Rolls
- 1 Pot Coffee

LUNCH
- 1 Dozen Cheezeburgers
- 1 1/2 Pounds French Fries
- 6 Chocolate Shakes

DINNER
- 1 Large Mixing Bowl of Salad
- 1 Tub full of Chicken
- 3 Pecks Potatoes
- 1 1/2 Dozen Rolls with Butter
- 4 Pies
- 2 Gallon of Iced Tea

Birthplace: Ohio
Weight at Birth: 14 1/2 Pounds
Age: 36
Height: 5 Feet 7 Inches
Weight: 750 Pounds
Waist: 100 Inches

around eastern Canadian midways. Joe's wife dressed as a nurse and stood alongside Tait, a life-size mannequin in a coffin with a breathing pump in its chest.

In 1959, Jim Steinmetz bought Joe Sciortino's Barnum's American Sideshow, which consisted entirely of life-size papier-mâché freaks made by Snap Wyatt. "Nothing but heat," Jim says. "People complaining there was nothing in there but a bunch of dummies! I finally sold it. They took up a whole semi and they were heavy." Jim

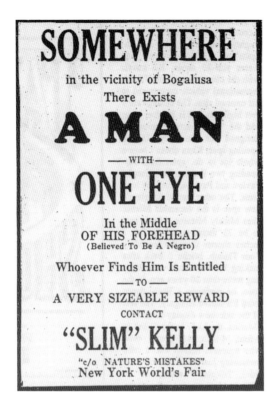

Ad placed by sideshowman Slim Kelly looking for this rumored One-Eyed Man.

quickly got some acts — fire-eater Andy Briskie joined, along with the Grady Stile's "Lobster Family," Shirley Hunter ("Charlie Hunter") in the blow-off, and a blade box — and the money started coming in.

"We always had fat people," Jim recalled. "They were easy to find and they liked the work. They just sat there, ate or read, gave a short spiel and sold their photo cards. They were happy to have a place where someone else was paying the grocery bill! We had a lot of working acts, sometimes a midget or gaffed-up dwarf. Giants were the best — people would always go in to see a giant. I liked Johann Petursson. He was very good to work with, easygoing, smart and a real nice person. I had giant Eddie Carmel with me for a long time. He was hard to work with — didn't want to stand up: just sit in a chair and sell his cards and rings. People paid their dollar to see him erect! I used to send my kids in there with a two-by-four to hit him on the legs if he didn't get up. He also sold more photos and rings standing up, but he was lazy."

Showmen watched for freaks with the same relentless attention that truck drivers spent following the highway's center line. Finding one was usually pure luck. In the early '30s, Dick Best discovered Betty Lou Williams by following up rumors about a four-legged baby born in the Georgia woods. Stopping at a general store, he inquired about such a person and the proprietor offered to get him help. The help was the local sheriff, who locked Dick up. The cop believed anyone looking for something as crazy as a four-legged girl couldn't be up to any good. Eight hours later, when Dick was freed from the Richland, Ga., jail, he doubled back to the general store. He gave a schoolkid a dollar

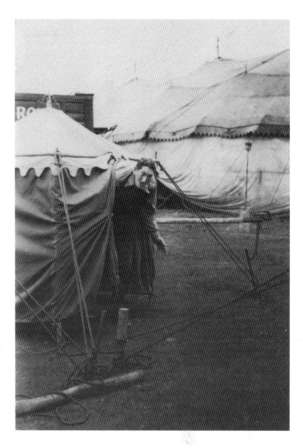

Giant Jack Earle somehow managing to get out of the small sideshow donnicker (toilet) tent on Ringling Bros. and Barnum & Bailey Circus lot September 6, 1938, in Columbus, OH.

and asked him about a four-legged baby. The kid led him to Betty Lou's home.

Oddities have walked up to the showman's ticket box seeking work, but usually it was the parents or siblings who

Jack Earle in the 1938 Ringling Bros. and Barnum & Bailey Circus backyard with Betty Broadbent's son in 1938.

The phenomenal "stump man" Barney Nelson was a feature freak attraction on early 10-in-one shows in the World War I era. He worked mainly for Pete Kortes sideshows into the early fifties. Here he is in the pit, sketching with a pencil held between his toes.

approached the showman. Some oddities came on the showground simply as patrons, and a showman saw something in their peculiar appearance and hired them. One afternoon in the 1960s, Earl Meyers was preparing to gather a tip in front of his sideshow when a couple walked up to him with a teenager. Could he put their son to

work? The kid's face was grotesquely swollen on one side, causing his mouth to droop unevenly, and one ear was much larger than the other. One side of his face looked normal, while the other looked distorted. Meyers turned him into "the Boy with Two Faces," and Bobby Livingston was not only a welcome addition to the show, but his parents

sent Earl money each week to enclose with their son's salary.

Dean Potter tells of how Randy Rosenson found Jimmy Ghassy ("Fat Jimmy") out in Vineland, N.J., when he pulled into a gas station one day. "This 700-pound-plus guy was sitting in a big chair between the gas pumps," said Dean. "He just reached out one way or

Giant Ray Johnson at 8-feet-tall was billed as the "Nubian Giant" when on the 1956 Clyde Beatty Circus sideshow. He was from Fort Dodge, Iowa, but left a job at a brickyard to tour with a sideshow. He worked on numerous circuses and carnival 10-in-ones. His last job was as a doorman at the Hollywood Plaza Hotel. He was forced into retirement due to bad health and ended up living in Riverside, Cal., with his wife and 10 children.

Slim Kelly is seen here in the centre on the bally stage of his 1936 10-in-one using the Ripley name. The only other freak shown besides the dwarf in front of Kelly is a young Dick Hillburn, sitting on the right ticket box. The fourth person from the right is "Shackles" the escape artist. One major freak who could actually entertain folks for a few minutes was all you needed.

another and pumped your gas. That was his job. Randy said to him, 'Boy, I'm going to make you a star.'"

But trouping for fat folks wasn't easy. On the 1915 Zeidman & Pollie Shows, 729-pound Elma was too big to get through the doors of

I don't think pitying these guys would have gone too well. They'd probably would have chased you away with a tent pole. Part of everyone's desire in the working world is to be part of the team. You can't argue these three didn't get some satisfaction from being "with it and for it."

The undertaker had to rig up a block and tackle and drag his body to the landing to slide it down on planks. The body was removed from the house out the back door and through a new opening in the fence. No hearse was big enough, so a flat wagon took his oversized coffin to the cemetery.

Exhibiting a legitimate human oddity or even a handicapped person billed as a freak begged instant controversy. Some promoters skirted the skepticism by adopting the attraction, and many acts stayed with one sideshow operator for life. Freaks, more than anyone in show business, needed a constant caregiver-companion along with someone to handle their business affairs. Many ticket sellers or talkers managed a freak, and some were married to one. The relations between manager and freak, like any other partnership, had its pros and cons, though most arrangements proved good and were long-term partnerships. However, life on the road was a grind for both. While the freak's challenges were social and physical, the manager always faced the possibility that his attraction might keel over at any minute.

the railway coaches. She was transported in a baggage car in a specially built chair. The *Clipper* obit for Furman Schenck, a black fat boy who died August 24, 1892, in New Brunswick, N.J., stated, "He was 500 pounds at age 14. He grew fatter and richer, leading

the life of a freak. On the show bills, his age was shown as 18, and folks not familiar with the business methods of the dime museum used to gaze up into his merry face and wonder what he would be when he grew up!" Furman died in a second-floor bedroom.

Laws governing what could or couldn't be done in exhibiting humans differed from state to state. As early as 1869, North Carolina passed a law making it illegal to exhibit any child under 18 who was mentally retarded, deformed or

It would be hard to pass these three characters on a sideshow bally without stopping. They were not only bally magnets but helped put the show up and down.

had a natural physical detraction. A New York State bill in 1894 required guardians of incompetent persons to account for all money earned by the service of such persons.

In 1921, the president of the American Association of Fairs and Expositions declared at their annual meeting, "Freaks in the future will be banished from fairs." This decision was supported by an article in the *Elmira Advertiser* the same year: "Nothing now makes anyone wonder or exhibit interest in freaks; the public is merely disgusted. The dime-store freaks have lost their public allure. Nor have showmen been converted to the uplift. The real situation that prompts the ban on freaks is that freaks yearly are becoming scarcer. Fewer births end away from normalcy. As a result, the sideshow is on its last pins. It has enemies, but leaving aside its mental or pathological influence, it certainly furnished a multitude of thrills for a generation now using hair restorer and leaning on canes."

But the October 1927 *Billboard* told a different tale: "Old-fashioned freaks have come back. The fat lady is back earning fifty bucks a week and cakes (eats) and the armless wonder is back in the pit painting landscapes with paint brushes held between the toes of his feet." The biggest draw seemed to be Baltimore's Johnny Eck, who had recently returned home after a Canadian tour that included Toronto's CNE, where he turned 12,000 a day at a dime each for a show that lasted 29 seconds. "Pass quietly, folks, to your left and make room for others to witness the world's greatest marvel in his unparallel act," droned the lecturer. "Don't forget to take with you a life-like photograph of the half-boy, only ten cents."

The U.S. government's stance on freaks, when putting together the unemployment

J.J.J. - C.N.E.

Johnny Eck posed out front of his show while on the Johnny J. Jones midway at the Canadian National Exhibition in Toronto, Ontario, Canada, 1927. Eck did so many things besides being exhibited as a half-person. He was in movies, worked with leading magicians, made models, led his own big band and painted door screens in his native Baltimore.

tax and social security act in the mid-1930s, was strange. Workers on percentage, like talkers, had to pay, while freaks and acts making their living from unusual feats were exempt. Oddities finding themselves out of work could not expect to obtain employment through regular state or federal channels. One

state classified "freaks" as sick people afflicted with illnesses, and therefore exempt from benefits. The government simply believed freaks were unemployable.

Yvonne and Yvette, twins joined together at the head, were born in L.A. to Willia Jones McCarther, a single mom with five kids. She

refused to have them institutionalized, telling doctors, "God gave them to me and I guess he will show me how to raise them." When the twins reached age two she placed them on exhibition to pay off medical bills. In March 1951 she signed with Nat Lorow, whose brothers ran the sideshow on Royal American

Armless Jose DeLeon playing cards with famed tattooed lady Betty Broadbent while with Lorow Bros. 10-in-one on RAS in 1952.

Hoyt Shumaker, a handicapped performer, is seen here working in Dick Best's 10-in-one on Royal American Shows in the early 1960s.

Shows, but earlier in the month a couple named Younger — who claimed to have a contract signed by the twins — had exhibited them at the San Bernardino National Orange Show for the first time. The Youngers arranged for Harry Golub to exhibit the twins in the Clyde Beatty Circus sideshow. Golub showed them in a separate tent joined to the sideshow top. People viewed the twins behind a four-by-six-foot Plexiglas window inside a specially built trailer called the "Twin Plex," air-conditioned and temperature-controlled. Beside the trailer, on a 20-by-40-foot stage, was an X-ray exhibit showing the growth of the twins, and registered nurses accompanied the pair at all times.

Lorow got a court judgement that upheld his contract with the McCarthers and the twins toured with Lorow's 10-in-one on RAS for a season. After a decade on exhibition across North America, the McCarther twins

Dick Hillburn and Carl the Frog Boy have rigged up their car so that with the two of them they can drive it and pull their house-trailer from spot to spot. This photo was taken at the Ottawa, ON, exhibition in the mid-1960s when they had their show with Amusements of America.

Percilla the Monkey Girl with her head and body covered up to hide her facial and body hair, is being led to the stage by a lady sideshow worker. Quite visible in the photo are both the teaser curtain and the cat walk at the front of the 10-in-one tent.

became gospel singers. They died at 43 and were buried in a double-size pink coffin. Their last few years had been spent in an apartment in Pacoima, Calif., where they lived off a disability pension. They had been due to grad-uate from a community college as children's nurses when they died.

Freaks were better off on shows than almost anywhere else. Unless a freak went out of his or her way to leave the lot, his only contact with towners was when he appeared on the sideshow stage. Freaks made out best on rail circuses that provided them with beds in railcars, a cookhouse on the lot and a gilly vehicle to transfer them

Thin man Gene Pulley was a regular on numerous circus and carnival sideshows from the 1930s into the '50s. Here is the pitch photo card he used while on Ringling in 1955.

Dolly Reagan was a fixture in Ward Hall–Cris Christ sideshows from 1972 until her death in 1991. Born Clara "Dolly" Scott in Saskatoon, Sask., in 1919 she was discovered by someone in the side show business at age 23 while selling raffle tickets at a fair. Some days the anklipsis of her joints made it hard for her to work but she hated not working and more importantly not having a chance to sell her photo pitch cards.

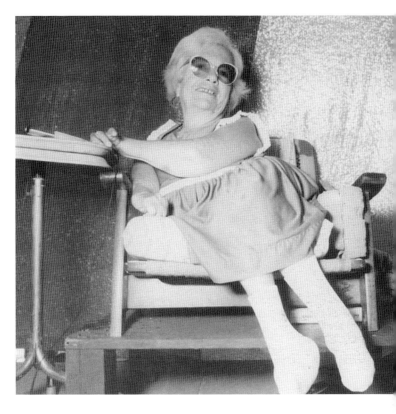

from the sleeping cars to the lot and back. Freaks with bad facial deformities found it hard to eat away from the lot and many of the large 10-in-ones of this era carried their own cookhouse — operators didn't want their featured freak scoffing food in public at a midway grab joint.

The house trailer was not only the best thing to happen to outdoor show folks in the 20th century, but a lifesaver for freaks. Walter Davis praised the arrival of house trailers in a 1936 *Billboard*: "For many seasons, such well-known freaks and physical wonders as Percilla 'The Monkey Girl' had been subject to much embarrassment by traveling openly on trains and buses. Now she is able to get a good night's rest after the closing performance on the lot last played, and the following

day can be driven to the next town in privacy, ready for the opening performance, without the prying eyes and jests of the public."

Talk of banishing sideshow freaks from fairs flared up in fall 1968 — and 15-year-old Carol Grant, a high school student in Raleigh, N.C., provided the match. She took offense when sideshow operator Slim Kelly was quoted in a local paper as saying, "When the current ones die off, that'll be the end." Grant, who was

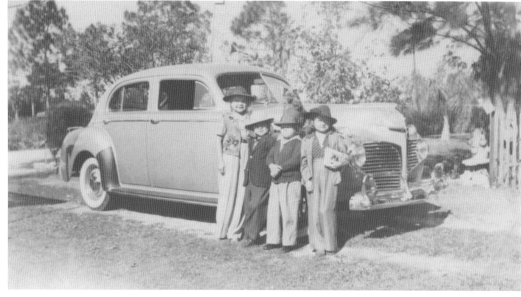

Armless performer Joanne Beach combs daughter Peggy Ann's hair beside a sideshow wagon on RAS in 1953. Obviously the show's press department was using this photo to send to the editors in charge of the "Women's Section" in various newspapers enroute, as it says on the back — "Woman's 2 col Tues noon."

Seen here in their Sarasota, Fla., driveway with their new car in 1938, the Doll family were long time R.B.B. and B. Circus sideshow performers. They not only changed their family name of Schneider to Doll but acquired new first names as well. Left to right they are Daisy (Hilda), Grace (Frieda), Harry (Kurt) and Tiny (Elly) Doll (Schneider).

born with arm and leg deformities, wrote to Agricultural Commissioner J. A. Graham, North Carolina Fair manager Art Pitzer and the governor's wife: "Figures show Mr. Kelly absolutely wrong. One in every 16 babies is born with a major birth defect; nearly 8,000 were born in North Carolina alone last year. One of every 10 families is affected in some way by a major birth defect." Grant continued, "Freak shows were geared to ignorant and uneducated people. The reason Mr. Kelly is going out of business is that people are realizing handicapped people are people, too!"

She had a point. Most attractions left billed as a "Frog Boy" or "Ossified Lady" weren't traditional freaks, but severely handicapped folks earning a living by exhibiting themselves. They certainly weren't freaks in the public's eye any longer, once municipalities led the way in providing special parking spaces for them, ramps into buildings, wider elevators, lower telephones and drinking fountains, and sloping street curbs. However, government still didn't provide enough money for them to live securely.

The *Raleigh News and Observer* commented, "We have learned there are more humane means for [the malformed] to earn a livelihood and contribute to the world than being gawked at for profit." However, the paper

Giants never lose their appeal. Giant Gilbert Reichert stands beside Cal Lipes who has one of his midget horses from his grind show on Royal American Shows in 1952. Reichert was with the Lorow Bros. sideshow.

Frank Lentini had three legs, two sets of genital organs, four feet and sixteen toes. Born in Sicily in 1889 he came to the U.S.A. ten years later where he soon became one of biggest sideshow attractions of all time. He owned a sideshow for a time and died while touring with Walter Wanous. You always see him wearing socks because he was embarrassed by a mole on one leg.

didn't suggest any. The politicians and the media never asked the freaks — you had to read the weekly *Amusement Business* to hear their voices. North Carolina showman Harvey Boswell, besides spending years as a back-end operator, was also wheelchair-bound. His August 1968 *Amusement Business* rebuttal stated, "I am stared at, but it doesn't bother me. Nor does it bother the freaks when they are stared at on the way to the bank to deposit the hundred, hundred and fifty, two hundred-fifty and even five hundred per week that some of the more sensational oddities receive for their showing in sideshows."

Esther Blackmon "the Alligator-Skinned Lady" wrote in to *Amusement Business*, "I entered the business at age fifteen, and until that time I was a real 'freak,' a misfit among normal people, not accepted anywhere at schools, socials, or the business world. Once I was introduced to show-business, however, life changed for me, and I was able to become a happy, adjusted person. I own my home and I have not done this through welfare checks or charity but through my own labors. I only hope I can live out the rest of my life with the dignity and meaning that show business has given me."

Many Siamese twins toured on American midways as single-O shows. Here are the Blzek Sisters on Wortham's World's Greatest Shows in 1922. They died the next year in a Chicago hospital.

Ronnie and Donnie Galyon were born in Dayton, Ohio, in 1951. They are the world's oldest living set of conjoined twins and presently the world's only male conjoined twins. For many seasons, patrons could look through one of the windows in an air-conditioned house trailer to see them. They each have a political vote, two social security numbers but only one passport and live well in retirement. They were one of the last big freak attractions seen on American midways.

Jack W. Donahue "the Human Balloon" wrote, "I've been a sideshow performer for the past 30 years." He related working with old Charley Porter "the Ossified Man": "One day, folks in the tip told Charley how sorry they were for him. They knew a young man in town with the same condition. The family had a special driveway built and mirrors arranged in his room so people could drive by and wave to him. Once a month an ambulance took him to a movie. Charlie laughed in their face. He told them he didn't want their pity.

For 50 years he had been on tour and owned his own car and home and had two people on his payroll to take care of him, so he wouldn't be a burden to anyone."

A 1902 Michigan law making it an offense to display a human oddity commercially lay in limbo until dusted off by an overzealous district attorney in the early '70s. During the state fair, some acts were arrested right off the bally stand. In the November 9, 1974, *Amusement Business*, Irwin Kirby wrote in his opinion column, "Early calls, shows without interruption, sometimes twenty-five to thirty a day, no time for meals, and on the platform for as long as fourteen hours! Do these things add up to exploitation or to show business?" Answering his own inquiry, he pointed out, "The current freak show operators all have acts and people that have been with them for years. They don't seem exploited. These people own their homes and own and drive cars and are raising families."

When freak exhibitions came under the gun in Florida a few years later, showmen Ward Hall, Chris Christ and Dick Johnson, aided by the newly formed Outdoor Amusement Business Association, challenged the courts. The law backed down. If the showmen's case had failed, they were prepared to argue that one couldn't discriminate against a person's physical size or appearance,

and to suggest that the Miss America Pageant was also a freak show, since some of the girls had modified their bodies with silicone breast implants, nose jobs, tummy tucks and other beauty adjustments.

My only run-in with freaks was when I befriended Percilla Bejano "the Monkey Girl" and her husband, Emmett, during the mid-'90s. I met them in the museum at the International Showman's Association Trade Show in Gibsonton, Fla., one afternoon. Percilla wanted to stay for the night dance, but their ride wanted to go. I booked her a cab and gave her $30 for the fare. After they had left late that night, Percilla paged me and said, "You didn't give me cab fare, I couldn't pay the man." A week later I went around to her house in Lutz and she was very apologetic. She'd found the money tucked down in her purse bottom. "Did you pay the cab company?" I asked. "No," she giggled. I doubt she ever did.

The Bejanos had a fenced-in lot and a small bungalow with a nice front garden and a backyard full of goats and yapping dogs, as well as their old Airstream trailer. When I stopped to see them the next winter, Percilla was upset. Emmett was in the hospital, and she couldn't find anyone to take her to see him. Again, I volunteered. Inside, I soon knew what it was like to be stared at. We made an odd couple — a lady with a shadow beard and a ratty old scarf draped over her head, shuf-

fling along the hospital corridors with a fat guy toward the ICU.

Emmett lay there motionless. Drips, tubes and wires ran from him and monitors stood at the top of the bed. He lay covered except for his feet. Percilla waltzed up to his side and called out, "Emmett, it's Percilla — your one and only!" No response. She sang out again. Nothing. She tossed off the blanket and felt his skin. "Too dry, too dry. . . . I told them they had to keep putting lotion on him!" As she inspected his feet, the toe on one foot moved. "He's alive!" she called out enthusiastically. "Did you see that, Al? He's alive." That was the only sign of life in Emmett. It may have been his last wave to her. We didn't stay long.

Back in the van she was upbeat. The toe wiggle had done wonders. She wanted a quart of ice cream. It had to be this store, this brand, this flavor. We drove there and I got it. Back on the road she asked, "How much?" I said, "My treat." I stopped beside her gate and went around, opened the side door and helped her down. We spent some time chatting in the garden. When I left, I heard all this jingling in the back of the van. I thought something had broken loose. I stopped, turned and saw large silver coins covering the floor and my bed. I scooped them up. Around $30 in 50-cent pieces. Percilla's old pitch money!

Emmett died a few days later.

Working Acts
The Real Sideshow Entertainers

Here are the acts with Jack Halligan's World Fair Freaks posed on the bally on the Conklin Shows midway in 1933. On the very left is showman, magician, sword swallower Joe Kara. Next to him is Andrew Gawley from Meaford, ON, billed as "The Man with Steel Hands." Note the big bell over the talker's head.

"The guts of the sideshow are the pitches and working acts," according to sword swallower, sideshow builder and operator Red Trower. "If you consider a bunch of people sitting around in wheelchairs entertaining, your idea of entertaining and mine are two different things. Unless you're a medical doctor eyeing them up for an operation, they are not entertaining. That doesn't mean they are not nice people — I have a lot of respect for them. They make for nice banners on the front that you got to have so you can sell tickets."

Sideshowmen were no different from any other under-canvas entrepreneur in wanting the most show for the least money. Here, the novelty or "working act" shone. Why hire a freak who occupied only one stage when you could get a versatile couple who covered half the banners on your front? A 1915 *Clipper* ad read, "Man and wife: can do — punch, magic, marionettes, fire-eating, vent, mind-reading, Hindu mysteries, sword-walking, cremation illusion, wife pianist, both glassblowers." Ed Wood's "At Liberty" ad in a June 1921 *Billboard* offered, "For ten-in-one show: five people. Magician, fire-eater, world's greatest rope escape and illusion and electric chair. Smallest contortionist, mind-reading and Buddha." Perhaps one of the most unusual help wanted ads was this one, placed by sideshow operator Joe E. Hilton in March 1949: "Wanted: armless woman to handle big snake."

"Specialties," as variety numbers were called in the mid-1800s, were the most enjoyable acts presented on the stages of small-town opera houses, crummy theaters,

Working acts on the bally helped sell the show since you couldn't bring a featured freak out there. You have an oddball assembly of humans here with whips, ropes, fire and steel swords that would capture just about anyone's interest. This is 10-in-one operator Carrol Miller's sideshow ballying on the 1953 King Reid Shows. Miller is kneeling on the right with his wife behind him.

An early electric act. Look closely to see the wire coming from the right side and wrapping around the man's left arm. It's supplying the electric current that's coming off his finger and lighting the cigar in his mouth.

dive saloons and early fairground and circus sideshows. Charlie Roark credits his versatility as a sideshow performer and talker to his medicine-show days. "Best place in the world to get an education," he declared. "The medicine show I was with came into a town for a week and stayed two if business was good, doing a different show every night. It had to be a good show to keep them coming back. I learned all those old skits, 'Three o'Clock Train,' 'Thieves in the Pawn Shop'— surefire skits of pure corn. I played straight

(Above) Punch and Judy became the standard circus sideshow act. During the days of sideshow grift it diverted the ladies and children away from the cooch area. Once a staple entertainment at holiday beaches, amusement parks and sideshows it got sabotaged by the 1960s political correctness movement. One of the last practicioners here is Brent (Cheeko) DeWitt.

(Left) Ward Hall and John Trower (Little Red) at the first sideshow convention held during the Inkin in the Valley tattoo event at Wilkes-Barre, Pa. John first worked on circuses but for most seasons he made his living on sideshows. He did sword swallowing and knife throwing, as well as being a noted builder of sideshow apparatus and illusions. He also operated his own sideshows.

man to Smokey Bickman the comic. When he was sick, I blackened my face and his wife would do the straight parts." The carnival 10-in-ones were closer to medicine shows than anything else in show business.

"People are fascinated by fire, knives and electricity," said Red Trower. "A good fire act is a strong act. People always like the electric-chair act. Sword swallowing is strong — knives again. An escape artist is a fair working act if it isn't too slow an escape. Working acts have to be quick and to the point — five minutes, tops. People get bored easily. The sideshow is built for X capacity per hour."

The sideshow's appeal was its something-for-everyone approach. Some routines were standards, but the range of oddball specialty numbers was huge. One act might have made your stomach muscles tighten, while another brought on fits of laughter.

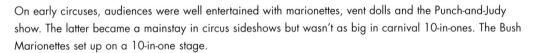

On early circuses, audiences were well entertained with marionettes, vent dolls and the Punch-and-Judy show. The latter became a mainstay in circus sideshows but wasn't as big in carnival 10-in-ones. The Bush Marionettes set up on a 10-in-one stage.

Melvin Burkhart was one of the best sideshow performers of his generation. Nobody was better at shoving an ice pick up their nose while making it look so pleasing. Here he is a few seasons after he retired in the 1990s having last worked for John Bradshaw in Coney Island. Showman Todd Robbins now wears Melvin's hat and carries on his legend.

The Punch-and-Judy act remained in circus sideshows to the end, but wasn't seen as much in later 10-in-ones. "People started to think it was too violent for the kids!" Red said.

"It got unpopular, like cigarette smoking." Over a century ago, New York City magic supplier W. J. Judd was the premier supplier of Punch-and-Judy accessories. Besides selling the carved figures, his 1874 *Clipper* ads offered foldable Punch-and-Judy frames to hold the small canvas puppet theater. Halifax, N.S., native Hal Harris, an old-time circus calliope player, was the last person advertising Punch outfits in *Amusement Business*. I bought the last one he made, in 1977 — the figures and theater all packed into a small wooden suitcase.

Sometimes in a carnival 10-in-one it was necessary to hold the tip for long durations. This called for a good "stall act." Dean Potter

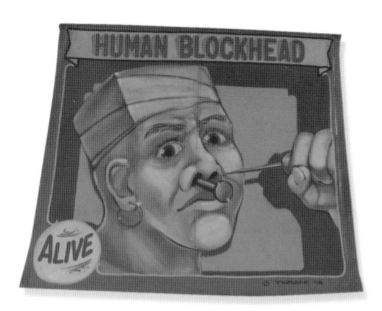

Blockhead banner painted by Ohio banner painter T. Frank was used on Tim Deremer's 10-in-one illusion show in the 1990s.

explained: "On Slim Kelly's sideshow we had Melvin Burkhart 'the Anatomical Man.' When we opened, Melvin would get up there and do magic, etc., for a half-hour. That helped keep folks on the catwalk. After that it was just bang-bang-bang — and you were set. I don't know if it would have worked if it wasn't for him working so long in the beginning."

Such stall acts had other uses. "Stall acts were used during the era of sex blow-offs," recalled Chris Christ. "We would keep something going on during the blow-off depending on what we had in the show. If the show was strong enough, we would do the electric chair.

Milo Vagge is seen here during his act in the Lorow Bros. 10-in-one on Royal American Shows in 1952. Club swingers and boxers were long-time favorites of sideshow audiences.

Regurgitation acts were unique and despite their suggested unpleasantness, went over well with sideshow audiences. The Great Waldo's specialty was swallowing mice but here he swallows differently colored ribbons and brings back up whatever color the audience calls for.

pitches. On Hall and Christ's sideshows in the '70s, Chris said, "I would always put the sword swallower on the 12-foot stage next to the fat man, then the fat man, then the blow-off. The sword-swallower would do his act and then lecture on the fat man and then make the blow-off opening from the stage steps. I had another stage down in that end of the tent for the knife-thrower. I would always have the fire-eater work on the blade-box stage before the blade box. Get them over there for an act first.

"We normally kept the show to 45 minutes, sometimes 30. In Dallas, on a big day during the peak periods, we took the blow and blade box out to make room for the people. Ward Hall got up there and moved the show. All the acts stayed on the stage. We could run through the show in 12 minutes."

Among the most dramatic working acts was gravage. Early circus sideshows often featured stone eaters — people who swallowed pebbles and other objects, then brought them back up. Other such "human ostriches" swallowed coins and live mice. In 1925, Hadji Ali, in his Coney Island show, swallowed 30 hazelnuts, an almond, three live goldfish, three silk handkerchiefs and 60 glasses of water. He brought the objects back up one at a time, in the order he swallowed them. A 1930s regurgitator known as "the Great Waldo" swallowed and brought back up

Today, acts do the glass box, nail board — stuff we kept in the truck for emergencies. We called them 'gazoonie acts.' We would have to get real short before we would use that crap. I preferred using illusions like 'Spidora' or 'the Headless Girl' as extras. We often had magicians who did

the lecturing and who did some acts, but I didn't use magic as an act itself because I didn't want to empty the tent out!"

Using whatever acts and freaks he had on hand, the sideshow operator would line up the performance, spacing out the dings and

The wave of new sideshow acts that started in the late 1980s and blossomed in the '90s has given the entertainment world many fine performers. Here is N.Y.C.'s Brian Bielemeier producing razor blades after swallowing them.

intact lemons, goldfish, frogs, rats and pocket watches. In another routine, he drank containers holding different colors of water and let the audience call out the colors they wanted him to shoot out of his mouth. These days, Todd Robbins' lightbulb-eating routine is a sideshow classic. "I have eaten enough broken glass to shit out a chandelier," he says. "When I fart, wind chimes play."

Old-timers used to swallow razor blades and a piece of string, then bring them back up with the razors evenly spaced out on the string. New sideshow acts today do the same routine with needles, as the old-fashioned razor blades are no longer easily available. Tim Cridland's routine of swallowing a piece of string and then cutting into his stomach flesh to pull it out is a tough act to watch, but the staging is brilliant. While the Great Hubbell stuck a rubber hose attached to a bicycle pump in his mouth and let an audience volunteer pump up his stomach to near-exploding size, Matt Crawley today goes the opposite way in blowing up a large rubber water bottle until it explodes.

As a teenager on Royal American Shows in the '40s, when his uncles the Lorows had the 10-in-one, Peter Manos assisted in the show's bullet-catch act. The Lorows had a guy with one of his front teeth drilled out so a .22 calibre bullet could fit inside. He'd get someone from the audience to drop a real bullet in the lower chamber of a rifle, then hand the gun to his wife and stand behind a small square of glass at the other end of the platform. She'd fire the gun, the glass would shatter, and he'd grab his face. After a few grimaces, he'd step to the front of the stage, remove his hands from his face and give the tip a big grin. The spent shell would be embedded in his tooth. He'd pull it out and pass it around. The act was a crowd-pleaser, as long as Peter yanked on the wire that ran the gimmick breaking the glass.

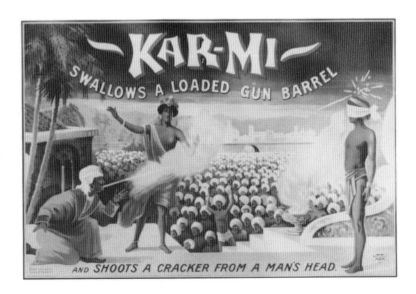

Shooting acts have been popular sideshow attractions. Shown in this photo given to me years ago is a poster used by the Great Kar-Mi swallowing a loaded gun and shooting a cracker from a man's head. The Kar-Mi were a 19th-century touring sideshow troupe.

One of the best sideshow bally acts were fire-eaters. On big fairs some sideshowmen would hire a couple of them so that a fire-eater could be on the bally all the time the show was open. At night there was nothing better than their flaming torches to stop a circus blow-off crowd or folks coming off the grandstand show at a fair.

Concealed in the stand that held the square of glass was a thin wire attached to a mouse-trap spring. The wire ran from its release mechanism down through a hole in the stage to where Peter sat, ready, underneath. When he heard the rifle fire, he yanked the wire. The guy onstage put the spent bullet in his tooth when he grabbed his face — his wife had palmed the real bullet and substituted a dummy blast.

Biting lead was okay, but the standard sideshow entree was either steel or fire. "I always thought the sideshow was naked if you didn't have a fire-eater and a sword swal-lower," Dean Potter said. "You needed them on the bally." Many sideshow operators hired an extra fire-eater or sword swallower for their big spots and kept one of them on the bally all the time. Henry Thompson preferred fire-eaters up on his bally when the night crowd exited the big top, because their burning torches were effective in stopping people long enough for him to launch into his opening.

Patience and persistence were needed in learning to swallow steel. Joey Givens said, "On Leola Conklin's sideshow I asked the sword swallower, 'How do you do that?' 'Tilt your head back and push,' he instructed. 'Get yourself a coat hanger and bend it and sand it. Get you a little rag with some corn oil on it and a garbage can. As long as you can get your gut, chest and mouth in a reasonably straight line, you've got it made. At first you'll gag and throw up, but you can unlearn the gag reflex.'" Consult a professional before trying this!

Chuckling, Joey added, "I learned standing over the garbage can going *whoo* — up, *whoo* — up, *whoo* — up. . . . But soon you don't need the corn oil. Once you've learned to swallow the coat hanger you can go on to a bayonet.

"I swallowed swords for Slim Kelly off and on for two years," continued Joey. "Whenever he needed someone, I'd swing in. That was a period when I wasn't doing an awful lot and was gaining weight. I didn't want to put on a dress! Previously I had worked as a lady sword swallower. Leona Lee was the best of them. She carried her own banner showing this blond girl standing there with a Model T-Ford above her. The

'kicker' on the banner read: 'The Only Woman in the World to Swallow a Model-T Axle.' She used a tent stake with the big gearhead on it, which she had sanded down and chromed. It was attached by two chains to a pole. She would get two volunteers from the audience to hold each end of the pole, while she would get underneath it. When she got into position she told them to lower away. She took about 18 inches of it in before signaling them to pull it back up."

Charlie Roark recalled another terrific old vaud specialty — Felix the Indian Clay Modeler: "While the sideshow band played for his act, Felix would take a big glob of clay and quickly fashion different animal heads. He told me that when movies first started, Edison made a kinescope movie of his act. He had played every variety theater in the country and worked on Ringling and many of the top sideshows and winter museums." Felix

Netzahualt's January 6, 1972, *Amusement Business* obituary gave his age as 96. He was a Pueblo Indian.

Another famous sideshow specialty act was that of Frank W. Blasser, known as "the Broom King" or "Yankee Whittler." His quick-carving act was a mainstay of dime museums

One of the longest-running sideshow acts was lightning sculptor Nabor Feliz, seen here in front of one of the R.B.B. and B. Circus bannerline wagons. Beside him is Sadie Anderson, the Leopard Skin Girl.

A 1920s sideshow on the C. A. Wortham Shows has a banner for J. C. Wood, one of the most interesting working acts of all time. His career went back to the early 1900s where right in front of you he would make a beard on his face of swarming bees. He also created a hat of bees and lay down on a cot covered in them. Afterwards he pitched the tip jars of honey.

and circus sideshows from the late 1800s until his death in 1921. And the 1908 Hagenbeck-Wallace Circus sideshow had no freaks but some outstanding working acts that included Veto Basile, "the Vegetable King," who sculptured faces out of vegetables.

Tank acts were also big on early circus sideshows — the larger shows even carried a glass-sided wagon for the "Man Fish" act. The

Musical acts were extremely good for sideshows as they could also create some excitement on the bally. Rudy Gaehler, shown here playing three clarinets at once, had been with the R.B.B. and B. Circus sideshow numerous seasons.

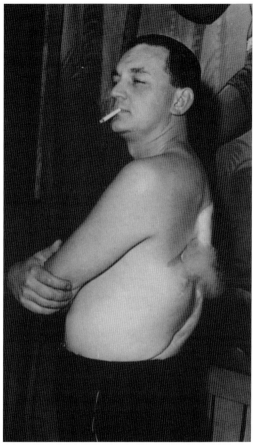

Earl Hall, billed as "the Man with Two Mouths" was a sensation on mid 20th-century sideshows. Today's anti-smoking crowd certainly wouldn't be interested in taking their kids in to see him.

performer smoked, drank and ate underwater, and some wrote on slates or read a book. Albert Kaylor's November 1915 *Billboard* ad

was straight to the point: "Cehio —'Human Fish': strictly sober, time underwater is two minutes. No tank. Ticket if far." A writer to

Billboard in that era commented, "In one day, the 'Human Fish' in the sideshow consumed underwater forty-eight bottles of soda water and a half bunch of bananas. The next day the sideshow had a sign on the glass pool — this show for sale!"

Clipper ads for cigarette fiends started appearing in the early 1870s. An act featuring a bony-framed person lying on a settee next to hundreds of cigarette butts went over well during World War I anti-smoking campaigns. In a May 1915 *Billboard*, Mose Wood's "At Liberty" ad stated, "Mose 'The Cigarette Fiend,' age twenty-seven, height five feet, weight sixty-three pounds, fourteen inches around waist, limbs the size of silver dollar. Have strong lecture."

Sideshow operator Jim Steinmetz, looking back to the '50s, recalled, "I used a working guy that was thin and looked emaciated as a cigarette fiend. We put some black makeup under his eyes, making him look gaunt and wasted. I sent the working crew out on the midway to gather up cigarette butts. We poured buckets of them on the stage and the ground around it. However, the public didn't like it. So we quit using that."

"I had 'Twisto the Human Pretzel,'" Malcolm Garey said. "This guy used to tie himself into a knot and then run through a barrel. He was so skinny I framed a show around him called 'Nicotine Nick — the

World's Worst Chain Smoker — Come in and See What Smoking Can Do to You!' The guy didn't smoke but was so skinny you could take your finger and thumb and circle his arm around the muscle. Nightly, he'd pick up cigarette buts off the midway and drop them around a big old chair that made him look even smaller. He had a TV, but mostly he would

Cuban Antonio Gawanda was a hit on the 1931 Ringling Bros. and Barnum & Bailey Circus sideshow.

220

be reading the paper. He had two cigarettes lit between his fingers like he was puffing them. Piles of butts lay around him in ashtrays and five-gallon buckets. He was a natural — quiet and didn't mind people staring at him."

Charlie Roark recalled a French-Canadian named Alfred Langevin. "He was an odd act that went over big on the Ringling sideshow when I was there. He'd been cartooned by Ripley. Alfred had a cigarette holder welded into the center of an eyewash glass. He put a cigarette in the holder, got it smoking and then held the glass up to his eye. Smoke came out his nose and mouth. He had an enlarged duct between the eyes and his nose and mouth cavities." Langevin would also inflate a balloon from a tube held to his eye as well as blow a whistle.

The hardest act to see in show business — trained fleas — always pulled crowds. They appealed to the whole family. A few dozen spectators crowded around a small table to watch "Tina the Wire-Walking Flea" do her act, followed by a crew of pests who kicked and juggled balls, pulled racing chariots, turned a gold merry-go-round and dived off a ladder into a small pool of water. A 1909 *Billboard* ad placed by Prof. Wilhelm Fricke offered showmen complete flea outfits. Claiming to have "the only flea act in America at this time," he revealed, "I use only

European fleas. No American or Sand fleas." Over the next 50 years there were plenty of other flea shows.

Irwin Kirby recalled European flea showman John Top going to see agent Irving Rosenthal about a location at Palisades Park. Unfortunately, John made the mistake of setting his satchel of large Belgian fleas on the office radiator and cooked his entire troupe! L.A. native Carl Lipes also trouped a flea show. After working Cleveland's Great Lakes Expo in 1936, he saw a doctor about red spots inside his arms. When the doc asked him what drugs he was shooting, Lipes replied that he fed his troupe of fleas there. The doctor told him, "You'd better find a doc specializing in mental illness. I'm just a GP!"

Easel acts were also good stall routines. An artist drew a sketch of a smiling face, then turned it over to show you the character frowning. Other artists could draw two sketches at once. Rag-picture artists used a large blackboard with pins driven into it. Rags of different materials and colors were put on the board in various ways to create scenes, landscapes and seascapes, plus bold images of animals or perhaps windmills. Sand drawing was a similar act using a special brush for applying the differently colored sands into the glass-fronted drawing surface set on an easel.

In one of the more unusual smoke acts, the performer created smoke pictures on an

One of the best sideshow entertainers was dwarf Bluey Bluey. He also worked in vaudeville and in movies. Showmen admired him for his sideshow magic, especially his "thumb tie" routine. Many showmen claimed he was the absolute best at performing it during the 1920s and '30s.

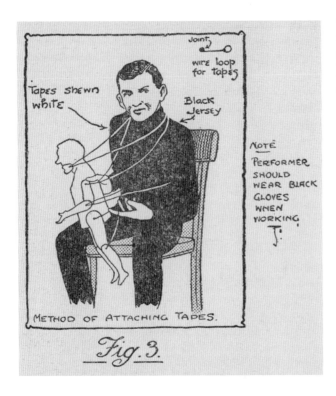

Joint

wire loop for tapes

Tapes shewn white

Black Jersey

NOTE

PERFORMER SHOULD WEAR BLACK GLOVES WHEN WORKING

J.

METHOD OF ATTACHING TAPES.

Fig. 3.

An instructional drawing showing how to work a shadowgraph figure.

stage for such a show was about twice as large as the Punch-and-Judy stage. The shadows of the performer's hands were thrown onto a white sheet across the little stage opening, and the act worked best at night when back-lit. Manipulation of the fingers created a few images, but top novelty silhouette workers used ready-made figures of stiff card or tin painted white. They were made to move, walk, talk and laugh by means of wires.

Some working acts were so unusual, they could have been billed as freaks. Andrew Gawley, billed as "the Man with Steel Hands," was 91 when he died in a Meaford, Ont., nursing home. He'd lost both hands in a buzz-saw accident at age 17, but managed to see America via the sideshow attraction route. His first artificial hands were carved from wood by his blind father, and were later used by a blacksmith as models for steel hands. The new hands, based on marionette mechanisms, gave him five separate grips, enabling him to even catch a ball. In the '30s, he worked for both Conklin Shows and Ripley's, and he later left the road to run a machine repair shop, fixing bicycles and sharpening skates.

William B. Doss, "the Man Who Grows" or "the Human Periscope," was featured in the early 1900s on Barnum & Bailey sideshows. A 1921 *Billboard* described his act: "Doss, a

enamel plate using a smoking torch. Lola Conklin, the famed half-and-half, besides working as a bearded lady and fire-eater, also created beautiful scenes on a porcelain plate using only her torches.

Hal Haviland, who presented a dog and pony act in the '60s and '70s, could add five minutes to a show by tearing a wad of newsprint and shaping it into a 10-foot-high tree. Paper tear acts were popular on early sideshows. In the 1920s, a Mr. Marshall in Wadsworth, Ohio, sold paper-tear designs fully

prepared and requiring no skill to work. For a dollar, he sent you 12 pieces — a skeleton, a monkey riding an elephant and ducks swimming. Patter came free with a $3 order. Other paper artists could quickly create flowers and other objects from colored tissue paper.

On a 1927 Coney Island sideshow, Professor Perry would cut out a silhouette of a person in the crowd and offer to do the same for others for a fee. "Shadowgraphs," or novelty silhouettes, were a popular late-19th-century act, but are scarce now. The

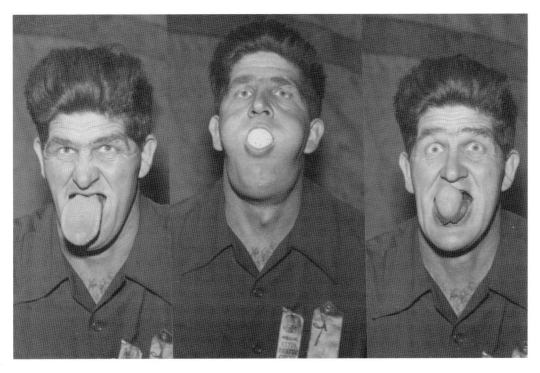

Along with "eye poppers" — guys that literally would shoot their eyes out of their sockets and pop them back in — were folks that stuffed huge amounts of balls and other objects into their mouths. This is the pitch card sold by Paul (Big Mouth) Williams. The writing on the ribbon pinned on him says Clyde Beatty Circus.

Pitch card for Solomon Stone, Lightning Calculator. Mental acts were good in sideshows and many who did them were also good lecturers. Their routines could certainly stretch the show when needed.

43-year veteran of circus and carnival sideshows, from his ordinary stature of six feet two inches gradually forces his head and body upwards to a height of eight feet! He can also extend the hand on his right arm a further eighteen inches." Another performer, Clarence E. Willard, could increase his height another two feet. He claimed he could accomplish this feat by stretching the muscles in his knees, hips, chest and throat.

A December 1921 *Billboard* announced that Johnny J. Jones's sideshow was offering the perfect act, "the Miracle Man." Baffling scientists and doctors, the performer's heart would stop beating for extended periods of time. You could hold a watch glass under his nose and no moisture would form. He would stop his circulation while a committee of men were asked to inspect him for a pulse.

Joe Kara and his wife Myril practising their "impalement act" in the 1930s. Joe was a Montreal magician known as KARS who could do most sideshow acts including sword swallowing. From the 1940s through the 1950s he toured his own girl shows and grind shows on Canadian midways.

Watching someone shove sharp pins through his flesh doesn't appeal to everyone, but human pin cushions went way back in sideshow lore. At the turn of the century, Shaw's *Book of Acts* recommended rubbing cocaine (available at the local drugstore) on your breast to dull the pain before inserting cut pieces of wire through the flesh. Pain acts were even seen on the family-oriented Ringling sideshow. One season during World War II, Kitty San Duna, a big, blonde German woman with blue eyes, worked there. "She would lay down on a nail board and her husband would place a big blacksmith's anvil on her chest," recalled Charlie Roark, who lectured for the act. "Two audience males were invited to hit the anvil with sledge hammers. One time there were no volunteers, so her husband and I swung the sledges. I missed the anvil and hit my foot. That was my last attempt at doing that. During her act the

In the early 20th-century, bird circuses were big on circus sideshows. They came along to replace rooster and cat orchestras. It was one of the sideshow acts that children could really enjoy. Note the fancy stitching depicting birds on the bird table stage cloth.

Through the 1930s and 1940s, Rasmus Neilsen spent numerous seasons on the R.B.B. and B. Circus sideshow billed as the Tattooed Wonder Man. However, his act was hanging weights from his various piercings.

sideshow band played the 'Anvil Chorus.'"

Showmen were continually coming up with gaffed or fake acts. Malcolm Garey described one he did himself in his sideshow: "I had to buy Sailor West's five-in-one to get him to teach the act to me. West had been bitten by a rattlesnake and the fingers on one hand were all messed up. He could no longer work the trick. He told me, 'If someone doesn't faint, leave the show or get sick right in front of you — you haven't done it right.' The secret was to not rush it.

"I would come out with the knife already in my wrist but under my cape. I walked along in front of the people and told them, 'I was in a severe automobile accident. When I woke up in the hospital I was informed they would have to amputate my hand at the wrist. Then, the medics felt that by doing invasive surgery they could save the hand but I would have a permanent hole through my wrist. Now I live

Nikola Tessla's patent for the electric coil goes back to 1859. Ads placed by Glen McWilliams in 1910 *Billboards* offered showmen an outfit for passing more than 500,000 volts of electricity through the body. Oil could be lit from the palms of your hands or an electric bulb while holding it in your mouth. The electric chair act is still with us.

can look at the knife, ask any questions you want, but *please* don't touch the knife! Any sudden movement in my wrist could sever an artery and I may bleed to death before you.' I would approach someone in the tip that was sweating or uneasy and stick the knife up close to them, then move the blade. The hole moved on the other side of my wrist and droplets of blood oozed out. I would scream, 'Oh my God, I hope it's not the main artery!' Then I would take the rest of the wraps off, quickly revealing the knife going in and coming out the other side of my wrist. It was all gaffed up with denture cream and iodine. The wrist looked all infected. That's when someone fainted or left the show quickly. Those who stayed went out talking about it."

Another sideshow standard was just as gruesome. The December 1888 *Clipper* announced, "Fred Wilson will surprise the amusement world with his patented electric act. The act will mimic in every way the electrocution of criminals as passed by the last legislature in this state (New York) which goes into effect January 1, 1889." The electric-chair act remains a staple in sideshow presentations. Mind reader Norm Johnstone recalls lecturer Don McGiver's masterful handling of the electric chair: "He would have a two-foot-long, four-inch-square piece of wood burst into flames when he turned the switch on. The lady sitting in the chair would

with this hole in my wrist. At school I would drop a coin through to impress other kids. I have been examined by doctors all over the country and they haven't proven it to be phony. If there is anyone in the audience with a bad heart, please don't look at this!'

"I would bring my hand slowly from under the cape and reveal the butcher knife stuck completely through my wrist, which was done up in some cloths. I slowly began unwrapping them while telling the crowd, 'I'm going to pass along in front of you. You go into agonistic convulsions while Don reached behind the curtain and threw a handful of horse hair on a hot electric grill, giving off a smell like burning flesh. People fainted."

As sideshows dwindled on midways, the last acts you saw on them were working acts. The rubber girl became the girl in the blade box, and Miss Electro was the old-time electric-chair act. Impalement acts — knife and hatchet throwing at a pretty assistant — were still around. People would still stop to see the fire-eater and be amazed by sword swallowers. Today there are more pain acts than ever. New sideshow performers eat light-bulbs, walk on glass shards, stick pins in themselves and lie down on beds of nails. While the freaks are long gone, the guts of the old-time sideshow — the working acts — are still with us.

Chapter 14

Dime Museums and Amusement Parks

Dave Rosen's 1930 Wonderland Sideshow at Coney Island Amusement Park didn't have the luxury of a 120-foot bannerline. Rosen's outfit is jammed in between a game booth and a hot dog stand. Doc Garfield, — the man without a skull — is the feature, and seen here wearing a sweater and skull cap on the bally. Doc went on to own numerous sideshows. Fat lady Jolly Viola is putting in her 7th season. Seated next to her is "Elephanto" The Elephant Girl while sword swallower "Grendol" stands behind her. Little Jenny is the dwarf lady. Not in the photo were Edema The Man with the Reversible Body and Princess Helena the "Miracle Girl" who was putting in her 9th year. The man with twisted legs may be Brownwell the Fish Leg Man. Note the signs proclaiming — No Extra Charge. This was after N.Y.C. authorities raised a big stink over extra charge blow-offs.

In the third quarter of the 19th century, the boom in dime-museum shows paralleled the growth in the outdoor sideshow business. Many sideshow operators, or those with experience on such enterprises, became owners of dime museums, where fairground and circus sideshow people found needed winter work. In the 1880s George Middleton, a privilege and sideshow operator, piloted the Kohl and Middleton dime-museum empire in Chicago and the Midwest.

After Barnum's New York City museum burned in 1865, one-time Barnum sideshow operator G. B. Bunnell became the Big Apple's "Museum King." Bunnell's Great Dime Museum opened in the Bowery in October 1879. Attractions were P. T. Barnum's great sensation "the Tattooed Greek," "the Marvel-lous Talking Bird with a Human Brain," "Toby the Wonderful Educated Pig," "the American Giantess," "the Circassian Princess," "the Bearded Girl," "the One-Pound Baby," "the Egyptian Juggler," "Winston the Humorist," "Punch and Judy," "Evarts the Magician" and "the Infernal Regions." Also on display were a baby elephant, humorous farces, panoramic views, statuary, paintings and hundreds of rare curios. In November, Bunnell opened a second museum on Brooklyn's Washington Street, and Bunnell's Touring Museum opened in December, in the Athenian Hall in New Haven, Conn. Then on to New Jersey and other New York state venues with the giantess "Ibonia," Zoa Melike "the Tattooed Man" and a bearded girl.

Early N.Y.C. Museum of Anatomy. The money in these operations came from patrons seeking consultation with resident doctors after seeing wax figures showing a wide range of diseases.

Front cover of the catalogue to Stanhope and Epstean's New Dime Museum in Chicago. Listed on the front are all the various departments. The key was having a central downtown location.

Capt. Costentenus's tours on various sideshows, including Bunnell's, lead the way for tattooed women and men to enter the sideshow exhibition business. In the 1870s, George Bunnell became the N.Y.C. museum king following in Barnum's footsteps.

Fairground showman Frank Blitz didn't miss a winter without having a show out in halls or stores. In October 1879, his Callander and Blitz Museum closed its summer season at the Richmond, Va., fair and opened the winter tour in November in Jersey City. The show went through the eastern states and into Canada, featuring Blitz's magic act, glass-blowers, a fire-eater, a juggler and marionettes. When the John Robinson Circus closed in Baton Rouge in December, its sideshow went on playing dates billed as "the

DON'T FAIL TO VISIT

London Dime Musee.

(INCORPORATED)

312=14=16 State St., Opposite Siegel, Cooper & Co.'s

CHICAGO

4 Large Curio Halls · 3 Theatres · Big Vaudeville Show

The Great Fitzsimmons Fight and The Original Midway Dancers

FIRST-CLASS FOR LADIES' GENTLEMEN AND CHILDREN

ADMISSION 10c TO ALL   OVER

NELSON & BRITT FIGHT

A small card-stock handout used in advertising the London Dime Museum in Chicago around the turn of the 20th century. Both the oriental dancers and the Great Fitzsimmons fight movie were draws on circus and carnival midways.

BARNUM'S AMERICAN MUSEUM,

Corner of Broadway and Ann Street,

NEW YORK,

Opposite St. Paul's Church and the Astor House, contiguous to the City Hall, Park Fountain; and in the immediate vicinity of the Irving House and all the Principal Hotels.

PHINEAS T. BARNUM, PROPRIETOR.

Sketch of Barnum's American Museum from the back of an 1850 pitch memoir of Robert Hale's the English Quaker Giant.

Creole Combination." It featured giant A. Belmont Creole, the Belmont Brothers (bar performers), Professor Dizatz "the Fire King," "the Hero Brothers" (black comedians), "Happy Jack Lawton" the clown and a demonstration of the phonograph.

In a December 1928 *Billboard* article, "The Good Old Days of the 'Dime Museum,'" Barry Gray described his 1879 visit to Worth's Museum at Chatham Square in New York's Bowery district. A dime got him in. Upstairs he saw Professor Hutchings's exhibition of lightning calculating, several freaks and Captain Contentatus "the Tattooed Greek." Downstairs, a half-hour variety show took place in the Bijou Theater, and "Dante's Inferno" followed in a smaller theater. Both theaters were at street level so patrons could be dumped outside easily on big days. The uppermost floor held the menagerie animals, slot machines, candy and food counters, a glass-blower's stand, shooting galleries and games of chance. Animal noises blocked out the moans of game losers. Circus owners often

(Left) Kohl and Middleton were both circus sideshowmen who parlayed their showland expertise into an 1880s chain of dime museums and theaters based around three dime museums in Chicago and others in Midwest cities.

(Right) Photo pitch card sold by dwarf Che Mah. He was two-foot-four. The back of the photo says it was taken in 1898 on his 60th birthday while he was with the Buffalo Bill Wild West Show. He was well off and later retired to Knox, Ind. He was born in Ningpo, China, and died in 1926.

placed exotic animals with museums over the winter, while Charles Reiche and other N.Y.C. animal dealers rented out animals for modest rates. Museum hours ran from 10 to 10, and Sunday crowds often covered the weekly nut. If there was a lineup to get into the variety stage show, the act that had just worked was put on again and again until the lingerers left and a new crowd came in.

Most dime museums were winter-only operations, but the July 1881 *Brooklyn Eagle* noted that the well-ventilated G. B. Bunnell's Washington Street Museum stayed open all year. The first-floor theater seated 200, and the basement held curiosities plus the

"grotto" of waterfalls and mechanical devices. The main draw that year was the Chinese dwarf Che Mah, who Bunnell claimed was paid $100 weekly in gold. Che Mah estimated his personal fortune at

This Oct. 19, 1885, four-page program for William Austin and Frank P. Stone's Boston dime museum lists Prof. Hutchins as the lecturer and Major Nutt as the reserve seat agent. All four pages are ringed with local advertising. One set performance of vaud and musical acts ending with a four-person comedy titled *Wanted — A Male Nurse* took place at 1:30, 5, 7:15 and 10 o'clock. Another set performance piece featuring Sam Lucas — colored comedian, the Human Python — Cheltra, and the resident stock company's one-act play, *Mike McCarthy at The Club*, went on at 11:15, 3:15 and 8:30.

$75,000. The show also featured two semi-nude Zulus who sang, did a savage war dance and hurled spears at targets. The next act, the decapitation of a man, was at the far end of the room. Some mediocre singers helped thin

The third page of the Oct. 19, 1885, Austin & Stone Museum program lists the museum department features that included Herr Haag the original "Elastic Man" and the held-over Fannie Mills — the girl from Sandusky, Ohio. Fannie wears 19" long shoes. Also in the line-up were Lewis C. Smith lecturing on his Arctic experiences, the bearded Mille Rosa and a Punch-and-Judy show. Coming up was the Fat Ladies Convention.

Pitch booklet of Che Mah the Chinese Dwarf. The Popular Publishing Co. of N.Y.C. specialized in the printing of these booklets and pamphlets for sideshow people.

A group of sideshow people working at Jack Schaffer's World Museum at Paterson, N.J., in 1939. The man standing is Keller-Relleck from Europe, billed as "the man that can pass through a keyhole." He carried a small plywood keyhole that he wriggled his body through.

the crowd and more people came in. Bunnell's averaged 700 patrons nightly.

Circus man W. C. Coup is credited with bringing dramas into dime museums. Freaks were considered window dressing as the money was made by presenting New York City plays (whose rights could be bought cheaply) after their boondock tours. Packing in drama crowds depended on selecting the right plays — believe it or not, the Brooklyn Museum's 5,000 weekly visitors favored Shakespeare! Patrons got into the gallery for a dime, and a second dime got them a better floor seat. Thirty cents secured a good chair in the orchestra and 50 cents more, a box seat.

In 1879, Dr. George O. Starr introduced continuous performances at Bunnell's Bowery dime museum, and other operators soon adopted the policy. Vaud theater king Franklin Keith brought the practice to vaudeville, whose arrival in the 1890s ended the dime-museum era. John Kodet, a former staffer at Worth's Museum, opened the Harlem Museum at 125th Street in 1913, later claiming, "I'm the man who brought museums back to New York City." Max

(*Left*) Keller — the man who can put himself through a keyhole — kept an autograph book containing photos and brief notes from those he worked with in circuses, dime museums and sideshows. I acquired it in the 1990s. Here is the page beside Frank Graf's photo listing the shows he was on at Coney Island.

(*Right*) Tattooed man Frank G. Graf was a fixture in the post-First World War I era sideshows at Coney Island. Many acts like Graf made their home in Coney Island or in N.Y.C. and its surroundings and were not interested in road work. They could work Coney Island in the summer and dime museums and vaud theatres in the city during the winter.

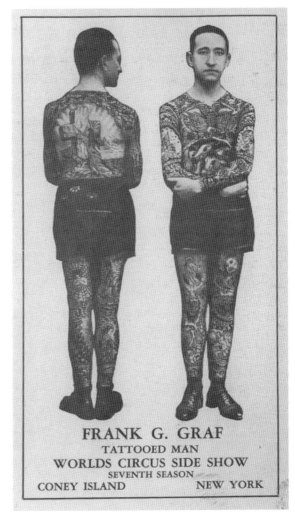

FRANK G. GRAF
TATTOOED MAN
WORLDS CIRCUS SIDE SHOW
SEVENTH SEASON
CONEY ISLAND   **NEW YORK**

Schaffer and William Schork opened Hubert's Museum in October 1925 on West 42nd Street where their colorful street frontage and enlarged lobby photos of acts drew punters inside. Seven stages crowded the 45-by-75-foot exhibition space. Adults paid 15 cents in the daytime and a quarter at night. Children got in for a dime anytime.

Hubert's became known for its performing fleas but other vermin also claimed the stage. The International Mutoscope Reel Co.'s 1933 *Billboard* ad read: "Cockroach Races!! An actual race track with ten live cockroaches running hell-bent for leather over hurdles." The average racer lived five months and the supplier shipped new ones promptly, though most operators likely picked up new thoroughbreds in their own tenement houses.

Robust Times Square action kept Hubert's and its last manager, showman Woo Foo, on life support until it closed on November 1, 1965. The place switched over to all games. Harold Smith, of magic and musical-glass fame, stayed

The following program is visible to the naked eye and must be seen to be appreciated.

Introductional Lecture of Training Fleas:

ACT I
Chariot Race

ACT II
Prince Henry, the Juggler

ACT III
Playing Foot Ball

ACT IV
Paddy Carrying a Flag and Jumping Through a Hoop

ACT V
The Flea Hotel

ACT VI
Rudolph Operating the Merry-Go-Round

ACT VII
Several Fleas Dressed in Costume Dancing to Music

The Flea Circus must be seen to be believed and once seen it will never be forgotten. It can all be seen without the aid of a magnifying glass. A very interesting lecture accompanies the performances.

SEE IT AT

HUBERT'S MUSEUM
228-232 West 42nd St.   New York City

TRAINED FLEAS
NOW SHOWING AT
HUBERT'S MUSEUM
228-232 West 42nd St.   New York City

Souvenir folder from William Heckler's flea circus at Hubert's Museum. One side lists the acts the fleas will do and the other side announces his lecture on the flea. His son Roy inherited the business and kept it going at Hubert's where it remained the main draw until a few years before the place closed.

(Left) Charlie Lucas as he appeared in Lou Dufour's "Africa Speaks or Darkest Africa" style sideshows. Charlie had been around sideshows since the late 1920s as an act and also as a manager of African-American entertainers.

on, managing two shifts of cashiers and change men. He noted in *Amusement Business*, "We're still getting asked where the fleas are."

The mecca for show folks was Coney Island, with its own style of banner painting and its milieu of game inventors and ride manufacturers. Unfortunately, the fall in popularity of Coney Island paralleled the demise of Hubert's Museum. My first visit, one rainy

(Above) Giant Buck Nolan working at Hubert's Museum, N.Y.C., in the late 1950s. The operation was winding down with Charlie Lucas (Woo Foo), the manager.

Some of the first sideshows at Coney Island were under tents and operated by road sideshowmen. Note the crude banners on this one on the Bowery area. Eventually the place would have its own banner painters, ride manufacturers and three amusement parks.

HUBERTS' MUSEUM – CONEY ISLAND.

SEASON – 1926

In the 1920s Coney Island could have three or four sideshows. Here's an interior view of Hubert's Museum on the boardwalk in 1926. The lecturer walked the patrons down one side and then out along the other side. Note the lights and mirrors on the building pillars to try to flash it up.

1930s amusement park sideshow. The show is in a permanent building but the operators have virtually copied a midway 10-in-one with the walkway (catwalk) and pit curtain. The double-sized banners tilted toward the crowd really help to sell it. Note the early "gyro" type ride in the background.

For a number of seasons (late 1930s to 1940s) Lou Dufour operated an all–African-American sideshow on the Conklin Shows midways and at the CNE in Toronto. The whole show was done by Charlie Lucas and several women, including his wife.

March morning in 1990, I didn't see it at its best. One was thankful for the light even a dull day provided, as this was no place to be after dark. Everything was boarded up or behind graffiti-covered steel shutters. Both the Astro Wheel and the Cyclone were just large, dull metal-and-wood silhouettes against a gray background. Hot-dog legend Nathan's Famous was barely open. Only one side of the joint served the lunchtime crowd — me and a crew of garbage collectors.

It was hard to imagine this place was once home to three amusement parks and many sideshows. Louis Hickman's Seaside Museum, the first sideshow, went back to 1886. Dreamland Park lasted from 1904 to 1911 and Luna Park from 1903 to 1946. Steeplechase, the longest-lasting, ran from 1897 to 1965.

In 1904, Sam Gumpertz became the manager of Lilliputia, a midget city, and the next year he exhibited a tribe of non–head-hunting

This is in one of Lou Dufour's African-American sideshows on Conklin Shows. Most of the acts were basic sideshow numbers including a wicked-looking sword ladder and nail board performed by lovely semi-nude ladies.

PROF. VICTOR A. PERRY

LECTURER & DEMONSTRATOR

RESIDENCE
254 W. 39 ST., N.Y.CITY

BOARDWALK SIDE SHOW
CONEY ISLAND

This photo and business card for Professor Victor A. Perry (the Candy Kid), a lecturer and demonstrator at the 1920s Boardwalk sideshow at Coney Island was also in Keller's autograph book. Note the gold-tipped lion's claw he's wearing, hanging from one button. Many showmen wore them or an Elk's tooth.

weeks in Cuba.

After World War I, the Coney sideshow field became crowded. Alexander Rosen opened Wonderland, and when he died, his son David ran it into the 1950s. In the '20s, Hubert Muller established Hubert's Museum on the boardwalk, where vet talker Jimmy Davenport turned 700 people an hour. Each turn grossed the show $70. Louis Newman and Sam Wagner opened World's Circus Sideshow on Surf Ave. in 1922, and later, Fred Sindell opened another seaside freak-a-torium.

In the late '40s, Wagner told an interviewer he had spent 35 of his 60 years running sideshows at Coney. He described himself as a simple, home-loving man whose job was a combination manager, nursemaid and advice dispenser to a mob of midgets, giants, bearded ladies, three-legged men and lion-faced boys. His building was big and airy, stretching from Surf Ave. to the Bowery, with entrances at both ends. Fourteen platforms — one for each act — were placed six feet apart. Wagner claimed he had exhibited over 2,000 freaks, with "Olga the Bearded Lady" being his best draw.

A 1938 *Billboard* article noted that Coney's 1,000-foot-wide, 2.5-mile-long amusement zone held 60 bathhouses, 70 ball-toss games, 13 carousels, 11 roller coasters, five tunnels of love, three funhouses, two waxworks, six penny arcades, 20 shooting galleries, three freak shows and over 200 eating joints. A 1956 *Variety* piece

Bontocs. He managed Dreamland Park until it burned down in 1911. "I just drifted into the freak game, ending up with a pit show due to a bad debt," he told an interviewer. "I made money. Now I have agents around the world keeping an eye out for unusual attractions." He opened his Eden Musée in 1916 and then his sideshow called Dreamland. The usual season was 20 weeks at Coney Island, then another six weeks of fairs, followed by 12

(Right) John Bradshaw makes the bally on his first full-season sideshow at Coney Island in a building leased by Dick Zigun. Behind him is Astroland Amusement Park and in front of him the boardwalk. A rainy Saturday or Sunday could ruin the whole week for him. Note the new "human cigarette factory" banner painted for Otis Jordon.

John Bradshaw from Richmond, Va., first worked on a Ward Hall–Chris Christ sideshow unit run by Dick Johnson in 1973. From 1974 through 1976 he worked for Whitey Sutton swallowing swords and doing the lecturing. Then he framed his own shows and except for a couple of missed seasons was out until 1992. He developed his sideshow skills on the Whitey Sutton side show in the 1970s. He's making an opening with sword swallower Diane Falk behind him.

called Coney the "popcorn peninsula," describing it as "drab as usual with overhead valentines extolling such virtues as elephant-skinned damsels, turtle lassies, human volcanos, three-legged men and sabre-swallowers. The resort is an architectural eyesore, a collection of flea-bitten, peeling fire-traps housing a motley assortment of dubious games of skill and dispensing heavily fried non-digestable comestibles. Nothing is being done by private

Mark Frierson banners are hung on the front of the boardwalk building John Bradshaw first used. There was no elevated bally; you were right on the boardwalk by the beach and the ocean.

This is Otis Jordon working on Ward Hall–Chris Christ sideshow. He was one of the last freak attractions driving his own camper truck and enjoying his life on carnival sideshows. In the early1980s he was stopped from working on the Sutton sideshow at the N.Y. State Fair at Syracuse. sideshow owner Elsie Sutton soon gave up and folded the show. There were no buyers for it.

Dick Zigun's Sideshow by the Sea Shore across from the famous Cyclone roller coaster continues to operate each season. Upstairs is a museum dedicated to Coney Island amusements and annually, Todd Robbins operates a summer sideshow school here.

enterprise to stem the decaying tide of Coney Island's shabby carnival chaos."

Bob Bells advertised for sideshow acts in a June 1975 *Amusement Business*, but sideshow operations wouldn't grace Coney for two decades more, when showman John Bradshaw, tired of road expenses, tried it. Dick Zigun, a former Yale student, rented an old arcade at 12th Street and

Boardwalk near the Astro Wheel. His plans were to put on art, musical and cultural events. Someone brought him and John together, and John brought a small sideshow in for Labor Day weekend as a trial. It did well enough for Bradshaw to come back the next season.

Zigun provided the space and ticket sellers, and cleaned the place for 40 percent of the first

Nothing has changed much in the sideshow world. If you are not doing anything, grab a snake and get out on the bally. Here EEK the Geek, an albino python and an Indian couple work the bally on Dick Zigun's Sideshow by the Sea Shore in 2004 when members of the Circus Historical Society visited for a day.

Burkhart working for me. He said, 'You're not scared to ask for the money!' 'Well, no business, no show,' I told him.

"Payroll was $2,225 a week. I needed $3,800 to break even. On a good Sunday you could take in $2,500 with tickets and the inside. Saturday was fair and the rest of the week slow. If you lost Sunday you were dead. Admission was a $1 on slow days and $2 on fast days. On the Fourth of July I started at $2 and went up to $3.

"Inside were 12 acts. Otis Jordon was the feature and a good worker. No trouble. He was 30.5 inches tall. When I brought him up to New York I changed his billing from 'Frog Boy' to 'the Human Cigarette Factory.' I had a new banner painted for him — he really liked that. Before, we pitched him as having the body of a frog and head of a human. He rolls a cigarette with his lips, lights it, swallows it, brings it out with the lighted end inside his mouth. He liked to dress in a shirt with a bolo tie and just socks, no shoes. He was a great

draw. People would come back and see him two or three times. When he pitched his photo card he asked for a donation. Most gave a buck. Often girls would come up and kiss him and give him $10!

"Everyone had to work bally," continued Bradshaw. "I broke in new workers to talk out front. When they finished their act I told them to grab a snake and a girl and get out there. After three weeks they would be giving a singsong spiel. I would change the pitch on them — 'Inside we have a man who drinks burning gasoline like you drink iced tea.' I used the two-headed pig in the blow and had the mouse pitch and the blade box. My blade-box spiel was short and to the point: 'This young lady makes her living this way. You can come up and see her with a donation of no less than 50 cents.' You had to use those exact words.

"Some days the inside did more than the tickets. It was a dollar to get in, a dollar on the blade box and the blow was 50 cents to a dollar. The blow only held 40 people or so. However, at 10 shows a day it was good money. Lots of great acts would come out from the city and want to work. They'd show me some spectacular trick. They'd work for three days but couldn't keep going. They would say, 'After the show we are going to party.' I told them, 'After the show closes we go to bed — beat!'"

$3,500 and 50 percent of proceeds beyond that. "First season there I didn't have a blow-off," said Bradshaw. "We took up a donation in the seats for the guy that did pins. I had Melvin

Chapter 15

Store Shows, Theaters and Whale Carcasses

In the 1920s–30s Fred LaReine had sideshows at various East Coast parks, including Coney Island. In the winter he had store shows and units out on vaudeville circuits. This is the cast at his March 1933 Paterson, N.J., Market St. Museum. Note Clicko in the center and the Men from Mars on the upper stage holding musical instruments. Note the difference in the half-and-half's legs. He/she is standing first on the left at floor level. No trouble assembling a big cast in the hungry 1930s, including two fat gals.

Unemployment was the greatest fear in poorly paid show business. Aerialists and elephant trainers had a tough time finding winter work. Freaks and sideshow hustlers were in some ways better off than the average performer, as there were many enterprises off the showground that could use their acts or services in the off-season. Winter sideshows turned up regularly in vacant stores on main-street America. This tradition of showing in vacant rooms here went back to the curiosity showmen of the early 19th century.

Booklet outlining the attractions inside Dr. Linn's Museum of Anatomy on Main Street in Buffalo, N.Y. The museum operated 9 a.m. to 10 p.m. daily with Fridays from 2–6 reserved for Ladies ONLY.

Anatomy store shows, which featured cases of diseased body parts, and usually ended with a consultation with a doctor,

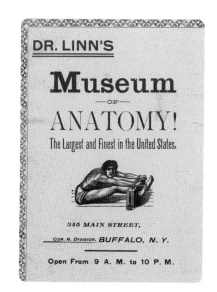

DR. LINN'S

Museum
—OF—
ANATOMY!

The Largest and Finest in the United States.

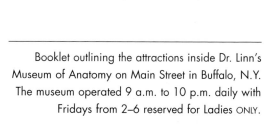

345 MAIN STREET,

COR. N. DIVISION. BUFFALO, N.Y.

Open From 9 A. M. to 10 P. M.

☞ No person should fail to pass an hour or two in examining the marvels and wonders of Nature displayed in this collection, comprising over

2 000 MODELS OF THE HUMAN BODY!
IN HEALTH AND DISEASE.

CURIOSITIES and MONSTROSITIES!

ILLUSTRATIONS OF PROGRESS OF LIFE.

PATHOLOGICAL CASES,
ILLUSTRATING HIDDEN LIFE WITHIN LIFE.

HIDDEN WONDERS OF THE WORLD
And Beauties of Nature now revealed, showing the Handicraft of Man.

☞ Striking unheard of sights never before exhibited to the public, comprising Phenomena almost Fabulous in the Annals of the World,

COLLECTED TOGETHER AT A COST OF OVER $200,000.00.

OPEN DAILY FROM 9 A. M. TO 10 P. M.
SUNDAYS 2 TO 10 P. M.   LADIES, FRIDAYS, 2 TO 6.

Back cover of a booklet describing the wonders of Dr. Linn's Museum of Anatomy that claims to have 2,000 models of the human body on display.

Broadside advertising the American Museum of Anatomy For Gentlemen Only. Added attraction — The Missing Link.

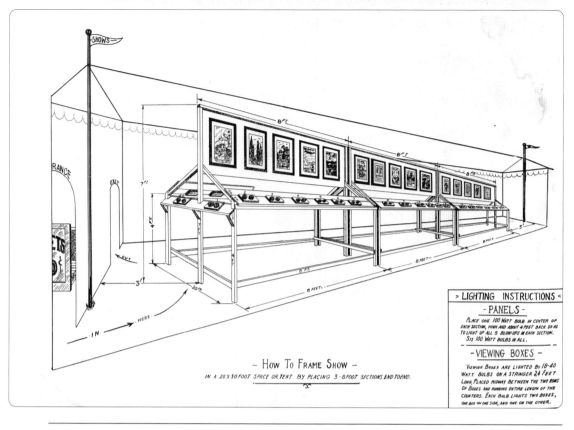

~ HOW TO FRAME SHOW ~
IN A 20 X 30 FOOT SPACE OR TENT BY PLACING 3 - 8 FOOT SECTIONS END TO END.

> LIGHTING INSTRUCTIONS <
- PANELS -
PLACE ONE 100 WATT BULB IN CENTER OF
EACH SECTION, HIGH AND ABOUT 4 FEET BACK SO AS
TO LIGHT UP ALL 5 BLOW-UPS IN EACH SECTION.
SIX 100 WATT BULBS IN ALL.

- VIEWING BOXES -
VIEWING BOXES ARE LIGHTED BY 18-40
WATT BULBS ON A STRINGER 24 FEET
LONG, PLACED MIDWAY BETWEEN THE TWO ROWS
OF BOXES AND RUNNING ENTIRE LENGTH OF THE
COUNTERS. EACH BULB LIGHTS TWO BOXES,
ONE BOX ON ONE SIDE, AND ONE ON THE OTHER.

A sketch showing how to set up one of Charles T. Buell's peep shows inside a tent or storefront. His *Billboard* ads claimed his shows could be operated with only two people with very little nut (expenses). His depiction on slides of Opium Dens, White Slavery and underworld gangsters did well anywhere.

always did well in rented rooms. The doctors (of sometimes questionable certification) charged a small fee for the consultation but made their money selling cure-alls. People feared sexual diseases and felt more at ease showing their ailments to a traveling doctor rather than their family physician.

Frank A. Robbins, on Parker Greater Shows, extended his 1918 pit sideshow season 15 weeks with a winter traveling museum. His acts only had two weeks off at Christmas. Besides sideshow operators, many hustlers exhibited wax outlaw outfits, miniature worlds, unborn shows, wildlife and stiffs inside stores over the winter. Although they couldn't put a Ferris wheel or merry-go-round in most stores, even small commercial spaces could be adapted for something like A.

T. Wright's "original, non-breakable laughing mirrors." As the originator and vendor of such an attraction, Wright claimed, "My mirror show is the best storefront show — only two people needed."

The Depression years saw almost all the summer sideshow people in store shows for the winter. As the 1931 season closed, Slim Kelly opened his November store show in Springfield, Mass., then moving to Richmond, Va., and Norfolk. He featured "Bluey-Bluey," "Coo-Coo the Bird Girl," John Williams "the Alligator Man," "Zipp the African Pinhead" and Mr. and Mrs. Cliff Karns with their "Fat Follies." A "Prison Show" and "Hidden Secrets" were extra attractions. Future 10-in-one operator and monkey speedway operator Glenn Porter was the inside lecturer.

After the Beckmann & Gerety midway closed its season, both Cash Miller and Pete Kortes took their sideshows indoors. Kortes' show opened in Port Arthur, Tex., going on to Galveston. "Victor-Victoria" was in the annex, and Eddie Breitenstine had his weird boys "Eko and Iko" there for a spell. Kortes's regulars were fat lady Alice from Dallas, Nabor Feliz "the Pueblo Indian Clay Modeller," armless artist Barney Nelson and Walter L. Cole "the Skeleton Dude." Miller's winter operation opened in Baton Rouge with future showman Ray Cramer on the front and wife, Mildred, as lecturer. The blow featured "Jean-Jeanette."

MILLERS TRAVELLING MUSEUM. WORLD FAIR FREAKS.

In the summer, Cash Miller and his wife operated sideshows and walk-through attractions on various midways and then inside stores during the winter. Cash is credited with framing Ripley's first touring road museum. Here is his crew standing around the blade box on his World Fair Freaks in the early 1930s.

Big-time 10-in-one operator Carl Lauther opened Lauther's All-Star Museum in November, in Bridgeport, Conn., on the second floor of a Main Street address. Laid out in a 60-by-80-foot space, the show featured Percilla "the Monkey Girl," the "Woo Foo" torture act, Laurello "the Man with the Revolving Head," two pygmies, an escape artist, a mentalist, a Buddha reader, a half-and-half in the blow-off plus a "Prison Show" and a unit of Dufour's "Naked Truth" shows. Whitey Sutton worked the front under a large electric sign composed of 265 lights. No

Most times, storefront showmen were lucky if they got a small vacant store space on the main drag. Ray Marsh Brydon has scored a big space on a corner for his World's Fair Museum. Adults 15 cents — children a dime. He claimed to square the Ripley's Believe It or Not name in his advertising by saying that many of the acts had worked for Ripley.

In the late 1920s Lou Dufour had put together a dozen or more Life Shows that he booked onto carnival midways. In the winter, he put them out as store shows or add-on blow-offs for sideshowmen operating winter-store sideshows. Here's one of Lou's outfits set up inside a building.

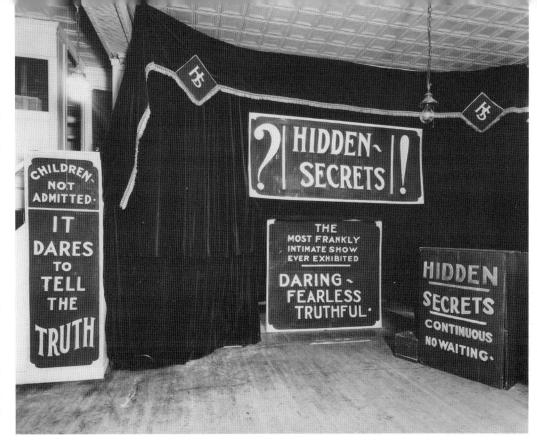

doubt the biggest job on teardown was packing away all those bulbs!

John T. McCaslin's Baltimore dime-museum sidewalk bally was stopped by police for too much noise. He moved it inside the lobby and found business improved because the talker could be heard more easily. Carnival owner John M. Sheesley opened a 12-stage store show on Buffalo's Main Street featuring "Gravityo the Man of a Thousand Thrills," Ernest Henderson "the Leather-Skinned Boy," Singlees the fire worker and Grace McDaniel "the Mule-Faced

Alex Linton was noted as a sword swallower who for years held a record for swallowing four 27-inch swords at once. Here he is in 1938 at the Newark Dime Museum throwing knives.

Woman." Acts got three weeks' work, with the program changing monthly.

Lou Dufour found winter homes for his dozen embryo shows, while circus man Sam Dock had his Punch-and-Judy and marionette show in stores for the winter. Doc Sesrad's "Man Frozen in Ice" attraction toured theaters, and at the Winnipeg, Man., fair he claimed to be the only person to "Freeze a Woman in a Block of Ice Alive!"

Max Gruberg's normal winter gig was working vaud with his "Jungle Oddities,"

The South St. Museum in Philadelphia in the 1930s had a nice space out front for a bally platform and ticket box almost like any sideshow operation at an amusement park. Here on the bally are Gertie the Pinhead and the Hindu Rubber Man sitting on the small platform. Bobby Hasson was the manager.

Workers on a storefront sideshow stretch out a python to ballyhoo the wonders inside.

featuring a tricycle-riding elephant, but he, too, got into the winter sideshow game. On Montreal's main drag, beside the Gayety Theatre, eight acts worked, plus the "Unveiled Show" behind a nice black-and-white front at the back of the room. In the windows, mother and baby monkeys drew the tip. A ticket box shaped like a circus wagon and a "Spidora" illusion made up the outside bally. Gruberg's other unit was on its 11th week in Philadelphia. It featured Mortardo, whose impressive lobby display carried over to his act — with his wife

beside him dressed as a nurse, Mortado, wearing an immaculate white wardrobe, drank colored liquids and shot them out of holes in his body.

Alva's Museum, in High Point, N.C., was one of the few owned by a performer — "Alva the Alligator Boy" featured himself in the blow-off along with his sister, "Alice the Alligator Girl." Featured at the Harlem Mu-

seum in N.Y.C. were "Tony the Alligator Boy" and his first-class whistling act, along with Laurello, who twisted his head 180 degrees. Blow-offs were "The Third Sex" and Dufour's "Naked Truth."

During the Depression years there were so many winter sideshows out that Billboard started a museum page just to keep track of them. Midget promoter Ray Marsh Brydon

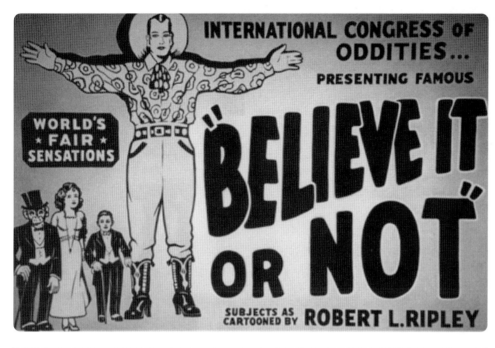

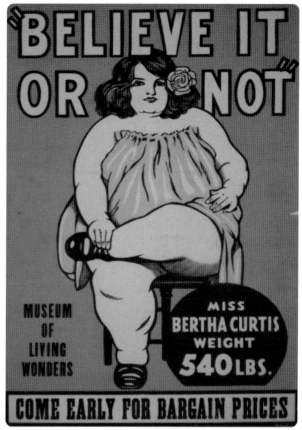

Ray Marsh Brydon store sideshow posters.

emerged as the leading store-show operator of the '30s and '40s. At age 11, he'd left home, working as an usher on the Sells-Floto Circus. A November 1929 *Billboard* noted that his "Freak Museum and Theater" had been in Indianapolis for seven weeks in a two-floor store with 80-foot frontage. The acts appeared on four-foot-high sideshow stages, and a glassblowing stand was at the back wall.

Brydon successfully promoted "Mike and Ike" the midgets for many years and on the store show with them were "Jolly Dolly" the fat girl, "Little Lord Leo" the English midget, Zip the "What Is It?" "Leo–Leola" the half-and-half, Professor Heuman the Russian instrumentalist, "Little San Toy" in the Chinese Torture Cabinet, "Ziki the Australian Bushman," plus a sword-swallower and snake handler.

A partner in both the mid-'30s Dan Rice Circus and the 1945 Allen King-King Circus, Brydon's expertise lay in his store-show presentations that employed the top bill posters, press and contracting agents from summer circuses and midways. He was also no slouch in getting publicity for his "International Congress of Oddities." For years, he had a chimp named Snookie that went everywhere his shows did.

HOLLYWOOD MASONIC TEMPLE

WORLD'S FAIR MUSEUM

PRESENTS

MAIN ENTRANCE

BIGGER THAN BARNUM'S *MORE THRILLS THAN A* CIRCUS

A NEW YORK WORLD'S FAIR PRESENTATION

OPEN DAILY
1 P.M. to 11 P.M.

LARGEST EXHIBITION OF HUMAN ODDITIES ON EARTH

LIVING CARTOONED ODDITIES *FROM THE EARTH'S* FOUR CORNERS

World's Fair Museum plays the Los Angeles Hollywood Masonic Temple, later known for years as the venue for the Oscar awards in the movie industry.

When Snookie died in 1936, Brydon had him embalmed, put in a casket and given a proper funeral with four midgets as pallbearers. The chimp was buried in Macon, Georgia's Central City Park — a famous circus winter grounds. The media ate it up.

At his peak in 1948, Brydon had freak units at Chicago's Riverside Park, one at Palisades Park, N.J., a sideshow and girl show at Savin Rock in West Haven, Conn., plus back-end shows at a dozen other venues. He began handling the back-end bookings for various large fairs, including Dallas. In 1951, his 22 shows grossed $186,000, setting a Dallas Fair record. At age 55 and at the top of his career, Brydon suddenly died in June 1954, in Indianapolis. Fellow troupers remembered him for caring little about money. That seemed to be true — when he died, his meager estate was traveling with him.

Robert Ripley's name is linked forever to the world of the bizarre. Born in Santa Rosa, Calif., in 1893, Ripley was a world traveler

Inside Lou Dufour's John Hix Strange As It Seems sideshow at the 1939 N.Y. World's Fair. Note the blade box at the back and the entrance to the blow-off behind it at the right side.

1937 *Billboard* ad placed by the management of Philadelphia's Eighth Street Museum opening on September 4th that season. Acts would be changed every two to three weeks. Most winter sideshow operations in this era were ones touring in stores put out by showmen that had existing 10-in-ones on carnivals in the summer. A few were permanent museums going like this one in Philadelphia, or ones in New York City and its surrounding cities.

and cartoonist of oddball subjects. In 1918, his sports comics about unusual athletic feats became the *Believe It or Not* strip, which at its peak appeared in over 300 newspapers. His first book of the comics sold over half a million copies. He also began cartooning sideshow acts and gave a huge boost to the freak business in the '30s, when his company began touring curiosities. His name brought notoriety to hundreds of attractions and some legitimacy to the freak game.

Ripley's "Believe It or Not" Odditorium at the 1933 Chicago World's Fair drew an estimated 2 million, then went on to fairs in Cleveland, San Diego, Dallas, San Francisco and New York. His shows were well-presented, with nice stages, good scenery, elaborate lighting and well-uniformed staff. Sometimes he had 30-plus acts. Despite his standard warning — "Anyone using my name will be prosecuted to the fullest extent of the law" — many sideshow operators adopted the title or versions of it.

Freak showman Cash Miller was given credit with getting Ripley's road show out, in the winter of 1933–34. At the 1935 California Pacific International Expo in San Diego,

255

Ripley's show had 11 stages, featuring anatomical wonder Anato Hayes, Roy Brad "the Ossified Man," Frieda Pushnik, Betty Lou Williams, fire-eater Singlee, Mimi Garneau, who swallowed a 22-inch neon tube, "Pin-Cushion" Leo Kongee and Dr. W. Mayfield lifting weights with his eyelids and tongue. Ripley's 1939 date at the San Francisco fair was almost as big as Chicago. The place was mobbed. Ripley's hoped to surpass its Chicago Century of Progress gross of $540,000.

In 1939, Ripley's applied for a site at the New York World's Fair, only to learn that Dufour and Rogers were putting their "John Hix's Strange as It Seems" show there. The best Ripley's could do was rent a former restaurant site on Broadway. Ripley partnered with John McMahon, who ran "Streets of Paris" at Chicago World's Fair, and Stanley Graham, who ran the "Midget City" there, and the Odditorium occupied 30,000 square feet and housed $2 million worth of artifacts collected by Ripley on his travels. Live acts worked on a revolving stage in a second-floor theater, while 40 lady guides added sex appeal. Adults paid 40 cents and kids a quarter. Today, there are dozens of Ripley museums in major tourist destinations around the world, including one in sanitized Times Square.

Sideshow attractions were everywhere. Jack "Abie" Tavlin's 1938 *Billboard* ad stated, "Wanted — Acts, freaks etc. for six weeks:

November 15 to December 24, Goldblatt's department store, Chicago." Charlie Roark had first seen his future wife, tattooed lady Betty Broadbent, there. "The store booked attractions in there at Christmastime," Charlie recalled. "They had the 'Del Rio Midget Show' free. When it was over, someone made a pitch for the sideshow in the next room. Patrons paid to see it. Big-name acts like sword-swallower Mimi Garneau. I was doing my Punch-and-Judy act and Betty Broadbent was booked in. When store management saw all her tattoos, they didn't let her work. They didn't think their young Toyland customers should see her."

A small 1922 *Billboard* ad read, "'Whale-Swallowed Jonah' — Build a whale out of canvas and let it swallow." Phony whales had a long exhibition history; real ones were better — you could smell them for miles. In July 1928, a kid sweeping up Harry Anfenger's Long Beach wax museum suggested, "Why don't you troupe a whale?" He'd been watching people line up to be ferried out to see a captured whale. Anfenger hustled up the money to buy a whale, but it instantly began rotting. The procurer, Cap Dietrich, suggested Harry get over to Ed Griffin — pronto. Ed stuffed deep sea fishermen's catches. While Ed was pumping vats of formaldehyde and salt solution into the carcass, it exploded. Cap's

next advice: "Get the stinking mess on a flat car and hit the road."

Huge crowds weakened the viewing platforms on their first venue. Within days, the whale repaid all expenses. Anfenger's Pacific Whaling Co. put out another unit and Griffin opened a school for whale embalmers. He cranked out whale carcasses with assembly-line speed. A double-length rail car was lowered into the water dockside, and a whale carcass floated onto it. Inside the shop, the whale was embalmed and the car's sides, ends and roof built up to create a temporary exhibition chamber.

Anfenger's eight units went on the road so quickly that they were severely undermanned until the American Circus Corp. (Ringling) shelved some circuses and turned loose much-needed contracting agents, sideshow lecturers, bill posterers and press agents. But forty tons of dead whale stunk, and fruit juice baths didn't help much. Anfenger's workers scooped out the whale's inards and reinforced it with wooden supports. The crew, equipped with 12-inch brass needles, gave it daily injections of embalming fluid.

In one season, 7 million people saw the whales, earning the company $2 million. Whale units were soon following each other into town. One showman had an 80-ton real whale on an auto trailer on the Beckmann & Gerety Shows in 1936. But the

Big crowds lined up in the 1920s and '30s to see whales carried on 80-foot-long railroad cars. Besides the whale inside, visitors saw all kinds of sideshow acts and were exposed to a blade-box presentation along with all the other sideshow-style dings and pitches. Note the electrician up on the pole tying in the light lines of individual bulbs above the exhibition area.

MONSTER CAPTIVE FINBACK WHALE EXHIBITION

THE PACIFIC WHALING COMPANY

On whale-car shows, the exhibition spaces for sideshow acts were small. They could be at the end of the car, opposite the entrance and exit ramps, or an area built off the side of the car, or in a small canvas-and-wood frame enclosure between the entrance and exit ramps by the ticket box. Here famed sword swallower Mimi Garneau helps to hold up an octopus on the whale show. You can see the edge of her her sword stand on the platform behind her.

"blubber boom" shrunk quickly once too many showmen began trouping whales whose ancestry could be traced directly to the pulp mill.

During the Depression and in between engagements, Charlie Roark worked on a Pacific Whaling Co. unit. "The whale generated a steady stream of customers, despite the

257

This 1940s newspaper ad advertises the appearance of the Godino Siamese Twins and their beautiful brides appearing for two days in a 1,200-seat tent behind the Cambridge, Mass. post offfice. Variety tent shows made good money as producers could have all the concessions plus pitch prize candy and sell photos of the acts.

overwhelming smell," he recalled. "One of the sideshows featured a dead octopus stuffed into a metal drum — it also stank. Near the end of the lecture on the whale, the lecturer would pick up a wad of stuff off the whale, explaining that it was ambergris, a substance used in perfume. The lecture[r] sold small bottles of whale perfume for a quarter. One mark told me, 'If that stuff from the whale could smell as nice as the whale stunk, it must be good stuff!'"

Many early midway operators, including wild-animal showman Frank Bostock, survived the winters by booking their attractions over the vaud circuits. Bostock promoted midget "Chiquita," "Wallace the Fighting Lion" and "Consul the Man-Chimp." In the summer, Leopold Singer and Ike Rose operated midget troupes on midways, and in the winter they went into vaud theaters. Stage audiences enjoyed the banter of Singer's midgets just as much as patrons of the sawdust world and roared at: "Bobby, what makes you so tall?" "I eat what's right!"

"Marjorie, what makes you so small?" "I eat what's left."

In booking oddities through theaters, agents and showmen took a softer approach than when placing them on the midway. Bostock's November 1910 *Billboard* ad promoting "Chiquita" read, "Not classed as a freak of nature, but properly termed 'The Smallest Representative of her Sex — A Gift of Nature.'" Photos show her wearing a stylish evening dress, and the text described her as "twenty-eight inches tall, weighing thirty pounds and perfect in form and figure, gifted with brains, faculties, and dignity."

In 1909, the *New York Dramatic Mirror* commented on the appearance of "Princess Susanna" at Brooklyn's Columbia Theater: "She is called 'The Doll Lady' and is thirty-two inches high and weighs thirty-two pounds. Her act consists of one song, 'A Little Boy Called Taps,' sung in a smart army uniform as she walks a wire. The act is good but depends more on the unique little personality and odd stature of the performer than any great cleverness she displays."

Vaudeville acts turned in wads of cash for their owners until movies threatened the grosses. Vaud theaters ran the same bill for a week, but started changing acts mid-week to stay in business. They needed exotic acts fast — ex-convicts, boxers and freaks became the new crowd-grabbers. In 1924, Loew

For a long time, movies faced stiff competition from live entertainment provided by touring shows, vaudeville and night clubs. Movie theater owners often hired live acts, including showgirl dancers and freaks, to bring in patrons. The owner of the Strand has added female impersonator Bobby Kork and another dancer to the showing of *Conflict* starring Humphrey Bogart.

Chiquita "The Living Doll" was born in Cuba in 1869. Frank C. Bostock, the English menagerie showman, first exhibited her in the U.S. as part of his early midway and zoo operations here. During the winter Bostock booked her in vaud theatres where she was a big hit, speaking and singing in Italian, Spanish and English. On stage she was always lavishly dressed and jeweled.

publicity chief Ted Turner plucked the conjoined Hilton Sisters off the C. A. Wortham Shows midway. Earlier, $500 would have secured them but the Loew's circuit paid them a grand the first week. By their third week, Loew's was shelling out $2,000 on any shows over four a day. Their run shattered all previous Loew's box-office records. Next winter they bombed out over the same route but were picked up by the William Morris Agency. Booked over the Orpheum Circuit, they generated huge audiences again and earned $3,000 a week.

Former burlesque worker Peter Thomas wrote me about the Hiltons: "Daisy and Violet Hilton worked in burlesque. In fact, they worked anywhere they could find work. I saw their act in a second-run vaud theater. They were nice-looking and wore good gowns. They sang 'My Blue Heaven,' played the saxophones and did a softshoe-and-tap type dance. Bob Johnston, who ran the Hollywood Burlesque in San Diego for 50 years, played them over and over. They came in on a two-week contract and always did business for him.

"Years ago some bright manager put them with the two Filipino brothers — possibly the Hartman Twins — who played accordians," Thomas continued. "They were booked into small-town movie theaters — a matinee and two evening shows with a film. They could work in a small space in front of the movie screen. Since the boys supplied the music, no band or pianist was needed. The agent said the act did very well and toured for months. Another act I knew had toured with the Hiltons, reported they were cheerful girls. They had to send out for food except where there was a cheap cafe next door or down the block. However, it must have been hard for them — just carrying around the knowledge that if one died the other would slip away shortly."

In May 1929, Turner signed male conjoined twins Simplicio and Lucio Godino. Their tour of Loew's vaud theaters featured a 14-piece band that accompanied them playing saxophones. The parents of American Siamese twins Mary and Margaret Gibbs approached Turner to do the same thing for their girls. He put them in a N.Y.C. apartment with a piano teacher, and after two years of preparations, they opened in Hoboken, N.J., and played area theaters for

Big-lipped female members of the Ubangi tribe were publicity-getting curiosities on the 1930–31 Ringling Bros. and Barnum & Bailey Circus. Parents inserted the disks in female babies because the Ubangi tribe believed that the women with the biggest lips were the most desirable.

$2,150 a week.

Loew died, and in 1929 Turner's assets got wiped out. Broke, he teamed up with Lou Dufour to pilot a "Birth" movie. Backstage,

Lou's jarred embryos were the perfect blow-off. Turner convinced the son of France's postmaster general to help him bring Ubangis (members of the Saharan tribe by the Ubangi River) from French equatorial Africa to the United States. The Ubangis landed in Brooklyn in 1931 and opened in a Philadelphia theater. The first few days were terrific, then business slumped. Beyond the first eight rows of seats, you couldn't see the big-lipped gals. Turner and Dufour managed to offload the Ubangis onto the Ringling show.

Besides Siamese twins, vaudeville audiences saw entire freak units. In 1927 Fred LaReine had three "Coney Island"–titled sideshow units in vaud. The next season he had two units titled "A Night in Coney Island" on the Loew's circuit. All carried banners, special lobby displays and pulled off outdoor stunts for publicity. Albert-Alberta on one unit was heavily promoted and the show's closer. Next season, Fred sent a unit to England, where Albert-Alberta's antics roused the ire of the conservative press and literally stopped the tour. Various New York showmen, including Frank Bostock's nephew, J. Gordon Bostock, and the Wagner Brothers of Coney Island fame had freak units out on Loew's and the Keith-Albee theatre circuits through the '20s.

In 1936, *Billboard* reported that agents were placing more freaks and sideshow acts with film studios. An early short made in 1919 had shown clips of Leopold Singer's midget troupe at home and on the road. When the 61-minute Todd Browning movie *Freaks* was first released in New York in 1932, the *New York Times* stated, "The difficulty is in telling whether it should be shown at the Rialto

This is the outside view of Fred LaReine's Paterson, N.J., Market St. Museum in spring 1933. Note the performing bear lying down. The secret of operating a store show was location, location, location. You wanted to be on the city's main business street as close to Woolworth's as possible.

A 1950s brochure promoting Lou Dufour's Big 4 Unit Show featuring on stage the joined-at-the-head twins — Yvonne and Yvette — plus Frankie and Johnnie, the two-headed baby, plus two films — *Nature's Mistakes* and another depicting the sex lives of Hitler and Mussolini.

A large Montreal theatre crowd watches as Giovanni Iuliani lectures on freaks before the viewing of Todd Browning's movie *Freaks*. Banned in theaters for years, it was revived in Canada in 1965 by Cineplex under the title *L'Amour Chez les Montres (The Loves of Freaks)*. Note Giovanni's wife dressed in a nurse uniform at the left of the stage in case anyone faints!

Theater or the Medical Center." Quickly banned here, the film wasn't allowed into Britain until 1963.

Lou Dufour coupled film and live freaks together in a 1956 road show he titled "Nature's Mistakes." It featured many top

freaks, including "Schlitzie the Pinhead" and a Browning made film based on Todd Robbins' story "Spurs," but it was one of Lou's few

Giovanni Iuliani explains how Siamese Twins come about while his wife is busy selling a special souvenir freak booklet to the audience. The combination of lecture, film and live freaks ran for months in various Montreal theatres setting box office records. Outside of Quebec and without the live acts, the film tanked.

The newspaper ad for *Love of Freaks* playing two days at the Palangio's Empire Theatre. In Ontario, without the live freaks, the tour promoter added another movie to the bill — *The Horrible* directed by Alfred Hitchcock — but business was minor compared to Quebec where the live freaks on stage drew sellout crowds.

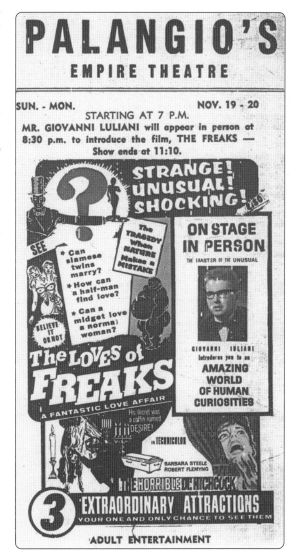

losing ventures. A decade later, Cineplex did better. The Canadian company paid MGM $5,000 for the Canadian rights to *Freaks* for five years, inspired after its staff visited the Grand Guignol crime theater in Paris. A French soundtrack was made for Browning's film in France, and Montreal sideshow talker Giovanni Iuliani was hired to do the lecturing. Dick Best rounded up Bob Melvin "the Man With Two Faces," "Sealo," Esther Blackmon "the Alligator Lady," fat woman Mary King and midget Jimmy Wilson as live stage acts.

When Cineplex wanted something to pitch, Iuliani came up with a booklet of freak photos, and 10,000 copies were printed. Iuliani recalled the printer saying, "You better have a big enough storage cupboard for these, because you won't sell that many!" The show opened simultaneously at Montreal's Chateau and Francais theaters, three shows a day, drawing 120,000 viewers in just over five weeks. Browning's *Freaks*, renamed *L'Amour Chez les Montres* (*The Loves of Freaks*), soon buried the big Hollywood movie *My Fair Lady* in Montreal. Another 10,000 pitch books were needed.

Before each film screening, Iuliani introduced his wife, Susan, dressed in a nurse's outfit. If anyone in the theater felt uncomfortable, they were to signal her. That is, if you could get her attention, as most times she was busy selling freak booklets. The pitch book cleverly had a sealed centre section — you had to cut the pages open to see the lady with extra breasts. Iuliani pitched, "Don't forget we have a shock section. We do warn you, if you are weak of heart, do not look at it. Keep it away from children."

Eighty-thousand shelled out a deuce to see the show at the Chateau Theatre on Montreal's Rue St. Denis. The film and live acts played every spot with a theatre in Quebec, but once out of the province and without the live component, the film did very little box office. Iuliani went on to be a ringmaster on various circuses, including my own Martin and Downs and Super Circus International (Super Cirque).

Up until the old Madison Square Garden was replaced with the one now, there was room in the basement for a menagerie and a sideshow during the Ringling Bros. and Barnum & Bailey's annual spring N.Y.C. run. In the late 1950s and early '60s, various sideshow producers including Nat Eagle brought a dozen or so acts in. Charlotte Vogel "The Elephant Skin Girl" poses for a photo during one of those years. Note the card on the chair advertising her life story and photo for a dime.

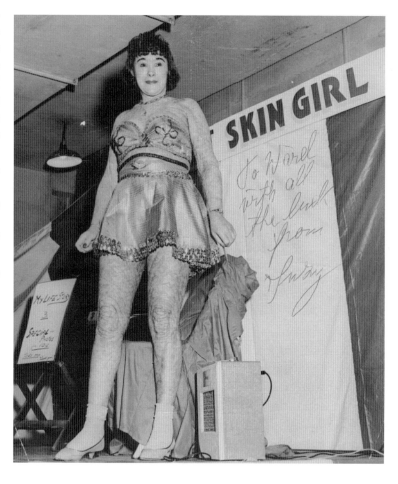

Many arenas and buildings that indoor circuses play hardly have room backstage for anything — and owners are lucky if the animals can stay inside. Regardless, indoor circuses often found space for a sideshow. For years, each spring Ringling offered the public a free menagerie and sideshow at the Madison Square Garden and the Boston Garden dates before the tenting show began. The Madison Square Garden sideshow was dropped in 1968, when the new Garden building had no space for it.

Many other indoor circus promoters had sideshow units on their dates. At the 1947 Cleveland Shrine Circus, producer Achmed "Doc" Hagaa's sideshow offering had Dolly Reagan "the Ossified Lady," Melvin Burkhardt doing magic and lecturing, Dorothy Lauther with rag pictures, novelty act "the Musical Reeses," Dolly Joyce "The Atomic Wonder Girl," Gilbert Ray "The World's Tallest Man," Paula Alley "the World's Smallest Girl," plus "the Anatomical Wonder," Punch and Judy, a blade box and a "Mickey Mouse Circus."

(Left) In 1974 the management of the Ringling Bros. and Barnum & Bailey Circus asked Ward Hall to produce a sideshow for their date at the Washington Armory. In the strong lineup of freaks were circus and carnival sideshow veterans Cliff and Mamie King. Cliff was a good outside talker and inside lecturer.

(Right) Lou Dufour on the bally outside his John Hix Strange As It Seems show at the 1939 N.Y. World's Fair. Besides being a midway showman, Dufour was a well-educated promoter who had staged Crime Doesn't Pay and Darkest Africa shows at other world's fairs here and in Belgium. He beat Ripley's into this one. Ripley's rented a space near Times Square.

An April 1974 *Amusement Business* story noted that Ringling Bros. and Barnum & Bailey were putting the sideshow back to work after many seasons, and would play the Washington Armory that month. The sideshow was provided by World Fair Attractions, owned by Ward Hall and Chris Christ. Performers included lecturer Milt Robbins, the Christophers' knife-throwing act, "Lady Sandra Reed" — an albino sword swallower — armless wonder Emmett Blackman, Johann Petursson "the Viking Giant," contortionist Francis Duggan as "Bobo the Rubber Man," fat lady "Jolly Dolly" and fat man "Big Jim," Fred Lulling "the Fire-Eater Mephisto," dwarf clown Pete Terhurne and "Cairo the Egyptian Giant" — a strong lineup that kept up with Ringling sideshow quality.

While mainly associated with outdoor circuses and carnivals, sideshows and those working in them cropped up in many other forms of entertainment. Stints on vaudville and movie stages, in storefront sideshows, Christmastime department-store promotions and even as extra-charge attractions on whale-car shows kept sideshow acts, lecturers and talkers employed in response to their "At Liberty" ads.

MAIN CIRCUS SIDE SHOW

STRANGE PEOPLE

Chapter 16

Strong Enough To Be Exhibited Alone

In 1954, Bobby Hasson's 10-in-one on Royal American Shows featuring Johann Petursson the Viking Giant. Bobby is standing on the ground far left while his brother Bill is ground level far right. Next season Bobby gave up his deal with Royal American Shows (RAS) and went over to manage the Ringling–Barnum & Bailey Circus sideshow only to see the show close under canvas mid-1956 season. He bought the Ringling custard truck and went back onto RAS until he retired in the late 1970s.

Midway showmen with novel attractions and major freaks have always done well. During a one-week Topeka, Kan., street fair in 1900, over 11,000 people paid 15 cents each to see Frank and Louise Blitz's showing of Carolina siamese twins "Millie-Christine." Frank did the outside spieling, Louise handled the lecturing, and show folks claimed she made the twins rich from pitch-card sales. The Blitzes had one of the strongest freak attractions on tour at the time, enabling Frank to be fiercely independent and allowing him to avoid exhibiting on the carnival's midway at agricultural fairs. He took pride in paying fairs only 10 percent of his gross. His 1900 *Clipper* ad warned, "Remember, we do not show on a midway, as ours is not a midway attraction. Don't sign any contract with a midway company that prohibits you from letting on any attraction except what they furnish."

Fifty years later, showman Harold Overturf's philosophy was similar to Blitz's. Harold's "Little People" were usually found back by the fair's cattle barns, on what showmen and fair boards called the "independent midway." In protest of high rents and percentages charged by carnival companies on the main fair midways, Overturf gathered showmen with midget horses, menacing alligators, tiny people and fat folks, and booked them into various fairs on the fairs' independent midways.

Originally, fairs booked all their attractions, but when midway companies came along and offered to handle this chore, many fairs were

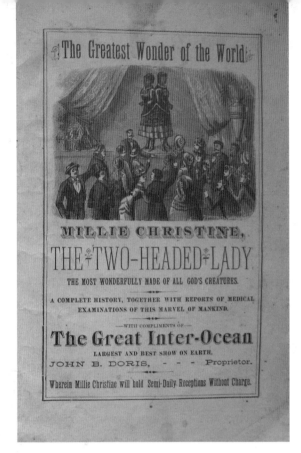

(*Left*) Pitch booklet for the conjoined Carolina Twins — Millie-Christine — while appearing with John B. Doris's The Great Inter-Ocean Circus. The attraction was seen twice daily free of charge. No doubt the little pitch booklet sold well.

Billboard ad placed by Frank R. Blitz reminding fair managers that many midway companies only have one or two show-owned shows and the rest are booked on independents. Why not cut out the midway and book shows like his "Millie-Christine" directly? Blitz encouraged fairs to keep an independent midway for showmen who preferred to stay off the carnival midway.

glad to let them. Midway owners wanted the "X," or exclusive rights to the whole grounds, where everyone paid them rent. Besides taking in more revenue, midways would then control what games and shows were on the lot and make sure no fly-by-night grifter got the carnival's flat and alibi stores closed, and no strong cooch show closed down their girl shows.

However, this arrangement hurt the local church and service club stands that couldn't afford midway footage prices. Since fair-board members had to live with these folks, most fairs began reserving a small area away from the main midway for these tenants, but soon showmen, pitchmen, demonstrators and various other hustlers took advantage of the low rent on

"independent midways." These days, some grind showmen still prefer to book their animal oddity shows there — feeling they'll do better than on the midway, where today's fairgoers assume everything is fake.

Many major freaks on American midways were exhibited "single-O" style, the showman's term for any attraction strong enough to be shown alone. Alice Elizabeth Doherty

Besides being good sideshow blow-offs, the flea circus (like Professor Alexander's) made ideal single-O shows. Flea performances don't last too long. Their only drawback was that only a few dozen people could view them at one time. It truly was a grind show.

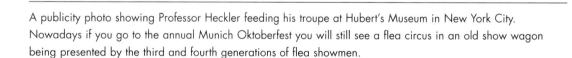

A publicity photo showing Professor Heckler feeding his troupe at Hubert's Museum in New York City. Nowadays if you go to the annual Munich Oktoberfest you will still see a flea circus in an old show wagon being presented by the third and fourth generations of flea showmen.

did extremely well as a single-O. She was the 1880s freak sensation known as the "Minnesota Wooly Baby." Born in March 1887 in Minneapolis, she had fine white hair adorning her entire body. By the time she was 16 months old, this otherwise healthy little girl was blanketed in hair that even covered her face and clogged her ears. Many exhibitors made offers to her parents to let them display her, but the Dohertys refused, saying they loved her too much to be separated from her. The city's dime-museum operators, Kohl and

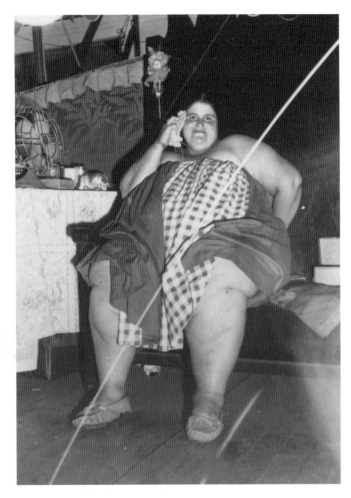

He was a nice guy but he couldn't win a dime as a single-O. At a big state fair, Jerry Lipko had a phony two-headed baby sitting next to Lentini, outgrossing him terribly. In this case it wasn't sitting beside the fake two-headed baby that did the harm but the fact that Frank's three legs were just too unbelievable. The marks had heard about two-headed babies being born, but nobody with three legs."

Midgets and fat folks have always done well in the single-O. Slim Kelly, Dick Best, Lou Dufour and other operators often carried a fat single-O show along with their 10-in-ones. "Slim's fat show with Mary King was only 10 cents," Dean Potter recalled. "One day in Raleigh, N.C., they were short of help and Slim said to me, 'You're going to have to go over there and sell tickets on that fat show.' I sold 10,000 tickets! You hardly looked up. She was selling her picture inside for a dime. Almost everyone bought a picture."

Seasons back, Ward Hall put resident side-show fat man Bruce Snowdon in a single-O. Banners called him "Falstaff the Fat" and "Sir Lunchalot," showing him fully clothed in period English costume. Ward admitted, "That was a mistake. He should have been painted in a bathing suit to show off all that flesh!"

Back-end showman Tim Deremer had to field two or three grind shows along with his large string illusion show to get the nut in the 1980s. He operated a "Mermaid Show," a

Middleton, got around that problem by hiring the whole family. On tour, the mother told the visiting public that the reason her daughter was hirsute was that two months before giving birth she had been frightened by a small dog. In 1894 Alice's sister Agnes took over her management and toured her as "Alice the Dog-Face Girl" or "Alice the Bearded Lady" until Alice's death in 1933.

Not all attractions worked single-O style were a guaranteed success. Dean Potter said, "I worked with 'Lentini the Three-Legged Man.'

A *Billboard* ad placed by Betty Lou Williams warning that she had contacted a law firm who will prosecute anyone using a gaff to present an act advertised as having a double body or four legs. The gaff was simply a headless rubber baby that was glued onto the person's stomach or fitted into a corset-like garment that could be worn. Mary Clark was a notorious offender.

"Girl to Gorilla," a "Zoma" (geek) attraction and for a short time a "Fat Show." When I asked him about exhibiting fat people, there was dead silence on the phone. Then, choking up, Tim replied, "I had a fat man out a year or two before. I spotted a very huge person walking down the Meadowland's Fair midway. I sent an employee after this fat kid to ask if he would be interested in a job. The guy had never left Brooklyn but took the job and came down to Ohio on Amtrack. We trained him to do the act — told him what to do and how to do it. He loved it. He thought it was the greatest thing in the world. We then went to the fair in Columbus, Ohio.

"Day six of the fair, the fat boy dies in his sleep during the night. When I stepped out of my trailer that morning a lady shoved a microphone in my face, demanding to know, 'What killed 'Billy Pork Chops'? Front pages of the local newspapers read, 'Billy Pork Chops a.k.a. David Fleischman of Brooklyn, New York, dies at Ohio State Fair.' He weighed almost 600 pounds and he died inside a trailer — it took seven roughies to get him out. We put a wreath out front of the show and kept it dark for a couple of days."

One of Walter Wanous's strongest features was his brother-in-law Dick Best's disovery, Betty Lou Williams, the Four-Legged Girl. She was 14 months old when she appeared at the 1933 Chicago World of Progress Fair in Ripley's "Believe It or Not." Walter recalls, "She was very young. Her father use to carry her onstage in his big hand. People really got a kick out of her. We had some slow days on the 10-in-one at this one date, so I would pick one person out of the tip and send them in to see her. I asked them to come right back out and tell the rest what they saw. They all came back raving about Betty Lou Williams.

"We got the idea to make her into a single-O feature on her own from that. Later,

Betty Lou Williams in 1952. She did very well in a sideshow or single-O. Her money supported her parents and siblings back home. Sadly, she died in her early 20s in a New York City hotel room.

An impressive five-banner front for the Betty Lou Williams single-O show on the Cetlin & Wilson Shows midway in the early 1960s. At the time, there were only a handful of freak attractions as strong as her.

she would phone up and say, 'I got to get out of this town, it is driving me crazy. I don't care if you pay me or not.' But she still got $500 weekly from us. She made enough to buy her daddy a 155-acre peanut farm and to send all her brothers and sisters through school. She died in a hotel in Trenton, N.J. She was only 24."

Another four-legged person made out better. Ernest Leonard Defort was born in 1931 in Winnipeg's St. Joseph Hospital. Many showmen approached his parents about

showing him, and the Deforts decided to let Canadian midway owner Patty Conklin handle Ernie's career. Conklin first placed him in the sideshow on the Conklin & Garrett midway in 1933, and the next season he was switched to a single-O setup and exhibited that way until he left the midway. Although the show was titled "Ernie-Len," Ernie called his malformed twin "Lester." During the off-season he went to school in Winnipeg like other kids, except for a few months in 1937 when his parents took him to Europe hoping surgeons there

could remove the second body. All of them said it would be fatal to do so.

Patty Conklin had quietly put aside some money from exhibiting Ernie, and Ernie's parents came up with the balance necessary to send Ernie to the Mayo Clinic in Rochester, Minn., in 1943. Toronto papers reported that his operation, performed by Dr. Henry W. Meyerding, lasted from 7:30 a.m. until 2 in the afternoon. The partial siamese twin attached to his body at the lower chest and upper abdomen was successfully removed. "Lester" had well-developed pelvic bones, hip joints and legs, but the abdomen, chest, arms and hands had failed to grow.

A month later, Ernie was back home in Winnipeg. Newspaper stories led one to believe that was the end of it. However, Ernie explained to me that the hole in his chest wouldn't heal. He had to wear and change special bandages continuously. When better antibiotics came along in 1950 he had a final operation that fixed him completely, and soon he graduated from high school. In 1951 the family moved and his days as an attraction ended, but Ernie remained a carny. For two years, he ran the "Roll-O-Plane" ride for Conklin at Crystal Beach, Ont., and another three summers were spent working diggers and a gaming wheel for Harry Shore in Montreal. He then went into banking. In June 2008, he was 79 with no regrets about his

Pre–World War II, Ernie-Len, the Double-Bodied Boy, is on display inside this platform-style show on the Conklin & Garrett midway. The enclosure is a joint frame with a canvas top and sides. Originally, Conklin exhibited him in the sideshow but soon featured him, single-O.

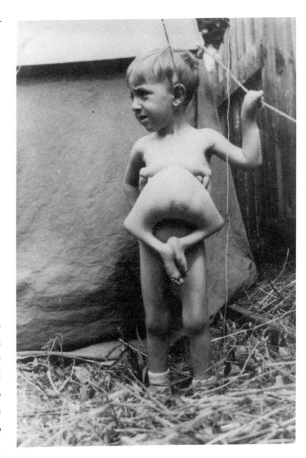

(Left) The bulky sweater that Ernest Leonard Defort is wearing helps to hide the partial twin body growing out of his chest. When he was in his early teens, the twin was successfully removed at the Mayo Clinic in Rochester, Minn.

(Right) Young Ernest Defort shows off his parasitic twin whom he called Lester. After a brief career on the midway, Ernest had surgery to remove the twin. He ended up a healthy normal citizen who worked in a bank for most of his adult life and who is still doing well in retirement.

life, having accomplished what some oddities may have secretly dreamed about — becoming "normal."

As sideshows shut down on circuses and dwindled on midways, and many of the remaining top freaks saw their main employment venue vanish, some took the opportunity to put out their own single-O shows. When the circus I was on played close to Royal American Shows at the Regina, Sask., fair in 1964, fire-eater Carlos Leal took me with him to visit his friends there. Leal's first stop was to see the giant, Johann Petursson. Glen Porter of sideshow and monkey speedway fame had helped the giant go on his own that year. Patrons bought a ticket, then entered the show between the legs of an

In 1964 I saw the Viking Giant at the Regina, Sask., Exhibition. You entered and exited the show trailer through the painted giant's legs. The back side of the trailer was built with a hydraulic awning that opened up revealing an exhibition space where Johann Petursson could sit in his large chair and sell his giant rings. The roof on Johann's truck rig was raised so he could get in and drive it and his show semi-trailer from town to town.

enormous cut-out of a Viking painted on the show front.

Grind showman Lee Kolozsy recalled, "When Johann had the show himself, the grind tapes were still Glen Porter's voice. Johann's show was built on a semi and pulled by a special Ford tractor that had its roof cut and raised so Johann could fit in and drive it.

"One time I visited him and he was having trouble with kids sneaking under the sidewall, so he got a garden hose with lots of pressure. Soon as the sidewall lifted, he soaked them. The last time I saw Johann was at a flea market between Gibsonton and Tampa. He had his big chair and was selling his souvenir rings. He was all stooped over and the hump on his back was higher than his head."

It was around the same time that showman and circus performer Eddie Pedrero ran one of the best single-O attractions. On circus bookings he travelled extensively throughout Mexico and Central and South America. In 1959, while in Managua, Nicaragua, Eddie saw a man with huge feet begging outside the circus. He convinced Francisco Sandoval Rios to come back to the U.S., then built a special show for him. Eddie showed him as "the Snowman," "the Abominable Snowman" and "Big Foot."

Although the rest of his body was normal, Francisco's feet were deformed, with his left foot hugely misshapen. His deformities were

Eddie Pedrero built this grind show that he titled Abominable Snow Man to exhibit Francisco Sandoval Rios. The show was built onto a truck with living quarters for Rios. The basic colors were blue and white.

not from crippling elephantiasis but from a gland dysfunction. His nickname in Spanish was "Patica," meaning "small feet." His feet continued to grow larger. Doctors told Eddie that Francisco's left foot weighed 17 pounds and his left leg over 150. He could walk but had to stop and rest often. Eddie had special shoes made for him, but the poor circulation in Francisco's left foot caused it to become hot and ulcerated. Doctors told Eddie that if they tried to amputate Francisco's feet, his chances of survival were slim.

On exhibition, Francisco sat with his back to the midway. He told people his name and

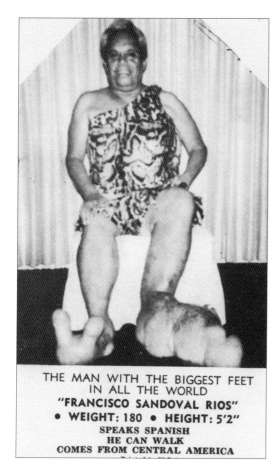

THE MAN WITH THE BIGGEST FEET
IN ALL THE WORLD
"FRANCISCO SANDOVAL RIOS"
● **WEIGHT: 180** ● **HEIGHT: 5'2"**
SPEAKS SPANISH
HE CAN WALK
COMES FROM CENTRAL AMERICA

Francisco Sandoval Rios's pitch card. Showman Eddie Pedrero found him in South America while on tour with a circus. Besides operating back-in units, Eddie and his relatives built back-end units and fun houses for other showmen in the 1960s.

touched his feet so the crowd could see they were real. Signs explained his medical condition, and he sold a postcard photo of himself for a quarter. Eddie boasted to a reporter, "We got inside what we advertise on the outside. He's real and he's alive . . . living and breathing." When the reporter asked how much Francisco made, Eddie retorted, "He makes a good living. We both make a good living if business is good. If business is bad, we both don't do so good. He always makes enough money so he can go for four or five months to Nicaragua and live well. I make sure of that."

Mickey Saiber had been a professional swimmer prior to landing in the freak exhibition business. Over the phone, he related how he had spent thousands of dollars to frame a fat-man show and then within weeks put the fat man on a diet to improve his health! I had to meet him. Sitting beside his wave pool in Butler, Penn., Mickey explained how he'd caught the midway bug. "During high school, for a summer job, I helped a guy who traveled for Globe Import Export," he began. "They sold slum and jewelry to carnival game operators. My employer started sending me out alone. I got to know various carnival people, including the 'special people.'"

"One job outing I met and became friends with Randy Rosenson, who had two bogus attractions — 'the Little People from Australia' and an 'Egyptian Giantess.' I watched him sitting in his trailer while people kept coming in with boxes of money. I thought, 'What is this?' He was going for a quarter at the time and they were real beef shows. Then I met and became friends with giantess Delores Pullard, billed as 'the Tallest Woman in the World.' She stood eight-foot-two. The guy promoting her wasn't paying her what he said he would. She asked me, 'Why don't you build a show for me?'" Mickey and his partner Randy presented Delores Pullard until Randy dropped out.

Mickey described Delores as well proportioned with very lady-like hands. She had been confined to a wheelchair for 10 years due to a high school basketball injury. Delores got around in a car whose interior her husband had specially designed for her so that for five months each season she could work for Mickey, who framed a second show for her titled "Land of the Giants." Show painter Lou Stamm did the front and Mickey booked it on Royal American. Unfortunately, the life expectancy for a giant is short, and Delores's size-23 feet were an indication of her acromegaly problems. Her pituitary gland continued to secrete growth hormones, and on March 18, 1971, at age 24, she went into a Houston, Tex., hospital where doctors tried to remove a brain tumor. She didn't survive the operation.

Besides losing a friend, Mickey had a serious problem. He'd committed her show to the Florida State Fair. Showing up in Tampa

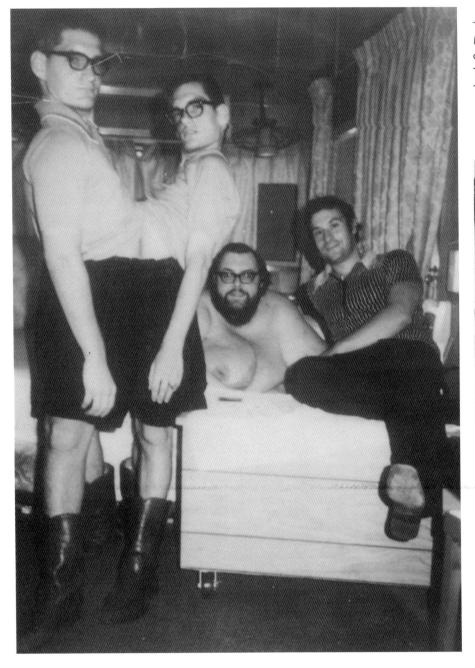

(Left) Mickey Saiber on the right with Mike Walker and Ronnie and Donnie Galyon. The Siamese Twins were the hottest freak attraction in the 1970s. They have now retired from the business.

The pitch card for Delores Pullard who Mickey Saiber billed as the Amazon Girl. She is sitting on the back of the car (her husband had re-built the interior so she could comfortably ride from spot to spot) when working for Mickey.

around to the big question, "I'm in a desperate spot here, John. Would you consider going in drag in my show?"

"Making him into a lady wasn't easy," explained Mickey. "John was very much a ladies' man. He didn't like being in drag. Normally he was good with people, talked and joked with them, but because he had a low, deep voice, he wouldn't talk with the public when in drag." Later, Mickey exhibited John as the "the Watusi Warrior." "I wanted 'the Watusi Warrior' to be bigger," said Mickey. "I had a pair of expensive custom boots made for him that made him over eight feet tall. He didn't like the boots, so I wore them."

Ward Hall told Mickey about a huge fat man living in Iowa, and Mickey hurried out there. "I walked into the room and he was immense," related Mickey. "I mean, the largest human being I had ever seen! He pleaded with me to take him on the road so he could make something of his life. He was tired of just lying in one room. I gave him the stage name 'Mike Walker.'"

Mickey and Frank Hansen became partners, presenting the "Mike Walker Drug Abuse Exhibit" in an exhibition trailer that doubled as an air-conditioned living unit and a mobile hospital. There have been hundreds of fat shows, but the Hansen-Saiber fat show was different. They were the first to fuse freakdom and drug abuse. Mike Walker was presented in 1971 as an enormous lost soul who had experienced one drug trip too many. When they played western Canada on the Royal American midway, *Amusement Business* magazine noted, "This new show is without a doubt one of the most powerful and highest-grossing units on the road today. In Calgary it made a laughing matter of a thousand-dollar daily earnings."

Saiber and Hansen's idea of stoned individuals ending up as freaks continued on midways. "Walker was exhibited inside the trailer on a big round bed," related Mickey. "People would come up the steps on the side of the trailer facing the midway and walk around the front to the other side. They could view him through three windows. The people he wanted to talk to he would invite inside. Parents took their kids in and he would lecture them, 'Look what's going to happen to you if you take drugs!' The back of Walker's pitch card read, 'A heavy man with a heavy message.' I tried putting my shows into the realm of being able to help other people. I became

without a giant would ruin his reputation. Desperate, he called up giant John Rankin, who stood seven-and-a-half feet — not overly tall alongside today's basketball players. Mickey hoped that with special shoes he would appear close to Pullard's advertised height. Duplicating her curves and pretty face was another matter! Finally Mickey got

The mobile medical and exhibition trailer that Mickey Saiber and Frank Hansen built to display the 1,187-pound Mike Walker. Patrons climbed the steps at the left and could look in both the side and end windows of the trailer to see Mike lying inside on a bed. If he liked you, he'd invite you inside.

aware of a heroin rehabilitation centre called Christian Farms that was taking people out of jails and rehabilitating them. I started donating a portion of our money to them."

Mickey used the same approach in exhibiting "Little Richard," a dwarf who had glaucoma. Mickey's grind-tape spiel for him urged people to sign their organ donor cards and donate their eyes to the eye bank. "Freaks have impacted my life," Mickey said. "I met a half-man named Dick Hillburn, and Carl Norwood billed as 'the Frog Boy.' Dick

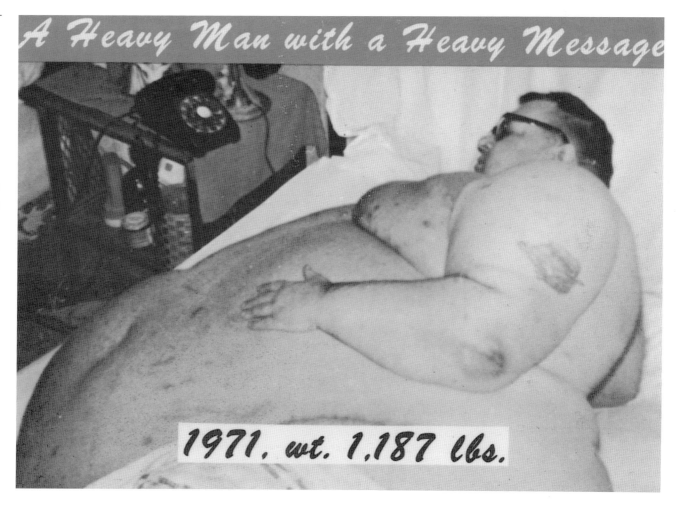

Mickey Saiber took this photo of Mike Walker when he first saw him. Walker told Mickey he wanted to make something of his life by going on tour. Mickey presented him as a victim of drug abuse, and that started a wave of drug abuse shows on American midways.

operated his own show, drove his own truck, built his own equipment and painted his own banners. Little Carl was adopted by Dick and his wife, Annie. They were financially smart and owned a diner, had property and saved their money. After Dick died, Carl and his adopted mother kept asking me to frame a show for them.

"Carl was inspirational. He was only a couple of feet tall. His little legs had no knees, just curves with feet on the ends. He had the best attitude toward life. No matter how bad

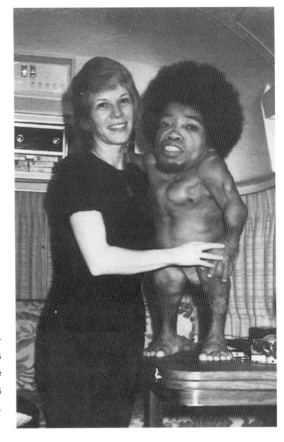

things got or whatever happened, he always looked at things positively. Here's a guy who has all these physical handicaps and he was always up." Carl Norwood was 38 when he died in Atlanta, Ga., in February 1976.

The illness or death of an attraction is an obvious freak exhibitor's worry, but Mickey Saiber told me about other problems. First he hesitated, perhaps mulling over what he was going to tell me: "There was something else. In the case of the men attractions, a number of women became attracted to them in a very, very odd way. I have walked up at times and looked in Mike Walker's window and had to close the show because he was having sex with a woman in there. He didn't care who watched. I exhibited him with just a towel over his privates. I have actually walked in on the dwarf Little Richard and seen him in the act, which was the most bizarre thing you could imagine. All you saw was Little Richard's head with the big Afro on this woman's stomach and his little butt bouncing up and down. There is a certain type of woman that is attracted sexually to freaks!"

Word travels fast on the carnival circuit about who to employ and who not to. If you

This is the grind-show trailer Prince Arthur and his wife were exhibited in, billed as The World's Strangest Married Couple. The basic colour is orange with yellow backgrounds for the pictorials and blue lettering with white trim.

hire certain people you must live with their habits. "'Little Richard' was completely frivolous," Mickey recalled. "All he cared about was sex. He was called the 'tripod' and you can imagine why! He would spend every dime he had on sex. No matter what responsibilities he had, whether the show was open or not, sex came first. Little Richard, the rogue that he was, would pretend he was sleeping on the floor with sunglasses on. He looked up ladies' dresses as they walked through the show." The last Mickey heard of Little Richard was that he had died while doing a sex act onstage in a New Orleans club. "I'm sure, in his mind, he was already in heaven," chuckled Mickey.

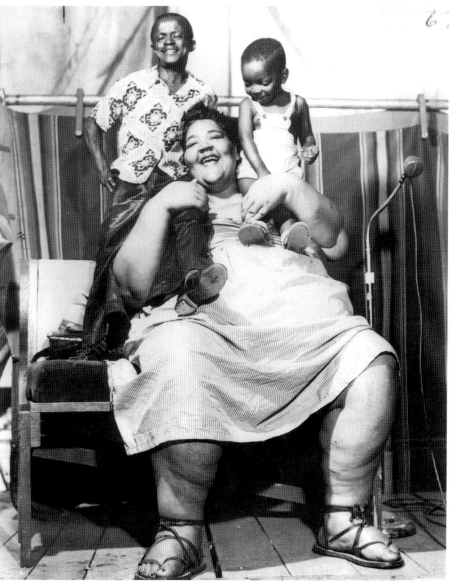

Prince Arthur and his wife and child posing inside their grind show on Royal American Shows in 1958. In those years, fat and little made for a good grind-show combination.

Chapter 17

Grinding Out a Living

The peep show, a small pictorial show in a box, may have been the original grind show. It was compact, portable, cheap to frame and easy to work, plus the crowd watching was visible and would attract more spectators. Henry Morley's *Memoirs of Bartholomew Fair* describes a 1728 peep show, "The Siege of Gibraltar": "The box sat on jacks. By working outside levers, the showman changed the scenes inside. Two viewing windows allowed two customers at a time." Peep showmen set up anywhere, usually for free, while curiosity showmen had to rent a room, employ a door talker and a lecturer. The peep-show operator was his own talker, money collector and lecturer, covering all the elements that later made grind shows profitable.

The biggest or the smallest have always been grind-show mainstays. In January 1950, T. S. Aylesworth built this panel front for L. Harry Cann's "Queen Jean" show. Cann had numerous back-end shows including sideshows and motordromes.

The forefathers of today's grind shows could easily have been the early peep shows carried from venue to venue on the exhibitor's back or pushed along in wheelbarrels. It was only a matter of time before showmen put larger peep shows on carts and widened their field of exhibition.

This seven-banner fronted show on the 1951 Cetlin & Wilson Shows' midway ballyhooed midget horses and cattle plus Rana and Piru, the Sacred Wolves from Tibet. Note the four reader boards out front. How could you go wrong for a dime?

French showmen captured the true spirit of grind shows by calling them "*entresorts*," or "in-and-outs." Grind shows have limited viewing space inside trailers or tents, as showmen want their customers to look and go. There's no bally — the talker's continuous short pitch or the repeating grind-tape spiel, aided by the artwork on the front or the banners attracts new customers. Midway economics in the 1960s made recorded spiels a must, and the continuous tape-loop machines revolutionized grind-show operations overnight.

Grind shows worked on volume guaranteed by a low admission ticket. For over half a century they barely rose above a dime, and even now admission is only 50 cents to a dollar. If they're on a midway using coupons, the price can equal a major ride. Carl Sedlmayr Sr., alluding to the uniqueness of grind-show attractions described his 1930s midway: "You will find enough meritorious sit-down shows at which you can spend an entire evening and enough grind shows to round out the spirit of the business." Sedlmayr Sr., once a grind showman himself, was an astute businessman who curtailed his sit-down shows' performances to under 40 minutes and didn't allow games to give away large prizes that might stop people from getting on the rides. His midway philosophy favored the in-and-out show.

When he was off the road, Kissimmee, Florida–based Peter Hennen sold new and used grind shows, grind-show attractions and taped spiels. His reputation for making the right grind tape for an exhibit was unequaled. He charged $25 and kept a copy on file in case more were needed.

By the 1980s, talking, as a profession, was dead. The frontman on a grind show was now a minimum-wage ticket seller and watch person. Most showmen soon used cassettes for spiels that lasted 30 seconds to a minute. The tape I recorded for my own circus snake show went: "See the giant python snakes . . . As big around as a man's arm. They are not poisonous. . . . They kill by constriction and by constriction alone. . . . They're not dead, stuffed or mummified. They're . . . A-L-I-V-E!" But grind tapes were not foolproof. Your spiel still needed the right words, and what the tapes lacked in spontaneity, they made up for by not taking any breaks, nipping alcohol or toking up.

Hennen's tapes were so good that the most skeptical midway walkers couldn't resist spending 50 cents to scratch their curiosity itch. "My phone would ring in the middle of the night," recalled Malcolm Garey. "It would be Peter: 'I got a good one! Listen: "See the little girl born to live her entire life under water. She can't come out or she will die. She's in there now. She goes to school in there. You can come in and see her. You can ask her questions. She may not answer you."'"

Master grind showman Peter Hennen working the microphone on his World's Strangest Baby show. Peter was a former Detroit radio announcer who took a tour around America's midways before deciding to get into the sideshow business. For years he wintered in Kissimmee, Fla., where he built and sold grind shows, their attractions and the best grind tapes in the business.

Malcolm laughed, shaking his head. "What is he talking about? Has he found a real mermaid? You went in the show and here was this big-ass fishbowl with some goldfish swimming in it, and a sign with this disclaimer: 'GOLDFISH DO SPEND THEIR ENTIRE LIFE UNDERWATER. THESE ARE GIRL GOLDFISH AND THEY GO TO SCHOOL. THEY LIVE IN SCHOOLS.'" Snickering, Malcolm wheezed, "Oh, the heat on that one!"

On hearing Peter Hennen's name, Chris Christ rolls his eyes: "Peter was a genius. Very

Peter Hennen on the front of his 10-in-one sideshow in the '60s. He had a regular gay crew that stuck with him year in and year out. At the peak of his midway career, Peter's shows made regular visits to the biggest fairs, including the Michigan State Fair and Toronto's Canadian National Exhibition.

clever, but he liked to take it over the line. His grind tapes were famous. They were good at putting asses past the ticket box. Peter had such a high-pitched, annoying voice, so annoying it really worked."

Grind shows could range from real human freaks to the ridiculous, but the "anything goes" atmosphere started fading in the '70s. Unfortunately, any showman who came up with a unique grind-show attraction soon saw it duplicated by others within a season. A good example was Doug Morgan's "Arabian Giantess," which opened

One of Peter Hennen's grind shows sporting a Johnny Meah–designed and –painted front. Inside was a guy sitting in a pit with some snakes. Peter's wording on his shows seldom failed to pull people inside them. Anyone would pay a quarter to see "The Last of the Tree People" — wouldn't they?

In 1968, Doug Morgan unveiled his Arabian Giantess show. It was an instant success on midways and soon imitated by other operators. There were so many imitations of it at one point that Irwin Kirby, the circus and carnival editor of *Amusement Business*, suggested they form the Arabian Giantess Society.

Ward Hall and Chris Christ framed this "LIVE" 2-Headed Girl exhibit on a former Godding Million Dollar Midway minstrel revue show front. Despite numerous refurbishings, the show never made any money. When they gave up on it, Chris lowered the trailer's frame and put their first museum-style show inside it. For a decade, it did nothing but make money for them.

in spring 1968. His fiberglass giantess was a large, mummified female figure with long eyelashes and big nipples. The show was truck-mounted and the paintings on the fine, three-dimensional front depicted an enormous girl leaping over desert sand dunes. The grind spiel said she'd been found buried in the desert, standing up. Business was brisk, but very soon other showmen had the same attraction.

One winter, Ward Hall had a Tampa artist make him a two-headed princess. "I had enough sense to pay the guy extra money to take a hammer and destroy the molds," Hall quips. No doubt Ward wanted to avoid the

Elaina-Maria inside the Hall-Christ Live 2 Headed Girl grind show. Next to animals the most often-used attraction in grind shows were illusions. However, it was often hard to keep illusion help. Very few workers wanted to stay in the illusion apparatus for extended time periods.

situation Peter Hennen, Micky Saiber, Dean Potter, Eric Rasmussen and Bernie Brusen found themselves in: they were all out at the same time with a "Giant Cleo show," a gaffed-up giant girl created by a New Mexico artist who had made six of them.

Most back-end folks are characters. Jack Sands and his wife, Ruth, are no exception. From the '40s to the '70s, they played hundreds of spots with their various homemade grind shows. June was a first-class painter and tattooer while Jack could frame anything. In February 2000, over lunch at the Giant's Camp on Route 41 as traffic whistled through Gibsonton, our conversation turned to hop-scotching around to avoid playing repeat spots. "Take that 'Vampira' show I had," recalled Jack. "In the wintertime I framed a little show to play two or three Florida fairs. I wanted to get the public's reaction and see what changes we had to make before we went north. We were playing up in Fruitville, 'Date City.' I'd played there with 'Vampira' — this time it was 'Phineas Hideous Tom.' I changed the whole front. It was red-and-white-striped and I painted it black. I changed the entrance

Jack Sands's "Vampira show" with a new coat of paint, title and different lettering. Vampira the Devil's Daughter became "Ampira the Mystery Girl."

Jack Sands's "Vampira" trailer-mounted grind show during the 1960s. Jack operated one or two shows each year up and down the East Coast. The challenge was finding a new non-living attraction each tour. The grind trailer or truck had to be redesigned and re-painted so people at the repeat fair dates wouldn't recognize the show from the previous year.

(Left) When "Vampira" lost its appeal, Jack Sands switched the show over to Phineas A. Fobb. Jack liked these low-nut shows. No animals to feed and no salary needed for the object being gawked at.

(Right) Jack Sands's Peek-O-Rama mainly consisted of Bernard Kobel's freak photos. Numerous back-end showmen used Kobel's photos as part of their exhibits and some made a whole show of them like Jack has done here. Pity the midway trotter that believed "Real and Authentic" meant the attraction inside was alive.

and the exit. I changed every conceivable thing so it wouldn't look like the same thing. Here come a bunch of kids: 'Oh, that's "Vampira,"' they shouted!"

"It's hard to fool a kid," continued Jack. "We're up in Massachusetts one time in the rain. It's a terrible Saturday night and we're getting ready to tear down. I'm stripping out the shows, she's selling tickets. Some kid comes along who had been walking around and around the midway. June calls him over: 'This is the last chance to see this show!' Looking at her, he says, 'No, lady, it's your last chance to get my quarter!'"

Jack framed a show he called "Empira, Queen of the Nile." Billed as a mummy, it was no more than a skeleton with yards of

Jack Sands's fine pickled-baby show mounted on the back of a small truck. This arrangement didn't take up a lot of midway footage and the front part of the truck could be used as a living space. A trailer grind show could be towed behind it. Numerous operators preferred this setup.

material draped around it. Leaning forward and lowering his voice, Jack said, "You could buy real bodies from Roger Livesey — he got them from India. It was customary to take the dead out to this island and leave them there, where birds and animals would remove the flesh and the sun baked the bones. Livesey had a contact who got the bones and shipped them to him in barrels. He put together skeletons to sell to medical schools. I tried to get him to make me an eight-foot giant skeleton, but he wanted too much money."

Many showmen weren't shy about taking your money to look at a phony exhibit. A sign in one guy's ticket box could only be seen on the way out: "Pay Your Money — Enter Quickly — Take Your Screwing Gracefully — and Exit Quickly!" Malcolm Garey points to a photo in one of his albums and said, "God, what a rip-off that was! That's Fat Usher's 50-foot 'Green Gardinia Hahoses.' I went in the show — dinosaur eggs, a two-headed baby, but nothing 50-feet big. I went back out. Fats was sitting in the ticket box. Lettering on all three sides read, 'World's Biggest Rip-Off — 50 cents. If you don't have the right change, it's a dollar.' I said to him, 'Your star attraction's missing.'

"'Wha'dya mean?' growled Fats.

"'Your Green Gardinia Hahoses.' He jumped out of the ticket box screaming, 'Oh my God, I forgot to put it in there!' He ran to

his house trailer and unhooked the garden hose he had rigged up to his shower and put it back in the exhibit area inside the trailer."

Midget horses and big horses, as well as giant pigs and steers, are still good attractions. "Giant rats" that lived in sewers from Paris to Moscow were steady earners. No doubt some showmen now have them crawling around "Saddam Hussein's Dungeons" or "Gitmo!" Malcolm Garey recalled the "Rats of Viet Nam" show he ran for Billy Burr's carnival playing New England fairs: "Midway-goers heard a recorded voice say, 'They eat the flesh, they gnaw the bones, they suck the raw blood from the body. The rats of Viet Nam.' It was pretty strong. Sometimes we got asked by committees to turn that tape off!"

Inside Malcolm's "Gallery of Freaks" show among the pickled and stuffed specimens were various live creatures including a five-legged dog, a big albino python and some freak chickens. The one questionable exhibit was his "Invisible Rabbit." Sometimes people didn't get the joke. Malcolm admitted, "I had a lot of fair managers tell me, 'We had complaints about your show!' They usually don't tell you that. I would take poop from the cages out back of the show where I kept the rabbits I fed to the snake, and put the poop and a water dish in the Invisible Rabbit's cage. People took pictures of it. One day a guy

Showman Malcolm Garey has exhibited all kinds of attractions. Some were legitimate like his Killer Frogs but many were Garey's own fabrications. He enjoyed turning a tabloid press story into a midway nightmare. Malcolm no longer has grind shows. He now tours his Frog Jumping Championships as a booked-on fair attraction.

comes out and says to me, 'You better get in there, I think your Invisible Rabbit's got out.' 'What do you mean?' 'Well, her door is open.' I look him in the eye and say, 'I'm not worried, it's happened before. She'll be back; she has babies in there and won't leave them very long.' He looks at me like I'm nuts."

At one town, Malcolm was beside Max Kitz's Log House. "The World's Largest Pig"

(Left) You can still see a huge pig grind show at some fairs. When Malcolm Garey put out the "World's Smallest Pig," showman Max Kitz told him: "You'll starve to death." Malcolm's "Poor Little Ernie Show," however, did big money and soon developed a reputation among New England show folks.

Malcolm said, "I'd get a baby pig from a farm and keep him about 10 weeks. When he was too big I'd get another Ernie. The Hormone Institute was doing research on old age and experimenting by stunting the growth of pigs. They wouldn't get any bigger than 15 pounds full-grown. I wrote them for information and used their letters

(Below) Malcom Garey's Killer Frog show did very well for him. The entrance banner is the artwork of banner painter Mark Frierson.

was across from them. They began jackpotting and Kitz said, "Look at that guy over there. He's making a fortune with that giant pig." Malcolm replied, "Why does eveything have to be big, giant or the largest? What's the matter with 'the World's *Smallest* Pig'?" Kitz retorted, "You can't make any money with that — you'll starve to death." Despite Kitz's skepticism, Malcolm went ahead and framed a midget-porker show. His grind tape went, "Poor little Ernie. His mother and father weighed several hundred pounds, but Ernie was born to be a mini-pig for the rest of his life. He will never grow up. He will never be any bigger than the palm of your hand. Come in and see him, now."

to flash the show. They wanted $300 or $400 for one of their pigs. I could get all I wanted for $10."

Malcolm's fondness for cheap and outrageous attractions resulted in many shows, including his "Two Hundred Pound Man Eating Plant." The show consisted of a guy sitting there munching on lettuce. Most were funny. In defense of such exhibits, Malcolm said, "I always tried not to rip off the public. I honestly believed in stopping the beefs before they started. Give them what you advertise and if you have to deceive them, keep them happy once they see it. Let them go away laughing about it. If you have to give them their money back because they came out of there like a screaming maniac, then give them their money back. At all costs keep them from running to the show office!"

One time Malcolm was trying to figure out what to do next: "I am listening to the radio. A song titled 'The Funky Chicken' comes on. A band's playing and this guy's going, 'Squawk . . . squawk, squawk, funky chicken!' Wow, that's all right. I'm playing Stamford, Connecticut, and there's a poultry market around the corner. I got six nice chickens and I started to build a 'Funky Chicken' show. I took some geek banners, turned them around and sprayed them with white paint, then lettered them, 'Funky Chicken.' I got the record and played it in the ticket box. I tie-dyed one

A media hurricane over the remains of a sea serpent that had washed up on a Maine beach prompted midway showman Malcolm Garey to quickly glue some cow bones from his granddad's farm into a look-alike sea serpent. The Child Who Never Grew Up was another on-the-spot show creation inspired by a story in a supermarket tab paper.

of the chickens different colors. He became the Funky Chicken. The rest of them were the harem running around in there.

"In the daytime, to get them to run around, I just threw some corn in there. As soon as the sun went down, they'd huddle in the corner of the pit, sleeping. This was no good. I came up with an idea to keep them moving at night: I buried a couple of hot plates in the pit, put a tin sheet over them and threw dirt over the sheet. Turned on the hot plates. It worked fine until I forgot to turn it off one night and cooked half the chickens. That left Funky and one of the white chickens. I go in the show the next day and the white

chicken had died. Funky got me through the weekend. We start to close up and my help comes out and says, 'Funky died!' We buried him on the lot."

Sometimes the idea for a show comes from a newspaper or magazine article. "I was reading in Enquirer about this nun who had given birth to a child," Malcolm recalled. "Embarrassed, she left it in a monastery cellar. It sounded like a hell of a show. I dropped the religous part and changed it to a brother and sister who had a child together. They kept it confined in the depths of their home until a fire exposed their secret. Unfortunately, the child, who was now 13 years old, died from

Malcolm Garey's last big show sitting in the Tampa Armory's parking lot in the mid 1990s waiting to be auctioned off. Small live animals were on display in the trailer. A 30-by-40-foot tent attached to the trailer held the museum artifacts. Malcolm would wait until he had 20–30 people gathered inside the show and then give them a lecture tour of the displays.

been chewed upon. In the beginning of the season I put 50 rats in there. By the end I had close to 300. . . . I was used to the smell and the money it made."

When it comes to the quality of shows, there have always been showmen with no qualms about stretching the perimeters around H. L. Mencken's line "Nobody ever went broke underestimating the taste of the American public." One of the last of the midway shockers was titled "Long Tall Sally — Home of the Whopper!" The attraction was a very tall guy named Zainer Laydick from Dayton, Pennsylvania. John Bradshaw recalled, "I set up one time at the Gateway Fair in Dubois, Penn., and right next to me was 'Long Tall Sally.' I had a sex attraction in the blow but wasn't exposing anything. I'm hanging around the top one day and the sheriff came up and was knocking on the door of her trailer. Zainer didn't answer. The sheriff asked me if I knew where that giant girl was, and I said, 'I don't know, I think she went to the store.' 'When she comes back, you tell her to wait for me because I have to talk to her.'

"After he left, I knocked on the door and said, 'Zainer, it's John Bradshaw.' He opened the door and I told him what the sheriff had said. He said, 'Let me get in drag real quick.' He went over and spoke with the sheriff and the sheriff told her she had to leave town by

shock after being out in society. The spiel said she was dead, but the creatures that roamed the darkness with her are still here inside if you look closely.

"I decked out the inside like a funeral parlor with the little girl laid out in a coffin.

Her parents, brother and sister — mannequins — stood there crying. Behind it all were crushed-velvet drapes. Very classy-looking until you looked closer and saw the fingers of the little girl mannequin were chewed off and everything else around had

Malcolm Garey sitting in the ticket box of his smaller version of the Killer Frog show. Once inside, people could pay Malcolm a dollar per mouse to watch them being fed to the frogs. These South American frogs can no longer be imported into the U.S.A.

In the 1970s, the feature on the Ringling Bros. and Barnum & Bailey Circus was a live goat with a horn coming out of its forehead ballyhooed as a "Living Unicorn." It drew plenty of media attention although some of it was not positive. However, controversial publicity is better than no publicity any day. Some grind showmen couldn't pass up the opportunity to put out their own "Living Unicorns."

sundown. 'What happened?' I asked. Zainer said, 'I flashed the mayor's kid.'"

At various Pennsylvania fairs Denny Gilli had worked beside Zainer who sometimes exhibited as "Helga Hess the German Giantess" in a little 20-foot-square top. Zainer worked with a microphone and would turn the treble switch on the amp up higher to make his voice sound more female, and he would say, "My name is Helga Hoffman and I am six-foot-six tall. I was born in Germany, la-la-la . . . I have been

married three times. I have been divorced three times. My last husband was a midget. When he divorced me, he had two complaints. One, when he kissed me, his feet were in it. Two, when he stood by me, his mouth was in it. If you don't know what I mean, you're going to before you waltz your ass out that fucking door,' at which time he would pull his little panel aside and spread his legs and show that big old gash he cre- ated, screaming, 'It's a whopper, not a chopper — it's a wonder my guts don't fall out!' People came out either mad or howling in laughter."

Chapter 18

Billy Reed Is Still Alive

Joe Kara was a Montreal, Quebec, professional magician and sideshow performer — circa 1930–1960. He put out girl shows and various low-nut grind shows such as Captain Bob Tait — the Ossified Man.

The decline in midway shows was a consequence of the cleanup of fixed games. As long as shows carried alibi and flat stores they needed back-end shows as heat deflectors. "I got front money," said old-time back-end showman Jack Sands. "So much a show out of the office. I didn't tell people what my deal was nor did I ask them theirs. The last few years on the road — and not on small shows either — I was paying no privilege and getting electric 24 hours a day!" Penn Premiere Shows' May 1962 *Amusement Business* ad offered a deal, guaranteed by the show office, for fat shows and sideshows that included complete outfits, new banners and props. Desperate to have a show on the back end, many carnivals only charged shows committee money for rent, foregoing any profit for themselves.

While '60s integration ended the black rock-and-roll midway revues, all other shows continued to do well. A February 1965 *Amusement Business* survey of independent showmen listed over 150 back-end shows. Since carnival owners were putting their money into rides, not shows, when fairs did want shows on their midways, carnivals had to book them in. In this situation, shows with salaries, such as sideshows, were still economically feasible, while grind-show exhibitors displaying fake giants, gangster cars, pickled babies, dead whales, live midgets, fat folks and other offbeat attractions made out like bandits.

Back-end showman Bill Siros was winning money with his fake "Bonnie and Clyde Death Car." A mark counted the bullet holes and informed Bill his car was one short. Next

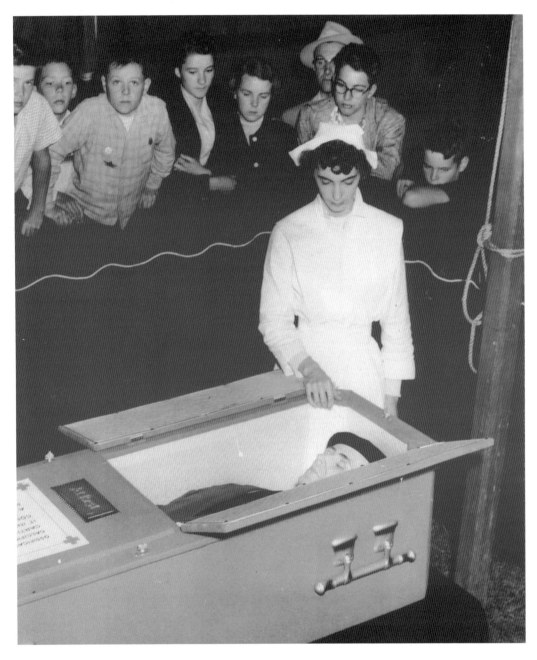

An attendant in a nurse's uniform looks over Captain Bob Tait and explains to the young on-lookers crowding the pit curtain that Mr. Tait was slowly turning to stone. Although he looked dead, a small motor raised and lowered Captain Bob's chest giving the impression he was indeed ALIVE!

morning, Siros came out of his trailer with a gun and added the extra bullet hole in the car's door. Arnold Raybuck's giant steer show and man-eating piranha exhibit did well, and Harvey Boswell had revived the museum-show formula, exhibiting live snakes, pickled punks and curios in sealed jars behind pit curtains. In the blow-off were stiffs Marie O'Day and Gold Tooth Jimmy. Not to be outdone, Carl Thierkauf framed a show called "The Thing." People looked into a pit at a round piece of foam covered in Naugahyde. A hidden air pump made "the Thing" rise and fall with the same steady rhythm that quarters dropped into Carl's ticket box.

These days, Jack Constantine tours more back-end shows than anyone. He stumbled into the business while working as a hotel dance instructor in Miami in 1972. At the Dade County Fair he became friends with back-end showman Randy Rosenson, who convinced Jack to fix up and tour a fake Egyptian giantess. They next partnered on a

(Above left) Veteran sideshowman Milo Anthony had his Monkey People from Tobacco Road on the 1959 Wm. T. Collins Show's midway. Inside were twin pinheads and a snake.

(Above right) "The Thing" appeared on the independent midway at the 1960 San Bernardino, Calif., Orange Fair. The live attraction was billed as having horns like a gazelle, the front of a buffalo, the rear end of a horse and the grunts of a pig. At a dime, few will pass it up.

Over the years, numerous back-end operators have exhibited alligators. They draw well on independent fair midways. This one appeared at the Elmira, N.Y., fair in the 1980s.

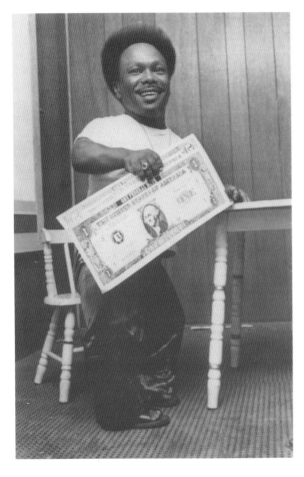

"Drug Abuse" show, and Jack opened with it on Murphy Shows in '73 at Grand Fall, N.D. It made $900 and Jack was hooked.

Next season he bought into Randy's "Little Man" show exhibiting Eddie Taylor and bought Eddie Pedrero's baby show, which he reframed into a fat-man show. His big break came when he landed a booking on Royal American. "Carl Sedlmayr Jr. listened to my pitch and looked at the photos of my show at his Tampa home," Jack recalled. "He kept looking at the photos and then back at me. Finally he said, 'Mr. Constantine, will you be traveling with these shows?' I told him I would be. He took another look at the photos, then stuck out his hand: 'You're booked!' I stayed there five years. After Royal, I just branched out and went everywhere. Now I play five fairs at once."

The show front for Jack Constantine's Fat Albert Show at the Canadian National Exhibition in Toronto, Ont., in 1982. Part of the success of this attraction was Fat Albert's pleasing personality. Anyone who went in and saw him was not disappointed in his size or his conversation.

The back of Fat Albert's pitch card reads: "I always like to meet new friends. God Bless You. Hey Hey Hey!" He sold a ton of these while making himself and Jack Constantine a very good living.

I had reached Jack in May 2000 at his Florida winter quarters, where he was waiting for his crew of "Little Women" from the Caribbean islands to arrive at the Tampa airport. Nearly half his shows featured them — they were his best attractions. Before them, a huge fat man was his mainstay. Kent Nicolson was born in Canton, Miss., but grew up near Jack in Astabula, Ohio. "The first year I called him Hank Jackson but he did that 'Hey-hey-hey' thing from the *Fat Albert* cartoon," Jack said, "so I changed his billing to Fat Albert. He was with me 14 years, went all over with me. His show had the highest single-day gross of any grind show in history on the Conklin midway at the CNE one year. I have had some good days with the 'little women' shows — but nothing like that!"

Customers going in to see Fat Albert, whose show front said he weighed 860 pounds, were greeted with his cheery "Hey, hey, hey." He would let patrons photograph him seated for 50 cents; if they wanted him to stand up for the shot, it was five bucks. It was

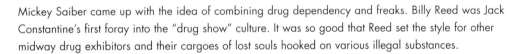

Mickey Saiber came up with the idea of combining drug dependency and freaks. Billy Reed was Jack Constantine's first foray into the "drug show" culture. It was so good that Reed set the style for other midway drug exhibitors and their cargoes of lost souls hooked on various illegal substances.

The pictorials on a grind-show front are one of the main reasons why potential patrons stop and consider going inside. Once they have stopped to look, the small signs (reader's boards) serve to suggest and verify the legitimacy of the attraction inside. This sign hanging above the viewing area of Billy Reed is a classic!

not unusual for Albert to come off the road with $40,000, and soon be phoning Jack for five grand more. When Jack asked what happened to all the money, Albert said, "When I makes big money I live big!" Sadly, Albert's dead, but his image lives on. A painting of him decorates Jack's museum-show entrance

banner, and inside a video of "Fat Albert" plays continuously on a TV screen.

Another winner for Jack was a drug show entitled "Billy Reed — Condemned to a Living Death." The show never failed to attract fairgoers and the media. In 1990, a story in the *Syracuse Herald-Journal* described Billy: "A sor-

rowful sight as he rolls back and forth in his wheelchair with a twelve-foot python slithering around his body. Billy wears a surgical gown. A blanket covers his legs. He stares blankly into space." And a sign inside the exhibit described Billy's downward spiral after his friend died of a drug overdose: "AFTER ONE

"HELLO' HIS name is BILLY WEST. HE was a "CRACK" addict. After smoking "CRACK" and using other drugs, "LSD" etc., HIS brain couldn't function ('FRIED') HE freaked out after HIS best friend died from an overdose. After 100 trips of "LSD" and "CRACK", Billy now believes this snake is a reincarnation of HIS best friend.
PLEASE - NO CONVERSATION WITH BILLY.

Billy Reed sitting in a wheelchair with a python draped around him. The signage behind him explains the snake's presence: "After 100 trips of LSD and Crack, Billy now believes this snake is a reincarnation of HIS best friend." Billy's hardest task was watching television for twelve-hour stretches! The TV is mounted above the viewing window, out of sight.

HUNDRED TRIPS ON LSD AND CRACK, BILLY NOW BELIEVES THIS SNAKE IS A REINCARNATION OF HIS BEST FRIEND."

On the outside of Billy's exhibition trailer were the words "Mobile Medical Unit No. 2," and a young woman in a lab coat with a stethoscope hanging around her neck ran the ticket box. When the Syracuse fair office received calls about Billy from patrons concerned about his treatment, a *Herald-Journal* reporter proclaimed, "Don't worry about Billy. He's just fine, the fair's crack-addict exhibition is a simulation. City health inspectors and State police visited Billy. Sgt. Robert Marquart, after his inspection, said, 'There's nothing criminal over there.' . . . Nightly, after the show closes, Billy strolls the midway, goes for a beer, eats a good dinner and then ambles off to sleep at a quality hotel."

Jack's biggest gripe is turning half his show's gross over to midway owners or fair boards. With most shows priced at a dollar or less, he needed a lot of customers to carry his nut and now only plays the bigger fairs and no still dates. He has slowly added shows, and some years are better for him than others. Recalling the previous season, Jack said, "I've had 29 good years up until last year. It wasn't a bad year, at least not for others, but I have a lot of shows and a heavy nut. If I lay dead for three years and then go back out, I would have a hell of a year. . . . If I could stay around New York City, I would be okay. In the midwest you do okay the first year, but the second year it drops to half. When I was on RAS years back I changed my show fronts every year. Now I change one here and there. It doesn't seem to help anymore. Once you play a spot for 10 or 15 years, they know it. Nowadays you have to keep your frontage small because rents are so high.

"The expenses eat you up. It's not only the footage or percentage, but the electric, garbage, charging you to stay on the lot, all the dings. Also the winter expenses plus insurance, taxes, phones, pagers, walkie-talkies, beepers, all those vehicles on the road. It all costs money to keep going."

What has he learned in the business? His response is instant: "Don't believe anything you hear and half of what you see." Recently,

This is Harold Overturf's West Indies Midget show in the early 1980s. The grind tape droned: "Little people — little people — look way down by your feet — little people — no higher than your knee." Inside were a small lady and two small men. The men wore boxing gloves, and periodically put on a boxing demonstration. After Harold died, Jack Constantine began using these folks in his shows.

In the 1990s Jack converted several of his little-lady show fronts into shows that looked like small houses. One is built on a very small trailer. This one is a solid-panel front with wood sides and vinyl roof. It is harder and harder for grind showmen to get good locations on midways. Their shows have to be adaptable to the spaces left between the rides and fun houses or in the case of Jack's midget horse show — in among the center joints.

Jack has been booking his giant rat, little horse, and "Little Women" shows on independent fair midways. "The shows have to be good quality and no heat for the independent midway," he confided.

Jack's expertise in show fronts is evident. "You got to be captured instantly by it and it has to say 'maybe' — it has to be believable," he articulated. "Why they say no to 'Space Aliens' and yes to 'Snake Girl,' I don't know. With the 'Snake Girl' [an illusion with the body of a snake and the head of a girl] you get all kinds of questions: 'How does she live?' 'How do you feed her?' 'How does she travel?' Actually, one in a thousand going through that show believe it!"

About the future of the back end, he said, "Regretfully, I'm afraid the back end for guys

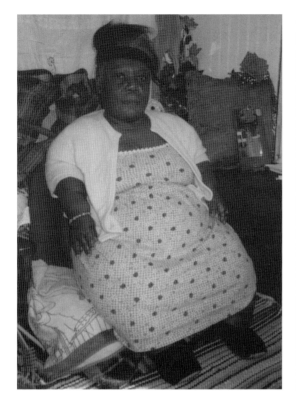

Jack's little ladies come from either Haiti or Jamaica. Little Gloria Rodent and her husband Sonny are Jamaican. Ruby Saddler, who was working for Harold Overturf, spotted Gloria in their hometown and recruited her at age 21. Gloria, who is two-feet-five inches high, is now in her early 50s. She wants to be a gospel singer. Note her color photo for sale beside her.

The front artwork of Lee Kolozsy's trailer snake show was done by Lew Stemm. The pit holding the snake is on the ground. No stairs to climb — no lawsuits if a patron falls down them. People looking into the pit are clearly visible to midway patrons which helps to draw others into the show.

like me is ending. I can only think of 10 people in all the country still doing it."

Lee Kolozsy is Jack's main contemporary. Originally from a circus family, Lee's a genius when it comes to grind-show constructions. His innovations in show-front designs for portable exhibition spaces have improved these shows as much as any other showman before him. I met Lee in the early 1990s at the Orlando Fair when he was setting up his snake show and I quickly recognized the show's uniqueness. A huge front served as a backdrop for the pit, where spectators stood on the ground and looked at the snakes. There were no stairs to climb and all the spectators were visible to those passing by on the midway. The front was close to 40 feet long and appeared to have been built on a large truck or trailer, but, surprisingly, Lee had framed it onto a small 14-foot utility trailer. Later in the summer, I saw his "Giant Rat" show. Built on a small pickup camper, the folding front,

This is the back of the large snake show built by Lee Kolozsy and set up at the Orlando, Fla., Fair in the early 1990s. The whole front collapses onto this little double-axle trailer. One thing you learn fast in outdoor show business — You don't want any trailer that doesn't have a double axle.

This is one of my favourite pit-show fronts. Lee Kolozsy built it on a small pickup truck. Using the outline of the huge rat as the show front is pure genius. The pit is on the ground. Black fencing with lampposts holds the non-paying public out of free-viewing range.

when erected, formed the outline of a giant rat. The pit was placed in front of the show front, with a semi-circle of fencing to keep non-paying customers from seeing the exhibit.

"I designed them out of necessity," Lee said about his innovative grind shows. "By the time I was full-time in the back-end business, the big rides with scenery started arriving on the midway. Show owners who had paid half a million dollars for a ride didn't want some booked-on rag bannerline blocking their big ride. I designed these shows where the pit was in front and the scenery behind. They could place my front in line with the back scenery of the ride and I wouldn't block anything. This was the only way you could get a good location."

The huge rats that grind showmen ballyhoo are neutrinos or capybaras from South America. They are usually of mild disposition and easy to feed and keep. Pete and Lee Kolozsy keep re-inventing the look of grind shows. Pete presently has a nice rat show on tour that is framed like a garbage dumpster.

This grind show featuring a $50,000 coffin appeared on the 1975 Century 21 Show's midway. Motorcycles, cars and other toys of the rich and famous were often grind-show exhibits as were their images in wax but this is the only playboy coffin on display that I know of.

"Carnivals started putting a lot of center joints down the midway, even in front of the shows and the fun houses," explained Lee. "Patrons were jammed in between the joints and the show bannerline. They didn't have the distance to get back and properly see the artwork on the banners. With my design, the scenery was set back 20 or more feet and you could see all of it on any midway layout. I designed those new pit shows so all you can see is asses and elbows. People say I'm the McDonald's drive-through of the back-end business."

What lures customers into grind shows? "You have someone walking down the midway and what gets their attention is the scenics, the flash, the artwork on the front," he said. "The midway patron looks at the front and then his or her eyes are quickly drawn to the people looking into the pit. They realize the only thing keeping them from looking in there too is 50 cents. Monkey see — monkey do. The worst grind show can have the biggest business imaginable if it has the right location where thousands of people are going by it.

"One key to the grind-show business is that you tantalize them," Lee continued. "You hold it just out of reach. Look at circus posters — they are similar to show fronts and banners. Both tell a quick story. The grind show is like hot pants and mini skirts. What makes them work is not what you see, but what you can't see. You got to make the public want to see it."

Around the 1970s, fairs and carnivals began charging showmen for having their house trailers on the grounds. Some tried to eliminate paying two rents by combining their show and their living quarters. Here, Peter Hennen has put his "Dracula's Daughter" attraction in the back room of his house trailer. To be in business, you just had to raise the blinds on the trailer's rear window and get in the ticket box out front.

Lee started working grind shows around 1963. "Bob Atterbury had one out on Hamid's Steel Pier," he recalled. "Bob had taken a janitor's storage area and put up three banners outside it. It had an 'Arabian Giantess' figure in there. It went for a nickel and was a real heater! I only worked it a few days and this mean-looking lady came up to the ticket box and rapped her nickel on the top. 'Son, is that giantess alive?' I told her, 'It's just like you and me.' She paid her nickel and went inside. A few minutes [later] she came charging out, screaming at me, 'I thought you said it was like you and me!' I said, 'That's right — just a couple of dummies.'"

Lee recalled the times when the last big 10-in-ones and illusion shows stood beside fake attractions of all kinds: "I was in Charleston, and our family's 10-in-one illusion show was set up there — shows were having a bit of a revival at that time. Jack Waller did one of the best ballies I ever saw. Jack's 'Rosemary's Baby' show was something else. This was when the movie of the same name was a big Hollywood thriller. The front part of the trailer was a party room — lots of girls and a variety of substances frowned on by the law. The middle held the illusion, and Jack slept in the back of the trailer. It was the

first place that I saw a motorized curtain. The room in the middle, used for the illusion, was draped off and had a gloomy look. The person working the illusion, once he was set in it, could push a button and the drapes around him would open so the marks could look in the window and see the attraction.

"Jack had two small banners and a ticket box out front. When someone bought a ticket, the girl in the ticket box pushed a buzzer and a bell went off in the front room of the trailer. Whoever was working the illusion got up, went back there and put his head on the block. It was a head on a sword and you saw this little devil body — this little made-up demonic character. The person whose head was in the illusion put on a pair of fake devil's horns. It was effective and people liked it. If they went into the 'Rosemary's Baby' show first, they would go to the other shows."

For the few back-end showmen left, the competition for the midway patron's dollar is greater than ever. They duke it out with big rides, three-storey fun houses, laser dark rides and a midway overflowing with game and food stands. Everybody has a sound system and is booming either music or a pitch at you. Jack Constantine's latest weapon in his attempts to maintain a suitable income with his shows relies on a simple sign on what he calls his "conversion ticket boxes." The sign hangs on the front of the box and in bold letters states "Special $1.00 — Today." In very small vertical letters are the words "Under 10 Years Old." In even smaller letters, a tiny sign

Fat Albert is still featured on Jack Constantine's museum entrance banner despite being long gone. However, inside, the late Fat Albert can be seen on video. Jack's latest weapon in maintaining high enough grosses to stay in business is the "conversion ticket box." The front reads "SPECIAL $1.00 TODAY." The small print down the side reads "Under 12 yrs old." When adults step up with a buck, they are shown a sign on the counter: "Under 12 yrs. old — $1.00. Adults — $2.00." It always pays to read the small print — anywhere.

on the top of the ticket box reads, "Admission $2.00. Children under 10 years old — $1.00." When adults and teenagers step up with a dollar bill in hand, the ticket seller simply points to the price sign and asks them for another dollar. Most shrug, pay up and go in.

The
AMERICAN
GOLIATH
TEN FEET FOUR
AND ONE HALF
INCHES HIGH

CARDIFF GIANT
WORLD'S GREATEST HOAX

DIMENSIONS
of GREAT GIANT
HEIGHT   10 ft 4½ in
LENGTH of ARM   4 ft 9½ in
SHOULDERS   3 ft 1½ in
ACROSS WRIST   5 in
LENGTH of FOOT 21 in
WEIGHT   990 lbs

EIGHTH WONDER
OF THE WORLD

CARDIFF GIANT

25¢
CARDIFF
GIANT

CARDIFF GIANT

THE AMERICAN
GOLIATH

CARDIFF GIANT

AS SEEN ON CBS-TV
YOU ARE THERE

Chapter 19

Stiffs, Stone Giants and Siberskoyes

Dead, stuffed or mummified attractions require no salary. Even if you don't use them they are good to carry as an insurance policy. You can never go wrong with a two-headed baby, devil fish, elephant children, shrunken cannibals and other grotesque wonders made of wax, papier-mâché or composite concoctions.

During World War II, Homer Tate was the showman's go-to guy for weird displays. Tate's creations have posed as ancient cavemen, Borneo mudmen, shrunken Japanese soldiers, lost aliens, shortened Amazon missionaries and Vietnamese foresters severely affected by Agent Orange. When not in use, these little people cost you nothing and wait quietly in their shipping boxes for their next role. They require only new labels and reader boards with newspaper clippings authenticating the attraction.

Morbidity appeals to much of the show-going public. During the 1920s, Dayton, Ohio, resident C. E. Warren advertised mummified Indians in *Billboard* for $25 each. In 1938, J. Omer Barnhart advertised "the best preserved real human mummified body ever shown the American public. Will stand close inspection by doctors or anyone else," and in 1975, *Amusement Business* carried this ad: "Mummified man: Genuine. Unwrapped in horror coffin. Used as theatrical and carnival attraction for a 100 years." Rumors still continue that John Wilkes Booth's body made the carnival circuit.

An ad in a September 1947 *Billboard* read, "The Most Talked-of Exhibition in Ohio — 'EUGENE'. . . . Over the past eighteen years, over seven hundred and fifty thousand people have

The author with Captain Harvey Boswell at Harvey's old roadside zoo in Wilson, N.C. Harvey had museum-style sideshows out years before it became the trend in the 1990s. His blow-off usually contained stiffs "Gold Tooth Jimmy and Marie O'Day." The sign leaning up against the tree came from one of Harvey's ding shows. Harvey died a few seasons back.

Harvey donated several banners from his museum shows to the carnival museum run by the International Independent Showmen's Association in Gibsonton, Fla. This one ballyhoos the famous toured stiff — Marie O'Day.

viewed the body at the Littleton Funeral Home. This exhibition is available for Homecomings, Street Fairs and Carnivals in Ohio, September, October and November. Displayed in 26-foot trailer. Write or wire R. Littleton." Directory assistance still had a number for Littleton; however it's his son Barth who answers when I call. "Do you still have Eugene?" I ask. Barth casually answers, "No." After I explain my interest in his father's popular exhibit, he kindly relates the

mystery man's history. On June 6, 1929, the body of a man in his mid-50s was found on the highway. The coroner said he had died of natural causes. A notebook scrap was found on him with the address 1118 Yale Ave., Cincinnati, but that turned out to be a vacant lot. The person living nearest this address was a man named Eugene Johnson, so Barth's father, Roger, his grandfather Harry and mortician Olin Moon called their corpse Eugene.

With no next of kin to be found, the black man's body was embalmed, and for the next 35 years Eugene lay in state inside a small house adjacent to the funeral home. Nearly a million visitors signed the register book. "Eugene received a new suit almost every year," Barth says. "Summer weekends saw lines of people waiting to pass by the bier. A few years back it was necessary to build a wire screen across the room to protect him from souvenir seekers.

Pranksters had taken him from the building several times. Once he ended up on the campus of the Ohio State University in Columbus." Afterwards, Barth figured it was time to bury Eugene. He purchased a regular plot in the local cemetery and bore all the funeral costs himself.

Dead bodies required no salaries. Much the same could be said of Log Houses. Cross-sections of huge trees turned into living spaces or "Log Houses" were low-nut exhibits. The Detroit News Tribune carried a 1905 ad for a "Mammoth Spruce Log" on exhibit on Gratiot Avenue for 10 cents admission. This Washington State log was 38 feet long, nine feet in diameter and weighed 15 tons. Inside was a parlor and office with furniture carved out of its walls. Also inside were two dens containing native wild animals, including "Teddy" the mountain lion.

Jamie and Dale Allen's Original Redwood Log House has been on display for nearly 60 seasons. An estimated 1 million people have passed through its bedroom, living room and kitchen. The log was the fourth one cut from a 1,900-year-old tree that was 14 feet in diameter at the stump and 267 feet high. The Allens' chunk measured 33 feet long and about nine feet wide. It took four months to hollow it out and remove 11,000 board feet of lumber.

At the 2003 Tampa Fair, their log house was on the independent midway. Relating its history, Jamie Allen said, "My grandfather actually had it prior to my father. My granddad couldn't

The exit end of Jamie Allen's famous Log House. You can see the wear on the top of the log where people have pounded it with their fist to see how strong it is. People go in without a ticket but are asked to contribute something on their way out. Most do.

afford a regular house and lived in this one for seven years. It doesn't have a bathroom. My grandparents went around to schools and town centers. I have older gentlemen come through now and they tell me, 'This log house came to my school when I was a kid. I paid a dime then and so, lady, I'm going to give you a dime now!' We run strictly on a donation basis."

Asked about other log houses, she said, "Used to be one up at Benson's Wild Animal Farm. The people who had it on tour left it there — nobody attended to it. Squirrels ate out the roof. It is now sitting in a museum in St. Augustine, Florida. Ours is the only touring one. The wear I have on it is where the big men come out and beat on the end of it — they want to see how solid it is. Redwood is a very soft wood, not a hard wood. Every time they do it, they weaken it a little more.

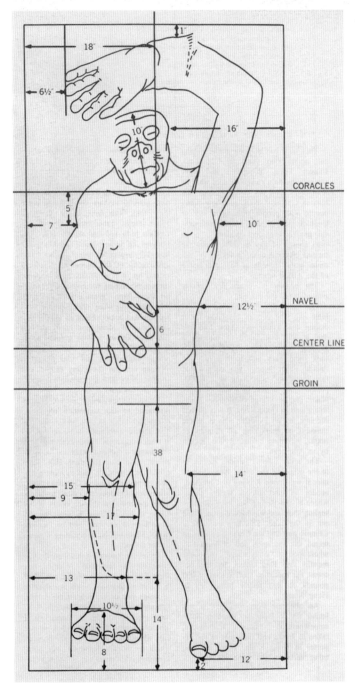

A drawing of the "missing link" as reproduced from Ivan Sanderson's *Argosy* article in Frank Hansen's promotional booklet. Sanderson's description included: "There is a comparatively fresh corpse preserved in ice, of a specimen of at least one kind of ultra-primitive fully-haired man thing that displays so many heretofore unexpected and non-human characteristics as to warrant our dubbing it a 'missing link.'"

"I cover it with a tarp when it rains or when I'm at home," she continued. "It doesn't leak but it absorbs water; then you weigh more at the scales! It weighs 36,000 pounds. I get two to three miles to the gallon pulling it."

Jamie works the Log house show with a ding. "I don't think I'm in the ding business," she said, smirking. "I raise money for non-profit organizations. That's what I do. I could charge all the people $1, $2, $5 to come in — whatever the going rate is out there. In my mind, when you pay for your wife or your husband and kids to get in the fair, pay to park, feed them once and let them ride, you have spent a good whack of money. I want everybody to see that log. If I didn't, I wouldn't have it out here. That guy who's got three little kids that all need new shoes can afford a quarter or 50 cents for his whole family to go through there. And if you can't afford to give me that dime, nickel, quarter — whatever — then you need it more than me and . . . have a nice day at the fair."

Not every attraction is as straightforward as a log house. Some attractions come with a complicated story line — perhaps to fudge the truth. The May 1969 *Argosy* magazine featured Frank D. Hansen's Siberskoye creature on its cover while posing the question "Living fossil: Is this the missing link between man and the apes?" One contempo-

Jamie Allen's Redwood Log House set-up at the Florida State Fair, Tampa, Fla., in the mid-2000s. Jamie prefers to stay off the midway. You pay less money on the independent areas at fairs that are usually less hectic than the midway where you can hear the attraction's grind tape better. Lately the "log" has been as far north as the Erie County Fair in Hamburg, N.Y.

The cover of the May 1969 *Argosy* issue containing the "Missing Link" story written by the magazine's science editor Ivan T. Sanderson after a visit to Frank Hansen's frozen creature. This is a brochure that Frank sent out to fairs and malls. Sanderson stated at the beginning of his *Argosy* article: "I must admit that even I, who have spent most of my life in this search, am filled with wonder as I report the following!"

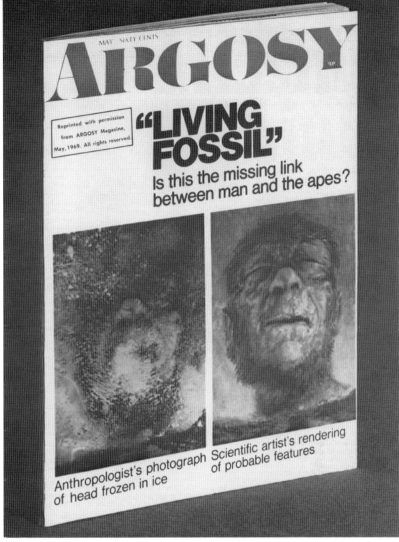

rary showman said of Frank's creature, "It was no more than a frozen overcoat." Quick research showed that Frank was still in his hometown of Rolling Stone, Minn. On the phone, Frank seems at first to be hard of hearing, then claims he can't remember much these days and repeats my questions to his wife to prove it. This act goes on for 15 minutes, until, about to hang up, I say, "Other show guys told me it was only a 'frozen overcoat.'" Frank groans, "Oh no! I never heard that. Anybody that said that was just jealous. There have been a lot of duplicates of it."

I tell him I can't find "Siberskoye" in the dictionary. What exactly was it? Chuckling, Frank replies, "Siberskoye was taken from the word *Siberia*. For a long time there was some

Back-end showmen Rick West and Frank Hansen shortly before Frank died. When I talked to Frank a few years back, he said he was not a carny. Maybe in his mind he wasn't but he was sure one heck of a showman. He knew how to keep the publicity kettle at a continuous boil. His stories, true or false, were always entertaining.

claim or opinion that this specimen that I am exhibiting came from the way northern areas. Where it came from has never really been proven or settled by any of this investigation. It is still a mystery — even to me. Dr.

Heuvelmans of Belgium and Ivan Sanderson, science editor for *Argosy*, declared it absolutely authentic. Siberskoye was really a name used to mean 'ape-like man.'"

I quote an article to him from the *Regina Leader Post* in which he stated, "I don't know the person I got it from." "Yep, that's exactly right," exclaims Frank. "The most important thing about this particular show is the fact that I as an exhibitor always presented it to the public as a mystery. In other words, I didn't know all the rudiments about it. I knew how I got it and where I was told it came from. When the scientists got involved with it, I told them the same thing.

"I was exhibiting the oldest John Deere tractor at the Arizona State Fair, and that's where I met the owner of the specimen. He was standing out in front of my tractor show, watching people go through it. He was not in it for the money," relates Frank, explaining that this nameless gentleman is a multimillionaire. "His whole motive was to determine people's feelings relative to the abominable snowman. Did they believe it or not? The Siberskoye was always exhibited as a 'What Is It?' I never made any claims to its authenticity or what it represented. I just listened to people and copied down what they had to say. It was a good exhibit because of the controversy it created. Fifty percent would say, 'Oh, anybody can see that it is made-up,' while the other 50

percent or sometimes 100 percent would say, 'No, you can see it's authentic. Look at this . . . look at that.' That's what made it such a promotional item — the mystery!"

Frank's creature was mysterious but not as foggy as his story. "I'll tell you, I never knew what it was," he says. "I never let the ice get down to where I could even touch it. It was always kept frozen, even when we were off the road. I had to build a refrigerated coffin. I kept that thing frozen from the time I made the decision to make it into an exhibit as the

In 1968 Frank Hansen started exhibiting "The World's Oldest John Deere Tractor" as a free attraction. It had been for a time on exhibit at the Smithsonian Institution. After Frank left the midway, he continued to travel to antique car and truck rallies and farm shows with the tractor. After the John Deere Co. disclaimed manufacture of it, Frank billed it as the "Mystery Tractor."

America's Number *1* Agricultural Attraction

Frank Hansen started exhibiting the Siberskoye Creature in 1967. Here is the creature at Frank's home in Minnesota, set up the way he exhibited it in malls. The attraction did well indoors or outdoors. Frank framed it right and spent big money in making it look legitimate. Everything about the frozen creature was first-class.

I'm not sure if this is Frank's creature show or an imitator's. There were a lot of copycats. Some duplicators simply placed an old fur overcoat in the bottom of an ice chest and sprinkled convenience store ice around it. Others had their own sculpted versions embedded in ice.

owner wanted."

The *Argosy* story propelled Frank's creature into the national spotlight and Sanderson went on Johnny Carson's TV show. Frank recalls, "That's when they broke their oath to me! I let them look at it with the agreement that they would not report anything about what they had seen or write anything about it without getting permission from the owner. They came to see it in the middle of the winter. They were looking at it and Huevelmans reached up and pulled this light I had hanging over it so they could see better and he broke the cord. He put the hot lamp down on the glass lid — it shattered. The most awful odor came out. Huevelmans said, 'It's real, it's real; that's what you call putrification. This proves for once and for all that the abominable snowman does exist.'"

After showing in Canada, Frank ran into trouble with customs officials on his way back into the United States. "The American government tried to take it," he says. Frank claims that

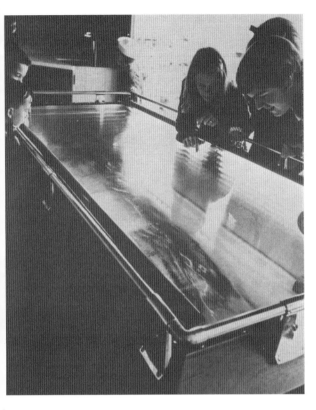

Minnesota senator Walter Mondale's office came to his aid, but his troubles snowballed until he simply wanted out. He finally found a museum owner in England who wanted the creature but the owner took it back. "He sent a refrigerated truck," Frank recalls. "The same day the story 'Creature That Is Not Man or Beast Vanishes' appeared in the newspapers, I was on my way to meet the owner's people to turn the specimen over to them. We made the switch inside a building. I don't know what happened to it. The scientists insisted it was absolutely authentic, but they couldn't get me to agree to that and they didn't know who the owner was. They couldn't get to the owner, so it passed away as a mystery."

Frank insists he isn't a carny, but he sure acts like one. Irwin Kirby wrote in his *Amusement Business* column that Frank had stopped exhibiting the frozen creature because so many other showmen were copying it. Complaining he didn't like the fakes out there, Frank says, "Many people were copying it and so badly. It is unbelievable what people put out there and tried to pass off as our specimen." One imitator made a creature from a stuffed rubber diving suit laid out in a freezer with a couple of bags of convenience-store ice cubes sprinkled over it.

Frank told everyone a phony story. Only near the end of the yarn that he spun, did he mention any hint of a second figure. "Right after the government tried to glom it, I had a model maker duplicate the creature," he claims. "Coming back from Canada, I switched it right away. I put the model in and continued to exhibit it that way. You couldn't tell the difference! I paid a lot of money for it; I left the real one at home." Frank finally stopped showing his frozen thing and switched over to a cryogenic show. Cryogenics was a hot topic at the time.

Back-end operator Rick West, who visited Frank in fall 2002, says Frank admitted the creature was a latex figure. "It is amazing that this latex figure stirred up so much controversy," Rick tells me. "What were those two scientists thinking when they looked at this thing? Of course latex smells, it gives off an odor. The creature had been stored for 20 years. It was lying in several inches of water when I saw it, but still looked good. . . . If it hadn't been frozen, it would just be another 'What Is It?' or 'Cardiff Giant' figure."

Down at the 2008 trade show in Gibsonton, Fla., back-end showman Pete Kolozsy mentioned that show artist Lew Stamm had painted Frank's various shows. He suggested I stop and see Lew near Knoxville, Tenn. Over pizza, Lew tells me about his experiences with Frank Hansen. "I asked Frank where he had the creature made and he blew up," Lew exclaims. "I'm staying in his basement. I saw a picture of it standing upright with a sculptor's rod through the main body. The creature was made in Hollywood by a scenic artist, using human hair. One hand half-covered the face. Frank's biggest challenge was getting the ice covering the creature clear so

After the Siberskoye Creature got too hot to handle, Frank Hansen replaced it with an exhibition of Cryogenic Suspension. Note the nude girl in one of the pictorials and the sign stating: "On view in a few pre-selected areas of the United States and Canada." I would assume those places would be the ones where grind shows did their best! Frank's shows always had that clean scientific look to them. This one is painted white and baby blue.

you could see it."

Laughing, Lew says, "Frank claimed he shot the creature out hunting one day. It fell in the water and they couldn't get to it. They went back in the winter and it was still there, frozen in the ice. They chipped it out and hauled it back to his farm."

Malcolm Garey recalls another hoax, this one perpetrated by showman Sammy Lewis: "Years ago he had out 'Dr. Schort's Miracle Discovery.' It was a fur coat he kept alive. He had an old housetrailer and you looked in the

Bob Foglesong's Snowman Show as it appeared on the California National Orange Show midway in 1970. Note the spelling of "Abomidable" on the sky board and "Abomindable" on the ticket box. Sometimes showmen mis-spell names to titillate and attract the public's attention — or perhaps their spelling is just abominable!

side window next to the door. The midway side of the trailer was painted orange and lettered, 'Dr. Schort's Miracle Discovery. What Is It? We Don't Know — Tell Us!' You paid him and walked around the ticket box and peered in the window. This thing is lying there and looks like it is breathing as it has a pulsating effect to it. Tubes are running in and out of it with a saline solution — blood!

"One day I went over to see him and knocked on his trailer door. He called to come in. Seated, Sammy said to me, 'Ya want something to drink?' 'Sure, why not.' He grabs this tube that was going into the thing and a glass and fills it up and hands it to me. I said, 'Look, I'm not into that!' He laughed, 'It's just fruit juice!' 'Holy Jesus,' I exclaimed. He showed me the rest of it. The fur coat was lying there with a vacuum-cleaner bag underneath it. He had some kind of rheostat attached to it so the bag would blow up and then collapse, over and over. This was the pulse of the monster. The buttons on the overcoat were the eyes. When he positioned the coat just right, you could see them. He had a shower curtain that went around the exhibit area by the side window. When he closed the show, he just pulled the window shade down. He ran that sucker for a long time!"

The biggest stiff on tour in the '60s was Jerry "Tyrone" Malone's frozen whale. In an unusual career shuffle, Malone went from selling motor homes to chauffeuring a 20-ton whale from town to town. In 1967, he and motor-home dealer George Zoaranian acquired one of the 200 sperm whales snared off the Californian coast that year. The whale was named "Little Irvy" after George's son. George put up the hundred grand needed to frame the show and Malone got a freezer company to provide the refrigeration unit in lieu of advertising. The show opened in July at Fisherman's Wharf in San Francisco in a special tractor-trailer unit. The Kenworth tractor, affectionately named "Big Blue," had six grand worth of chrome and four grand in paint and upholstery. In 1978, Malone told *Amusement Business*, "The people love the truck that carries the whale as much as they do the whale." The public's reaction to the truck led Malone to frame a "Boss Truck" as his next touring attraction.

The 1970 wide-nose, 13-speed, V-12–powered Kenilworth didn't go over too well at its first date — until he climbed into it and started revving the motor. That's what the crowd wanted. He drove the truck 114.89 miles per hour and set a speed record at

This is Jerry "Tyrone" Malone's frozen whale show in the 1970s when it was one of the hottest attractions on American midways. At one fair, a group of showmen in the show cookhouse spotted beside the "Little Irvy" show were ribbing Jerry about his whale being a replica. He jumped up and threw open the back doors of the reefer truck holding the whale. Immediately this terrible stench engulfed the area and knocked out business at the cookhouse for the rest of the day.

Snap Wyatt kneeling beside one of his papier-mâché sculpted Cardiff Giants. Snapp, who got his name from being able to paint signs quickly, was not only one of the best banner painters of all time but a real genius at crafting show attractions from papier-mâché. He wrote and sold a detailed manuscript on how to do it. His giants were easier to transport!

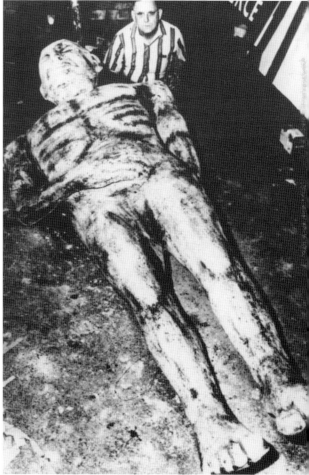

Bonneville Salt Flats. Next he was in the movie Movin' On, and from then on crowds showed up at fairs and sportsmen's shows to see it. His love of trucks also led to racing semi-trailer rigs. Unfortunately, Jerry was a big rounder who rarely passed a bar. He had driven up to see painter Lew Stemm, who was designing a truck museum Malone wished to install near Pigeon Forks, Tenn. On the way back to California, his car careened across the median and was crushed under a semi-trailer. Jerry died in the accident.

Many sideshows bore the "Barnum Museum" title and many freak animal shows were billed as "Barnum's Barnyard." Things smacking of Barnum history, including the Cardiff Giant, always did well. In the 1950s, banner painter Snapp Wyatt turned out papier-mâché Cardiff Giants. The original giant was 12 feet long,

Snap Wyatt's July 27, 1959, *Billboard* ad advertising his Cardiff Giants for sale.

almost five feet broad, and weighed nearly four tons. Made of gypsum in a barn near Quincy, Ill., by sculptor G. Fabricio Salawasout in 1868, it was hauled to Chicago, then shipped to Buffalo, down the Erie Canal to Cardiff, N.Y. Before burial, the giant was given long rubbings with sand and water. The pores in the skin were carefully created by picking the entire face with leaden hammers faced with needles. The peculiar gooseflesh look fooled many viewers. The figure was bathed in sulfuric acid to age it and then interred on farmland. A year later, well diggers uncovered the sleeping hoax.

The farm owners covered the giant's grave with a tent and were soon grossing two grand daily. Barnum heard about it and wanted it. Local citizens David Hannum, Dr. Westcott and Colonel Thorn bought a half-interest in the giant's future exhibitions and turned Barnum down. In 1869, a Dr. Judd was staying at the Utica, N.Y., Empire Hotel and the "Cardiff Giant" was on display just a few doors down,

The front and back of the pitch booklet being sold for the Cardiff Giant while on exhibition at 113 Washington Street, Boston, Mass. The Giant was discovered in 1869 and the sketch shows the raising of the giant on the Cardiff village farm thirteen miles from Syracuse, N.Y. Notoriety from the association with P. T. Barnum gave it a lasting appeal for both showmen and public.

inside a vacant shop. After viewing it, he returned to the hotel bar, where the talk in the room was about the giant. One of the bar patrons discussing the attraction said he was a sculptor and could make one just as good. Judd introduced himself and soon hired the

sculptor to create a replica giant out of concrete, which he then sold to Barnum.

Barnum did well with the replica giant, and when he tired of it, he leased it out to other showmen for 3 percent of the gross. B. C. "Doc" McKay went broke exhibiting it in

Macon, Ga., in 1880 and simply left it on a flat car in the rail yards. A 1934 *Billboard* story brought up the Cardiff Giant saga again. The original one, it was reported, had been stored in Iowa and was now being leased by the Syracuse Chamber of Commerce for exhibition at the fall State Fair there. Unfortunately, people weren't all that interested in the hunk of stone, and the carnival playing the fair didn't want it, as it was too heavy to move easily, so the stone giant remained under its canopy at the fairgrounds until the fair board threatened to drag it off the property. The Chamber of Commerce was last heard trying to get the salt museum at Onondaga Lake to take it.

A few winters back, I visited Ward Hall and Chris Christ at their Gibsonton home. Driving into their place, I almost collided with a huge gray object lying in the circular driveway. I got out and inspected it — it was their papier-mâché Cardiff Giant. As I walked toward their door, several birds swooped down and began drinking rainwater that had collected in the giant's navel.

That wasn't the last time I saw it. Showman Bobby Reynolds got hold of it and had it propped up at a 45-degree angle inside his "Believe It — You're Nuts" museum at the 1996 Hamburg, N.Y., Fair on the midway of the James E. Strates Shows. In a few days, the midway and Bobby's museum sideshow

What is odd about this Cardiff Giant show is the large chair between the ticket boxes. It is sitting there as if the 'stone' giant was alive inside and could sit in it. The center banner boasts: Barnum's $60,000 Cardiff Giant.

would be moving into Syracuse for the State Fair there. The Cardiff Giant would return to his beginnings.

There was no advance publicity about it. Forty years ago, carnival press agents Star DeBelle, Richmond Cox or Mae Hong, who were as comfortable handling the road company of a Broadway hit as they were ballyhooing the bearded lady, would have ignited a media storm over "The Giant's Return!"

It was just a fake replica, but remember — the replica was good enough for Barnum.

Chapter 20

The Last Docs, Professors, Colonels and Preachers

Chris Christ making an opening with armless wonder Louise Capps on the bally during the 1986 Texas State Fair (Dallas). Ward Hall and Chris Christ had played the fair for close to two decades. Their 1986 season was one of their last, with a big cast of sideshow performers. Midway economics no long favoured big back-end attractions with a lot of salaries.

Midway showmen should have had it easy in the '60s. Unfortunately, they were seeing their livelihoods eroding while the new generation of showgoers were tripping on free love and copious amounts of drugs. Even girl shows folded once guys could see strippers in bars. But somehow the sideshow Docs, Professors, Colonels and Preachers sporting paperless diplomas in markology held on. While the media and an uninformed public believed sideshows were becoming a thing of the past, the remaining ones were still among the 10 top-grossing attractions at major fairs. What finally did in back-end showmen was midway politics and economics. When the era of "spectacular rides" began in the '70s, all carnival owners cared about was obtaining bigger and newer rides so they could enhance their bidding power for the best fair dates.

Midways tried to outbid each other for fair contracts. The fairs won and the independent showmen lost as midway owners offloaded their high expenses onto their tenants. The biggest challenge for those left in the outdoor amusement business became finding enough workers for simple jobs like ticket selling. The solution was to eliminate individual ticket boxes for each ride and show in exchange for centrally located ticket boxes. Independent showmen no longer sold their own tickets at their shows. In 1977, Royal American was the last big outfit to switch over. Their accountant, Guy Gardner, told *Amusement Business,* "Universal tickets do save labor, provide better control, and limit

Today's old-timers include Ward Hall, whose sideshow career goes back to the mid-1940s. With his partner, Chris Christ, he has owned wax shows at seaside amusement areas, numerous grind shows, and at one time, four touring sideshows. Their 2009 edition of the World of Wonders sideshow is the last big show of its kind presently playing the midway circuit.

the tickets needed but at the same time they may hurt impulse buying which is the key to the sideshow operations."

To eliminate rolls of differently priced tickets, carnivals switched to coupons for rides and shows. Patrons could buy books of them. Once the 1975 Texas State Fair credited coupons with a 21 percent increase in

A strip of P.O.P. (pay-one-price) ride and show coupons.

their gross, there was no going back. Concessionaire Garnett Walker warned, "Anytime the kids are walking down the midway with coupons rather than cash, it's going to hurt the games." Shows were hurt too. Owners viewed shows and fun houses as vehicles for mopping up loose coupons like greasy-spoon diners used bread to soak up beef gravy.

The '80s brought pay-one-price promotions. Midway patrons were sold a wrist bracelet that allowed them unlimited ride and show visits. Sideshow owner Elsie Sutton rationalized, "Too many people wore out the show." People came in and out of the show when they wanted, avoiding the blade box and the blow-off dings. Normally they paid a buck and stayed for the 50-minute show. The decreasing gross from the quarter-priced blow-off and blade-box dings no longer justified Sutton staying in business and in 1985 she put the sideshow up for sale.

By this era, most of the old-timers — those who'd started in the early days of the 10-in-one business — were either dead or retired. Few newcomers arrived to replace them. Asked why no new showmen had come along, grind showman Lee Kolozsy replied, "Nobody wants to invest $50,000 to $60,000 in an unconventional piece of equipment. People going into the business

Elsie Sutton continued to run the sideshow after her husband Whitey died during the Clearfield, Pa., fair. She finally stopped touring in the 1980s. Here it is on the James E. Strates midway a few years before it closed. In the end, the bannerline was made up of banners representing painters Snap Wyatt, Sigler and Johnny Meah. Sutton and his partner Slim Kelly had stopped ballying long ago and relied only on the grind tape. Note the teaser curtain hanging down over the catwalk.

today would rather buy a food trailer or a ride from a manufacturer. Almost all the shows are made by the showmen who operate them. Nobody knows how to frame or operate them. Nobody wants to work that hard."

One new sideshow operator in the '80s was Rick Dennis. He put out a 10-in-one in 1984, but the next spring he wrote to Jon Friday, who had helped him, "We canceled the '85 season due to no reliable help and your bouncers and things are on the way to

THIS LICENSE MUST BE POSTED IN A CONSPICUOUS
PLACE AT ALL TIMES WHEN ESTABLISHMENT IS IN OPERATION

$30.00   STATE OF OHIO $30.00
RICHARD F. CELESTE, Governor

1989

Department of Agriculture
OHIO CONCESSION LICENSE

To Operate

Circus of Oddities

COST TO PARTICIPANT _$1.00_

Issued To   NON-TRANSFERABLE

FIRM NAME _Jon D. Friday_

STREET ADDRESS _69220 County Rd. #687_

CITY _Hartford_   STATE _Mi_   ZIP _49057_

DATED THIS _2nd_ DAY OF _August_ 19_89_

LICENSEE: _____ INSPECTOR _Art Lumm_

ANY CHANGE OF GAME PLAY OR PRICE SHALL VOID THIS LICENSE

$30.00 $30.00
AGR 1004 (Rev 11/88)   №   5239

Ohio Dept. of Agriculture Concession License for Jon Friday's Circus of Oddities sideshow in 1989. This is a gaming license but somehow the state managed to ding Jon a buck for it. Operating a show of any kind brings out a constant parade of health, tax and electrical inspectors — not to mention the SPCA, the fire and police departments.

Johnny Meah working on a banner at his workshop beside his home in Riverview, Fla., during the early 1990s. Johnny is still one of the premier show artists. For many years he was also a performer on circus and carnival sideshows and in show management roles. He is an author and a living book of knowledge on the business.

you pre-paid. We lost $2,000 with it. I'm stuck with a $300 python and enormous phone bills." Rick made more money renting tents, but stayed in the business running grind shows. Help problems continued, though — at one point he had to use a mechanical headless girl. However, a young pig he had thoroughly tattooed grew into a 1,000-pound pink-skinned art gallery that drew well.

Show owners have figured out new ways of getting the gross without letting the help handle cash. A few seasons back I was alarmed to see a teenager sitting in a ticket box before a grind show at the CNE with neither change nor tickets. Admittance was gained by handing him a small plastic card that was swiped through a machine called a "Blinkie" before being handed back. Take away handling cash and you take away the biggest lure for people to work on midways.

Many showmen blamed welfare, but it wasn't a new problem. "On some shows, paydays were hit-and-miss affairs," Charlie Roark said. "Ringling, like other shows, held back two weeks' pay; one was paid the second week before they closed and the other came with your last pay. Habib the Egyptian fire-eater got his first hold-back-week pay and blew. He figured that was all he was going to get, so why stick around? When I bumped into him in N.Y.C., Habib told me he had a great job — no work. It was called welfare."

With no freaks and few good working acts around, getting a gazoonie to work the nail board became impossible. "Show guys want to give them $100 a week and tell them to sleep under the stage," Dean Potter lamented. "They don't go for that anymore. People can get a couple hundred dollars a week washing dishes."

In spring 2002, I caught up with Dean again. He was preparing to leave for his 52nd season. His carnival career included being a half-and-half and a sideshow and freak-animal show operator. He was going out with his single-O snake show called "Big Mama." Why had he switched from human oddities to

The late Dean Potter standing beside the ticket box of his Bloody Mama snake show in the late 1980s. Dean's career as a back-end showman and performer spanned five decades. He owned sideshows, animal oddity shows and grind shows. Earlier in his midway life he had been one of the best half-and-half attractions. He's sadly missed by many show folks.

animal ones? "I'd rather shovel shit than take it," he said. "The secret to keeping a sideshow out was getting good help. It kept getting harder each year. You really have to love it or you wouldn't put yourself through all that.

Even when it is running at 100 percent, it's a nightmare. Nobody would be acting up and then you'd go into your biggest spot and the sword swallower would be drunk and the bearded lady doesn't want to work because she lost her boyfriend during the night. When I started in the business, if there weren't a half-dozen freaks on the stage it was a lousy show. Give the audience a good fire-eater and sword swallower and they're satisfied today."

As sideshows diminished, one of the better acts still working was Captain Don Leslie. Before he died a few years back, he recalled, "Norman Brooks wanted me to go with him in 1982 on his 'Strange People' sideshow. Norm had been out a dozen years with girl shows with drag queens and was a swishy queen himself. However, in a beef you wanted him on your side. I did swords and pins in the blow. My sister did the blade box and electric chair. Floyd Block did blockhead. Wayne, who Lady Diane had broken in to swallow swords, got cut up trying to swallow 16 blades, so he only did fire and magic.

"Then I went over to Jeff Murray's sideshow. Jon Friday was doing the outside openings and the blow and blade-box pitches. Murray sold tickets and made the freak-book pitch. The acts were me and one girl."

There was no question that a segment of the public were turned off sideshows, and

The bally of Norm Brooks's Strange People Show in 1982 with Ms. Joan (Sabrina) Leslie the electric girl, talker David King and sword swallower and sideshow performer extraordinaire Capt. Don Leslie. Brooks toured a first-class sideshow as the big 10-in-ones on midways were coming to an end.

some showmen blamed poor attractions. Irwin Kirby's weekly Opinion column in *Amusement Business* quoted a letter he had received from Jon Friday in March 1975: "Unfortunately for the outdoor show world the pickled punk, wax dummy and stiff back end operations have been living off the ignorance of the public for so long that large seg-

ments (especially teenagers and young adults) avoid the back end like the plague. No matter what you bring to a fair, when you set up in the back end you become one of them and in the same league."

With no freaks and few working acts, sideshows became smaller and smaller. During the 2008 Gibsonton trade show, artist Denny Gilli told me about having a small sideshow with a performer named David King: "King later had his own sideshow where he talked on the bally and then went inside and did all the acts except for the half-and-half in the blow. One day he's in the middle of the blow-off spiel and a guy in the tip interrupts him, saying, 'Now, buddy, I watched you out front talk about 10 acts. I paid my 50 cents. I didn't say anything when you did all 10 of them. Now you're telling me for another quarter I'm going to go in there and see a half-man, half-woman. If I go in there and you take your pants off, there's going to be trouble!'"

Many young midway owners grew up around midways that had no back ends. They held negative views about shows. If they wanted back-end shows, the advertised for "Family Oriented Shows Only." They didn't want to lose a date over a beef about a two-headed baby or a guy in drag billed as a bearded lady. But there were still a few show-friendly operators. An aging Harvey Boswell

Part of the Ward Hall–Chris Christ sideshow bannerline on the Gooding Million Dollar Midway during the 1969 Brocton, Mass., Fair. Note the striped teaser curtain and how close the bannerline is to the tent. You can just see the striped bally cloth of the long performer's stage running along the back of the tent.

had limited his tented museum walk-through to a handful of spots close to home. He had played some fairs with Amusments of America and wrote me in 1986: "We did pretty good, sold our own tickets and took their coupons. Best of both worlds."

The media didn't help. Fair newspaper stories applauded their nicer, politer and politically correct appearances with more

The bally on Sam Alexander's 1982 sideshow. Most of his performers were young people except for Poncho Raymond from Montreal who did knife throwing. Poncho had worked in the past for Sam at Montreal's Belmont Park. Sam's banners had been painted by Sigler and the overall color scheme of the show was green and orange.

Sam Alexander, the former two-faced man, in the ticket box of his sideshow on the Bill Lynch Show's midway at the 1982 Bridgewater, Nova Scotia, fair, shortly before he left the sideshow business. It was the first time I'd seen Sam without his mask on. He had gone through numerous operations to reconstruct his face.

flower tubs, litter barrels, rest benches and midways without freak shows. A reporter visiting the 1991 N.Y. State Fair wrote, "The demented thrill of yesterday is clearly absent, and it's not even too rough for kids. If your kid wakes up screaming the night after your family trip to the fair, it's more likely to be from an upset stomach full of curly fries and sno-cones thoroughly scrambled by a spin on the Paratrooper than because of a freak-

(Above) Tim Smith's big horse and big steer shows back on the Erie Country Fair's independent midway at Hamburg, N.Y., in the early 1990s. Tom Binborn was the first to design and pioneer these clean-looking steel-sided exhibition shows that looked like mini-barns. Numerous other operators copied them.

The daily record statements used by Deggeller Amusement Co. to keep track of attraction grosses. This one is for the Fat Show, booked into their date at Kissimmee, Fla. The ticket price was a quarter. Deducted from the gross were state taxes, the insurance charged by the carnival and the percentage paid the operator. The carnival ended up with over 40 percent of the gross.

show–inspired nightmare."

To find the last freak-animal shows at fairs you had to look around the cattle barns. Tom Bindborn was a successful grind showman exhibiting big and little horses and large steers housed inside compact metal enclosures painted up like barns. Many showmen copied his ideas, and his stepson Wayne Pies has done well following in his footsteps. And in 2000, there were six shows at the Erie Country Fair in Hamburg, N.Y. Jim and Suzan Kavalczik's Big Bear Country exhibit and Tim Smith's Giant Steer and Big Horse grind shows were way off the midway. Tim pointed out

that on the carnival midway many people believed his attractions were fake. His biggest problem was that people didn't know what a "steer" was.

Bobby Reynolds's large tent museum was set up near the Strates Shows' giant wheel. Several of his "Believe It — You're Nuts" show banners depicted what were clearly illusions, but inside all the public saw were the illusions apparatus up on a stage. Sitting kitty-corner from the show at a picnic table, he exclaimed, "Some people come out of that museum show after only being in there a few minutes. They complain there is nothing to see. I tell them, 'It took me 50 years to collect all that crap.'"

Admission to "Believe It — You're Nuts" was only a buck. Bobby's usual position inside was in a director's chair beside the fence enclosing his real two-headed baby, which was housed in a small trailer pushed into a corner of the tent. You paid extra and looked in the trailer's back window. While I'm talking with Bobby, a pudgy kid of about

Mickey Dales was one of the best broad tossers in the business. In 1950 he briefly owned Dales Bros. Circus. He ended on carnivals where they needed his grift experience to keep on top of the flat stores and alibi joints. When the rigged games and back-end shows started disappearing in the 1970s, many carnies claimed midways had lost their soul.

12 swaggers up and butts in: "Hey, mister, where's the World's Biggest Bat?" Bobby calmly points his finger to a large brown stump-looking object lying between two of the tent's center poles and says, "Right there!" No doubt this kid, seeing the text-only banner outside, had imagined a huge hairy upside-down creature — not 200 pounds of papier-mâché molded into a baseball bat and painted an ugly brown. The kid grinned and said, "Cool," before heading off to stare at the "Lady With No Middle." If more kids like him come along, the back-end business may have a future!

The Michigan-based Norton's Auction Company specialized in selling off used show equipment. Here one of their auctioneers is busy trying to sell Al Moody's famous two-headed bull during a Tommy Sciortino auction held in a tent behind the Tampa, Fla., chapter of the Showmen's League of America clubhouse in the 1990s. Tommy can be seen just behind the bull.

During February many showmen head to the Florida State Fair held in Tampa and to the trade show held at the International Independent Showmen's Association grounds in Gibsonton. On a sunny afternoon in the early 1990s a crowd gathered on the other side of town inside a tent behind the Tampa Showmen's Club. Lined up around the tent's perimeter were some of the last remnants of the back-end midway business — wooden

The Johnny Meah–painted front of the Hall and Christ "World Freak Museum" sideshow in Florida in November 1988. The operation was more of a walk-thru museum-style show than a stage sideshow. They still had the fat man, a tattooed lady and dwarf fire eater — and snake handler Pete Terhurne seen here on the bally.

carousel horses and old arcade machines had drawn the rich antique crowd. Freak-animal showman Dick Johnson kibbitzed with Ward Hall, Chris Christ and Malcolm Garey. Slowly they moved along, looking over the jars of pickled freak animals, an old blade box, the Sutton sideshow ticket boxes and banners showing that "Strange Girl EEKA" being captured alive. Ribald laughter punctuated their banter.

Carousel horses set sales records, and arcade machines sold high. Show folks held back patiently, waiting to bid on Al Moody's stuffed two-headed bull, its glass eyes reflecting the seated bidders. But the fast money soon dried up, and the showmen's bids failed to meet the reserved minimum. Al's son lugged the bull back home. I left the grounds feeling I'd been to a wake for the back-end business.

Ward and Chris are the senior citizens of the sideshow world. They have been out there longer than anyone still doing it. Ward, who started in a circus sideshow in the mid-1940s, is now in his 70s. Chris is a boomer. A Buffalo, N.Y., native, he joined Ward's show at 17 in 1965 and soon became his partner. At the top of their field in 1976 they had several grind shows, seaside wax museums and four sideshows. Their last big sideshow operation with freaks and working acts was in 1983. They survived bankruptcy

The 1986 Hall and Christ sideshow cast at the Dallas, Tex., State Fair. Top, from left: Mavis Johnson — illusions, Lorette Fulkerson — tattooed lady, Louise Capps — armless wonder, Dolly Reagan — the ossified lady, Malinda Maxie — beaded lady, bally girls Carrie Spears and Nola Capps. Front from left: Max — ticket seller, Ward Hall, Steve — snake handler, Todd Knight — pin cushion, John Trower — sword swallower, Bruce Hill — knife thrower, Chris M. Christ, Dick Tanas — front talker, James Soper — tickets. Very front: dwarf fire-eater Pete Terhurne, fat man Bruce Snowdon, frog boy Dickie Brisben.

two years later, after their tented illusion show — Wondercade — folded, leaving piles of bills.

They managed to hang on to the museum show they had framed on a semi-trailer in 1976. When they sold it in 1987 they kept the boxed "Two-Headed Princess" and "the Chinese Giant Lady." These exhibits, plus wax

The few midway sideshows left were filling their tents with dead, stuffed and man-created exhibits. Fewer acts meant less people to up and down the show. Hall and Christ survived by hiring more new-wave sideshow performers. Here posed with veterans fat Bruce Snowdon and Pete the dwarf are new recruits who included Stephanie Monseu and Keith Nelson of the very talented and successful Bindlestiff Family Cirkus on the back right.

For years Hall and Christ used only a grind tape to put people into their show. By the early 2000s the taped spiels no longer pulled in the crowd and they had to go back to continuous ballys to keep the tent filled. Three talkers were used in rotation. Ward and Pete Terhurne and a Coney Island show gal get ready for another bally at the Allentown, Pa., fair.

Another old favorite, the headless lady, was put back into the Hall and Christ sideshow. For a number of years the headless lady illusion had been used by several grind showmen. The original goes back to the 1930s.

(Below) Gary L. Syers cooked on tugboats hauling barges to Alaska from Seattle. In his off time he exhibited this grind show he had built. In 2004 Ward Hall and Chris Christ decided to leave the road and sell their show. The next year, Syers came along to buy it but ended up framing a new show with their help. After the Tampa Fair he sold it to Ward and Chris, who continue to tour it.

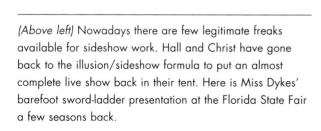

(Above left) Nowadays there are few legitimate freaks available for sideshow work. Hall and Christ have gone back to the illusion/sideshow formula to put an almost complete live show back in their tent. Here is Miss Dykes' barefoot sword-ladder presentation at the Florida State Fair a few seasons back.

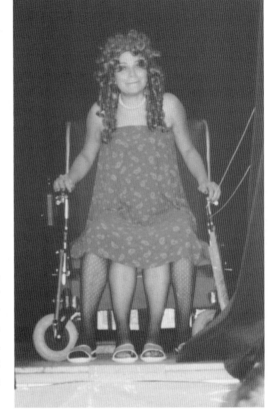

(Left) The Hall and Christ "World of Wonders" at the Florida State Fair in the early 2000s. Cases of artifacts plus a big live snake were still on view. Acts did fire-eating, sword swallowing, human pin cushion, knife throwing, and the electric lady routine plus fat man Bruce Snowdon held down his position near the exit. People liked the live portion of the show.

(Right) The four-legged girl is another act/illusion added recently to the Hall-Christ sideshow. The extra-wide wheelchair is a nice touch. Johnny Meah's banner out front depicts the four-legged girl in a shoe store. The clerk had to get different-colored shoes to supply her shoe needs.

Hollywood stars transformed into freaks, were the basis for their new canvas banner-line museum/sideshow. With few acts around, the museum format was the only way to continue.

"With the museum show, we had our biggest year in 1987–88, the first time we had it out," quipped Ward. "The grosses have gone down because we have been going over the same route for 12 years." Most of the show was in glass cases, but a few live acts were retained. Some were also impossible to work with. Ward recalls the trouble he had with bearded lady Malinda Maxie (Vivian Wheeler): "I got a complaint about her. I

Archie and Mae McCaskill's illusion sideshow. In the 1950s it was one of the premier back-end units. Illusion sideshows were very similar to a 10-in-one in that they often had the same dings and pitches including the blade box and a blow. The only difference was that they didn't have any freaks.

investigated it. She was sitting on the stage up there with not a real short dress on, but it was above her knees. When two guys came in, she spread her legs and flashed them. She didn't have any panties on. I told her, 'You can't do that.' She replied, 'They don't believe I am a real woman!'"

In the early '90s, they still had dwarf Pete Terhurne on the bally. Inside, pin cushion and sword swallower Red Stuart and Lorette, the tattooed lady, worked on a small stage near the exit, while fat man Bruce Snowden occupied a chair in front of the stage. The only other breathing occupant was a python. In 1998 on teardown Sunday at their Meadowlands, N.Y., date they couldn't find any extra help, so they posted a $500 bond with a temp labor agency. They wound up with a guy on steroids who couldn't lift and another chap toting a briefcase. They didn't get off the lot until late Wednesday and blew the opening days of their next fair.

To get the show up and down, Hall and Christ had to put more live acts back into the show. In 2000, Ward said, "I had three young sideshow performers from San Fransico plus a couple of old-timers and it went over well. We couldn't get any roughies, so the sideshow acts saved us." The blow-off was back in the show but still no blade box. Chris confided, "We couldn't have two dings in there and still run three shows per hour. The only reason I put the live blow in was so we could have a crew to move it. It basically paid for the crew. The morning you told them they wouldn't have to do a show anymore, all they had to do was move it — they would all leave."

Not only had the inside of their show gone through various changes but the outside changed as well. In 1995 the show became an illusion sideshow using the old stage along the back wall, and the front was comprised of two semis with fold-out banners painted by Johnny Meah. The show had seven girls and two magicians and was managed by magic veteran Floyd Bradbury and his wife, Cherri. The only working act was a girl in the blow billed as a "Torture Act." She walked on broken glass and laid down on the nail board. The show was too expensive to operate and the next year they went back to the museum format and Meach repainted the front. The show remained the same through 2003, when Ward and Chris tried unsuccessfully to sell it.

In the fall of 2004 a buyer turned up. Gary Syers had long been interested in sideshows and had framed a small grind show he worked on the West Coast between stints as a cook on a boat pulling barges up to Alaska. The show was rebuilt that winter with a huge canvas bannerline painted by Bill Browning, and Johnny Meah painted new entrance banners. World of Wonders opened at the Tampa Fair Febuary 2005 and did well. However, Gary decided he didn't want to tour it and sold it back to Ward and Chris. The show is mostly illusions worked by several girls, with a smattering of sideshow working acts. The blow-off varies from a live pin-cushion act to pickled bouncers. The blade box has been reinstated, as well as a few cased curios.

Chris and Ward know the spots to play and exactly where on the midway the show has to be to do the best business. They don't need John Kenneth Galbraith to tell them the economy is in trouble. They know things are tough when they see a lot of worn and old bills show up in their ticket aprons. They adjust their prices to the different areas of the country and to the various promotions run at each fair. "On one-third of the biggest fairs in the country, you can't book sideshows on them," griped Ward. "Most of the biggest midways don't want shows."

Ask Ward what he missed about the old-time shows and he'll tell you there was nothing prettier than a canvas sideshow tent with stars around the poles, a flashy fringed valence around the sides and sawdust on the ground. Chris remarked, "The thing that I used to enjoy in the business that you don't get anymore was competition. As long as it stayed above board. No cheap shots, just going head to head. Eric Rasmussen was the guy we'd go head to head with and then go out and drink beer together. It was just one-upmanship. At the Columbus, Ohio, fair he would have his illusion show across from our sideshow. I had a four-by-four easel board painted up and placed on our bally. It read: 'ALL LIVE FREAKS — NO ILLUSIONS.' Eric got a piece of four-by-eight plywood and painted on it: 'ALL ILLUSIONS — NO SICK OR DISEASED PEOPLE!'"

Chapter 21

Sideshow Hoi Polloi

An evening out to enjoy new-wave burlesque can often end in a brawl between masked Mexican wrestlers. Intermission at the revived roller derby can include someone swallowing swords and a woman twirling tassles with her ample breasts. At an upscale fundraising dinner, fire-eaters often replace the after-dinner speaker.

These days, attractions long associated with midways are more often found off them than on. At the 1999 Edmonton Fringe

Publicity still taken by Alison Braun for the Jim Rose Circus Sideshow. *(Left to right)* Mr. Lifto (Joe Hermann) in drag, Matt "the Tube" Crowley, Jim and Bébé Rose, the Torture King (Tim Cridland) and the Enigma (Paul Laurence).

An advertising card for Lucha Va-Voom featuring masked Mexican wrestling and the Velvet Hammer Burlesque troupe at the Palace in Los Angeles. The Velvet Hammer was one of the first of the current burlesque-rival troupes.

One of the most popular exhibits during the 2008 Toronto Nuit Blanche all-night art romp was Roy Kohn and Kate Vasyliw's "Meeky" show set-up near the Ontario parliament buildings. Roy painted the banners, created the wax Meeky figure and shot the documentary film shown outside to the tip. An estimated 6,000–7,000 saw Meeky. The film was recently screened at the 2009 Coney Island Film Festival.

Festival, spectators paid a dollar, entered a tent and gawked at a four-minute act called "the Cobra Girl." The midway snake-girl illusion was presented by Ghost Writers Theatre Company, headed by magician Ron Pearson. In true sideshow fashion, Ron told spectators that Cobra Girl was the result of an experiment that went horribly wrong when an

American scientist tried to create a super-woman by injecting her with cobra venom.

And in the cafeteria lunchrooms, while some teenagers responded to calls of "Yo, geek" with smiles, others bandied about the word "freak," as their parents had done during the hippie era. Over in Spokane, Wash., high school officials were trying to ban

informal dances called mixers. The problem was a dancing style called "freaking." One school official described it as "having sex with your clothes on." New York City clubbers called it "grinding."

Real bearded ladies made a comeback. Bearded Jennifer Miller, who John Bradshaw had pulled off the Coney Island boardwalk

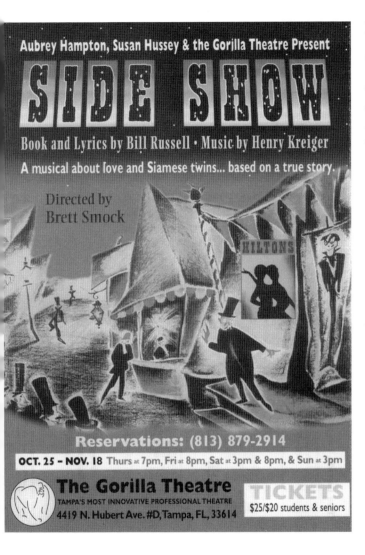

The Tampa, Fla., Gorilla Theatre playbill advertising the play *Side Show*. Sadly, audiences didn't warm up to *Side Show* quickly enough to keep it going. The story was based on the lives of conjoined twins the Hilton sisters.

Circus Historical Society member Ed Todd and bearded lady Jennifer Miller upstairs in the Coney Island Museum during the 2004 visit by CHS members.

some years back, had a part in the musical *Side Show* about the lives of the conjoined Hilton Sisters. When it opened at N.Y.C.'s Richard Rodgers Theater, Miller told the *New York Times*, "I thought there should be a real bearded lady in the house, just to keep them honest."

By 2005, Dr. Gunther von Hagens of Germany had drawn a worldwide audience of 17 million to his anatomical exhibitions of human corpses. When his scientific wonders hit Toronto that fall there was a firestorm of publicity. A *Globe and Mail*

The brochure advertising Gunther von Hagens' BodyWorlds 2 exhibit held September 2005–February 2006 at the Ontario Science Centre. The old-time anatomy show was back doing gangbuster business just like in the old days.

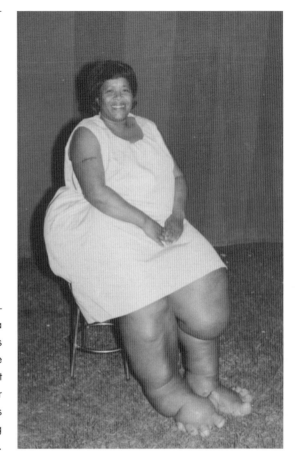

Sylvia Porter, the elephant foot girl, was a terrific sideshow attraction in the 1950–60s era. People today assume diseases like elephantiasis have disappeared. A recent Canadian initiative successfully treated over 80 million people with elephantiasis. There is hope that the world's greatest disfiguring disease can be eradicated in 20 years.

article entitled "Honey, I Scared the Kids," reported, "A Science Centre show has parents asking if corpses are family viewing." By replacing their natural fluids with fluid plastic, the process von Hagens calls "plastination" turns corpses into remarkable anatomical models. Before hardening, the "plastinates" or bodies are fixed into life-like poses.

Sideshows have been without legitimate freaks for a long time, and medical people are doing their best to keep it that way. In 2005, televised news informed us that Egyptian twins who were joined at the head had been surgically

The author and Todd Robbins during Todd's inside tour of Coney Island for members of the Circus Historical Society in 2004. Years before the new-wave sideshow performers came along, Todd was busy keeping the sideshow arts alive on the midway and in clubs. In past summers he has passed on his performance skills to those attending the summer Coney Island Sideshow School.

A booking brochure used by the renowned British performance artist Lucifire. She is now married to Dave Tusk and together they present the "The Fire Tusk Pain Proof Circus." Lucifire is one of the world's top performers of sideshow, burlesque and nouveau-vaudeville. Her truly inventive fire acts have advanced the sideshow arts to a higher performance level.

separated in 2003 at a Dallas, Tex., hospital and were going home. An October 2005 *Globe and Mail* story, "Hope for fixing birth defects," pointed out that U.S. surgeons have pioneered a technique to repair birth defects with custom-made tissue from an unborn child's own fetal cells. A month later, the world got its first face transplant recipient in Amiens, France. Pre-natal imaging that allows parents to decide if they want a defective baby born has also played a large part in reducing the births of freaks.

While sideshows were almost gone from midways, appearances of sideshow acts on club and theater stages increased. "If you've been waiting to see a man put out a lighted cigar on his tongue, chew up and swallow a light bulb and hammer a nail up his nose into his skull, then congratulations, your patience has been rewarded," screamed a September

2003 *New Yorker* blurb for Todd Robbins's *Carnival Knowledge* at the Soho Playhouse. Seats went fast at $35 to $45 a pop.

Few suspected tattooing would become the fastest-growing fashion trend since baseball caps. Nor did folks suspect the tattoo crowd was dragging a bunch of sideshow geeks and sword-swallowing wannabes with it. However, body modification and sideshows went together like hot dogs and mustard. Nose rings and nipple piercings quickly spread from a few devotees to becoming a common look.

The true venue for the reborn freak-a-toriums were bars that hosted bands with names like Tit Fuck Me Jesus. The audiences weren't reading *Amusement Business* or *Variety* but flipping the pages of *Tattoo Art International*, *Shift*, *Implosion* and *Juxtapoz*, and appreciating the carny-circus–inspired artwork of geniuses like Joe Coleman. Those really in the know were getting Chris Fenner's fanzine *Freaks*.

For a time, the sideshow stew simmered in underground clubs waiting for something to bring it to a boil. That catalyst was the Jim Rose Circus Sideshow. The troupe started in Seattle, Wash., in 1991 and the next year, tour-managed by Jan Gregor, they went on their first tour, criss-crossing Canada playing rock rooms. By the time they returned to Seattle, they were riding a tidal wave of publicity and were booked on the rock festival Lollapalooza.

Rose started out as a performance poet

Jim Rose and his crew's big break was getting on the Lollapalooza tour. The crowd had no idea what they were watching but they were bowled over by the sideshow acts. Here, Jim Rose eggs the crowd on while Matt Crawley blows up a water bottle until it explodes.

and soon added fire-eating to his poety readings. Lava-like patter has been flowing from him ever since. Onstage with him are Mr. Lifto, who hangs an anvil from his penis; Matt the Tube Crawley, a regurgitation specialist who blows into a hot water bottle until it explodes; and Tim Cridland the Torture King, who sticks long needles through various parts of his anatomy. Adding sex appeal is Rose's soul mate and assistant, Bébé the Circus Queen. Seeing the show at the Network Club in Buffalo, N.Y., in October 1995, *Art Voice* writer James Moss

wrote, "They eat worms and slugs, chomp on lightbulbs, drink quarts of bile, put their hands in rat traps, swallow razor blades and drive nails up their noses. They're crazy!" And he added, "They are nice, gracious, intelligent and entertaining as hell."

The Jim Rose Circus Sideshow's first Toronto date was promoted by Gary Cormier at the Olde Brunswick House, a student watering hole featuring Friday-night dwarf tossing. Rose's last Toronto venue was in 2002 for Gary at the Opera House, a venue that had descended from opera to Asian porn before

An ad from *NOW* magazine for the last appearance of the Jim Rose Circus Sideshow at the Opera House in Toronto for promoter Gary Cormier. Most new-wave sideshow acts depended on club promoters for dates but often the venues were small and profits not that big. High gas prices combined with the long distances between gigs still makes touring tough.

being turned into a dance club. When I saw Jim in the under-stage dressing room, he started waving pages of his contract at me. It called for Rose's $3,500 guarantee off first, then the promoter's costs, and then a percentage split on the remainder. Pointing his finger to a figure, Jim exclaimed, "Look at this! Eight hundred bucks for this venue. Now, I know he isn't paying $800! I know and he knows I know, him and the bar owner are partners. The owner's happy with the booze money. Look at this! Nine hundred and something for advertising. The only ad I saw was about four lines. Same old shit. . . . Now, tomorrow night we will pick up $10,000 easy in Boston. But you know I love Gary Cormier. He and a promoter in Vancouver really put me on the map."

In 2001, GWAR front woman Danielle Stampe put out the Girly Freak Show. Except for Zamora (Tim Cuidland), all the performers were women. Seen here on the nail board is Camanda Galactica who had formerly been with the Know Nothing Sideshow troupe which was infamous in punk circus circles.

The sideshow business today is still as itinerant as the original freak museums attached to circuses were in the beginning. Numerous attempts at putting live sideshow productions in permanent venues have been short lived. "Shock!" featuring Tim Cridland playing at the Greek Isles Hotel and Casino in Las Vegas was another fleeting endeavor.

It was a good show. The young hipsters, goths and punkettes in their late teens and

Danielle Stampe is simply a "show broad," which is one of the highest compliments you can give a female trouper who has done it all to keep the show moving. She's performed in music gigs, wrestling matches, striptease spectacles and with many sideshow troupes, including her own.

20s liked it. Lifto's act — hooking a large anvil to the ring in his penis and swinging it between his legs — topped bug eating, razor blade chewing and other acts of depravity. The two heavy Mexican transvestite wrestlers were less impressive, while Rose's 480-pound yo-yo guy held the audience spellbound. His yo-yo tricks, many of them bordering on the impossible, were audience favourites. He captured the spirit of the old-time sideshow.

When the club owner came by, I asked her how well she did at the door. She replied: "Around 500 people," adding: "Two girls asked for their money back, saying they were waiting for the big moment and it never came." If Lifto's stretched-out and weighted dick, arching over the stage apron, wasn't "a moment," I wonder what those girls were expecting. I could hear Ward Hall's voice echoing in my ears: "No matter what's in the sideshow you always get beefs!"

The last thing Jim said to me as I left was: "I'm 45 years old. How much longer can I do this? This is my grab-it-all tour." Next time I heard of Jim and Bébé, they were trying their routines in comedy clubs. The idea was to work in the same venue for four or five days. They'd hired the Lizard Man, but after a few gigs he blew. They cancelled the rest of the tour. That's the sideshow business for you — the fat man dies and the party is over. No wonder old-timers married the midget lady!

In winter 2001, Torture King Tim Cridland played a campus pub at Toronto's York University with Matthew "Molotov" Bouvier and his partner Felicity Perez. During Tim's 90-minute show he breathes fire, stands on a carton of eggs without breaking them, walks on freshly broken glass, lies on a bed of nails and lets a woman from the audience jump up on down on his chest. Hot dogs held against his chest are chopped off with sharp hacks of a meat clever. Pokers are heated until glowing, then licked, and heated flat steal is bent by stomping on it with his feet. He lies backwards on four sharp swords while four big guys from the audience stand on a board laid across his chest. Near the show's end, when Tim shoves a long surgical skewer under his tongue and through his lower jaw, the college males who'd been heckling during the first half of the show began cheering, "You da man!" and

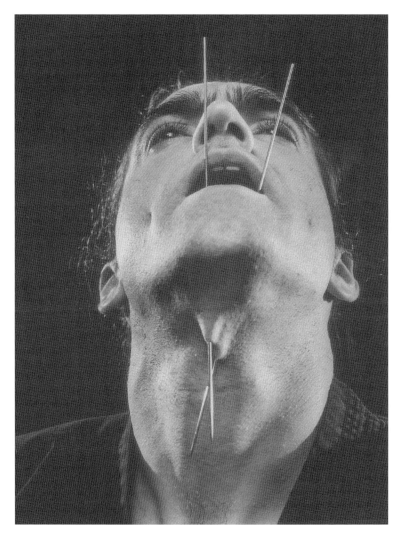

The late Mighty Jack Hartley was a true sideshowman. He painted first-class banners, made his own gaff exhibits and was the co-founder of the Bros. Grim Sideshow. Sadly, Jack died shortly after the Bros. Grim Sideshow got going.

"Wicked!" For his finale, Tim swallows string and retrieves it by cutting into his stomach. By this point the skeptics are either out cold or digging in their pockets for cash to buy a T-shirt for him to sign.

Matt did sword swallowing and knife throwing while Felicity walked the sword ladder and sat in the electric chair. Felicity also stole the show as Matt's knife-throwing target: she stood with her back against the circular knife board, and Matt hid her from his view with a paper screen. He then stepped back, and as he threw the knives through the screen, they outlined her body. She emerged from behind the paper topless,

Rock drummer and circus/carnival collector Ken Harck along with Jack Hartley founded the Bros. Grim Sideshow. Here, talker Smiley Davis is making his opening while Jack Hartley threatens the tip with a length of chain and the Enigma waves a chainsaw around at the Milwaukee Great Circus Parade grounds in early 2000s.

except for pasties. After the show, she told me she had worked at the California-based Lusty Lady peep theatres but originally studied method acting at the Lee Strasberg school in Hollywood.

"There are two kinds of people doing the modern sideshows — magicians who mix magic and sideshow routines and groups doing the modern primitive–style shows," says Tim. "At the former, audiences leave thinking the whole thing is fake. At the latter, the primitives cut themselves on broken bottles and are surprised when people walk out. They miss the whole point: the main focus has to be to make it entertaining." As an example of a troupe that mixes the entertaining and the shocking, Tim names the Know Nothing Circus Sideshow: "They have some good acts but it is gross stuff. One act has a guy gargling his own urine. One guy lies on a bed of nails and fellates himself."

Matt Bouvier and Felicity Perez had felt they were not legitimate unless they had spent time working on a real under-canvas midway sideshow. They had come along at the right time — the midway needed them and Ward Hall and Chris Christ were only too happy to hire them for a 2000 tour. "We wanted to learn," Matt explains. "I wanted to see what the carny sideshow was like first-hand. I feel I got the whole enchilada. The weird bosses with mood swings, the crazy fat man, the alcoholic dwarf and the hierarchy and pains in asses you had to deal with each day. I thought I'd be going there and drinking beer. You weren't allowed to do that. I wanted to stay to say I made a full season.

"It was harder work than I had ever done in my life," Matt says adamantly. "It really gave you an idea of how different generations view hard work. We did everything — unloaded and set up. Nothing was light. All steel. In the show we did seven acts. We had the fire-eating, the electric chair, the tongue lift and the tit pull, plus the bed of nails, the sword ladder and glass walking. Jack (Frankenstein)

who did the blow-off came out and did blockhead. Petey worked a little bit in the beginning doing the iron tongue, fire-eating and holding the snake, but he really wanted to be on the bally where Ward was, so he was planted on the bally doing fire-eating.

"The fat man had a photo of an electric wheelchair and did a charity pitch, claiming he was saving up for one. Actually, he already had one, as a mark who fainted found out. It got real hot one day at the Meadowlands. This one show we had 35 to 40 people inside the blow-off. Some were drunk. When

(Above) A publicity photo for the sideshow performance team of Felicity (Cha-Cha) Perez and Matt (Molotov) Bouvier. They started out working clubs and new-wave sideshow gigs. For several seasons they were the mainstays on the Hall-Christ World of Wonders.

Veteran sideshow performer Fred Lulling works under the name "Mephisto." He has spent numerous seasons with the Hall-Christ sideshows performing fire and pin-cushion acts. He is shown here inside the World of Wonders as he begins to drive a long spike up his nose in front of one of many tips each day at the 1999 Florida State Fair in Tampa.

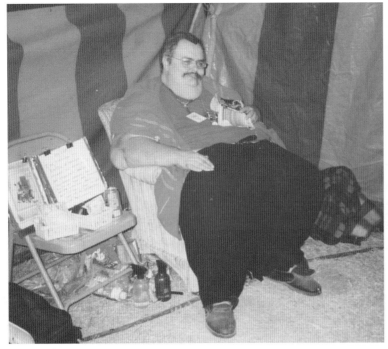

Fat man Bruce Snowdon sits near the exit of Hall and Christ's World of Wonders during the Tampa Fair in the early 2000s. Bruce came to work prepared with dozens of beverages and snacks, lots of pocket books and plenty of his pitch cards. Note the sign explaining any spare change would be used to buy a deluxe wheelchair, although he had a good one already.

Felicity Perez eating fire along with ZiZi Zpheem inside the Hall and Christ sideshow in the early 2000s. The small stage for the acts was in the center of the tent with the cased artifacts along the perimeter wall. The front was still made up of two steel semi-trailers with banners painted on them.

Jack the Pin Cushion took the needle out of his arm, this guy fainted. He fell out through the sidewall, hitting the fat man's wheelchair, breaking a steel peg off with his head. Blood's coming out of his head and we are like, 'Jesus Christ, we are screwed!' The guy gets up and says, 'I'm fine, I'm fine,' and then stumbles out of the tent onto the midway, never to be heard from again.

"After Petey went out on the bally, Felicity took the blow-off money and I did the pitch: 'Ladies and gentlemen, we have one act left to show you and this one is by far the most shocking and unusual thing we have yet to show you. It is so strange, so weird, that we have to keep Dr. Frankenstein in the small tent directly behind me. Now, Frankenstein's act is so graphic, so unusual, that we have not been allowed to present it on any fairgrounds in any state for the past eight years. Because this year is the last time we will be taking the big tent out with the big show, the fair board here in Bloomsburg have allowed us to show you Dr. Frankenstein, but under one condition . . .

"Folks! If the sight of blood makes you faint, you probably shouldn't go back there. But if you would like to see our most shocking, most unusual act, Dr. Frankenstein doing the exact same act in its shortened form that he did while he was on tour with the Circus of Horrors throughout Great Britain in 1999, please step right over to the lady. Now, folks, Dr. Frankenstein is a separate attraction in a separate tent. And for this reason we do charge a separate admission price of just one dollar to see him. Now, that dollar you spend you will soon forget about, but the look on your friend's face when he sees what Dr. Frankenstein does — *that* you will remember the rest of your life. Real and alive, Dr. Frankenstein is going to be starting his act in just a second.'

"Inside the blow, the tip hears Ward's voice on tape: 'Hi, my name is Frank. Middle initial N. Last name Stein. Frank N. Stein. I'm a good Jewish boy from Brooklyn, N.Y.' Then Jack, as Dr. Frankenstein, showed his chest where he had a button sewn to it. He spoke this line: 'My girlfriend said she doesn't want to go out with me anymore because my socks fall down, but I have a solution. Take a pin and — BAM, WHAPPO! — my socks don't fall down

anymore.' He would push the pin through his sock into his leg. We told him just go through the sock — how the hell is the tip going to know? But Jack was real macho. He wanted to go through the leg every single time. He'd jam the pin in there and say, 'That looks like blood there, smells like blood there, tastes like scotch!' He would then take a needle that was put in his arm from the last show and take it out, saying, 'Looks like I'm a quart low.' He would push another needle through his arm and say, 'Thank you, folks. If you have any questions, please feel free to ask and leave by the same way you came in.'"

Another new sideshow performer who has worked on a real side is George the Giant. I spoke with him before he began his day at the Osmond Theater in Branson, Mo., where he was the Ripley's Live show's ambassador of goodwill. George McArthur stands seven foot three inches in stocking feet and over seven foot seven inches in shoes. He says, "You gotta get shoes." In true show-giant tradition, George believes it is not a bad thing to alter your height. He had done many sideshow acts, but the producer only wanted him to do sword swallowing and pose in the lobby for people to take photos. In George's own words: "Just be tall."

The cast was strong. It included magician and sideshow performer Todd Robbins. Rick

In the 1980s, Doc Swan worked in my circus sideshow one season. He was one of the few young performers doing sideshow routines and had worked on some of the last big midway sideshows. Today you can see him entertaining folks of all ages at fairs, variety shows and clubs with his comedy sideshow/circus acts.

Basil escaped from chains and handcuffs while spinning around in a commercial clothes dryer. The famous Mexican-born Wolf Brothers, whose faces were covered in hair, did a trampoline act. Packaged by

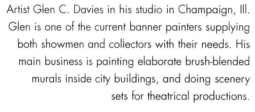

Dwarf Danny Black, George the Giant and the author at the first sideshow convention in Wilkes-Barre, Penn., in 2002. Besides being tall, George is a very accomplished sideshow performer whose numerous routines include sword swallowing and fire-eating.

Artist Glen C. Davies in his studio in Champaign, Ill. Glen is one of the current banner painters supplying both showmen and collectors with their needs. His main business is painting elaborate brush-blended murals inside city buildings, and doing scenery sets for theatrical productions.

Legends in Concert producer John Stuart, the show lacked live music and the sideshow acts were slowly being replaced by circus acts. "Originally Todd Robbins hammered a nail into his head but that was stopped," George recalled. "Todd's fire routine has been left out because the producer felt it was boring. The biggest problem in Branson is it is really the belt buckle of the Bible belt.

We have had to change costumes for our dancers so many times — too revealing, too seductive — it's ridiculous."

The Ripley Live show's changes to attract the blue-rinse bus-tour crowd seem bizarre until George relates his journey into sideshows. "I was born in Bakersfield, California, in 1969," he said. "When I was 12 years old we went to the fair and there

was a sideshow tent. I wanted to go in, but my brothers and sisters didn't want me to. They said I would be scared. I only saw the bally fire-eater and the sword swallower. I was amazed at what the human body could do. When I was 21, someone broke into my brother's home, tied him up, lit him on fire and left him to die. It left us with a fear of fire. I am one of those idiots that's afraid of heights, so I bungee jump. I also decided to learn fire-eating. I found some websites and I did everything you shouldn't do, including doing fire blasts with Coleman fuel!"

Despite setting his face on fire opening for a rock band, George went on to work for famed sideshowman Bobby Reynolds, joining that show in Amarillo, Texas. "I do the fire-eating, the blockhead and the balloon thing," George explained. "Bobby comes in the tent and tells me I am talking too much. I tell him when I am doing all these tricks I need a little buffer between them. Bobby yells, 'No talking, just do the damn trick and get it over with. Get them in and get them out.' Spectators would ask if I was going to do anymore, and I would tell them, 'Look, man, you only paid a buck!'

"Sideshow for me was a great weight loss program," George said, grinning. "Every time I went out with Bobby I lost 10 pounds. It's the best friggin' training I ever had. I am very thankful for Bobby. I learned a speech pattern when performing. It was a lot different than working in bars. The second time I went out with him I had some stuff under my belt. I wanted to try and do my straitjacket escape, so I did it 20 times a day. Why? Because I could! Bobby really made me understand what show business is."

The week after terrorists hit the World Trade Centre and the Pentagon, several circuses closed early and went home. Crowds were dismal at big Southern fairs. However, in a small theater in an Oregon city, the Bindlestiff

The Bindlestiff Family Cirkus as photographed by Raymond Pumilia for one of their early promotion cards. Described as a vaudevillian's variety of audacious amusements, performers Philomena, Mr. Pennygaff, SXip, Scotty the Blue Bunny, Rocket Johnny and Feather more than lived up to their billing.

Cirkus had a full house. This wacky troupe has been on the road for five years and offer up a real spectacle. The bullwhip act is followed by a chick doing psychic surgery on herself. After swallowing worms, she makes a small incision in her stomach and removes them. Your stomach returns to normal when a male performer comes out and manages to keep five plates spinning on rods at the same time. But just when you think you are comfortably back watching a regular circus-style act, his lovely assistant opens her dress, does a flip and ends up doing the splits on the floor. She then leans back and spreads her legs — no panties. The

Several years back, the ghosts of Hubert's Museum lingering around Times Square were happy to see dime-museum culture returned briefly to N.Y.C.'s West 22nd Street. Sadly, the Bindlestiff's Palace of Variety and Free Museum of Times Square was too good to last in today's Disney-fabricated Times Square.

Eric Sprague, a.k.a. the Lizard Man, is totally tattooed, and sports a split tongue plus forehead bumps. He is seen here performing on the nail board during his show at the 2002 Sideshow Gathering. He puts on a good show but freaked out a lot of people when they learned he holds a Ph.D. in the philosophy of art!

plate spinner leaves one of the rods with its spinning plate, and crowd sees that it has a rubber dildo on the end. He rubs it with lubricant and inserts it into her vagina. The audience is slack-jawed.

The Bindlestiff Cirkus is orchestrated by Stephanie Monseu and Keith Nelson, who appears as Mr. Pennygaff and Kinko the Clown. Pennygaff swallows swords, lighted neon tubes and to the audience's dismay, balloons, which he blows out his nose. Monseu is billed as Philomena, the show's onstage mistress of ceremonies. The show is European cabaret blended with *The Rocky Horror Picture Show*, Belgium beer halls, American carnival sideshow and cooch shows, in a rich sauce of circus acts. Everyone should see it.

During the summer of 2000, the buzz in the sideshow community was the upcoming sideshow convention at Wilkes-

One of the most interesting things about the hippie era was the artwork that came along with it on album covers, underground newspaper and concert posters. In the same vein, the artwork advertising today's tattoo, burlesque, roller derby and sideshow gigs is a joy to behold.

John (Red) Stuart is a midway sideshow veteran and without doubt one of the best sword swallowers of our time. He's a big supporter of the Sideshow Gathering and in the past has raised money for it by donating just-swallowed swords or by letting people staple paper money to his body. That's a twenty pinned to his forehead.

Barre, Pa. I headed there Labor Day weekend. Landmarks going into Wilkes-Barre, Pa., were not inspiring. A crumbling brewery with a name I couldn't pronounce. Old rail cars painted a sickly yellow piled up beside one of the main streets. Downtown, most stores were vacant. The

hotel sat on the city square, around which were metal signs affixed to poles: "If you pass this sign three times in a half-hour period you can be charged for cruising." An attempt at cleaning up the city's hooker or drug trade? It looked like any trade would greatly improve downtown.

My apprehensions proved unnecessary, though — the square's farm market was fun. Best of all, I became friends with a small guy with a big heart. Frank (Franco) Kossa and his partner Marc Fairchild had been putting on the Inkin' in the Valley Tattoo Convention for a decade before Franco made the move to add the sideshow

An advertising sticker from Tyler Fyre's Lucky Devil Circus Sideshow. Fyre's acts have been a mainstay at the Coney Island Sideshow by the Seashore for numerous seasons.

Business card used by The Amazing Boobzilla (The World's Strongest Breasts). For several years she was one of the acts with the Denver, Col.–based Crispy Family Carnival.

Ses Carny (Jesse House) describes his show as "Buckle Up. We're going on a runaway train ride and the brakes are broke." A seasoned performer, Ses has enhanced his sideshow reputation over the past few seasons by appearing on the Hall and Christ sideshow.

crowd. Tattooed guys and gals drifted past banners of two-headed children hanging in the lobby. The sideshow folks cruised the convention-hall tattoo booths. Some got tattooed. One elderly bus tourist emerging from the lobby elevator froze as if she had pushed the "M" button for mezzanine but the lift shot skyward dumping her on Mars. Later, she told me it was the most fun in a hotel she'd experienced in years.

As a circus person I'm used to five o'clock calls, but when I walked into the lobby around seven o'clock Saturday morning it was empty. Just overflowing ashtrays and empty Yuengling bottles. I figured tattooists were like carnies and rock musicians — they didn't stir until the afternoon. I spotted the Icelandic guy I had seen in the sideshow room the night before. His body must still

(Left) Banner painter, artist and illustrator Toni Lee Sangastiano continues to do banners for showmen and for the sideshow fan. Her quirky drawings and vivid color combinations make her banners outstanding.

(Right) Insectavora and Tyler Fyre can both deliver the unusual at short notice. They have been a fixture at Dick Zigun's Coney Island sideshow emporium in past seasons and have performed at several Sideshow Gatherings.

have been on Euro time. He had taken part in the "Big Swallow!" Friday night, during which 19 sword swallowers crowded the stage as Ward Hall counted down: "Three, two, one . . . Down the hatch"! All 19 held their swords down for photos before bringing them back up. Natasha, a busty blonde who also did a wonderful belly-dancing act, had swallowed 11 swords. Ward

asked if anyone felt they could swallow any more steel to up the total count. On the second try, the sword swallowers reached the 50-sword mark without any blood spitting.

The sideshow convention offered performances by various groups and individual artists. Watching people shove spikes up their noses in back-to-back shows may have seemed a bit much, but each troupe or act

had its own way of doing things. The sideshow convention caught on, and it's still going. New acts and fans show up each year. It's always edgy and funny. Sexy too, with all those tattooed girls and guys floating around. One sideshow artist that has been there a few times is a gal who calls herself Insectavora. She has worked at the Sideshow by the Seashore at Coney Island. At the end of

Ricky Hale is better known for his large freak-animal midway show but one year in the early 2000s he had this first-class sideshow at the Erie County Fair, Hamburg, N.Y. The small cast made up of new sideshow performers delivered a fast, funny and very entertaining 20-minute show.

expected her to strip nude, lean back on a chair and shoot flames from her crotch. Some blow-off!

Those mourning the disappearance of sideshows, circuses and traveling midways can take comfort in the words of the late George Carlin, social satirist and comedian: "When you are born, you get a free ticket to the freak show. Sit back and enjoy the ride."

Showmen discussing the decline of outdoor show business often say, "Don't worry, they can't put a Ferris wheel in their living room." But the real sadness lies in the fact that there are fewer and fewer traveling tented shows each season. While some show folks were born into the racket, the majority were towners who were fleeing bad homes or aching to sow their wild oats. Gays were just glad to find somewhere that welcomed them. And then there was Sam Alexander, 28 when a propane explosion blew away half his face. Nobody would hire him until he saw an ad for sideshow attractions. Later Sam related, "The sideshow owner said, 'You're the Man with Two faces.' I started at $75 a week. More important, I was finally accepted somewhere."

the evening at one convention, she charged those who wanted to go outside behind the hotel five bucks to see an unusal performance. She was a good fire-eater, but nobody

Glossary

ANNEX: Some circuses referred to their sideshow as the "Annex." The word was also used as a gentle way of saying the blow-off inside shows and particularly on 10-in-ones in the 1940s and '50s.

BALLET GIRLS: Show girls in the circus who rode elephants and horses and who presented the "aerial ballets" of choreographed aerial numbers on the Spanish web or swinging ladders. Ballet girls also enhanced the show with their presence in the show's costumed walk-arounds and parades known as "SPECS."

BALLY: The free show on a platform stage outside of any show.

BARNUM & BAILEY CIRCUS — "The Greatest Show on Earth": This circus was operated by James A. Bailey and P. T. Barnum from 1888 to 1890. From 1891 James E. Bailey, with several other partners, owned the show. In 1908 it was bought by the Ringling Bros. but continued to operate as a separate circus until 1918. In 1919 the show was combined with the Ringling Bros. Circus to form one circus titled Ringling Bros. Barnum & Bailey Circus — "The Greatest Show On Earth." After 1919 outdoor showmen often referred to it as just Ringling, Big Bertha or the "Big One."

BLOW or BLOW-OFF: Sideshow operators enhanced their inside money by charging patrons extra to see an attraction closed off in one end of the tent.

BUTE BOARD: A small padded board used as a surface for grifters to play three-card monte and the shell game. You needed the padded softness so you could press the shell down to kick the pea out into your hand. The board was set on a TRIPE.

CANDY PITCH: Showmen sold packaged candy with a prize inside on circuses and on carnival girl shows and other carnival attractions.

CAT WALK: Wooden viewing platform on a 10-in-one side show that is slightly raised off the ground and runs the length of the open front of the tent.

CHINESE: "Doing CHERRY PIE" at a circus meant doing extra jobs besides the one you were hired for but you got paid for them. Doing "Chinese," on the other hand, was work you were not paid for that you did in exchange for your room and board in the show's sleepers and cook house. On Sells and Gray Circus in the 1960s my Chinese as a candy butcher included setting up the sideshow bannerline, the big top marquee, setting the long side reserve chair grandstand and hanging the big top side wall. That was all done before you unloaded the concessions, set them up and began to make candy apples and popcorn.

CONCERT: A special short show put on after the main circus performance. It was advertised during the circus and tickets were sold in the seats during the show. When the main show ended, concert ticket holders were ushered into the best seats for the "after-show." Early concerts were mainly variety programs. Wrestlers, boxers and wild west movie stars were big concert draws in the first half of the 20th century.

COSMORAMAS: Scenes of cities, natural settings or scenes from a story that were painted on long expanses of canvas or paper. Audiences viewed the scenes as they were rolled from one roller to another one across a proscenium opening.

DING: To ask a crowd inside a sideshow or midway show for extra money. Ding shows were those that proclaimed on their outside advertising — No Tickets Required. However, once inside someone at the exit asked you for a donation. Being "dinged" is when the carny owner asks you to contribute to the showman's club or buy a yearbook ad.

DOLLAR STORES: A con game using a drop case.

FAIRIES: References to fairies on circuses as sideshow attractions in the 19th century usually meant midgets.

FAKIR: An early name used by showmen for a grifter.

FIELD BOX: A third sideshow ticket box set up further along from the two that normally are on either side of the bally platform. It is literally at the top of the midway — in the field. These boxes were usually not solid-sided boxes like the usual sideshow ticket boxes but just a frame with a small counter and a board for the seller to stand on like those used inside the big top to sell reserved seats from. They could be quickly folded up and put away.

GAZOONEY or **GAZONNIE:** Working man, roughy, lowly help, carnival ride worker.

GILLY BUS: Rail circuses carried a bus or station wagon to transfer its performers and executives from the train coaches to the lot show morning and night.

GRIFTERS: Name given to pickpockets, short change artists and operators of controlled gaming devices around touring entertainments. Showmen referred to their operations as "grift."

HAND BILLS: Small hand-out flyers advertising a show.

IMPALEMENT ACTS: An early name for knife- and hatchet-throwing acts.

INSIDE MONEY: The money the sideshow operator gets from the sales items, pitches, dings and blow-offs inside his sideshow as opposed to ticket box money that he has to share with fair or carnival owner.

JAM: Originated in the late 1920s by Thomas (Slim) Kelly and Whitey Austin as a means of keeping a crowd lined up along the front of their pit sideshow. After doing a bally out front, the talker would inform the tip (crowd) that he would halve the admission price for the next five minutes — forcing the crowd to go in right then as opposed to grinding them in slowly when not doing a bally.

LADY GYPSY SHOWING MARK HER PUSSY: Getting a male mark alone and asking him if he would to pay extra if she showed him her pussy went back as far as European vaudeville team the Barrisson Sisters. They would ask their audience the same question, then would lift their skirts to reveal kittens placed in pockets sewn into their undergarments.

LAY-OUT MAN: On circuses this can be the general superintendant or in many cases the twenty-four hour man. Everything is meas-ured out with a measuring tape. The lot person uses layout pins (a steel pin about a half inch in diameter pointed at the bottom end) about four feet high pushed into the ground to mark the locations of tent center poles, stake lines, the length of the sideshow bannerline, width of the midway, etc.

LIBERTY HORSES: Act in which four or more horses work "at liberty" — meaning without reins in the circus ring. They do various maneuvers guided by the presenter in the center who uses body posture along with two long whips as directional wands.

LOT and LICENSE: Most circuses rented a field and bought a local license to show in a town. When telephone solicitation crews came along in the 1950s, many circuses dropped lot and license policies and switched their operations to a telephone operation. The circus advance agent contracted a local sponsoring organization in each town. For a small portion of the circus ticket sales, the sponsoring club provided the lot and license and allowed a "phone crew" to use their name in selling kid tickets to local businesses. The phone sales pitch informed the potential buyer that if they wished, the tickets could be given out by the local club to "under privileged children" in the community. Show folks simply called them UPC tickets.

LOT LICE: What show folks called towners that hung around the circus lot.

MARKS: Towners, suckers or victims of confidence games.

MONSTROSITY SHOWS: Circus showmen in the 1870–80s sometimes referred to the sideshow as the monstrosity show because of the many disabled or freak acts in the performance.

MUSEUM: In the early days of showmanship a "Museum" referred to a collection of anything — be it stuffed animals or living attractions. Circus sideshowmen often painted the word on their doorway entrance banners to promote their show as being both uplifting and educational.

OUTSIDE SHOWS: Small freak and curiosity shows that were set up around the grounds outside the main circus tent. They were often independent of the circus and not included in the price of the circus ticket.

PATCH: The legal adjuster or "fixer" on circuses and carnivals.

PAVILLION SHOWMEN: A name given to the first showmen exhibiting circus and menagerie attractions under a tent.

PIG PEN: Some 10-in-one operators liked to hold up new customers coming into the tent when the blade box and blow-off presentations were going on. Holding these people up outside at the edge of the tent was called "Putting Them in the Pig Pen."

PRIVILEGE: Circus and carnival owners collected a fee from operators who operated shows, concessions and services on their lots. Showmen called this rent money a privilege fee or privilege money.

PUNK PUSHER: Circus worker who was in charge of organizing and bossing the kids helping to set-up the circus who were paid with a "working boy pass."

RESERVE SEAT SQUEEZE: Many circuses only sold reserve seats inside the big top. Entering the big top, the patron was immediately confronted with two men standing up on ticket boxes placed only a few feet apart so that people had to squeeze by them. The reserve seat sellers continually spieled that if you didn't buy a reserve seat, your seats would be way, way, way back in the far end of the tent! Fifteen minutes after the show started, the ring announcer made a pitch for the un-sold reserve seats at a discounted price which was known as the "Sheriff's Sale."

RESERVE SEATS: Reserve seat areas included those on the short side of the tent (the side of the tent broken up by the performer's entrance[s] and the bandstand) and the long continuous rows of seats on the opposite side known as the "long" side. These were the best areas to see all three rings of the American tent circus. General admission seating was limited to plain wooden plank seats in the end of the tent referred to as "the blues." Reserve seats could be plain planks (vendors rented out cushions) but most shows used individual wooden chairs or planks with folding back rests. The latter were called "starbacks" because the manufacturer of such seating often decorated the folding back rests with a painted star.

SKILLO: A controlled gambling wheel.

SONGSTERS: Small program-sized booklets containing the words to popular songs were sold on touring shows including circuses into the early years of the 20th century.

STICK: A person playing a game or going into a show that appears to be just a crowd member but is actually working for the show or the grifter.

STONE EATER: An early regurgitation act in which the performer swallows stones and then brings them back up.

STRING SHOW: Name given to early carnival 10-in-ones because of the long skinny tent in which the acts worked in pits along the front pit curtain. Viewers lined up along the tent's front pit curtain and looked inside.

SUCKER NETTING: Net sections like tennis netting but much taller were used to keep towners out of circus behind-the-scenes areas on the show lot. It was also used on the circus "midway" to keep towners from exiting the midway anywhere along it except back up at the beginning where they came on to it.

SYNOPSIS SHEETS: These were a set of instruction sheets for each town filled out by the advance agent when the town was booked months before the circus arrived. They were kept in the circus office wagon and listed all the things circus management and bosses needed to know about each lot and town on show day.

TEASER CURTAIN: A piece of canvas hanging down from the front edge of a sideshow tent so that midway walkers can't see the acts on stage inside. It also partially hides the spectators standing on the show's cat walk so their backsides and legs are visible to midway walkers as enticements to go inside and join them.

THE "X": Carnival owners would offer various showmen the "X" or exclusive on their midway for operating certain games, shows, etc. Usually having the "X" didn't hold at fair time.

TRAILERS: What show owners called those that followed their shows but set up off their lot to avoid paying privilege fees.

TRIPE: Portable set of three legs used to set the BUTE board that the grifters used as a playing surface.

WORKING ACTS: Non-freak acts in sideshows that actually perform such feats as swallowing swords, eating fire, knife throwing or magic.

Index

Hall, Earl (Man with Two Mouths), 219

Hall, Ward (sideshowman), 68, 69, 79, 80, 84, 86, 116, 136, 138, 141, 146, 168–170, 178, 185, 186, 194, 207, 211, 214, 243, 244, 265, 270, 279, 289, 290, 325, 326, 328, 333, 339, 340, 341, 342, 344, 354, 356, 365

Halligan, Jack (World's Fair freaks), 209

Hamilton, Claude (early 10-in-one showman), 118

handbills, 3, 7, 198

hand-organs, 26

Hankins, Doc (*Madame X*, blow-off), 183

Hansen, Frank D. (grind showman), 279, 280, 316–321

happy family (cage of assorted animals), 15

Harlem Museum, 234

Harris, Freddie (Manipo), 60, 79, 185

Harris, Hal (Punch-and-Judy maker), 212

Hart, Tommy (sideshowman), 60, 79, 84

Hartigan, Mike (carnival owner, artist), 26

Hartley, Jack (banner painter, strong man), 355, 356

Hasson, Bobby (sideshowman), 60, 70, 86, 140, 192, 252, 267

Haviland's Museum, 94

Hawaiian performers, 28, 35, 40, 44, 53, 60, 61, 63, 64, 66, 80, 70, 185

Hawkes, Clayton (showman), 96

Haworth, Joe (Big, fixer), 65, 69

Hayden, E. J. and Co. (show scenic firm), 25

Hayes, Analto (anatomical man act), 164,

256

headless lady (illusion), 341

Heckler, William (flea circus, store showman), 236, 269

Hennen, Peter (sideshowman), 182, 183, 184, 286–288, 290, 310

Hennies Bros. Shows, 135

Henshaw, William (sideshowman), 23

Heth, Joice, 8

High Grass Circus (NFB documentary film), 76

High Grass route, 49

Hillburn, Dick (half-man, sideshowman, sign painter, diner owner), 197, 202, 280, 282

Hilton Sisters, Daisy and Violet (conjoined twins), 130, 259, 260, 349

Hindu Basket trick, 166

hippopotamus, 58, 78, 98, 99, 102

Hix, John (Strange As It Seems, sideshow cartoonist), 184, 255, 256, 265

Hodges, Charlie (sideshowman), 144

Hoffman, Joe (sideshowman, circus owner), 63

homopongodies, 102

Hopwitt, Adelaide (fat lady), 16

Horne's Zoological Co., 94

Horrell, Shackles (escape act), 60

Howdy Doody, 59

Howe, J. R. and William Jr. and Co. Menagerie, 4

Howe, Seth B., 8

Houdini (escape artist, author), 148, 160

house trailers, 203, 310

Hoxie Bros. Circus, 85, 102, 169

Hubbell, Art (Human Bellows), 37, 42, 43

Hubert's Museum, 82, 146, 152, 176, 235, 236–238, 240, 242, 269, 362

Hughes, Charles (English showman), 3

Hugo the Great (regurgitationist), 39

Hunt, William (Signor Guillermo Antonio Farini), 8

Hunt Bros. Circus, 50

Hunter, Charlie (Charlotte the Gorilla Girl), 73, 177, 178, 180, 195

Hunting's Circus, 25, 27, 28

Hutchins, Prof. (lecturer, Lightning calculator), 146–147, 231, 233

Hutchinson, James L. (circus owner, sideshow operator), 24

Ike and Mike (look-alike midgets), 189, 190, 253

independent midway, 267, 268, 301, 306, 315, 335

individual sideshow stages, 79, 116, 138

Ingalls, Clyde (sideshowman), 38, 46, 53

Insectavora (performance artist), 365, 366

inside money, 85, 144, 151

invisible fortune paper, 157

Italian Bands, 27

Iuliani, Giovanni (showman, only North American clown with face on postage stamp), 262–264

Bibliography

Books that best explain the business of entertaining people have been those written by the showmen themselves. For those deeply interested in researching outdoor amusements, your education should begin by reading the N.Y. *Clipper*, the *Billboard* and *Amusement Business*. These weekly trade publications covered the American amusement world from mid-1850s until the mid-1990s.

Barnum, P. T. *Struggles and Triumphs or Forty Years' Recollections of P. T. Barnum by Himself*. Buffalo, N.Y.: Warren Johnson, 1873.

Bone, Howard. *Side Show: My Life with Geeks, Freaks, & Vagabonds in the Carny Trade*. Northville, Mich.: Son Dog Press, 2001.

Chubbuck, Ted. *Sounds of the Jenny*. New York, N.Y.: Vantage Press, 1972.

Dufour, Lou with Irvin Kirby. *Fabulous Life: A Showman's Tales of Carnivals, World's Fairs and Broadway*. New York, N.Y.: Vantage Press, 1977.

Gregor, Jan. *Circus of Scars*. Seattle, Wash.: Brennan Dalsgard Publishers, 1998.

Hall, Ward. *Struggles and Triumphs of a Modern Day Showman*. Carnival Publishers of Sarasota, Fla., 1981.

Holtman, Jerry. *Freak Show Man: Uncensored Memoirs of Harry Lewiston the Incredible Scoundrel*. Los Angeles, Calif.: Holloway House, 1968.

Horne, Marcel. *Annals of a Fire Breather*. Toronto, ON: Peter Martin Associates, 1973.

Iano, I. David. *A Wandering Showman*. East

Lansing, Mich.: Michigan State University Press, 1957.

Jay, Ricky. *Learned Pigs & Fireproof Women*. New York, N.Y.: Warner Books, 1988.

Lambert, William (Will Delavoye). *Show Life in America*. Self-published. East Point, Ga., 1925.

Mannix, Daniel P. *Memoirs of a Sword Swallower*. (Photo illustrated edition) San Francisco, Calif.: V/Research Publications, 1996.

Norman, George. *The Penny Showman: Memoirs of Tom Norman — The Silver King*. London, Eng.: Norman-Noakes, 1985.

Roberge, Marc. *Confidences de Giovanni*. Laval, QC: Éditions Neptune, 1975.

Rose, Jim. *Freak Like Me: Inside the Jim Rose Circus Sideshow*. New York, N.Y.: Dell Publishing, 1995.

Rowe, Joseph Andrew. *California Pioneer Circuses*. San Francisco, Calif.: H. S. Crocker & Co. 1926.

Steimeyer, Jim. *Hiding the Elephant*. New York, N.Y.: Carroll and Graf, 2003.

Stencell, A. W. *Girl Show: Into the Canvas World of Bump and Grind*. Toronto, ON: ECW Press, 1999.

Stencell, A. W. *Seeing Is Believing: America's Sideshows*. Toronto, ON: ECW Press, 2002.

Thomas, Gordon. *Bed of Nails: The Story of the Amazing Blondini*. London, Eng.: Allan Wingate, 1955.

Trav, S. D. *No Applause — Just Throw Money: The Book That Made Vaudeville Famous*. New York, N.Y.: Faber & Faber, 2005.

Trefflich, Henry and Edward Anthony. *Jungle for Sale*. New York, N.Y.: Hathorne Books, 1967.

Others

Bogdan, Robert. *Freak Show: Presenting Human Oddities for Amusement and Profit*. Chicago, Ill.: University of Chicago Press, 1982.

Bondeson, Jan. *The Feejee Mermaid and Other Essays in Natural and Unnatural History*. Ithaca, N.Y.: Cornell University Press, 1999.

Brigham, David R. *Public Culture in the Early Republic: Peale's Museum and Its Audience*. Washington, D.C.: Smithsonian Institution Press, 1995.

Dennett, Andrea Stulman. *Weird and Wonderful: The Dime Museum in America*. New York, N.Y.: New York University Press, 1997.

Denson, Charles. *Coney Island Lost and Found*. Berkeley, Calif.: Ten Speed Press, 2002.

Drimmer, Frederick. *Very Special People*. New York, N.Y.: Amjon Publishers, 1973.

Freaks, Geeks & Strange Girls: Side Show Banners of the Great American Midway. Honolulu, Hawaii: Hardy Marks Publications, 1995.

Fried, Fred and Mary Fried. *America's Forgotten Folk Arts*. New York, N.Y.: Pantheon Books, 1978.

Frost, Thomas. *The Old Showmen and the London Fairs*. London, Eng.: Chatto and Windus, 1881.

Gibson, Gregory. *Hubert's Freaks*. Orlando, Fla.: Harcourt, 2008.

Gold, Herbert. *The Man Who Was Not with It*. New York, N.Y.: Avon Books, 1956.

Goldston, Will. *How To Make Sand, Smoke, and Rag Pictures — Also Novelty Silhouettes, Clay Modelling*. London, Eng.: The Magician Ltd. Robin Hood Yard, no date.

Hill, J. Lee. *Freaks and Fire: The Underground Reinvention of Circus*. Brooklyn, N.Y.: Soft Skull Press, 2004.

Kunhardt, Philip B., Jr., Philip B. Kunhardt III, and Peter W. Kunhardt. *P. T. Barnum: America's Greatest Showman, An Illustrated Biography*. New York, N.Y.: Alfred A. Knopf, 1995.

Laurie, Joe, Jr. *Vaudeville from the Honky Tonks to the Palace*. New York, N.Y.: Henry Holt, 1953.

Levenson, Randal, and Spalding Gray. *In Search of the Monkey Girl*. Millerton, N.Y.: Aperture, 1981.

Lewis, Arthur H. *Carnival*. New York, N.Y.: Trident Press, 1970.

Lewis, Robert M., editor. *Travelling Show to Vaudeville: Theatrical Spectacle in America*

1830–1910. Baltimore, Md.: The Johns Hopkins University Press, 2003.

Lindfors, Bernth. *Africans on Stage: Studies in Ethnological Show Business*. Bloomington, Ind.: Indiana University Press.

Lindsay, David. *Madness in the Making: The Triumphant Rise and Untimely Fall of America's Show Inventors*. Authors' Guild Back In Print Edition, 2005.

Mitchell, Michael, editor. *Monsters: Human Freaks in America's Gilded Age. The Photographs of Chas. Eisenmann*. Toronto, ON: ECW Press, 2002.

Modern Primitives: An Investigation of Contemporary Adornment & Ritual. San Francisco, Calif.: RE/Search Publications, 1989.

Montagu, Ashley. *The Elephant Man: A Study in Human Dignity*. London, Eng.: Allison & Busby, 1972.

Page, Brett. *Writing for Vaudeville*. Cambridge, Mass.: Home Correspondence School, 1915.

Peacock, Shane. *The Great Farini*. Toronto, ON: Penguin, 1996.

Pilat, Oliver and Jo Ranson. *Sodom by the Sea: An Affectionate History of Coney Island*. Garden City, N.Y.: Doubleday Doran, 1941.

Primack, Phil. *New England County Fairs!* Chester, Conn.: The Globe Pequot Press, 1982.

Quigley, Christine. *Modern Mummies: The Preservation of the Human Body in the Twentieth Century*. Jefferson, N.C.: McFarland, 1998.

Sappol, Michael. *A Traffic in Dead Bodies: Anatomy and Embodied Social Identity in Nineteenth-Century America*. Princeton, N.J.: Princeton University Press, 2002.

Sloan, Mark, Roger Manley and Michelle Van Parys. *Dear Mr. Ripley: A Compendium of Curiosities from the Believe It or Not Archives*. Boston, Mass.: Bulfinch Press, Little Brown, 1993.

Standage. Tom *The Turk: The Life and Times of the Famous Eighteenth-Century Chess-Playing Machine*. New York, N.Y.: Walker, 2002.

Stearns, Marshall and Jean Stearns. *Jazz Dance: The Story of American Vernacular Dance*. New York: Da Capo Press, 1994.

Taylor, James and Kathleen Kotcher. *James Taylor's Shocked and Amazed: On & Off the Midway*. Guildford, Conn.: The Lyons Press, 2002.

Thayer, Stuart. *Annals of the American Circus 1793–1829*. Manchester, Mich.: Rymack Printing Co., 1976.

Thayer, Stuart. *Annals of the American Circus*. Vol. 2. 1830–1847. Seattle, Wash.: Peanut Butter Publishing, 1986.

Thayer, Stuart. *Annals of the American Circus*. Vol. 3. 1848–1860. Seattle, Wash.: Dauven and Thayer, 1992.

Thomson, Rosemarie Garland, editor. *Freakery: Cultural Spectacles of the Extraordinary Body*. New York, N.Y.: New York University Press, 1996.

Photo Credits

Amusement Business: 67 (lower right), 80 (ad), 183 (ad), 320 (left), 322.

Argosy magazine: 316.

Beckmann & Gerety Shows: 1936 pictorial magazine: 133 (top).

Billboard magazine illustrations: 43, 60 (right), 70 (lower mid), 95, 101,108, 110, 114, 118, 134, 135 (two ads), 136, 152 (left), 159 (upper ad), 165, 189, 255 (right), 268 (right), 271 (left), 324 (left), 337 (left).

Bob Blackmar Collection: 41 (right), 83 (right), 84 (right), 86 (lower right), 102 (lower), 127 (lower), 137, 138, 150 (right), 151 (left), 167, 169 (right),174 (left), 178, 179 (left), 184 (right), 210 (right), 221, 254, 257 (left), 296 (left), 325, 350 (right), 358 (right).

John Bradshaw: 243, 346.

Brian Braithwaite: 285.

Alison Braun: 346.

Circus World Museum Library, Baraboo, Wisconsin: 35 (illustration), 68, 115 (lower).

Barbara Fahs Charles: 104, 107, 111, 115 (top).

Bill Cooker: 125, 253, 275.

Karl Cullison: 180.

Glen C. Davies: 173.

Brent De Whitt: 211 (right).

Diane Falk: 168 (right).

Richard Flint Collection: 4 (right), 6 (ad), 7, 9, 10 (left), 11, 14, 15, 18, 20, 30, 31, 93, 96 (left), 106 (right ad), 107 (ad), 109, 144, 146 (bio), 149 (left), 193 (left), 223 (right), 230, 231 (right), 234 (left), 247, 248, 249, 268 (left), 324 (right).

Malcolm Garey: 292, 293 (right), 294.

Richard Groggin Collection: 237 (right).

Jan T. Gregor: 352, 353 (lower left).

Paul Gutheil: 351 (left).

Ward Hall and Chris Christ Archives: 79 (upper right), 126, 127 (upper), 139, 142, 146, 150 (left), 153, 169 (left), 194, 197 (right), 202 (right), 203 (right), 206 (right), 264, 265 (left), 289 (right), 290 (left), 326, 328 (left), 333, 338, 339, 340 (left).

Charles L. Hanson: 59 (upper right).

Ken Harck: 238, 246, 261.

Bob Harris: 44 (right).

Mike Hartigan: 26.

Illinois State University's Special Collections, Milner Library: 33, 47, 66 (right).

Giovanni Iuliani Archives: 262 (right), 263.

Jason Jones: 132 (right), 148, 154.

Kinder von RAS: xii (lower), 22 (upper right), 131 (left).

Lee Kolozsy: 321, 353 (lower left).

Mahatma magazine: 190 (right).

Peter Manos: 164, 165.

Joni Moriyama: 348.

Jeff and Sue Murray: 288.

Fakir Musafar: 355 (left).

Nelson Enterprises: 159 (lower two).

New York Clipper: 22, 29 (ad), 59 (ad).

North American Carnival Museum, Ottawa, Ontario, Canada: 130, 158 (left), 177, 184 (left), 192 (right), 214, 237 (upper left), 240, 241, 251 (upper), 255 (left), 265 (right), 273, 343.

Lucy O'Neil (Luxifire): 351 (right).

Ottawa City Archives: xi (upper), 202 (left), 216 (right), 270.

Bob Paul Collection: 36, 42 (right), 135 (lower right), 158 (right), 161, 182, 196 (right), 212 (right), 219, 225, 226, 250 (right), 252 (right), 274.

Barbara Pedrero: 276, 277.

Fred Pfening II: 51 (contract).

Diana Philips: 212 (right).

John Polacsek: 232 (left).

Faye Renton: 121, 122, 128, 188.

Rick and West: 318 (left), 319 (left), 323 (left).

Mickey Saiber: 278, 279, 280, 281, 282.

Jack and Ruth Sands: 162 (right), 290 (upper/lower right), 291.

Pattiann Sciortino: 312.

Richard Snyder: 81.

Somers Historical Society: 3, 8.

Strand Magazine: 24 (illustration).

Doc Swan: 359.

Gary Syers: 341 (right).

Remaining photos are from the author's personal collection.